D1705350

The Self and Self-Knowledge

The Self and Self-Knowledge

EDITED BY
Annalisa Coliva

UNIVERSITY PRESS

OXFORD
UNIVERSITY PRESS

Great Clarendon Street, Oxford, OX2 6DP,
United Kingdom

Oxford University Press is a department of the University of Oxford.
It furthers the University's objective of excellence in research, scholarship,
and education by publishing worldwide. Oxford is a registered trade mark of
Oxford University Press in the UK and in certain other countries

© The several contributors 2012

The moral rights of the authors have been asserted

First Edition published in 2012

Impression: 1

All rights reserved. No part of this publication may be reproduced, stored in
a retrieval system, or transmitted, in any form or by any means, without the
prior permission in writing of Oxford University Press, or as expressly permitted
by law, by licence or under terms agreed with the appropriate reprographics
rights organization. Enquiries concerning reproduction outside the scope of the
above should be sent to the Rights Department, Oxford University Press, at the
address above

You must not circulate this work in any other form
and you must impose this same condition on any acquirer

British Library Cataloguing in Publication Data

Data available

Library of Congress Cataloging in Publication Data

Data available

ISBN 978-0-19-959065-0

Printed in Great Britain by
MPG Books Group, Bodmin and King's Lynn

Acknowledgements

I would like to express my gratitude to the Fonds national suisse and the Institute of Philosophy, in collaboration with Arché at the University of St Andrews and the British Academy, for their financial support for the conferences from which this volume stems. Thanks are due also to Gianfranco Soldati, Tim Crane, Shahrar Ali and Crispin Wright for their efforts to secure funding and for their help in organizing these events. Some of the participants to the conferences, who are not present in this volume, contributed immensely to the success of those occasions. So, once more, I would like to express my gratitude to Gianfranco Soldati and Crispin Wright, but also to Eva Picardi, Barry Smith, and Jim Pryor. Finally, I would like to thank Ted Parent and Chris Peacocke for their invaluable comments on the *Introduction* as well as Alessia Pasquali for enormously helpful editorial assistance.

Contents

List of Contributors — ix

Introduction — 1
Annalisa Coliva

Part One: The Self and its Individuation

1. Does Rationality Enforce Identity? — 17
   Carol Rovane

2. The Conceptual Origin of Subject–Body Dualism — 39
   Martine Nida-Rümelin

3. Subjects and Consciousness — 74
   Christopher Peacocke

4. Does Perception Do Any Work in an Understanding of the First Person? — 102
   John Campbell

Part Two: Consciousness, Action Awareness, and Their Role in Self-Knowledge

5. Consciousness and Self-Awareness — 123
   Jane Heal

6. Reasons and Self-Knowledge — 139
   Conor McHugh

7. Knowledge of Actions and Tryings — 164
   Lucy O'Brien

8. Conscious Events and Self-Ascriptions: Comments on Heal and O'Brien — 180
   Christopher Peacocke

Part Three: Self-Knowledge: Robust or Fragile?

9. Externalism and Skepticism: Recognition, Expression, and Self-Knowledge — 189
   Dorit Bar-On

10. One Variety of Self-Knowledge: Constitutivism as Constructivism — 212
    Annalisa Coliva

11. How to Think about Phenomenal Self-Knowledge   243
    Paul Snowdon
12. The Unique Status of Self-Knowledge   263
    Akeel Bilgrami

Author Index   279
Subject Index   281

List of Contributors

DORIT BAR-ON is Professor of Philosophy at the University of North Carolina at Chapel Hill. She is the author of *Speaking My Mind: Expression and Self-Knowledge* (OUP 2004). She is presently working on a book manuscript, tentatively titled *Expression, Action, and Meaning* as part of a large-scale collaborative project on *Expression, Communication and the Origins of Meaning*, as well as on another book manuscript (with Keith Simmons), *If Truth Be Told*.

AKEEL BILGRAMI is Johnsonian Professor of Philosophy and Director of the Heyman Center for the Humanities at Columbia University. He is the author of *Belief and Meaning* (Blackwell 1992), *Self-Knowledge and Resentment* (Harvard 2006), and *Politics and The Moral Psychology of Identity* (Harvard forthcoming). He is presently working on a long project on the relationship between value, reason, and agency.

JOHN CAMPBELL is Willis S. and Marion Slusser Professor of Philosophy at the University of California, Berkeley. He is the author of *Past, Space and Self* (MIT 1994) and *Reference and Consciousness* (OUP 2002).

ANNALISA COLIVA is Associate Professor of Philosophy at the University of Modena and Reggio Emilia. She is the author of *Moore and Wittgenstein: Scepticism, Certainty and Common Sense* (Palgrave 2010), *I modi del relativismo* (Laterza 2009), and the editor of *Knowledge, Meaning and Mind: Themes from the Philosophy of Crispin Wright* (OUP forthcoming).

JANE HEAL is Professor of Philosophy at Cambridge University and Fellow of St John's College. She is the author of *Fact and Meaning: Quine and Wittgenstein on Philosophy of Language* (Blackwell 1989) and of *Mind, Reason and Imagination: Selected Essays in Philosophy of Mind and Language* (CUP 2003).

CONOR MCHUGH is Lecturer in Philosophy at the University of Southampton. He has published widely in epistemology and philosophy of mind and he is the editor (with Ezio Di Nucci) of *Content, Consciousness and Perception: Essays in Contemporary Philosophy of Mind* (Cambridge Scholars Press 2006).

MARTINE NIDA-RÜMELIN is Professor at the University of Fribourg in Switzerland. Her research focuses on the status of conscious individuals. Most of her work has appeared in collective volumes and international journals. She is the author of *Farben und phänomenales Wissen: Eine Materialismuskritik* (1993), *Der Blick von innen: Identität bewusstseinsfähiger Wesen über die Zeit* (Suhrkamp 2006, English version in preparation).

LUCY O'BRIEN is Reader in Philosophy at University College London. She is the author of *Self-Knowing Agents* (OUP 2007) and co-editor, with Matthew Soteriou, of *Mental Actions* (OUP 2009). She works on the philosophy of mind and action, focusing in particular on self-consciousness and self-knowledge.

CHRISTOPHER PEACOCKE is Professor of Philosophy at Columbia University and holds the Richard Wollheim Chair of Philosophy at University College London. His books include

Being Known (OUP 1999), *The Realm of Reason* (OUP 2003), and *Truly Understood* (OUP 2008). He is currently completing a book on the first person, the self, and self-representation.

CAROL ROVANE is Professor of Philosophy at Columbia University (NY). She is the author of *The Bounds of Agency: An Essay in Revisionary Metaphysics* (Princeton 1998) and *For and Against Relativism* (forthcoming).

PAUL SNOWDON is Grote Professor of Mind and Logic at University College London. Before that he was a fellow of Exeter College, Oxford. He is the author of several papers on the philosophy of perception, the mind–body problem and personal identity. Some of his writings on perceptions are about to be published under the title *Papers on Perceptual Experience* (OUP forthcoming).

Introduction

Annalisa Coliva

The Self and Self-Knowledge brings together eleven new essays and one substantial reply by some of the major theorists working in the field. It stems from two conferences held in Bigorio (Switzerland) in 2004 and at the Institute of Philosophy in London in 2008.[1]

The rationale of the conferences and of the book comes from noticing that programs that seek to reconcile the nature of the mind with a broadly physical, causal, and non-perspectival account of the world dominate current research in philosophy of psychology. However, our self-knowledge—characteristically expressed in *self-ascriptions* of mental states with propositional content, like "I hope my flight is on time" and "I was relieved to find my luggage waiting for me"—seems to be prima facie unsuited to causal, purely third-personal forms of explanation.[2] The problems here are not—at least not in the first instance—scientific. Rather, *philosophical* analysis is needed. More specifically, any satisfactory account of self-knowledge needs to provide philosophically defensible models of three main aspects:

1) how it is possible to have non-inferential but perspectivally *first-personal* (or *de se*) thoughts—thoughts characteristically expressed by means of the first-person pronoun and resting on no other mode of thinking about oneself; and, consequently, what notion of the self emerges from reflections on the possibility and features of first-person thoughts;
2) how one can know the *kind* of mental states one is in—how does one know that one's state is one of wishing for something, for instance, rather than expecting it?;

---

[1] These events were respectively made possible by the generous contribution of the Fonds national suisse (project number 1115-05572) and of the Institute of Philosophy, in collaboration with Arché at the University of St Andrews and the British Academy. I hereby express my deepest gratitude to all these institutions for their support.

[2] For a critical assessment of causal and otherwise naturalistically oriented accounts of self-knowledge, see Bar-On, D. 2004 *Speaking My Mind. Expression and Self-Knowledge*, Oxford, Oxford University Press; and Bilgrami, A. 2006 *Self-Knowledge and Resentment*, Cambridge (Mass.), Harvard University Press.

3) how one can have knowledge of the specific *propositional content* of a mental state one is in—that one is hoping, for instance, specifically for one's flight to be on time.

The third issue has received a lot of attention in the last three decades, especially in light of the problem of reconciling knowledge of one's mental states with *semantic externalism*: the now dominant view, originating in the work of Hilary Putnam and Tyler Burge, according to which the content of one's thoughts is at least partially determined by causal and sociological factors that are external to individual minds. However, the first two issues—how subjects are able to direct their thought onto themselves, and what view of the self that entails, as well as how they can know the kind of intentional states they are in—remain comparatively poorly understood, with little consensus emerging in recent research.

These latter two issues are the themes at the heart of the present volume, although one essay will be concerned with an account of the compatibility between semantic externalism and an expressivist explanation of self-knowledge, for reasons which will become apparent in the following. The way in which they will be approached, moreover, will be entirely philosophical in an attempt to elucidate the kind of *conceptual* and *methodological* considerations which should be brought to bear on an account of first-personal thoughts and, therefore, on the explanation of the nature of the self, as well as on the understanding of how it is so much as possible for us to know what kinds of mental state we are enjoying.

As anticipated, their specific differences notwithstanding, all contributors to the volume share the view that there is a distinctively first-personal perspective that philosophy is concerned to characterize and explain. That such an approach should make its voice heard (or, even, re-heard) is especially needed at this particular moment in time when considerable enthusiasm is placed on the idea that empirical inquiry and data could solve the problems of the self and self-knowledge, and even rebut some central tenets of the philosophical approach to these issues, such as the fact that there is a distinctively first-personal access to our own mental states.

Just to make a couple of examples: so-called "theory theories"[3] claim, roughly, that our knowledge of our own intentional states is the result of the tacit application to ourselves of a theory about the mind that we elaborate by means of observation and inference and fully develop around the age of 3 to 4. Self-knowledge would therefore be secured very much like our knowledge of other people's mental states. Hence, the idea that our own intentional mental states are often transparent to us and that we are mostly authoritative with respect to them is an illusion fostered by, on the one hand, the fact that we have become proficient in applying the theory of mind we have

---

[3] See, for instance, Gopnik, A. 1983 "How we can know our minds: The illusion of first person knowledge of intentionality", *Brain and Behavioral Science* 16, 1–14.

elaborated and, on the other, the fact that we are constantly around ourselves so that we tend generally to get ourselves right, as it were.

Alternatively, think of so-called "simulation theories".[4] Arguably, they don't deny the existence of a distinctively first-personal perspective. However, their internal differences notwithstanding, they all place knowledge of other minds in forms of simulation which already presuppose knowledge of our own mental states, one way or the other. They then nowadays tend to ground the latter knowledge in our instinctive, biologically based neural responses to stimuli which are, in turn, replicated by so-called "mirror neurons", when they occur in other subjects and make themselves manifest in relevant forms of behavior.[5]

As is well known, all these theories are subject to criticisms stemming from the other camp, and different versions of each have been proposed so that it is still unclear which one will prevail, if any.[6] Yet the point is not to deny that our mental states are physically realized in some neural configuration or other. Nor is it to deny that we have instinctive, biologically determined reactions to other subjects' characteristic behavior, or that children undergo considerable psychological development, also with respect to mentality. The point, rather, is that none of this fully and adequately accounts for our ability to make and understand *psychological self-ascriptions*, particularly of intentional mental states, which exhibit full mastery of the first person concept, as well as of a wide and fine-grained variety of psychological concepts.

Now, to clarify things perhaps at the cost of some simplification: if knowledge is understood as *propositional* knowledge and concepts are required to have it, any account of subjects' information processing or psychological abilities that fall short of the ability of making and understanding psychological self-ascriptions, *ipso facto* isn't an explanation of self-knowledge (as well as of knowledge of other minds). Of course these accounts may be illuminating and important, and no doubt the relevant concepts may be grounded in the ways in which subjects acquire and process information about themselves and others, or in their ability to have first-order mental states and to form expectations about other subjects' behavior. Yet, part of the philosophical work which needs to be done in this area is precisely that of clarifying the scope, the nature, and the role of these interconnections.

Furthermore, nothing in present-day psychological theories accounts for the role psychological self-ascriptions play in our communicative exchanges, or for the features

---

[4] See, for instance, Gordon, R. 1996 "Radical simulation", in P. Carruthers and P. K. Smith (eds.) *Theories of Theories of Mind*, Cambridge, Cambridge University Press, 11–21; Goldman, A. 2006 *Simulating Minds: The Philosophy, Psychology and Neuroscience of Mindreading*, Oxford, Oxford University Press.

[5] It is well known that mirror neurons have been discovered by the Italian research group led by Rizzolatti, based in Parma. Since then, various joint publications between members of the group and theorists of mind have appeared. See, for example, Gallese V. and Goldman, A. 1998 "Mirror neurons and the simulation theory of mindreading", *Trends in Cognitive Science* 2, 493–501.

[6] See, for instance, Carruthers and Smith 1996, op. cit. Davies, M. and Stone, T. 1995a (eds.) *Folk Psychology: The Theory of Mind Debate*, Oxford, Blackwell; and eid. 1995b *Mental Simulation: Evaluations and Applications*, Oxford, Blackwell.

that are characteristically accorded to them (by no means exclusively) within that practice, such as authority and transparency, as we will presently see. Connectedly, none of this explains the role that such a practice can and does play in allowing us to individuate mental states, with the fineness of grain our psychological self-ascriptions typically manifest.

Moreover, it is only by developing a philosophical account of reasons—broadly understood—that the connection between being in a given mental state and the corresponding self-ascription may (or may not) be characterized in epistemic terms, so as to motivate the idea that what goes by the name of "self-knowledge" is indeed a genuine kind of knowledge.

Finally, it merits note that the first person concept, which is necessary in order to make the relevant psychological self-ascriptions, is more presupposed than elucidated by current empirical research in psychology. Of course scientific inquiry can and does illuminate the various sensory, perceptual, proprioceptive, and memory-based modalities which ground first-personal attributions of various properties, both physical and psychological. Moreover, it surely shows which anomalies can sometimes affect our capacities for self-ascriptions of both kinds of properties, due to different kinds of malfunctioning.[7] Yet, for the reasons reviewed so far, a lot of work remains to be done to characterize adequately the possession conditions of such a concept and the implications a specification of such conditions has for our notion of the self, if any.

The essays contained in this volume are intended as a contribution to these preliminary and necessary elucidations of our first person concept and the conception of ourselves it underwrites, as well as of the distinctive features of psychological self-ascriptions, which characteristically express full-blown knowledge of, in particular, our own intentional mental states. Yet, as we shall review in a moment, even on this front consensus is hard to come by.

The background to the volume

As said, the contributors to the present volume share a general perspective onto the problems of the self and self-knowledge and on how best to investigate them. That is to say, they all agree that there is a distinctively first-personal perspective and that philosophical elucidation of its constitutive conditions may be relevant also to scientific inquiry at least in the following sense. Having a clearer grasp of it can shed light on how best to interpret the bearing of scientific results onto the issue of first person thoughts, self-knowledge, and the metaphysics of the self. However, they are also representative of different philosophical positions on each of these topics. In what follows, a brief sketch of their views is presented so as to make apparent the interest of a volume which

---

[7] Just to give a couple of examples, take the phenomenon of thought-insertion, considered as one of the distinctive features of schizophrenia, which impairs our ability to self-ascribe certain psychological properties. Or else, think of ascriptions of sensations in one's missing limb.

brings their perspectives together. In the last section I will then present in more detail their specific contributions to the present volume.

The self

As noted, no account of our ability authoritatively to self-ascribe intentional states would be complete unless it provided an explanation of how perspectivally *first-personal* thought is possible in the first place. The discussion of what is required in order for a subject to have a concept of *him/herself* is traditionally intertwined with the metaphysical issue of the nature of persons: are selves essentially identical to human beings (a kind of animal endowed of physical and psychological properties), or are they essentially rational, deliberative agents, or else centres of phenomenal awareness, who could transcend, at least in principle, their bodily limitations? Most importantly, what sort of considerations should we appeal to in order to decide this difficult issue, and what consequences would an answer to this question have with respect to the nature of first-personal thought?

One approach, manifest in what is perhaps the currently prevailing tendency in work on this topic, is purely *metaphysical*, seeking a resolution to the issue by appealing to our intuitions about counterfactual cases: about whether, after undergoing a number of hypothetical—either physical or psychological—changes a given subject would still be regarded as the same person, or indeed as a person at all. Martine Nida-Rümelin favors this approach and thinks it can be used to support a form of subject-body dualism.[8]

However, some theorists are weary of the methodology behind the metaphysical take on the issue because "intuitions" in this area of philosophy are characteristically conflicted and unstable. They therefore favor different approaches, which might respectively be called the *normative*, the *phenomenological*, and the *epistemological* approach.

Carol Rovane favors the normative one. This approach is distinctively non-naturalist, since it individuates selves on the basis of their "commitment to achieving overall rational unity".[9] Whenever this normative commitment is met, then, according to Rovane, there is one single *agent* and, therefore, one single *person*. It is a result of this view that if, for instance, the various personalities of subjects affected by multiple personality disorder were able to form plans and to devise and sustain ways of carrying them out, they should be regarded as specific, distinct persons. Conversely, if a group of human beings were capable of devising and carrying out plans, as one, so to say, they should equally be considered as one single person. Thus, more persons could inhabit one and the same body and more bodies could make up to one single person.

---

[8] Nida-Rümelin, M. forthcoming *The View from the Inside: Transtemporal Identity of Sentient Beings*, (a previous German edition has already appeared in print).
[9] Rovane, C. 1998 *The Bounds of Agency: An Essay in Revisionary Metaphysics*, Princeton (N. J.), Princeton University Press, 8.

The normally one-one relationship between selves and human animals is, on this view, a metaphysical contingency.

The phenomenological approach, advocated by Christopher Peacocke,[10] has it that selves are individuated by integrated apparatus that operates to produce conscious states. An implication of this view is that the ability to have first person thoughts such as "I am sleepy" does not depend on thinking of oneself as an embodied entity. Rather, possession of the first person concept requires no more than the ability to apply it when the thinker of *this* very thought has the property in question. While the view is hospitable to the possibility that selves might not be embodied, it is actually not committed to Cartesianism about the self. Indeed, on Peacocke's view, since some of the conscious states subjects enjoy represent parts of their bodies as, for example, aching, or represent other bodies as being variously located with respect to them, it actually follows that selves are embodied.

Proponents of the epistemological approach, finally, such as the late Gareth Evans, John McDowell, José Luis Bermúdez, John Campbell, and Lucy O'Brien, argue that in order for first-personal thoughts to be objective,[11] subjects must necessarily think of themselves as inter-subjectively accessible items in a public world. They take it to follow that for such thoughts to be possible at all, selves must conceive of themselves as necessarily embodied entities, and, in particular, as specific human beings. But it is important to stress that this conception of personal identity, also known as "animalist", need not be in any way hospitable to the idea, very much favored by hard-core naturalists, that selves should be identified with more fundamental and merely physical entities, such as functioning human brains. For all philosophers in the animalist camp endorse the view that persons—that is, human beings with psychological properties— are irreducible to more basic kinds of physical entities.[12]

Finally, although the proposals reviewed so far have a different take on the conditions of individuation of the first person concept, as well as on the metaphysical nature of selves, they also present common elements insofar as most of them consider selves to be capable of some kinds of action, which typically involve their being accessible to one another. So, to put it perhaps contentiously, it may not be a constitutive feature of selves that they be identical to human beings, and it may be that subjects need not think of themselves as specific living human animals in order to have the first person concept. Yet, it may nevertheless be a contingent but (mostly) unavoidable feature of selves that

---

[10] See Peacocke, C. 1999 *Being Known*, Oxford, Oxford University Press; and Peacocke, C. 2008 *Truly Understood*, Oxford, Oxford University Press.

[11] Evans, G. 1982 *The Varieties of Reference*, Oxford, Clarendon Press; McDowell, J. 1998 "Reductionism and the first person", in his *Mind, Value and Reality*, Cambridge (Mass.), Harvard University Press, 359–82; Bermúdez, J. L. 1998 *The Paradox of Self-Consciousness*, Cambridge (Mass.), MIT Press; O'Brien, L. 2007 *Self-Knowing Agents*, Oxford, Oxford University Press.

[12] Some elements of a non-epistemic defense of the animalist conception of the self can be found in Coliva, A. 2012 "Which key to all mythologies about the self?—A note on where the illusion of transcendence comes from and how to resist it", in F. Recanati and S. Prosser (eds.) *Immunity to Error Through Misidentification: New Essays*, Cambridge, Cambridge University Press, pp. 22–45.

they be realized in particular living human bodies, as well as a contingent, but nearly always actual aspect of first person thought, that subjects think of themselves as such.

Self-knowledge[13]

Since the 1970s, much of the philosophical discussion about self-knowledge has been conditioned by a trichotomy: that such knowledge can only be based "on observation, or on inference, or on nothing".[14] As we shall see in a moment, contemporary proponents of naturalistic accounts of self-knowledge have tended to favor refined versions of the first two kinds of explanation—accounts which try to assimilate self-knowledge to familiar, perceptual, or inferential ways of achieving knowledge of other kinds—while non-naturalist theorists have tended to favor the third: the idea that self-knowledge is, one way or another, based on no real cognitive achievement. However, this last kind of proposal, once regarded as liberating, is now coming under pressure in its turn, and non-naturalist yet somewhat epistemic accounts of self-knowledge are currently being advanced. The dialectical situation is quite complex, and the reasons behind the various trends are in need of clarification.

Naturalist accounts range from proposals like David Armstrong's refined observationalism, which postulates the existence of a reliable mechanism that produces beliefs about one's first-order mental states any time one has them, to the kind of inferentialism suggested by Alison Gopnik,[15] which sees self-knowledge as the deliverance of a personal psychological theory which one tacitly applies to one's own behavior and non-intentional mental states. However, such proposals seem generically out of kilter with some apparently *constitutive* and therefore a priori aspects of our basic psychological self-ascriptions, such as *transparency*, according to which if subjects have propositional attitudes they know they do; the *groundlessness* of our psychological intentional self-ascriptions, which, at least in most cases, don't appear to be based either on introspective awareness of intentional mental states, or on the observation of our own behavior, or brain states,[16] from which we should know inferentially what we are feeling or thinking.[17] Finally, these accounts have trouble in accounting for the fact that psychological self-ascriptions seem to be constitutively and not merely contingently *authoritative* insofar as a subject is normally treated as if an expert about her own

---

[13] Valuable recent introductions to the state of art are Gertler, B. (ed.) 2003 *Privileged Access: Philosophical Accounts of Self-Knowledge*, Aldershot, Ashgate, in particular the introductory essay; Gertler, B. 2011 *Self-Knowledge*, London, Routledge. A new collection of essays related to many of the issues at the heart of this volume is Hatzimoysis, A. (ed.) 2011 *Self-Knowledge*, Oxford, Oxford University Press.

[14] The trichotomy originates in Boghossian, P. 1989 "Content and self-knowledge", *Philosophical Topics* 17, 5–26 (at p. 5). It has been taken up by Peacocke, C. 1999, op.cit., 231.

[15] Armstrong, D. 1968 *A Materialist Theory of the Mind*, London, Routledge; Gopnik 1983, op. cit. A proposal similar to Armstrong's is Lycan's 1996 *Consciousness and Experience*, Cambridge (Mass.), MIT Press.

[16] This criticism is directed at Gopnik's account, not at Armstrong's, which is characterized by avoiding introspectionism (as well as inferentialism, of course).

[17] Of course cases of inferential self-knowledge may be possible. Yet, they usually presuppose non-inferential knowledge of the mental states which figure as premises of those inferences.

mental states: we usually take it for granted that if a subject says that she thinks that *p*, then it is the case that she thinks that *p*. To clarify: obviously there may be cases of self-deception. Yet they are normally considered cases of *irrationality* and not merely of brain-mechanisms' malfunctioning, as Armstrong's perspective would have it, or of mistaken theorizing about ourselves, as Gopnik's theory would predict.[18]

Responding to the perceived shortcomings of naturalist approaches, theorists writing in the 1980s started to propose so-called *constitutive* models of self-knowledge. The common core of all these accounts, variously advanced by philosophers such as Sydney Shoemaker and Crispin Wright,[19] is that self-knowledge—in fact our psychological self-ascriptions especially of intentional mental states—isn't the result of any cognitive achievement whatsoever. Indeed, it is somewhat of a misnomer to call it "knowledge". Rather, what goes by the name of "self-knowledge" is a by-product of *conceptual* relationships between first-order and second-order mental states—corresponding in fact to the three above-mentioned features of self-knowledge.[20] These relationships are sometimes expressed in the form of a single biconditional (known as the *Constitutive Thesis*):

Given certain conditions C, one ϕs that *p* if and only if one believes that one ϕs that *p*.[21]

Various readings of the Constitutive Thesis have been proposed. Some theorists, such as Shoemaker, have accorded priority to its left-to-right direction (transparency).[22]

---

[18] Peacocke 1999, op. cit., 224, insists on the rational aspect of self-knowledge which observationalism of Armstrong's reliabilist variety doesn't account for. Similar points are raised in Zimmerman, A. 1996 "Basic self-knowledge: Answering Peacocke's criticisms of constitutivism", *Philosophical Studies* 128, 337–79, and also in his "Self-knowledge: Rationalism vs. empiricism", *Philosophy Compass* 3/2, 325–52.

[19] Shoemaker, S. 1986 *The First Person Perspective and Other Essays*, Oxford, Oxford University Press; Wright, C. 1989 "Wittgenstein's later philosophy of mind: Sensation, privacy and intentions", *Journal of Philosophy*, LXXVI, 622–34, and "Self-knowledge: the Wittgensteinian legacy", in Wright, C., Smith, B. and Macdonald, C. 1998 (eds.) *Knowing Our Own Minds*, Oxford, Clarendon Press, 13–45.

[20] I am here referring to Shoemaker's (1996, op. cit.) groundbreaking work. In more recent pronouncements, however, he has maintained that there is a substantial epistemology of self-knowledge, although the details of what such an epistemology would look like are somehow left in the dark (Shoemaker, S. 2003 "Moran on self-knowledge", *European Journal of Philosophy* 11/3, 391–401, esp. at pp. 391, 400–1). This would place Shoemaker outside the circle of constitutive theorists as I have characterized them. This, however, is not the place to engage in a detailed examination and reconstruction of Shoemaker's position.

[21] Where ϕ ranges over propositional attitudes only.

[22] Richard Moran 2001 *Authority and Estrangement*, Princeton, Princeton University Press, as is well known, has forcefully defended transparency. Yet he is no constitutive theorist, since he denies that what goes by the name of "self-knowledge" is just the conceptual truth expressed by the Constitutive Thesis (cf. also Moran, R. 2003 "Responses to O'Brien and Shoemaker", *European Journal of Philosophy* 11/3, 402–19). Furthermore, it is important to keep distinct the notion of transparency from what Moran calls "the transparency condition". The latter consists in an *explanation* of how we have immediate knowledge of our beliefs along the lines provided by Gareth Evans. Notoriously, he held the view that in order to know our beliefs, we need not look within ourselves, but outward, at the world, to see whether there is any evidence that supports *p* so as to form the belief that *p*. If so, then we can just preface *p* with "I believe that" (Evans, op. cit., 225). Still, simply to hold that propositional mental states are transparent to their owners is not yet a commitment to the kind of explanation of how that is the case, which stems from Evans' position (and that Moran is concerned to elaborate at length). One reason to keep the two issues separate is that there is no agreement that Evans' account of transparency is correct, especially for other kinds of propositional attitude

Some, in contrast, like Wright, have given priority to its right-to-left side (authority).[23] Others, like Bilgrami, have accorded no priority to either.

Moreover, the Constitutive Thesis can be read as carrying different metaphysical commitments. It may be taken to imply that first-order mental states are (at least partially) *constituted* by the corresponding second-order ones, and so could not so much as exist without the corresponding states of awareness. Or else, it could be taken in a more deflationary way, as merely stating conceptually necessary and sufficient conditions for self-knowledge.

Another issue at the heart of the debate among constitutivists concerns the details of the C-conditions under which the biconditional is supposed to hold. Wright's, Bilgrami's, Heal's, and Coliva's views[24] all differ with respect to this issue, the proffered explanations ranging from the appeal to characteristic features of our linguistic practices of ascription of propositional attitudes to the conditions of deliberative agency.

It is, at present, still uncertain what is the most resilient form of the constitutive proposal, and what its metaphysical significance might be. But this kind of direction has in any case suffered something of a backlash, with many theorists increasingly uncertain whether any form of it can do justice to the stubborn impression that first-order and second-order mental states are *separate existences*: that infants and intelligent animals, which, arguably, lack the capacity for self-conscious thought, are capable of beliefs and desires; that a whole host of intelligent intentional states may well be *unconscious*, yet operative in shaping our own behavior; and, connectedly, that subjects may be *self-deceived* about their own intentional states and hence believe that they ϕ that p when in fact they do not. For all these reasons, it is tempting to make it a datum of the problem that it is one thing to have first-order mental states and quite another to *know* what they are.[25] It is true, to be sure, that the constitutive theorist has room for manoeuvre over these considerations by dint of the relativity of the biconditional to the obtaining of the so far unexplained conditions C. But some theorists are doubtful that there can be any satisfactory and substantial explanation of what those conditions might be, to bolster a constitutive account. And even if there can, it still remains natural to conceive

---

beside belief. For a sustained defense of the transparency method, see Fernández, J. 2003 "Privileged access naturalized", *Philosophical Quarterly* 53, 352–72, and Byrne, A. 2005 "Introspection", *Philosophical Topics* 33, 79–104.

[23] Notice that although Burge has maintained that there are self-verifying psychological self-ascriptions, he wouldn't count as a constitutive theorist, because he wishes to retain the idea that self-knowledge is indeed a form of genuine knowledge. To such an end, he has elaborated a (partially externalist) notion of entitlement as a form of epistemic support, which does not require a subject who has it to have an understanding of it (Burge, T. 1996 "Our entitlement to self-knowledge", *Proceedings of the Aristotelian Society* XCVII, 91–116).

[24] Wright, op. cit.; Bilgrami, op. cit.; Heal, J. 2001 "On first-person authority", *Proceedings of the Aristotelian Society* CII, 1–19; Coliva, A. 2009 "Self-knowledge and commitments", *Synthese* 171/3, 365–75.

[25] See, for instance, O'Brien, L. 2003 "Moran on agency and self-knowledge", *European Journal of Philosophy* 11/3, 375–90.

of self-knowledge as somehow *brought about* by the obtaining of the first-order mental states it concerns.

Recent non-naturalist, non observationalist, non-inferentialist, yet somehow *epistemic* accounts of self-knowledge,[26] such as, for instance, Christopher Peacocke's, Richard Moran's, and Lucy O'Brien's,[27] are intended to respond to these misgivings, and to provide a fourth way beyond the trichotomy "either by observation, or by inference or by nothing". According to proponents of this new model, self-knowledge consists in making judgements about one's own first-order mental states on the basis of having them and *for the reason* that one has them. Self-knowledge is thus a modest, yet genuinely cognitive accomplishment that consists in immediate, non-observational judgement about one's own mental states that is nevertheless rationally grounded in the obtaining of those very mental states. This new proposal, in distancing itself from the naturalist and constitutive accounts, and thereby from their special problems, is apt to impress as welcome—provided of course it does not encounter equally serious objections of its own.

There is, however, one salient potential trouble-spot:[28] the need to explain how a first-order mental state can count as *a subject's own reason* for ascribing it to herself, without thereby presupposing that she has anterior *knowledge* of it. For, otherwise, epistemic accounts would bluntly presuppose the very thing that they try to explain. Facing this concern, theorists of epistemic leanings, within the broadly speaking internalist camp, such as Christopher Peacocke and Jim Pryor,[29] have suggested that the mere occurrence of a first-order mental state can immediately justify its self-ascription, provided the state is *conscious*—that is, provided it contributes to a subject's occurrent phenomenological state. But this proposal in turn needs to be further clarified. For one thing, an account is now owing of how a belief, for example, can be an item of consciousness in a manner falling short of its being an item of self-knowledge. For another, while it is pretty much unquestioned that outer and inner sensations—like sensing red and being in pain—have a distinctive phenomenology, it is much more controversial that the same holds for propositional attitudes such as beliefs, desires, hopes, and wishes. And even if there *is* something it is phenomenologically like to believe that the present US President is a Democrat, say, it seems questionable

---

[26] I label them "epistemic" because, while recoiling from observationalism and inferentialism, these accounts are united in denying that what goes by the name of "self-knowledge" is just a conceptual truth captured by the Constitutive Thesis. They all share the view that our psychological self-ascriptions, when true, and epistemically grounded in the corresponding first-order mental states, express genuine knowledge of them.

[27] Peacocke 1999, op.cit.; Moran, op. cit.; O'Brian 2007, op. cit. Bar-On, op. cit., in contrast, presents an interesting combination of an expressivist view, according to which all avowals replace prior forms of linguistic and non-linguistic behavior, and have essentially an expressive role, with an epistemic account, which makes use of the notion of entitlement. So, in her view, being in the mental state which brings about the avowal also entitles the subject to it. Finally, for the reasons offered in fn. 23, also Burge would count as an epistemic theorist on the characterization of this position I have been offering.

[28] See Coliva, A. 2008 "Peacocke's self-knowledge", *Ratio*, 21/1, 13–27.

[29] Peacocke 1999, op. cit.; Pryor, J. 2005 "There is immediate justification", in M. Steup and E. Sosa (eds.) *Contemporary Debates in Epistemology*, Oxford, Blackwell, 181–201.

whether this phenomenological character is sufficiently fine-grained to underwrite all the distinctions we characteristically straightforwardly master between various psychological self-ascriptions with the same content—for instance, between a hope that that will be so, as opposed to a desire that it will, or the wish it will.

Of course it is open to an epistemic theorist to opt for an externalist construal of the notion of (non evidential) reason in this area, along the lines suggested by, for instance, Burge (1996, op. cit.). But the account must be such as to avoid the objections raised against crude forms of externalism, such as Armstrong's—in particular, that they don't account for the rational dimension of self-knowledge. At present, it is still uncertain whether this project can be successfully brought to completion.[30]

The foregoing should have made apparent the complexity of the issues at the core of this project and of the dialectic in the debate. A complexity that can only be treated with refined conceptual tools. It is therefore entirely appropriate that leading figures in the field should have the opportunity to deepen their reflections. Thus, the aim of this book is not to launch a new trend in the areas researched but, rather, to deepen the rationale behind some of the main already existing positions in the debate, by presenting new arguments which can lend support to these views; to develop some of their details by confronting new objections; and, finally, to raise challenges for opposite views which, meanwhile, have appeared in the literature. Hence, the proposed volume testifies not only to the complexity of the issues researched, but also to the kind of mature outlook that some of the main players in the field have reached.

The structure and content of the book

The book is divided into three, interrelated parts. The first part of the volume—*The self and its individuation*—contains four essays which address the topic of the nature of selves as well as some methodological issues relevant to the debate in this area. Two of them (Rovane and Nida-Rümelin) argue for a non-animalist account of selves, although by appealing to altogether different considerations. The third one (Peacocke's) mainly reacts against the no subject view to be associated to Hume, Kant, and the early Wittgenstein. Finally, the fourth essay (Campbell's) favors the animalist view. Let us present them in more detail.

In her "Does rationality enforce identity?", Rovane thinks that the impossibility of "quasi-reasoning", recently discussed by Tyler Burge,[31] brings grist to the mill of a neo-Lockean account of selves, according to which the latter must be individuated on the basis of their ability to have a unified rational point of view. She then argues that

---

[30] According to some remarks in Gertler 2011, op. cit. it is uncertain whether the rational elements to Burge's notion of entitlement play any significant epistemic role.
[31] See Burge, T. 2003 "Memory and persons", *The Philosophical Review*, 112/3, 289–337. Quasi-reasoning consists in reasoning out of attitudes that aren't strictly one's own, but that in fact derive from someone else's mental life, although they appear to be one's own.

this shows that there are three ways to conceive of the first person point of view—as a phenomenological point of view, determined by a single consciousness; as a bodily point of view, determined by the human animal which realizes it; or else, as a rational point of view. Rovane favors the last one, and therefore holds that personal identity is not a metaphysical given, but, on her account, a product of effort and will, which can transcend bodily and phenomenological limitations, so as to allow for the possibility of group and multiple personhood.

Nida-Rümelin, in the paper titled "The conceptual origin of subject-body dualism", argues that a criterion-free understanding of what a subject is, is deeply incorporated in our first-personal way of thinking and is in fact constitutive of our first person concept. On her view, this can be shown by considering several counterfactual scenarios. She then uses her diagnosis to develop a new argument in favour of a conceptual version of subject-body dualism. While, on Nida-Rümelin's view, such a version of subject-body dualism is not in itself a version of its metaphysical counterpart, it is consistent with it.

In "Subjects and consciousness" Peacocke claims that *de se* contents are individuated by the condition that they refer *de jure* to the owners of the mental states or events in whose contents they feature. This idea is then brought to bear on the issue of the ontology of subjects, which are conceived as metaphysically interdependent with conscious mental states and events. The view is then applied to a critical discussion of the positions of Hume, Kant, and the early Wittgenstein, to oppose the idea that there is no such thing as a self. As remarked in the previous section, Peacocke's account of the constitutive conditions of the first person concept does not make reference to subjects' abilities to think of themselves as embodied. Nevertheless, he thinks that among the conscious mental states subjects enjoy, some involve a representation of subjects as embodied. He therefore favors the metaphysical view that selves are embodied.

John Campbell, in his "Does perception do any work in an understanding of the first person?", challenges non-animalist accounts and presents a new and surprising argument to support animalism. On his view, grasp of the first person depends on an ability to use perception, not only to plot one's route through the world, but, interestingly, to gain the very knowledge of one's own mental states his opponents take to be fundamental to a grasp of the first person. For, on Campbell's view, knowledge of one's own mental states depends on knowledge of their causal connections and this, in turn, requires grasp of the role of perception in shaping our beliefs. But, in its turn, this presupposes grasp of the role of the world with which we, human animals, physically interact.

Part two—"Consciousness, action-awareness and their role in self-knowledge"—contains three papers and a substantial reply. Two essays react critically to the new epistemic paradigm, largely associated with recent work by Christopher Peacocke that has lately emerged as an alternative to the well-known trichotomy that self-knowledge should be based either "on inference, or on observation, or on nothing".[32] On such an epistemic, yet neither inferentialist nor observational model, knowledge of our own mental states should be based on an awareness of them, and knowledge of our mental actions on the awareness of our tryings of bringing them about.

Thus, in her "Consciousness and self-awareness", Heal presents a case of Freudian unconscious mental state, which supports the view that Peacocke's account of psychological self-ascriptions as non-inferentially justified on the basis of having first-order conscious mental states, stands in need of refinement. In particular, further work seems to be needed on the notion of what it means for a mental state to be conscious, and on the very idea of non-inferential justification. The paper concludes by outlining some possible developments of these two key-notions.

In the paper "Knowledge of actions and tryings", O'Brien, in contrast, considers the problem of how we can know our mental actions. She concedes that Peacocke's account would represent an improvement over a related proposal, but argues that it remains wanting. For, on her view, it must make room for the possibility that tryings cause action awareness, while failing to cause the action itself. O'Brien deems such a gap implausible in the case of mental actions.

Conor McHugh, in his "Reasons and self-knowledge", defends the approach to self-knowledge championed by Peacocke by presenting a "reasons account" of self-knowledge. Accordingly, certain conscious states and episodes can give their subjects reasons to self-ascribe corresponding propositional attitudes to their contents. He critically reacts to objections raised by Coliva,[33] and closes by presenting a distinction between various kinds of epistemological internalism, as well as an internalist conception of epistemic warrant that may have application in further domains.

The section ends with Peacocke's response to the criticisms raised by Heal and O'Brien, titled "Conscious events and self-ascriptions: Comments on Heal and O'Brien". Peacocke clarifies and deepens his account of consciously experiencing something as *F*, as opposed to having in consciousness manifestations of an unconscious state of *F*; as well as his account of the differences between apparent action awareness and apparent perceptual awareness.

Part three—*Self-knowledge: Robust or fragile?*—contains four papers that debate whether the characteristic features usually attributed to our knowledge of our own mental states—that is, transparency, authority, and groundlessness—and which are taken to set it apart from, and to make it much more robust than, any other form of knowledge are indeed secure.

On the one hand, Bar-On, in her "Externalism and skepticism: Recognition, expression and self-knowledge", explores the bearing of her neo-expressivist account of self-knowledge on the issue of semantic externalism, which is traditionally thought to pose a problem for the authority of self-knowledge. Bar-On claims that

---

[32] Cf. fn. 14. [33] Coliva 2008, op. cit.

neo-expressivism can make better sense than its alternatives of how attitudinal self-ascriptions can be especially authoritative and yet compatible with an externalist account of their content.

On the other hand, Coliva, in "One variety of self-knowledge: Constitutivism as constructivism", argues that for constitutive positions to stand scrutiny and to retain their distinctive metaphysical claim that, at least in some cases, one's own first-order mental states are constituted by one's own corresponding self-ascriptions, they should dramatically restrict their scope to some specific kinds of attitudinal self-ascriptions only, and endorse a rather radical form of constructivism. That way also transparency, authority, and groundlessness would indeed be secured as a matter of conceptual necessity. As a consequence, however, it is claimed that a unified account of our knowledge of all kinds of mental states we can enjoy—sensations, perceptions, emotions, and further sorts of propositional attitudes—is not forthcoming, and that we should therefore be hospitable to pluralism in this area.

The last two contributions discuss whether self-knowledge is indeed special compared to, and more secure than any other kind of knowledge, as many have argued, and whether, in the Wittgensteinian spirit endorsed by constitutivists, it would best be approached and investigated by paying close attention to *avowals*, that is, to first-personal, primarily verbal psychological self-ascriptions. Paul Snowdon attacks this view, in his "How to think about phenomenal self-knowledge", with special reference to so-called "phenomenal" avowals, that is, avowals of sensations and of other occurrent mental events with an experiential content to them. By presenting some counterexamples, he further contends that self-knowledge isn't as robust as constitutivists tend to think.

Akeel Bilgrami—a well-known champion of the constitutivist approach—responds in his "The unique status of self-knowledge". He defends the characteristic robustness and immediacy of central forms of propositional self-knowledge. Finally, Bilgrami offers further support to his preferred version of constitutivism, which makes essential reference to the notion of responsible agency.

PART ONE

The Self and its Individuation

1

Does Rationality Enforce Identity?

Carol Rovane

Locke asked us to envisage an imaginary case—the prince and the cobbler—in which the consciousnesses of two persons are switched, each into the other's body. He took this thought experiment to show that personal identity is not the same as animal identity, because he took it to be intuitively obvious that after the switch each person—the prince and the cobbler—would persist in a new and different body (cf. Locke 1975). Neo-Lockeans have asked us to envisage a much stranger form of personal survival—not merely life in a new and different body, but a life in which we face the prospect of a branching future, with more than one "descendent self" who will be psychologically related to us in roughly the same way that we find in the normal case where we have just one future self.[1] So-called "animalists" reject all versions of Locke's distinction, along with the possibility of a branching future, because they view the person as a suitably endowed animal whose identity is biologically given in the way that animal identity generally is (cf. Shoemaker 1970; Parfit 1971).[2]

One striking—you might even say, disconcerting—aspect of the philosophical dispute that Locke inaugurated with his thought experiment is that there is so little agreement about what would count as an adequate reason for taking sides in it. Animalists tend to insist that we mustn't stray too far from the facts of human psychology as we actually find them because, after all, the only *known* cases of personhood are normal adult human beings. Although proponents of Locke's distinction tend to agree that we should *start* with the actual case, they also find it appropriate to consider counterfactual cases. No doubt, the interest of the counterfactual approach depends upon the extent to which it sheds light on actual cases. But this, I think, is precisely the spirit in which Locke and neo-Lockeans have put us through the paces of so many thought experiments. They aim to show us something about what really

---

[1] For early important elaborations of this claim, see S. Shoemaker (1970) and D. Parfit (1971).
[2] There are so many proponents of the animalist view, that any list would either be too long or too incomplete. In this paper, I will be particularly concerned with a general line of argument for the animalist view that has been pursued by both John McDowell and Tyler Burge.

matters to us when we anticipate our futures in the distinctively first personal way that persons alone are able to do; and, according to them, this requires psychological continuity over time, but not the same body, nor even strict identity. Animalists clearly don't find themselves instructed, and as I've said, one central reason why is that they regard the counterfactuals that Locke and neo-Lockeans have asked us to envisage as too distant from the actual case to reveal anything about it.

There is good reason to regard this dispute as a stalemate. Prima facie, each side can offer an internally coherent metaphysical account of personal identity, and each can also claim significant support from common sense. Yet this doesn't mean that our only choice is to wallow in conflict. We can still seek reasons for taking one side or the other, so long as we properly understand our methodological predicament. We need to acknowledge that no matter what reasons we find for taking a given side, they will not suffice to *refute* the other side, except in a way that the other side would regard as question-begging. Because this is so, we cannot expect to resolve this dispute with the usual philosophical strategy of shifting the burden of proof to the other side, for that strategy will leave each side standing as unrefuted by its own lights. Or, to put the same point in another way: if strict proof involves the non-question-begging elimination of alternatives, we shall have to settle for something short of strict proof in the dispute about personal identity. We shall have to adopt a different philosophical methodology, that grants that no matter which side we take we'll be offering a *recommendation* rather than a demonstration. Furthermore, this recommendation will, unavoidably, be *revisionist*. Why? Because it will have to select some consistent subset of the conflicting strands in our commonsense thinking about persons, while rejecting the rest.

Thus, Parfit misled us when he declared his own view to be revisionist, insofar as that would naturally be taken to suggest that there is a non-revisionist view available. There are (at least) two respects in which his view is clearly revisionist: it denies that the identity of a person is all or nothing, affirming instead that it is a matter of degree; and it allows that persons might have something as good as personal survival without identity. I will focus on the second respect, arguing against Parfit's view of survival without identity by bringing to bear the metaphysical consideration to which my title refers, concerning whether rationality enforces identity. Normally, when philosophers argue against Parfit on this point they take themselves to be recovering a more commonsensical view of personal identity that is not revisionist. But my remarks in the preceding paragraph should make clear that this is not the spirit in which I insist that rationality enforces identity. I will show that a proper appreciation of this point entails a startlingly revisionist conception of personal identity, as well as a novel interpretation of Locke's distinction between personal and animal identity.[3]

---

[3] As an aside, let me clarify that there are certain metaphysical advantages that animalists have claimed for their view that I don't be discussing at all in this paper, except to note briefly why I'm setting them aside. One is that the animalist view would allow us to preserve *more* of our commonsense beliefs about persons than the Lockean and neo-Lockean views do. Obviously, this is an advantage only if we are bound to preserve as

In Section 1, I'll review the familiar contours of the philosophical discussion surrounding the defenses of Locke's distinction that were put forward by Parfit, Shoemaker, Perry and others.[4] It is well known that they have had to introduce some conceptual revisions in order to make sense of how, in a branching case, an ancestral self might have something like a first person relation to more than one descendent self, by introducing notions like quasi-memory and other quasi-attitudes. The main line of objection to these innovations has been much as I just described above: neo-Lockean innovations are deemed too unlike the first person point of view as we find it in the lives of actual persons, which of course do not branch. But neo-Lockeans don't find this objection persuasive, and the upshot is the usual stalemate.

In Section 2, I'll turn my attention to an issue that Tyler Burge briefly raised in the course of an unusually rich discussion of the first person (cf. Burge 2003). The bulk of that discussion is devoted to bringing various empirical considerations—which are drawn from both human and animal psychology—to bear against Parfit's ideas about branching. Although these considerations are in many ways novel, as well as intrinsically interesting, their ultimate significance for the philosophical study of personal identity is not entirely novel. In the main, they lend additional empirical support to the sorts of reservations I discuss in Section 1 that philosophers have already registered concerning the extent to which we can make sense of quasi-attitudes like quasi-memory, which Burge, like other opponents of Parfit, alleges we cannot do owing to the ways in which first person modes of thought are situated in animal life. But along the way, he also raises a specific objection against the possibility of quasi-*reasoning* that is somewhat different in character, insofar as it rests on normative rather than empirical considerations. The objection is that the norms of rationality require the strict identity of the reasoner. I will devote Section 2 to showing why Burge is absolutely right about this.

Although Burge is right that there can be no such thing as quasi-reasoning, I will show in Section 3 that he draws the wrong metaphysical conclusion. He takes it to follow that Locke was wrong to draw a distinction between personal and animal

---

much of common sense as possible, and I simply don't see why philosophical inquiry should be so bound, any more than scientific inquiry is. Much depends upon whether there are internal problems within our commonsense views and, also, upon whether further inquiry—whether it be scientific or philosophical inquiry—might offer an improvement on them. A second alleged advantage of the animalist view is that it coheres better with other important metaphysical commitments, most especially with an essentialist metaphysics that portrays persons as instances of a natural kind. Yet even if *some* sorts of entities are best understood as instances of natural kinds, others may not be—clubs for example—and I myself think it would be unwise to proceed on the assumption that persons must be of the first sort rather than the second. In any case, my strategy in this paper will be to focus on issues that have more directly to do with the nature of persons—in particular, issues having to do with rationality—and leave others to sort out broader metaphysical issues like essentialism as they will.

[4] The central text is D. Parfit (2004). An important early anthology of classic papers is edited by J. Perry (1975a).

identity. Whereas, what really follows is a *normative account of personal identity*, which brings in train a novel interpretation of Locke's distinction (cf. Rovane 1998).

This normative account of personal identity derives its primary motivation from an assumption about persons on which both proponents and opponents of Locke's distinction implicitly agree, which is that a person is a reflective rational agent. It goes together with this assumption that each person has a separate point of view from which it deliberates and acts. But there is a second assumption that all parties to the dispute about personal identity generally make as well, which is that the point of view of a person is a phenomenological point of view—in other words, the assumption is that each person has a separate center of consciousness, which is the site of its deliberations, and which constitutes the point of view from which it acts. What divides the parties is whether each such phenomenological point of view is necessarily rooted in a particular animal life. Animalists hold that it is, whereas Locke held that it is not, claiming instead that the same consciousness can persist in a new and different body—from which he concluded that there is a distinction between personal and animal identity. When Locke drew this conclusion, he took a stand on what is arguably an empirical issue that is better left for science to settle, concerning the nature and basis of consciousness. In contrast, the normative account of personal identity is entirely silent on this empirical issue, and indeed entirely independent of it. Rather than focusing on the nature of consciousness, it focuses directly and exclusively on the nature of reflective rational agency. Here is its central claim: *wherever there is a commitment to living up to the normative requirements that define individual rationality, there is an individual person.* Exactly what this central claim of the normative account of personal identity means will come into better focus as the paper proceeds. For now, I'll say just a bit more about its primary motivation, as well as its main implication about personal identity.

I've already indicated what the primary motivation for the normative account is, namely, the assumption that a person is a reflective rational agent. What makes this assumption an especially appropriate starting point for an account of personal identity is that it suffices to capture, or track, the distinctive ethical significance of persons that follows upon their distinctive social capacities. Reflective rational agents are the sorts of things that can treat one another specifically *as persons*, by engaging one another in distinctively interpersonal ways—such as conversation, argument, criticism, cooperation, competition, bargaining, and promising. This automatically entails the central claim of the normative account that I just spelled out above, because the main condition that an individual person must meet in order to be engaged in these distinctively interpersonal ways is that it must be committed to meeting the normative requirements that define individual rationality. In turn, this central claim entails a novel interpretation of Locke's distinction, because the commitment to meeting the normative requirements of individual rationality need not fall in a one-to-one way with individual human beings, but can fall many-to-one and also one-to-many. In the former case, this defining commitment of the individual person, in the light of which it may be regarded and treated as a person, would arise within parts of human beings so as to give rise to *multiple persons* within that human being; in the latter case it would arise within a group of human beings so as to give rise to a *group person* that comprises all of those human beings. In such cases it wouldn't be the individual human beings who could be engaged in distinctively interpersonal ways, but rather parts and groups of them.

This novel interpretation of Locke's distinction rests on a highly voluntarist conception of personal identity, according to which it is up to persons themselves to draw the boundaries within which they reason and act. They do this through *acts of appropriation*, in which they *commit* themselves to taking certain attitudes as a *normative basis* from which to deliberate and act. Through these acts of appropriation, each person comes to have its own distinctive point of view and, thereby, its own identity. So the normative account gives us the following picture: on the one hand, rationality *enforces* identity, in the sense that each person can reason only from its own attitudes; but on the other hand, each person's identity must also be *forged* through acts of appropriation by which the attitudes from which it reasons come to be its own. The normative account entails the twin possibilities of group and multiple personhood because these identity-constituting acts of appropriation may and can occur within different boundaries, thereby giving rise to persons of different sizes. Each such person has its own point of view in the rational sense—a point of view from which to deliberate in accord with the requirements of individual rationality. But this rational point of view need not coincide with either the bodily point of view of an individual animal, or the phenomenological point of view of a single consciousness. It is to be understood in purely normative and practical terms.

Admittedly, the main implications of the normative account—the twin possibilities of multiple and group persons, along with the voluntarist conception of personal identity on which those possibilities rest—are highly counter-intuitive. I suspect that they may seem even more counter-intuitive than Parfit's original claim about branching, to the effect that we can have something as good as ordinary survival without identity. Be that as it may, I'll proceed in Section 4 to critically assess his claim by bringing the considerations that drive the normative account to bear. My aim in doing so is not to show that we ought to refuse to contemplate the scenarios in which he thought branching would occur, such as bodily fission. We can and should try to work out the true metaphysical significance of those scenarios. What I want to bring out is that if we reflect on them with due care, we shall find reason to take seriously a suggestion that David Lewis made early on in response to Parfit (cf. Lewis 1976). Instead of viewing these scenarios as *branching* scenarios, in which a single ancestral self gives rise to several descendent selves, he suggested that we view them as cases in which several selves exist all along, initially co-existing within a single body and then continuing to exist later in separate bodies. Lewis's suggestion was not without its own metaphysical difficulties, and I won't be recommending that we adopt it in exactly the form—or even the spirit—in which he intended it. Nonetheless, he was right on one point: persons cannot and do not branch, even in cases where they co-habit the same body.

It will emerge from my arguments in this paper that the branching scenario is even more complicated than it has previously emerged as being. Previously, what seemed complicated and, to some, objectionable about Parfit's suggestion was that if subjects were to survive without identity, then they could not think about their own pasts and futures in a first person way without having to do some *self-individuating* work—for example, a person who anticipates a branching future would need to bear in mind that she is planning for two future selves rather than for one, and to keep straight which plans are for which future self. But as I shall explain at the end of Section 4, the prospect of bodily fission also presents many more *choices* than is generally acknowledged. The reason why is that persons are *always* presented with more choices than is generally acknowledged, owing to the ways in which they can forge the sort of rational unity that is characteristic of the individual person within different boundaries. This is just the voluntarist aspect of the normative account of personal identity to which I have already drawn attention: even though it is a fact that rationality enforces identity, this fact doesn't circumvent the role of choice in forging personal identity.

1. Can there be quasi-first person relations?

Before broaching the problem of branching self-consciousness, I want to set the stage by reviewing its Lockean sources.

Locke actually *conflated* the metaphysical condition of personal identity with the epistemic condition in which a person is aware of its identity through consciousness. Although it was objected in his own time that it is always wrong to conflate knowledge with the thing known, he didn't seem to view it as a mistake, but rather as a deep fact about the nature of the person—that what a person *is* is inseparable from its knowledge of itself. In a way, then, Locke was even more Cartesian than Descartes himself—not because he affirmed dualism, but because he endorsed the thesis proclaimed in the title of the second *Meditation*, that the mind is better known the body. Locke was not led to endorse this claim on the basis of Descartes's method of doubt, but rather on the basis of his empiricism, which led him to suppose that there is *nothing more to the self*—or really, I should say that there is nothing more to the *idea* of the self—than what the self *directly knows* of itself through consciousness. Locke's empiricism also led him to be somewhat cautious about Descartes's equation of the self with an immaterial thinking substance, since such a substance is not directly known through consciousness. Locke's caution on this metaphysical point eventually gave way to Hume's skepticism about the self, and both of these early empiricist moves constituted important first steps toward the reductionist conceptions of the self that Parfit and other neo-Lockeans put forward much later.

If all there were to choose from were Locke's original view of personal identity and the animalist view, it would make sense to choose the latter. It is simply going too far to make his conflation, since doing so would deprive us of the resources with which to make sense of the possibilities of ignorance and error with respect to ourselves—of forgetting and delusion. In contrast, animalists clearly have the resources with which to make sense of these epistemic imperfections. When we equate personal identity with animal identity, there is an actual history to which a person's beliefs about itself must answer, and of which they may fall short—whether it be by omission or misrepresentation.

However, neo-Lockeans are not generally tempted to make Locke's conflation. They are driven by quite other metaphysical considerations—usually, a tendency to Parfit-style reductionism together with some form of supervenience thesis (cf. Lewis 1976). When we think of persons as "nothing but" certain sorts of events standing in certain sorts of relations, and when we think of these events and relations as psychological events and relations that supervene on physical events and relations, then we have the materials with which to conceive the possibility that the life of a given person might diverge from the biological life of a given animal—though it requires thought experiments in which we imagine such things as brain transplants, brain re-programming, and molecule-for-molecule duplication. The problem of accounting for the distinction between self-knowledge and the thing known gets solved within such a metaphysical picture through two related moves. With respect to the first problem, of ignorance: the psychological relations that hold events together within a single life include many other relations besides personal memory, so that it becomes intelligible that past events may belong to a given person's life even if there is no present access to them through memory, or in other words, even if they have been forgotten. With respect to error: there is a reliable causal process through which veridical memories of earlier events are typically generated, in the light of which some apparent memories may fail to be veridical (cf. Perry 1975b).[5]

Of course, animalists tend to be unimpressed by this neo-Lockean response to the objection that Locke was wrong to conflate a person with its knowledge of itself. In their view, the only causal process that can generate memories is the causal process that we actually find at work in normally developed human beings. But neo-Lockeans are well within their rights to suppose that something can perform the function of human memory even if it isn't in every respect just like human memory, and so the line of objection I've just considered, concerning the defeasibility of self-knowledge, doesn't clearly resolve the dispute about personal identity in favor of the animalists.

One line that animalists have pressed in counter-response is that the account neo-Lockeans offer of the distinction between real memory on the one hand, and forgetfulness and delusion on the other, fails to capture adequately the first person character of the memory relation.

---

[5] See J. Perry (1975b) for a thorough and convincing account of memory within a Parfit-style reductionist framework.

This last charge is best understood in connection with the so-called "duplication objection" that has so often been raised against Locke and neo-Lockeans. The objection comes in two stages. The first stage observes that the identity relation is one-to-one, whereas the psychological relations in terms of which Locke and neo-Lockeans propose to analyze personal identity may be one-many—that is, they may take a branching form. Shoemaker responded to the logical problem that branching presents by proposing to analyze personal identity in terms of *non-branching* psychological continuity (cf. Shoemaker 1970). But his response didn't fully cope with the question: what would it be for persons to actually *live* the branching scenario? Parfit faced the question more squarely when he reasoned that dying a death of branching wouldn't be like ordinary death, because one would be psychologically related to several future persons in much the way that an individual person is typically related to her one and only future self—or, as he liked to put it, we would have what really *matters* in personal survival, only twice over (or perhaps more than twice).

There is a very powerful intuition, however, that the way in which a person is related to her own future thoughts is a *first person* way, and that it is impossible to bear a first person relation to such future thoughts without assuming one's continued identity over time as the same subject, both of one's present and of one's future thoughts—and, indeed, of one's past thoughts as well. This seems to be partly a *conceptual* point: when a person anticipates her future thoughts and actions, or remembers her past thoughts and actions, she thinks of them in a first person mode, as what *I* will think and do, or what *I* already thought and did, where the pronoun "I" expresses this identity over time. Furthermore, the psychological concepts that we employ along with the pronoun "I", such as memory and intention, likewise presuppose a strict identity over time: I can remember only my *own* past thoughts and intend only my *own* actions.

Neo-Lockeans do not take themselves to be constrained by these conceptual truths, because they maintain that it is possible to revise our concepts as needed in order to make sense of the branching scenario. They have introduced concepts like quasi-memory and quasi-intention, together with a quasi-first person pronoun "I*".[6] I have contributed a detailed account of how persons might employ these conceptual innovations in their actual lives in order to cope with the branching scenario—so that an ancestral self who faces the prospect of branching might think, *I intend that I* will do such and such after my body divides*, and descendent selves who recall the time before branching might think *I remember when I* did such and such* (cf. Rovane 1990).

This brings us to stage two of the duplication objection. Here we find many variations on a common theme of complaint, which is that we cannot really make sense of the possibilities that neo-Lockeans are asking us to envisage, because the conceptual revisions that they require take us too far from the only cases of personhood with which we are actually acquainted. Here are just a few sample complaints:

---

[6] The conceptual innovation of "quasi-" attitudes owes to Shoemaker (1970). The pronoun "I*" was originally introduced by Alan Sidelle.

Ordinarily, when I remember a past event, this puts me in a position to refer to myself without having to do any individuating work because the reference is, as Evans put it, "identification-free"—where the sign of such identification freedom is that it doesn't make sense to say, "I remember such and such", and then go on to ask, "but did it happen to *me?*" This question would certainly arise for descendent selves who can quasi-remember the life of an ancestral self to whom they are not identical, since they would have to work out whether the quasi-remembered event happened to *them* or to their ancestral self—in other words, to *me* or *me**. Similarly, when I frame an intention to do something, I generally don't have to specify *who* is intended to do it because there too, as in the case of memory, the reference to my future self should be identification free. Yet I would have to do such individuating work in cases where I anticipate having more than one descendent self, for then I must frame quasi-intentions, and quasi-anticipate that they will be quasi-remembered by more than one descendent self, and I will need to somehow specify which self is quasi-intended to do what. Finally, my concern for my own future well-being is driven by the thought that it will be *I* who will fare better or worse depending upon how well I plan. Yet this thought will be missing in cases where I must plan for more than one descendent self, since I will be constrained to think of those descendent selves as *not me*.[7]

If all that were on offer with these various complaints was the observation that the branching scenario would differ significantly from life as we know it, then we should not be impressed. When neo-Lockeans ask us to envisage the possibility of something as good as survival without identity, they know very well that they are asking us to think through a counterfactual case that departs significantly from the actual case. Yes, there would be more self-individuating work that a user of the pronoun "I*" would have to carry out, as compared with the ordinary case in which persons of human size use "I" to refer to themselves throughout their lives. Yes, the branching case would not afford what is called "identification-free" self-reference, but would involve a rather more complicated task of keeping track of psychological relatedness over time, and attending to whether and when it takes a branching form. And, yes, it is hard to keep hold of the idea that we can bear something like a first person relation to future selves with whom we are not, strictly speaking, identical—precisely because they are not *me*. But all the same, it hasn't been shown that it is impossible to do the requisite self-individuating work that would be required for successful uses of "I*", or to develop a quasi-first person relation, toward more than one future self, including quasi-self-concern.

I should register that these responses don't generally satisfy the animalists who raise the objections to which they are responses. Their positive view is that we cannot gain a proper understanding of the nature of the first person without taking due account of how it is situated in animal life. This is the line of argument for the animalist view that

---

[7] This line of objection is developed by J. McDowell (1997) and it is also endorsed by T. Burge (2003).

I mentioned in footnote 3 above, with which I said I would be especially concerned in this chapter. So what I'm registering is that the considerations that drive me to set aside that line of argument do not move committed animalists in the way that they move me. But this should not be surprising, given what I said in my introductory remarks about the methodological predicament that we face in connection with the dispute about personal identity. Our predicament is generated by the fact that neither party in the dispute can reasonably expect to refute the other, at least not in a way that the other would regard as non-question-begging. So the best we can hope to accomplish is to offer compelling reasons on which to recommend taking one side in the dispute rather than the other, even while granting that they fall short of strict proof.

This last point about our methodological predicament brings me to an aspect of my larger argument in this paper that is liable to be misunderstood. As I'll go on to explain in the next section, I see the specific case against quasi-reasoning as being decisive in a way that the general case against the quasi-attitudes that I've been discussing in this section is not. In other words, when I say that there is no such things as quasi-reasoning, I am not merely making a revisionist recommendation about how we should view rationality; I mean to show that we cannot make sense of quasi-reasoning at all. Yet somewhat surprisingly, this does not provide us with a basis on which to settle the dispute about personal identity in a way that animalists would be compelled to regard as non-question-begging. I'll say a bit more about why this is so at the very end of the chapter.

2. Why there is no such thing as quasi-reasoning

Why should the case for quasi-reasoning be any different from the cases I just considered, for quasi-attitudes? It will take both this section and the two that follow to answer this question. I'll begin in this one by drawing attention to the conceptual ties between the normative requirements of rationality on the one hand, and the concept of an individual person on the other.

The sort of reasoning I have in mind is the sort that a person engages in when she deliberates in a fully reflective way, about what to think and do. Reasoning in this sense presupposes a commitment to meeting various normative requirements of rationality, such as the following: to be consistent in one's beliefs, to rank one's preferences transitively, to accept the deductive and inductive consequences of one's attitudes, to evaluate one's ends by reference to the means that must be employed in order to achieve them, and to evaluate one's ends by reference to the foreseeable consequences of achieving them. There are real and hard questions about what, precisely, the list of requirements should include and how the requirements should be understood. But fortunately, my argument in this paper doesn't require me to offer or defend detailed answers to these questions. I need only attend to a much more general point about the connection between the various normative requirements of rationality and the concept of a rational individual.

The best way to understand this connection is by attending to the sense in which deliberation is first personal. When a person deliberates, she is really addressing a first person question, namely, what would it be best for *me* to think and do, all things considered. The scope of the "all" in her all-things-considered judgements is determined by her identity, for a person is not required to take into account literally *everything*, but only *her own* attitudes. Thus, the question before a deliberating agent is, what would it be best for *me* to think and do in the light of all that *I* believe, want, etc? A person proceeds to answer this question by striving to meet various specific requirements of rationality, such as those I listed above—consistency in belief, transitivity of preferences, etc. Here too we find that the identity of the person is centrally at issue. There is no failure of rationality if *you* think p is true and *I* think not-p is true, or if *you* think p is better than q and *I* think q is better than p. Such inconsistencies and intransitivities are failures of rationality only when they occur within a single person. This is really just a way of getting at the same point I just made about how the scope of the "all" in a person's all-things-considered judgements is determined by the person's identity. Just as rationality requires me to take all of my own attitudes into account when I deliberate, so also, rationality does not require me to take anyone else's attitudes as the basis of my deliberation. This shows that rationality in the sense that I'm concerned with is, as a matter of conceptual necessity, an entirely individual affair.

It may not yet be evident why this conceptual point cannot be *re*-conceptualized to suit the needs of the neo-Lockean view, along roughly the same lines as quasi-memory, quasi-anticipation, and so on. After all, it could equally be said of memory that it too is an entirely individual affair since, strictly speaking, only *I* can remember *my* past. But here we must ask, what is involved in supposing that I might deliberate in a way that takes into account attitudes that are not, strictly speaking *mine*, in a fashion analogous to how a descendent self might quasi-remember past thoughts that are not strictly speaking *hers* but only *hers**, because they were the thoughts of her ancestral self with whom she is not strictly identical? What I've said so far is this: If I were to take such thoughts into account, then I would be committed to reasoning *from* them in accord with the normative requirements of rationality, and since those normative requirements define what it is for an individual to be fully rational, I would have to think myself as one and the same subject throughout the time spanned. But here is a slightly more metaphysical way of putting the point: suppose that, after bodily fission occurs, I am aware of earlier thoughts that had occurred prior to fission in the way that most theorists would describe as quasi-remembering—if I were to reason from those earlier thoughts I would thereby *appropriate* them as my own, in the sense that I would take them as the basis of *my* deliberations, and then I wouldn't be thinking of them as *mine**, but would be thinking of them as *mine*.

This conclusion might seem too quick. Don't we routinely take into account in our deliberations attitudes that are not our own—as, for example, when I take my daughter's desires into account as well as my own?[8] But here we must ask in response, what are we doing when we take another's attitudes into account in our deliberations? In answer, I want to emphasize that we are precisely *not* getting into a quasi-first personal relation to those attitudes. Rather, we are taking them into account in something like the sense that we take *facts* into account. What the normative requirements of rationality require is that we take all and only our own *attitudes* into account. Obviously, I am not transgressing these requirements when I take the weather into account, even though the weather is not, strictly speaking, an attitude of mine at all. What I am taking into account are my *beliefs* about the weather. Similarly, when I take my daughter's desires into account, what I am really taking into account are *desires of my own* to satisfy her desires. It is important to see that this is not mere double counting. When I deliberate from these desires of my own, I am reasoning from *altruistic* desires, and their normative force is quite different from what it would be if I were deliberating from non-altruistic desires that made no reference to anyone else's desires.

To see why, consider the following facts about my actual attitudes: In my view, the only good reason to undertake leisure travel is to gain an experience of other cultures that one could not otherwise have. When I deliberate from this attitude, I can see that I have a prima facie reason to go India but not to Disneyland. However, as it happens, I also believe that my daughter would very much like me to take her to Disneyland and, furthermore, I also wish to make her happy. When I deliberate from all of these attitudes together, I may rationally conclude that, all things considered, I should go to Disneyland—provided that I rank my altruistic desire to satisfy my daughter's desire to go to Disneyland ahead of my other relevant desires. But note that this ranking wouldn't require me to *give up* or *revise* my views about what makes travel worthwhile. I can rationally act on my altruistic desire to satisfy my daughter's desire to go to Disneyland while also retaining a sense of *disagreement* with her about what makes travel worthwhile. In contrast, I cannot rationally take on board a direct, by which I mean non-altruistic, desire to go to Disneyland while retaining a sense of a disagreement with *myself;* rationality requires that I revise my background attitudes about what makes travel worthwhile in order to render them consistent with going to Disneyland.

It may not be entirely perspicuous why this digression about the difference between the normative force of altruistic desires and other desires addresses the specific issue at hand, which concerned the possibility of quasi-reasoning. The whole point of introducing the notion of quasi-reasoning—just as in the case of quasi-memory and quasi-anticipation—was to preserve all of the features of the first person *except* strict identity. In other words, the point was to introduce something *like* reasoning from one's own attitudes, which is also *unlike* reasoning from altruistic attitudes—a sort of middle ground, as it were, between intra- and inter-personal relations. The claim I'm working

---

[8] This discussion is a response to very helpful critical feedback that I received in an earlier correspondence about these themes with Sydney Shoemaker.

up to is that there is no such middle ground in connection with reasoning, and this makes for an important contrast with phenomenology. There may be conceptual room for the idea that I might have phenomenological access to past thoughts that are not *mine* but rather *mine** because they were thought by an ancestral self with whom I am not identical. But there is no conceptual room for a parallel idea in connection with rationality, as opposed to phenomenology. I cannot take *any* thought as a basis for my deliberations without appropriating it as, quite literally, *mine* in a sense that implies strict identity.[9]

This claim will come into better focus over the course of the next two sections. It is very much *the* claim that drives the arguments that I will be giving in those sections—arguments *for* the twin possibilities of multiple and group persons, and also *against* the possibility of something as good as survival without identity.

3. Why there can be multiple and group persons

Unfortunately, there isn't time to give the full argument for the possibility of multiple and group persons here, nor even to illustrate them with vivid examples. I can only sketch the basic outline.

The argument starts with a simple and familiar criterion of personhood, which elsewhere I have called an *ethical* criterion of personhood.[10] The reasons for calling it that have already emerged in my introductory remarks: persons have a distinctive ethical significance that follows upon the fact that they and they alone can engage one another in distinctively interpersonal ways, such as conversation, argument, criticism, etc. These forms of engagement are possible when, and only when, we find a subject of address who is committed to satisfying the normative requirements that define individual rationality. And this is the basis on which the ethical criterion distinguishes and individuates members of the kind 'person'.

The argument for multiple and group persons proceeds by establishing that parts of human beings and groups of human beings can satisfy this ethical criterion of personhood—that is, they can be committed to satisfying the normative requirements that define individual rationality, and by virtue of that commitment they can be engaged and treated as individual persons in their own rights.

I'll discuss the group case first. It is well known that when human beings engage in group activities, their joint efforts can take on the characteristics of individual rationality. Think, for example, of marital partners who deliberate together about how to manage their homes and families and other joint concerns. They may in the course of such joint deliberations do as a pair all of the things that individuals characteristically do in order to be rational: they may pool their information, resolve

---

[9] This point constitutes a departure from—and indeed a correction of—the view for which I argued in C. Rovane (1990).
[10] I elaborate and defend this criterion at length in C. Rovane (1998, ch. 3).

conflicts between them, rank their preferences together and, even, arrive at all-things-considered judgements together about what they should together think and do—where the "all" in question comprises all of their pooled deliberative considerations. The same can also happen in a less thoroughgoing way when colleagues co-author papers, or when teams of scientists design and run experiments together, or when corporations set up and follow corporate plans. We tend to assume that such joint endeavors leave human beings intact as individual agents in their own rights. Insofar as that is so, it should be possible to engage those human beings separately in conversation, argument, and other distinctively interpersonal relations. But, sometimes, this is not possible. Sometimes, marital partners won't speak for themselves. Their commitment to deliberating together is so thoroughgoing and so effective that everything they say and do reflects their joint deliberations and never reflects their separate points of view. The same can happen to co-authors, team members, and bureaucrats. The kind of case I have in mind is not one in which human participants simply wish to give voice to the larger viewpoint of the groups to which they belong. The kind of case I have in mind is one in which the human constituents of the group are not committed to deliberating separately on their own. That is, these human beings are not committed to meeting the normative requirements of rationality within their separate biological lives. Yet it is not because they lack rational capacities. It is because those rational capacities are directed in a different way, so as to help fulfill a larger commitment on the part of a whole group to meet the normative requirements of rationality within it.

I propose to model *all* cases of rational agency on the group case. On this model, rational agents aren't metaphysically given in the way that animals are. Rational agents come into existence when there is a commitment to meeting the normative requirements that define individual rationality within certain boundaries. The point is that when agents do this, they are *forging* an identity through their intentional efforts. This is true not only of group persons, but also of persons of human size, or even smaller size. Thus, an initially impulsive human being might forge an identity by deliberating as one within different spans of time—within each day, or week, or month, or year, or even a whole life-time. The last goal was celebrated by Plato as part of the just life and by Aristotle as part of the virtuous life. In a less high-minded way, we now typically pursue the project of living a unified human life for the sake of other more specific projects such as life-long personal relationships (friendships, marriages, families) and, also, careers. But what I want to emphasize is that these are *projects* and they are *optional*. A human being who lacks such 'life-projects' is not, therefore, *irrational*, any more than a group would be irrational if it failed to have projects of the sort that would give it reason to deliberate and act together as one at the level of the whole group. The exercise of rationality is always the same, no matter which boundaries it is exercised within. And it can be exercised within boundaries that are smaller than a human life, as well as larger. In such a case we would, of course, have multiple persons within a single human being.

The only cases of multiple personhood that are generally recognized in the popular imagination are pathological ones—cases that we used to call "multiple personality disorder" and now call "dissociative identity disorder." This diagnostic category is notoriously controversial. But I'm mentioning it nevertheless because it helps to make vivid how the ethical criterion of personhood can be fulfilled in the multiple case—how there can be than one subject of address within the same human body, who can be separately engaged in distinctively interpersonal ways. We have no difficulty in understanding portrayals of the therapeutic situation in which a clinician must separately address distinct alter personalities, even though they co-exist within the same body. My claim is that there are non-pathological conditions in which this might be true. If a human beings' projects are numerous, and if they have nothing to do with one another, this may make it pointless to strive to deliberate as one over the course of that whole human life. And it may be a rational response to let go of the commitment to doing so, and to deliberate only as the need and occasion arise—in each case taking into account only what matters to the project at hand. If this were to happen, then a single human being would house a number of separate persons, each of whom could be engaged separately in her own right.

These arguments for group and multiple personhood are not sufficiently developed here to be persuasive. I suspect that the case for multiple personhood will seem particularly weak. Who would deny that human beings typically deliberate in the way that I've attributed to multiple persons, taking into account only what matters to the project at hand without really striving to meet the normative requirements of rationality over the course of their whole lives? I don't think we should presume that this actually weakens my case, so much as weakens the case for saying that human beings are *one*, in the sense of qualifying as individual rational agents over the span of their biological lives. *Qua rational agents* human beings may be less whole within themselves, or separate from others, than is normally thought.

4. A return to something closer to Lewis's picture of survival and identity

Armed with this picture of rational agency, let's try to imagine what it would be to confront the so-called branching scenario, in which we would face the prospect of bodily fission.

Suppose I tried to enter into Parfit's positive attitude. Suppose I reasoned that this would not be like ordinary death, because all that matters in my personal survival would be preserved, only multiply. This would leave me with the task of *planning* for such a future. When we presume that our identities are metaphysically given, then it seems unavoidable to presume that what we would be planning for is exactly what Parfit described—having *more than one descendent self* with whom we are not identical, but at whom we might direct quasi-intentions which will later be quasi-remembered and acted upon. In Section 1, I referred to my own past effort to solve the problem of distinguishing distinct branches for the purposes of directing separate quasi-intentions at each of them. I won't rehearse that effort here, but will take it for granted that this individuating work can be done. I want to move on to a different and, I now think, much more interesting issue. When I direct a so-called quasi-intention at one of my so-called future selves, not only do I quasi-anticipate that it will be quasi-remembered by her; I also quasi-anticipate that when she quasi-remembers it, she will regard it as a normative basis from which to deliberate and act *then*. I also quasi-anticipate that there is much else that she will quasi-remember, which I do not quasi-intend that she should regard in the same way, as an appropriate basis for her deliberations and actions—I'm referring here to quasi-intentions that I have directed at *other* descendent selves rather than at her. So, when we try to imagine the situation with hindsight, from the perspective of my so-called descendent selves, it is clear that they should *not* appropriate *all* the attitudes they quasi-remember as *theirs*, in the normative sense that involves a *commitment* to taking them into account in their respective deliberations and actions. But likewise, when we consider the situation in prospect, from the perspective of the present, it is clear that there isn't really *one* deliberator to begin with, even though I've been describing the situation in that way. There is a single body and, also, a single center of consciousness, which I've been describing as a single person. But I've also been describing this presumptively 'single' person as making separate plans for each of her so-called descendent selves; and those separate plans mandate separate commitments to taking *some* present attitudes into account together with *some* anticipated future attitudes, and *other* present attitudes into account with *other* anticipated future attitudes. So although we find it almost irresistible to think of her as *one* prior to bodily fission, her deliberative life would not really be the deliberative life of one. She would already be deliberating *for*—and I think we should say *as*—many. Insofar as that ever comes to pass, there will already be multiple persons co-existing within the same body prior to fission.

When Parfit first raised the branching scenario, he suggested we might take solace from the fact that we would no longer have to choose between certain projects, but could pursue both. For example, I might not have faced the prospect of sacrificing music for philosophy, but could have resolved that one of my so-called descendent selves be a musician and the other a philosopher. The point for which I just argued is that if I were to take certain steps in the present to bring about that outcome—by pursuing musical training and philosophical studies—I would already be fragmenting into two independent agents who first co-exist within a single body and then later continue to exist in separate bodies. As I've already noted, we find it nearly irresistible to describe this situation, in which I am suggesting that there are multiple persons within a single human being, as a situation in which there is really just a single person with multiple projects. But compare the following case. Suppose I thought—as I do in fact think—that my talents and values together speak in favor of putting all of my efforts into philosophy rather than music. And suppose that, when faced with the prospect of bodily fission, I resolved to pursue philosophy single-mindedly. I could easily anticipate that, after fission, there would be a common pool of attitudes from which it would be possible to continue to pursue philosophy as a single—albeit dual-bodied—person, for there would be common memories of past philosophical projects and a common sense of how to continue to pursue them. In such a case, my *oneness* as a deliberator prior to fission would be facilitated in part by my expectation that I would continue as one afterward as well. So, at the very least, I think it is fair to say that this second case is a clearer case of oneness prior to fission.[11] I also think it is fair to say that in the first case, the segregation of effort that would be mandated by planning for a future in which there is both a philosopher and a musician compromises the sense in which we have a clear case of oneness prior to fission. When we bear in mind the ways in which different moments of deliberation prior to fission would involve an identification with one of those future persons to the exclusion of the other, it becomes clearer why this segregation of effort deserves to be classified as a case of multiple personhood.

The deep conceptual tie between the normative requirements of rationality and the concept of personal identity speaks against Parfit's view of the branching scenario, but it doesn't speak so clearly against Lewis's. Lewis was not entirely impressed with Parfit's claim that persons can have something as good as personal survival except without identity. Yet this didn't lead him to dismiss the branching scenario as impossible in quite the same spirit in which animalists have recommended that we should. Instead, he sought a way to preserve the link between survival and identity in that scenario, which he did by suggesting that in cases where the body divides, there are two persons who exist all along, first co-existing within the same body and then subsequently existing in separate bodies.

Lewis's suggestion faces (at least) three metaphysical difficulties. They are: 1) the distinct persons who are supposed to co-exist within a single body prior to fission would be indiscernible—thereby violating Leibniz's law; 2) the number of such indiscernible persons who would exist prior to fission would be a function of how many persons would exist after fission—thereby making the present and past depend upon the future; 3) such distinct but indiscernible persons who would exist prior to fission would share the same token thoughts in common—thereby violating our intuitions about the exclusive proprietary relation that each subject has to her own thoughts. In my assessment, these difficulties arise for Lewis because he, like Shoemaker, was more directly focused on the logical and conceptual difficulties presented by the branching scenario than on the practical difficulties that it would present for living a life. Thus, when Shoemaker initially proposed to define personal identity in

---

[11] Not every project that a person pursues as a single-bodied person could effectively be pursued in the event of bodily fission with this commitment to remaining one, in the sense of becoming a single, dual-bodied person. Although philosophical projects probably could, many projects associated with love and friendship could not. It is important to see, however, that this does not in any way compromise the general claim being argued for here about group and multiple personhood. It is in the nature of the case that different sorts of projects are open to persons of different size.

terms of non-branching psychological continuity, he didn't do enough to address the question of how we ought to respond to the branching scenario should it arise—even though he did share Parfit's positive attitude toward that scenario. Similarly, when Lewis reasoned that personal survival *must* involve identity, he didn't do enough to address the attendant practical difficulties that arise when we try to imagine what it would be like to cope with the prospect of bodily fission from a first person point of view. The three metaphysical difficulties that I just raised above may appear to be quite independent of such practical concerns, but it isn't really so. If we try to imagine our way into the branching scenario and consider how we might actually respond to it, we shall be able to see that the first and second are not really difficulties at all, and the third promises to be quite manageable. In order to see all of this, we shall need to bear in mind how rationality enforces identity, and how this goes together with the normative account of personal identity, which entails the twin possibilities of multiple and group persons.

Consider the first difficulty, concerning the alleged indiscernibility of persons who co-habit the same body prior to bodily fission. If they really are distinct, then they will be discernible by the usual test that the normative account of personhood employs, of whether they are available as separate subjects of address for the purposes of interpersonal forms of engagement, such as conversation, argument, criticism, and the like. So in short, if there are indeed distinct persons co-habiting the same body prior to fission, they will be discernible as multiple persons. The second difficulty for Lewis simply doesn't arise on the normative account, because how many persons exist at a given time will always be a function of how many persons exist *then* and not a function of how many persons exist later. Of course, persons can form intentions in the present which are aimed at forging identities over time, and whether their intentions are realized is something that can emerge only in the future. But the important thing to bear in mind is that if it should later turn out their intentions are not realized, this will not change the facts about the present. So for example, if, when faced with the prospect of bodily fission, I fragment now so as to create multiple persons who plan for separate futures, their separate existence in the present will not be undone if later, after fission, there emerges a single, dual-bodied self. Similarly, if I resolve now to remain one after fission, this will serve to reinforce my oneness now; but the fact that I am one now will not be undone if, after fission, there emerge two single-bodied selves instead. As for the third difficulty, which would arise if persons were to share token thoughts in common, it seems to me that it could in principle be handled in two different ways. On the one hand, we might insist that whenever multiple persons cohabit the same body prior to bodily fission, they always reason from distinct token attitudes, and this is so even in cases where they reason from attitudes of the same type. On the other hand, we might allow that they can overlap, in the sense of sharing token attitudes—indeed, for all I know, further reflection on the cases of group and multiple persons will bring to light very general reasons why we should allow this. The point that I want to emphasize is that, whichever hand we take, Lewis's response to the so-called branching scenario was closer to the truth than Parfit's: persons can't really branch. However, the deeper reason why doesn't owe to the general logical and metaphysical considerations that drove Lewis's response, but owe rather to considerations that have much more to do with the specific nature of persons, namely, how rationality enforces identity.

5. The variety of first person relations and the call for revision

I claimed at the outset that our commonsense thinking about persons is sufficiently multi-faceted that it can provide some support for both proponents and opponents of Locke's distinction. This claim harmonizes well with another one that has been central to my argument in this paper, which is that there is a variety of first person relations.

There are two kinds of first person relation that I'm especially concerned to distinguish: phenomenological relations of direct epistemic access through consciousness, and normative relations of commitment from which deliberations and actions proceed. The fact that there are these two kinds of first person relation doesn't by itself *prove* the point from which I started: that our commonsense thinking about personal identity is conflicted. Even if common sense supported only the animalist view of personal identity, we would still have reason to distinguish phenomenological first person relations from normative first person relations. Indeed, we would have reason to distinguish them no matter what view we took about personal identity. Everyone should be prepared to allow that having direct phenomenological access to an attitude through consciousness doesn't necessarily bring in train a commitment to appropriating it as a normative basis from which to deliberate and act—otherwise, we would have to be committed to reasoning from misleading states of consciousness like optical illusions and cravings. Conversely, everyone should also be prepared to allow that it is possible to appropriate certain attitudes as a normative basis from which to deliberate and act even though we lack direct phenomenological access to them through consciousness—the obvious case here is a long-term intention that one is liable to forget unless one records it in one's datebook.

The bare distinction between phenomenological and normative first person relations does not suffice by itself, therefore, to establish the radical-seeming conclusions of this paper. They follow only when we add a highly voluntarist picture of agent-identity. On this picture, it is up to rational agents to determine their own identities by setting the boundaries within which they deliberate; this is something they do through acts of appropriation and commitment, and it leaves them free to form multiple agents within a single human being, and group agents composed of many human beings.

Although these claims about the nature of rational agency may seem radical, they are not revisionist recommendations in the sense that I clarified in my introductory remarks. If others should deny that there can be multiple and group *agents*, they would be making a *metaphysical mistake*. While it is true that I think they should revise their views, I am not merely making a recommendation that they do so. I have offered an argument that leaves them no other option but to revise their views, because otherwise, as I just said, they would be making a metaphysical mistake. Specifically, they would be denying a *fact*, which is that it is within our power to draw and re-draw the boundaries of the rational points of view from which we deliberate and act. It can seem as though this is not a fact, because it can seem to individual human beings as though their specific identities as reflective rational agents is a metaphysically given fact—just as it is a metaphysically given fact that they have separate bodies and separate centers of consciousness. But even if any given human being does happen to believe this, she still surely cannot deny that it lies within her power to reason together with other human beings—not in the mode of arguing from her own point of view and persuading another whose point of view is distinct, but in the mode of figuring out together with another human being what rationally follows from all that they think with respect to the deliberative and practical problems before them. Due reflection on this evident human capacity brings to light that its application is wider, and more general, than we generally take for granted. Human beings who remain individual agents in the course of their lives must also exercise the very same human capacity in order to remain one over time—by deliberating from attitudes that span significant portions of time, in order to coordinate the exercise of their agency over time. This doesn't just *befall* us, but rather it is something we are taught to *do*. At our point in history and culture, we are explicitly taught to do this, and to believe that if we fail we have failed to live up to an individualist ideal, which is to lead a life that is a *whole* human life, unified within itself and separate from others; and furthermore, we are taught to do this in a way that obscures that there are any other options open to us. But once we understand how the separateness of our bodies and consciousnesses does not prevent us from deliberating and acting together with others from a common point of view, we can begin to appreciate what is required for *any* such rational point of view to come into being— namely, *effort* and *will* to deliberate and act within particular boundaries by taking all that belongs within those boundaries into account *together*. So to reiterate, it is a philosophical, and also in a sense a psychological, mistake to deny this.

However, the same charge cannot be levied against the main disputants in the philosophical dispute about personal identity as it is currently understood—about whether there is any distinction at all between personal identity and human (animal) identity. It is understandable that philosophers who are strongly inclined by their own intuitions to take one side in this dispute would like to show that the other side is indeed mistaken. But the unfortunate fact of the matter is that they cannot show this. Common sense provides significant support for both sides, and each side can draw on those aspects of common sense that support it in order to develop an internally coherent account of personhood and personal identity. As a result, the most that anyone can do in order to defend their account is to explain why they are privileging certain strands in our commonsense thinking about persons over others—where this amounts to justifying a revisionist recommendation. I have recommended that we privilege the strand in our commonsense thinking that equates persons with reflective rational agents; and the grounds on which I am recommending this equation are avowedly ethical—because when we link personhood with reflective rational agency we isolate a distinct ethical kind whose members can all *engage* one another specifically *as persons*.[12] I do not believe that those who reject the equation of persons with reflective rational agents are guilty of a metaphysical mistake. It would be perfectly coherent for them to recommend that we equate persons with human beings (or other suitably endowed animals), and in doing so, recommend against my conclusion that there can be multiple and group *persons*. What they cannot coherently do, however, is deny the metaphysical possibility of multiple and group *agents*.

When I reflect on the more specific philosophical debate about the branching scenario, I find a strange mix of metaphysical mistake and ethical choice. As I just made clear, it is coherent to hold that personal identity is the same as human (animal) identity, and to view bodily fission accordingly, as a form of death—no metaphysical mistake so far. Yet animalists *do* make a metaphysical mistake when they deny that there can be anything that deserves to be called a first person relation that spans from before until after bodily fission. It is possible to bear *normative* first person relations to a post-fission self in the ways that I described in the last section, in which it is effectively intended, prior to fission, that one's present attitudes will serve as a normative basis for future, post-fission deliberations. When animalists deny this, they are really making *choices*, and furthermore, they are making *two* choices. First, they are refusing to exercise their agency in such a way as to embrace any post-fission future at all. Second, they are refusing to allow that any such exercise of agency would be a form of personal survival. The first would be a personal choice that reflects their own view about what sort of life is really worth living. It is important to see that one could make such a personal choice even if one accepted my revisionist recommendation to equate persons with rational agents—in such a case one would be acknowledging the twin possibilities of multiple and group personhood, along with the possibility of embracing some form of life that continues after bodily fission, while at the same time choosing against all of these

---

[12] It is precisely because our primary task in the philosophical study of personal identity is one of justifying a revisionist recommendation that I find it appropriate to bring ethical considerations to bear. Many philosophers disagree. This isn't because they don't attach great ethical significance to the *outcome* of the dispute about personal identity. But they insist that the ethics should follow upon the metaphysics and is not a proper basis for it. Of course, even if we think—as I myself do—that such philosophers are wrong to exclude ethical considerations as an appropriate basis on which to resolve the dispute about personal identity, anyone is obviously within their rights to explore whether more narrowly metaphysical considerations might suffice.

In the past, Donald Davidson, David Wiggins, Derek Parfit, Tyler Burge, and John McDowell have all personally registered disagreement with me about the appropriateness of turning directly to ethical considerations as a primary defense for a philosophical account of personal identity. Younger philosophers now working on the subject seem to be much more receptive to this strategy, which was visibly at work in at least three of the papers that were presented at a conference on personal identity at the University of Sydney in December of 2008.

possibilities in favor of a human-size life. I think animalists fail to see that this would be a choice at all, because they wrongly see it as precluded by their view of personal identity, which equates it with human identity. But that view is also a matter of choice, since anyone who wishes to embrace a coherent view of personal identity must decide to privilege some part of our commonsense thinking about persons and let go of the rest. Neither of these two choices that animalists want to make could properly be called metaphysical mistakes. Mistakes arise on their part only insofar as they fail to understand the true nature of reflective rational agency, and the roles that it affords for choice both in life and in philosophy.

So to sum up: Animalists are free to reject life after bodily fission, and they are free to equate personal identity and human identity. But it does not lie within in their power to change the nature of rational agency. With respect to that nature, they've got one thing right and another thing wrong. They are right that the exercise of rational agency involves an identity-carrying first person relation. But they are wrong to think that this provides any support for their view of personal identity or against the view proposed in this paper.

References

Burge, T. 2003 "Memory and Persons", *The Philosophical Review* 112, 239–337.
Lewis, D. 1976 "Survival and Identity", in A. Rorty (ed.) *The Identities of Persons*, Berkeley (Calif.), University of California Press, 17–40.
Locke, J. 1975 *An Essay Concerning Human Understanding*, P. H. Nidditch (ed.), Oxford, Clarendon Press.
McDowell, J. 1997 "Reductionism and the First Person", in J. Dancy (ed.) *Reading Parfit*, Oxford, Blackwell, 230–250.
Parfit, D. 1971 "Personal Identity", *The Philosophical Review* 80, 3–27.
——2004 *Reasons and Persons*, Oxford, Oxford University Press.
Perry, J. (ed.) 1975a *Personal Identity*, Berkeley (Calif.), University of California Press.
——1975b "Personal Identity, Memory and the Problem of Circularity", in J. Perry (ed.) Berkeley (Calif.), University of California Press, 135–155.
Rovane, C. 1990 "Branching Self-Consciousness", *Philosophical Review* 99, 355–95.
——1998 *The Bounds of Agency: An Essay in Revisionary Metaphysics*, Princeton (N. J.), Princeton University Press.
Shoemaker, S. 1970 "Persons and their Pasts", *American Philosophical Quarterly* 7, 269–285.

2
The Conceptual Origin of Subject–Body Dualism

Martine Nida-Rümelin[1]

1. Introduction

Conscious individuals are characterized by having experiences and by being active in their behaviour.[2] Subject–body dualism is the view that conscious individuals are something over and above the matter that constitutes their body. According to subject–body dualism, an elephant, for instance, is an experiencing subject *having* a huge body. According to that view, the elephant is not identical to its body or any part of it, and the elephant is not constituted of its body at a given moment.

Subject–body dualism is unpopular in contemporary philosophy for many well-known reasons. Nonetheless, I am convinced that a specific version of subject–body dualism needs to be developed and can be successfully defended.[3] The present paper,

---

[1] In writing this chapter I realize how much I owe to critical comments from audiences at various places where I presented related material in the past two years: at Rutgers in March 2008, at the conference underlying this volume in London in May 2008, in our Research Colloquium in Fribourg in November 2008, in Barcelona in November 2008, in Munich in January 2009, in Frankfurt at a symposium on 'Der Blick von innen' in January 2009, in Regensburg in January 2009, in Konstanz in February 2009, in Canberra at the ANU in March 2009, in Geneva at the SOPHA conference in September 2009, in Bern in November 2009, and in Luzern in December 2009. I would like to thank all these audiences for helpful remarks that helped me a lot to improve on earlier formulations of the here presented material. I am aware that I learned a lot from comments by people whose identity I cannot remember. I would like to thank the following people for conversations that helped a lot to develop the view here presented: Barry Loewer, Kati Balog, Max Drömmer, Julian Nida-Rümelin, Christopher Peacocke, Gianfranco Soldati, Jim Pryor, Jiri Benovsky, Sven Rosenkrantz, Stephen Yablo, Godehard Link, Anne-Sophie Meincke, Jasper Liptow, Gerson Reuter, Andreas Kemmerling, Logi Gunnarson, Ralf Busse, Tobias Rosefeldt, Wolfgang Spohn, David Chalmers, Fiona Macpherson, and Stephan Leuenberger. I would like to thank the participants in my francophone seminar in spring 2008 for their interest, their questions and their critical comments. I owe the insight that counterfactual thought is more relevant for my theoretical purposes than transtemporal thought to a conversation with Sven Rosenkrantz in Barcelona in November 2008. This insight motivated the new formulation here developed which expands and modifies my earlier view on transtemporal identity (compare M. Nida-Rümelin 1997, 2001, and 2006a).

[2] It is crucial, I believe, to include the capacity of being active. For some remarks about the relevant sense of being active, see M. Nida-Rümelin (2006b, 2007).

[3] Compare ch. 5 in M. Nida-Rümelin (2006a), translation in preparation, and M. Nida-Rümelin (2008).

however, will not defend that view. I will focus on conceptual observations. My purpose is to uncover the conceptual origins of subject–body dualism. I will describe some particular features of thought that may be seen to underlie the intuitive appeal of subject–body dualism.

Most contemporary philosophers are likely to deny that subject–body dualism has any intuitive appeal. Many non-philosophers have no opinion on the issue. These psychological facts do not undermine the claim that subject–body dualism is in fact intuitively attractive. The intuitive appeal of subject–body dualism needs to be detected upon careful reflection. The intuition is not present to us 'on the surface' but it is, as I am going to argue, deeply incorporated into our thought. The conceptual observations developed in what follows may lead some reader, I hope, to discover an intuition he or she may not have been fully aware of, but that he or she will recognize as having been present under the surface all the time. The paper thus has a double function: it describes the conceptual origin of an intuition, and in doing so uncovers the intuition itself.

2. Transworld identity of microphysical particles

Let me start with a case which has nothing to do with consciousness: there are two boxes each containing nothing but one particular microphysical particle. Box 1 contains particle A, box 2 contains particle B. A and B are fundamental: they are not composed of further microphysical particles and not composed of any stuff. It does not matter for the present purposes whether there are fundamental particles in this sense. Apart from their different locations, A and B are perfectly alike.

Let us now consider the following counterfactual circumstances: boxes 1 and 2 do not exist and there is a different box, box 3, containing a particle C which is perfectly like A and B. We may ask the following question about this counterfactual possibility: is the particle in box 3 particle A (possibility P1) or is it particle B (possibility P2) or is it neither of the two? It is a plausible thought that P1 and P2 are genuinely different possibilities. But if so, what does the difference between these possibilities consist in?

This question cannot be answered using the assumption that a given particle is identical to the counterfactual particle C if and only if it is composed of the same stuff: the reply is excluded by the stipulation that A, B, and C are fundamental. Assuming that the counterfactual case is a way our world could have developed, one may propose another simple answer: C would be the actual particle A if and only if—in the counterfactual case at issue—it would stand in spatiotemporal continuity to A. We exclude this simple reply by a further stipulation: C in the counterfactual case comes into existence at the moment in which A and B actually start to exit.[4]

---

[4] In the formulation of the example, 'A' and 'B' are rigid designators but 'C' must be understood as an abbreviation of a non-rigid definite description. Otherwise the necessity of true identity statements formulated using rigid designators would create trouble for the example (compare the famous results in S. Kripke (1980)).

Having excluded these two replies one may wonder if there is a genuine difference between P1 and P2. Do we understand what the alleged difference consists in? There is no descriptive difference between P1 and P2: P1 and P2 are not distinct by virtue of C's respective qualitative properties. The only way to describe the difference is by reference to the real particles A and B. We can describe the difference, for instance demonstratively referring to particle A saying that *this* is the particle contained in box 3 in possibility P1; analogously we may characterize possibility P2 demonstratively referring to B. In order to describe the difference between the counterfactual possibilities P1 and P2 we must use some rigid designators for the real particles A and B.

If P1 and P2 are genuinely different possibilities, then we may say that the individuality of fundamental particles transcends any description: we cannot describe by reference to any qualitative features of possible worlds what the difference between a world in which A exists and a world in which A does not exist consists in. One may be sceptical, however, about whether P1 and P2 really are genuinely different. The fact that we cannot give an informative answer to the question of what would make it the case that C is numerically identical to A rather than to B may invite the following reaction: there really are no two distinct possibilities. Once we have described the possible world at issue, we cannot introduce a distinction between genuinely different subcases by the assumption 'C is A' and 'C is B' respectively. It may seem as if these were two different possibilities, but the appearance is an illusion.

I will not take a stance on this issue here. I share the intuition that there is a genuine difference between P1 and P2. On the other hand, it seems to me, the hypothesis that the intuition is illusionary must be taken seriously. It may well be that the intuition just outlined is part of an inadequate understanding we tend to have of fundamental particles. We tend to conceptualize fundamental physical particles as genuine individuals and this might be a mistake. Quantum physics may be taken to show that microphysical particles are not individuals in any ordinary sense. What follows does not depend on whether we accept or reject the metaphysical claim that the individuality of fundamental particles transcends any description. The conceptual reflections presented in what follows will lead to the conclusion that an analogous metaphysical claim for conscious beings is deeply incorporated in our cognitive architecture; according to that claim the individuality of conscious individuals transcends any description in a sense that will be explicated more carefully. In this respect, conscious individuals might share their special ontological status with fundamental particles. Despite this plausible commonality there is an important difference between the two cases which will become clear in what follows: the reasons in favour of the claim that experiencing subjects have a non-descriptive individual nature are fundamentally different from those supporting the analogous thesis with respect to microphysical particles.[5]

---

[5] In conversation after my talk in Canberra in February 2009, Fiona MacPherson proposed the plausible hypothesis that the special ontological status here at issue might be characteristic of fundamental individuals.

3. The individuality question

What makes the table in front of me the table it actually is? What features of a counterfactual situation constitute that the table in front of me exists in those circumstances? What are the conditions an individual thing existing under counterfactual circumstances must satisfy in order for that thing to be the table in front of me? These questions are different formulations of what I will call the individuality question for a particular individual. Asking the individuality question we are searching for an understanding of the individual nature of the thing at issue.

In most cases there is an informative answer to the individuality question. The best informative answer might still be imprecise. The answer may involve an open list of conditions, a sufficient number of which has to be satisfied for the individual in question to exist in counterfactual circumstances. In the case of the table in front of me this is plausibly the case. For some table T' in counterfactual circumstances to be *this* table T, T' must have a sufficient number of properties in common with T—properties that certainly concern its origin and the material it is made of. It seems clear that we can give an informative answer to the individuality question in the case of artefacts, plants, mountains, and other macrophysical objects. We are able to mention certain properties which, if exemplified by some thing in counterfactual circumstances, guarantee that the thing is identical to a given object of the relevant kind in the real world, and we can use those same properties to say appropriately that a given thing does not exist in counterfactual circumstances if none of these properties is exemplified by any particular under those circumstances. We may summarize these observations by saying that regular macrophysical objects have a descriptive individual nature; their individuality does not transcend any description; in their case the individuality question does have an informative answer.[6]

What about our own case? Upon reflection—in the way outlined in what follows—one may come to the following insight (or apparent insight, to say it in a neutral manner): there is no informative answer to the individuality question in our own case and in the case of other conscious individuals. If this is a genuine insight then we may say: the individual nature of conscious individuals is non-descriptive; what makes a conscious individual the individual it actually is transcends any description. Subject–body dualism is a quite immediate consequence of this result. Material objects do not

---

I owe the insight that fundamental physical particles are plausible candidates for that status to critical remarks in the discussion after that talk by Frank Jackson and David Chalmers.

[6] The issue is controversial in the present debate (cf. R. M. Adams 1979, 1981). What I will say about the conceptual contrast in the following sections does not depend on the metaphysical thesis here outlined which serves simply for introductory purposes. In the current debate, discussion about transworld identity is often replaced following Lewis by discussion about counterparts of actual individuals in other possible worlds (compare e.g. D. Lewis 1971); in this paper I mean to talk of numerical identity of individuals across different possible circumstances. Other possible worlds (counterfactual cases, counterfactual circumstances) will be understood as ways the actual world could have developed, in a way which is opposed to the realist understanding of possible worlds famously defended by David Lewis (1986).

have that feature: their individuality does not transcend any description. So, one may conclude, conscious individuals are not material objects.[7]

As noted earlier, however, it is not my purpose here to defend any metaphysical or ontological claim. I wish to describe the way we naturally understand our own individuality and the individuality of others that we take to be conscious. My claim is rather that a non-descriptive understanding of our own individuality and the individuality of other conscious beings is deeply incorporated in our cognitive architecture. According to our natural understanding the individual nature of conscious beings transcends any description. This claim will be supported in what follows using various thought experiments.

4. The individuality question concerning the table Tavola

The features of thought which lead in a natural way to subject–body dualism will become more easily recognizable when confronted with the way we think about normal macro-physical objects like artefacts used in daily life. I therefore introduce an example using a table named 'Tavola'.

Tavola has been constructed by Paolo in April 2010 on a beach near Lissabon. It was a warm and sunny day. This is, let us suppose, what actually happened. Let us now consider a counterfactual possibility: on the same day and in the same place Paolo constructs a table in the same way with the same intention, using the same material. The day is windy and cold; the sun does not appear. Would Tavola have come into existence? It seems obvious that the answer is positive.

One might consider other slightly different counterfactual circumstances, for example a counterfactual possibility in which Paolo constructed a table in the same way but with a different intention, and then go on to ask the same question: would Tavola have come into existence? According to a plausible intuition the same table could have been constructed by Paolo with a different purpose. Considering slightly different ways in which the world could have developed we can vary many details which have no bearing on the existence of Tavola. There are, however, limits to what is compatible with the existence of Tavola in counterfactual circumstances. As a clear example, consider circumstances in which Paolo never builds a table, no table remotely resembles Tavola, and no table is ever constructed out of the piece of wood used by Paolo in the real world. The intuition is clear: Tavola does not exist under these circumstances.

It is not, however, this uncontroversial claim I am interested in here, nor is it the fact that we can easily agree on that claim which is relevant for my purposes. I wish to focus on a different conceptual observation: we do not have any understanding of how the

---

[7] For more about how subject–body dualism follows from the result just mentioned, see the last section of M. Nida-Rümelin (2008).

counterfactual circumstances under consideration would have to be for the contrary claim (Tavola exists under those circumstances) to be true. Suppose someone were to seriously consider that Tavola could have existed under circumstances C that satisfy the above mentioned conditions: (a) No table has been constructed in C out of the wood Tavola consists of in the real world, (b) Paolo never constructed a table and (c) There is no table existing in C that remotely resembles Tavola. A person who seriously considers this possibility has to believe that there is some feature F the circumstances C might fulfil *in addition* which would make it true that Tavola exists in C despite the fulfilment of (a), (b), and (c). But what could that feature consist in? We do not have any positive understanding of that supposed additional feature. For Tavola to exist in C there would have to be some object (supposedly a table) quite different from Tavola in its form, composed of different stuff, having a different origin, which nonetheless *is* the individual table Tavola existing in the real world. We have no idea, no positive conception or understanding, of any additional feature of the counterfactual situation C which might render it true that some table existing in situation C would be Tavola, the concrete object we refer to in the actual world, although it does not share any relevant property with that particular real object. We do have *linguistic* means to 'express' that *supposed* additional feature. We might specify a table that would exist under the counterfactual circumstances C by some definite description D, and then describe the supposed additional feature pointing to Tavola, uttering '*this* is the table satisfying D under the circumstances C'. Our capacity to apparently express the supposed additional feature, however, should not be mistaken for a positive conception of it. What about the table satisfying D (which is constructed out of different stuff and shares no relevant properties with Tavola) could nonetheless make it true that it is Tavola? We certainly have to admit that we have no idea. This is the conceptual observation relevant for the present purposes. Its content is quite obvious and not surprising. It is not this observation about counterfactual thought with respect to non-conscious normal macro-objects in itself which deserves philosophical interest, but rather its contrast to what can be discovered upon reflection about counterfactual thought with respect to conscious beings developed below. In order to get a precise understanding of that contrast it will be helpful to explicitly formulate the observation just arrived at in a general way:

Conceptual Observation 1 (CO1):

X is a macro-physical thing existing in the real world of which we know that it is not endowed with consciousness.[8] L is a language containing no expression which can be used to rigidly refer to X.

---

[8] The formulation 'endowed with consciousness' is used in a way here which leaves it open whether conscious individuals are macro-physical objects (a claim which is denied by subject–body dualism). A subject body dualist may interpret the locution as meaning that there is a subject having the macro-physical object as

Using language L we can formulate non-trivial conditions C such that we do not have a positive understanding of what must be fulfilled in addition to C under circumstances where (i) none of these conditions is met and yet (ii) X exists in those circumstances.

According to this observation we need *not* refer to X in order to express that X does not exist in these circumstances. In a simplifying approximation one might put the point saying something like this: in the description of counterfactual circumstances it is possible to formulate conditions—without reference to X—which conceptually exclude that X exists in the circumstances thus described. The latter formulation may give a helpful rough understanding of the content of the claim but it is not a precise reformulation and misses an important aspect. To say that we *conceptually* exclude the existence of X invites the idea that the conditions at issue are in logical or conceptual contradiction with the existence of X. But this is not the point I wish to make, which is rather about what we are able to *positively conceptualize*. According to the observation CO1 we do not have the conceptual tools to conceive of any possible additional feature (additional to the relevant conditions described without reference to X) which could render it true that X exists despite the fulfilment of these conditions. Contrary to this, as will be argued below, when X is a conscious individual, we do have the conceptual capacity to conceive of the analogous additional feature in a parallel case.

It is necessary to talk of 'non-trivial' conditions in the above formulation for the following reason: One might exclude the existence of X by the assumption that the counterfactual conditions do not contain any individual of the kind X essentially belongs to. If X is Tavola, and if we suppose that Tavola is necessarily a table, then we can trivially exclude the existence of Tavola (in the relevant sense of 'exclusion', the additional feature at issue is not positively conceivable) by the assumption that there are no tables under the described circumstances. The sense of 'non-trivial' for the purposes at hand may thus be explicated as follows: 'trivial conditions' include for some necessary property P of X (a property X cannot fail to exemplify) the assumption that there are no entities with property P.[9] Another way to trivially exclude the possibility of Tavola's existence under counterfactual circumstances is more artificial: for each individual thing which might be accepted as a candidate for identity with Tavola one might stipulate its identity with some *other* object in the real world. Circumstances fulfilling a description of this kind will be counted as 'trivial' in the present context as well.

In this chapter I will contrast features of counterfactual thought about conscious individuals with features of counterfactual thought about macro-physical objects without consciousness. The same contrast could be described using features of counterfactual thought about socially constituted objects (like, for instance, a soccer club, a

---

its body; a materialist or a property dualist may interpret it as meaning that the macro-physical object is itself a conscious individual.

[9] More precisely one has to say this: 'where it is a conceptual truth that P is a necessary property of X'.

philosophy department, or a political party), or about entities which are in part socially constituted (like, for instance, a restaurant); a claim analogous to CO1 applies to entities of the latter kind as well.

We just considered conditions the fulfilment of which conceptually excludes the existence of Tavola. Let us now consider conditions with the opposite feature: they exclude Tavola's non-existence. More precisely, let us now focus on conditions of the following kind: we do not have a positive understanding of the additional feature counterfactual circumstances would have to fulfil if these conditions are met and yet Tavola does *not* exist under those circumstances. Again, we do not need to rigidly refer to Tavola in order to formulate circumstances of the relevant kind. We can simply say something like this: suppose the weather had been a bit different but Paolo had constructed a table of the same shape out of the same material and with the same purpose. That table would have been Tavola and, more importantly, the contrary assumption is not positively conceivable: we do not have any conceptual grasp of any additional feature which might render it true that Tavola does not exist under those circumstances. We can now formulate the parallel claim about the 'exclusion' of Tavola's non-existence in a more general way:

Conceptual Observation 2 (CO2):

X is a macro-physical thing existing in the real world of which we know that it is not endowed with consciousness.[10] L is a language containing no expression which can be used to rigidly refer to X.

Using language L we can formulate conditions C such that we do not have a positive understanding of what must be fulfilled in addition to C under circumstances where (i) these conditions are met and yet (ii) X does not exist in those circumstances.

5. Objections

It is quite commonly accepted that the content of demonstrative thoughts cannot be captured when the demonstrative element is replaced by some description. This insight about demonstrative thought might appear to be incompatible with the above developed observations about counterfactual thought with respect to normal non-conscious individuals.[11] This objection can be articulated saying that we are able to express the alleged additional features using a demonstrative:

---

[10] The formulation 'endowed with consciousness' is used in a way here which leaves it open whether conscious individuals are macro-physical objects (a claim which is denied by subject–body dualism). A subject body dualist may interpret the locution as meaning that there is subject having the macro-physical object as its body; a materialist or a property dualist may interpret it as meaning that the macro-physical object is itself a conscious individual.

[11] I would like to thank Jiri Benovsky and Steven Yablo for having attracted my attention to this potential objection independently in conversation.

THE SELF AND ITS INDIVIDUATION   47

(D1) 'Such-and-such table in the counterfactual circumstances considered is *this* one' (referring to Tavola).
(D2) 'There is no table in the counterfactual circumstances considered which is identical to *this* one' (referring to Tavola).

Assuming that the demonstrative elements in (D1) and (D2) cannot be substituted by any description without thereby changing their cognitive content, one might be led to the following results:

(R1) There is no contradiction in the assumption that counterfactual circumstances in which there is no table remotely resembling Tavola might still fulfil D1.
(R2) There is no contradiction in the assumption that counterfactual circumstances in which there is a table exactly like Tavola even in its material constitution might still fulfil D2.

R1 might appear to contradict CO1; R2 might appear to contradict CO2. It is important to note, however, that both claims are in fact compatible with the two theses developed about features of counterfactual thought. Lack of a contradiction in a description of a counterfactual situation does not imply that we have a positive understanding of the feature which would render the description true. CO1 does not imply the negation of R1. CO1 may be taken to be neutral about R1. CO1 makes a more specific claim: we do not have any positive conceptual grasp of the additional feature a situation must fulfil if D1 is true, although there is no table remotely resembling Tavola in that situation. To clearly understand the content of CO1 (and the difference to a negation of R1), it is helpful to try to switch between the two relevant 'possibilitites' in a concrete example. Think of a 'world' where Paolo has constructed a table like Tavola out of the same stuff under the same circumstances. Now try to switch in your thought between two 'possibilitites': the table he constructed is *this* one (referring to the real table Tavola*)*; the table he constructed is not *this* one. You will notice that you do not know what to do. You are asked to conceive of a particular objective feature of the 'world' at issue which constitutes the difference. You are asked to think of a case where, in addition to the facts about Paolo just mentioned, that feature is present, and to think of a case where it is not, and you are asked to switch between the two cases in thought. It is easy to note that this is something we are unable to do. We may demonstratively refer to Tavola and stipulate that it is one particular table in counterfactual circumstances, one of those that have nothing in common with Tavola. But the stipulation—even though it may be said to involve no contradiction—does not create a positive understanding of what it is about that other table which would render the stipulation true. CO1 states that conceptual incapacity; R1 does not imply that we have the relevant capacity; so there is no conflict between CO1 and R1. As argued below, the situation is quite different in the case of conscious individuals. Thinking about conscious individuals we easily manage to switch back and forth between the two analogous possibilities. One may assure oneself in the same way that R2 and CO2 are perfectly compatible. There is no contradiction, we may assume, in the assumption that a table exactly like Tavola in counterfactual circumstances, even in its origin and material constitution, is nonetheless not identical to *this* one (referring to Tavola). But the lack of a contradiction does not imply that we have any grasp of the difference between a case where a table exactly like Tavola, even in its origin and in its material constitution, is *not* identical to Tavola, as opposed to a case where it *is* identical to Tavola. We may introduce two distinct possibilities here by stipulation without contradiction (or so one may claim following R2); but the capacity to stipulate that difference must not be conflated with genuine positive understanding.

To avoid misunderstandings I would like to address a second objection. The two examples, so the objection goes, do not in fact support the two claims for the following reason: in introducing the example, reference to the real table Tavola could not be avoided. The first counterfactual situation, for instance, was described saying that Paolo constructs a table out of the same material (the material *Tavola* is actually made of). So a rigid designator for the relevant object, the name 'Tavola', was used in the description of the counterfactual situation. The answer is that in order to describe the relevant conditions we need to rigidly refer to the material Tavola is made of, but we need not rigidly refer to Tavola. We only use the term 'Tavola' to pick out the material Tavola is made of in the real world in order to then refer to that particular material in thinking or talking about different possible circumstances. It should be reminded at this point that the two claims CO1 and CO2 do not state that no rigid designation is needed at all in order to formulate conditions that exclude (in the relevant sense) the existence or non-existence of Tavola. They only state that no rigid designator of Tavola is needed to accomplish the respective task.

6. Counterfactual thought about oneself (part 1: no entailment of one's own existence by 'descriptive' conditions)

Let us now turn to the case of conscious individuals and, as a first step, reflect upon examples involving one's own existence or non-existence in counterfactual circumstances. The following examples will be presented in the first person. The reader should reflect upon these examples as examples about him- or herself.

I am born in the beginning of June and I was about ten days late. So my biological origin lies in the end of August of the preceding year. Suppose my mother had got pregnant in the end of July in the same year instead. A different human body would have evolved from a different fusion of cells. A child would have been born about a month earlier with different genes, different physical properties, and different psychological dispositions.

I thought a lot about this possibility when I was a child. I then wondered about the following question: If my mother had got pregnant a month earlier, what would have happened to me? Here are two possibilities: (P1) In that case I would not have been born. I never would have experienced anything. Instead of me someone else would have started to exist and to discover the world. (P2) I would have been born a month earlier. In that case, of course, I would look different; I would have different talents and different psychological dispositions. Yet, it would have been me who would have started to exist and to discover the world.[12]

Most of us will agree that P1 is the correct answer. P2 appears absurd, a hypothesis only a child could seriously consider. I will not argue that P2 might be correct. The crucial point is rather that we *understand* the difference between P1 and P2. Reflecting upon the example from the first person perspective, we have a clear understanding of what would render P2 true. P1 and P2 are exactly alike with respect to the properties of the child born a month earlier. Nonetheless we can switch in thought between two distinct subcases: the child is someone else (P1); the child is me (P2). Thinking about the question in the first person mode, we have a clear understanding of the additional feature which would render P1 true, and we have a clear understanding of the additional feature which would render P2 true. This conceptual observation about counterfactual first person thought might be summarized as follows: we have the conceptual capacity to grasp the difference between P1 and P2.[13]

How do we conceive of the difference between P1 and P2? Our conception of P2 ('I am the child born a month earlier') may be described as follows: we refer to the body of the child born a month earlier and conceive of that body as 'my body'. We conceive of a human body as 'my body' by entertaining the thought that I am the one who sees the world from its perspective, that I am the one who feels pain when it is hurt, that I am the one who moves its limbs, etc. In this particular way each of us can conceive without effort of counterfactual circumstances in which he or she would exist as a conscious being, even though he or she would be radically different. We conceive of P1 in a similar way. We then suppose that the body of the child born earlier is *not* my body and that I do *not* come into existence. We conceive of that possibility by entertaining the thought that I do not feel anything when that body is hurt, that I do not see the world from its perspective, that I do not see the world from any perspective, that I do not experience anything. Once we have conceived of the two possibilities in that way from the first person perspective we can easily switch in thought between the two. We then at least appear to be able to grasp a substantial difference between the two possibilities, P1 and P2.

When confronted with thought experiments of that kind, some people tend to declare themselves incapable of developing any clear understanding of the difference

---

[12] I wish to thank my childhood companion and brother Julian Nida-Rümelin for a long discussion we then had about the issue which I still clearly remember in many details.
[13] This formulation presupposes the metaphysical claim that there is a genuine difference between P1 and P2, a presupposition that could be avoided by a more cautious formulation: '...the difference or the apparent difference between P1 and P2...'; for simplicity I ignore that complication here and in some other places in the present chapter.

between P1 and P2. It looks as if they thereby disprove the general conceptual thesis at issue about human counterfactual first person thought. The contradiction, however, might be only apparent. There is in fact no contradiction between their self description and my conceptual claim if the way I wish to use 'clear understanding' here is not the use these people have in mind. By the claim that we have a 'clear understanding' of the difference I do not wish to exclude that we are puzzled when we reflect about it; I do not exclude either that we have reason to doubt the existence of a substantial difference; and I do not mean to imply that we have anything like a theoretical account of what the relevant difference really consists in.

By 'clear understanding' in the present context I mean something like this: reflecting upon the two cases, we are under the cognitive impression of grasping a substantial and real difference in a clear manner; this cognitive impression is forced upon us; we seem to conceive of a real and substantial difference and cannot get rid of that cognitive appearance. That cognitive impression is compatible with being puzzled upon further reflection. I will not try to give a theoretical account of the relevant sense of 'clear understanding' here. A closer look upon the cognitive situation created by the thought experiment might, however, help to avoid misunderstandings.

There is a sense in which we *are* unable to understand the difference between P1 and P2: reflection upon the difference creates puzzlement: we quickly realize that we lack any theoretical understanding of its nature. We are puzzled as soon as we realize that we do not seem to be able to give an informative answer to the apparently legitimate question: what does the difference consist in? It is not a difference between the physical or psychological properties of the person in the first possibility and the person in the second. They share all relevant properties. It is not a difference in the organic stuff the human organism in the one and the human organism in the other situation is composed of. So what might constitute the difference? It looks as if we cannot give any answer at all.[14]

The cognitive situation when we reflect upon the difference between P1 and P2 may be described a bit more precisely as follows. In a first step we immediately understand or seem to understand what the difference consists in. In P1, I never would have had any experience; in P2 I would have the body born a month earlier. This is, for me, a radical difference. It is the difference between 'eternal nothingness' and life. It is clear what the difference consists in when I consider the two possibilities 'from my perspective'. In a second step, of course, one might well wonder about what that difference which appears so obvious on the first level of reflection might consist in. One will then realize that there is no informative answer. The alleged difference cannot be described without reference to oneself saying 'that child is me' or 'I do

---

[14] One has to be careful though with the latter formulation. It is true that we cannot give an informative answer, but at least misleading to say that we cannot give any answer at all. Who wishes to understand the nature of the difference must conceive of it in the way described. The best answer, therefore, that can be given to the question about the nature of the difference is to ask the one who is enquiring about it to reflect upon the difference from the first person perspective.

not exist'. One may then come to the conclusion that there cannot be an objective difference between P1 and P2 after all. (This tempting conclusion which I wish to resist is endorsed by many philosophers.[15]) Furthermore, upon reflection, on the second level so to speak, some may lose sight of what they originally, in the first step, understood so well. It may happen, I suppose, that on the second level of reflection the thinker 'loses cognitive hold' of what appeared to be there 'on the first level'. Going back to the 'first step' the difference will again be obvious. Some who reflect upon the issue might switch back and forth between the two intuitions, 'there is a difference' and 'there is no difference'; maybe some people can stay aware of their own conception of the difference on the first level of reflection only when they are 'in the first mood'.[16]

The puzzling situation which emerges in the second step, however, should not blind one with respect to the first step. To become aware of the conceptual insight here at issue about the way we think of ourselves it is necessary to clearly separate the two steps. One may have well-founded doubts about whether P1 and P2 are genuinely different possibilities. In order to become aware of the conceptual capacity at issue, the reader should however put these doubts aside.

If there is a genuine difference between P1 and P2, then the difference transcends any description: there is no difference between P1 and P2 with respect to the distribution of qualitative properties and with respect to the constitution of matter. The claim of this section may be put as follows: any human being (and indeed any being capable of self-conscious thought) has the conceptual capacity to clearly conceive of that difference. The empirical fact that people often deny having that conceptual capacity is not a serious problem since there is a plausible explanation of this reaction which is perfectly compatible with the thesis at issue: we are puzzled by the apparent difference upon reflection when we realize that we cannot account for the difference in the usual descriptive manner. This puzzlement plausibly motivates the description that we lack a clear understanding of the difference. That puzzlement, however, is perfectly compatible with using the conceptual tools we all have for grasping the difference when we consider the example from the first person perspective.[17]

---

[15] A famous example is D. Parfit (1984) who endorses the parallel claim for transtemporal identity.

[16] This description of our cognitive situation (or something similar) emerged in a conversation with Jiri Benovsky.

[17] According to an anonymous referee—in order to be of any interest—these conceptual observations need to be tested by empirical investigation in the spirit of 'experimental philosophy'. Otherwise (as the referee puts it) 'all we have is the observation of the author'. This reaction is, in my view, symptomatic of a common misunderstanding of the role of intuition as well as phenomenological reflection in philosophical texts and in philosophical research. When an author explicates and defends an intuitive judgement, then he or she thereby asks the reader to engage him- or herself in intuitive testing. Analogously, when an author makes a phenomenological claim about human experience, then he or she thereby asks the reader to engage in phenomenological reflection in order to test that claim. If the author is successful, then, in both cases, the reader comes to the same conclusion on the basis of his or her own judgement. In that case, although there is no empirical investigation involved, the reader has a rational basis for agreement with the author. In the same way, the above observations invite the reader to engage in a certain cognitive activity. He or she is asked to

52   THE SELF AND SELF-KNOWLEDGE

7. Counterfactual thought about oneself (part 2: no 'entailment' of one's own existence by 'descriptive' conditions)

The preceding section was about our capacity to conceive of the counterfactual possibility of being a person who is radically different from the person one is in the real world. Let us now turn to the opposite case. We consider a possible situation where there is someone who shares all important or even all properties with me in the real world. Again, the reader is asked to think of the case in the first person mode. We all agree, I suppose, that under all circumstances in which the world would have developed in such a way that there would be someone just like me and with a body grown from the same biological origin, that person would be me. This plausible assumption will not be doubted in what follows. Rather, the issue is, once again, about whether we can conceive of the contrary. The claim is this: we have the conceptual capacities to conceive of a counterfactual situation where there is someone exactly like me and yet the person is not me. To illustrate this conceptual thesis I would like to remind you of an interesting passage in a classic paper by Thomas Nagel:

consider everything that can be said about the world without employing any token-reflexive expressions. This will include the description of all its physical content and their states, activities, and attributes. It will also include a description of all the persons in the world and their histories, memories, thoughts, sensations, perceptions, intentions, and so forth. I can thus describe without token-reflexives the entire world and everything that is happening in it—and this will include a description of Thomas Nagel and what he is thinking and feeling. But there seems to remain one thing which I cannot say in this fashion—namely, which of the various persons in the world *I* am. Even when everything that can be said in the specified manner has been said, and the world has in a sense been completely described, there seems to remain one fact which has not been expressed, and that is the fact that I am Thomas Nagel.... It is ... the fact that *I* am the subject of *these* experiences; this body is my body; the subject or center of my world is this person, Thomas Nagel. (Nagel, 1965, pp. 354ff)

As will become clear in what follows, I do not agree with the way Thomas Nagel puts his observation. However, he is drawing the reader's attention to a specific feature of first person thought which I believe to be precisely the one I am trying to express. Thomas Nagel's formulation of that thought is, however, problematic for the

---

find out—considering the relevant examples—whether he or she can positively conceive of the relevant possibilities. The way in which he or she then will conceive of them will reveal to him or her that the capacity to do so is no individual skill which other self-conscious humans might lack. Like in the cases of phenomenological reflection and intuition, the reader is asked to test my claims on the basis of his or her own judgement; once again, no empirical research is required for the observation to be valuable in the context of a rational debate. (The conceptual observations here at issue are not, however, arrived at by phenomenological reflection, nor are they the content of rational intuition in the usual sense, but—as these remarks suggest—there are similarities to both categories). These quite complicated meta-philosophical issues deserve closer examination and are relevant to support the reasoning elaborated here. I have to leave this, however, to another occasion.

following reason: he allows for the use of the name 'Thomas Nagel' in the description of the actual world. But the name 'Thomas Nagel' rigidly refers to the same person (the same subject of experience) Thomas Nagel refers to when he uses the word 'I'. Upon reflection we realize, therefore, that no fact appears to be left open when the world has been described without using token reflexives. We do not need token reflexives in order to express the fact (or the apparent additional fact) at issue. Some rigid designator referring to the thinker himself is sufficient for that purpose. Here is a corrected version of Thomas Nagel's formulation:

> consider everything that can be said about the world *without employing any rigid designator referring to me or to any other person*. This will include the description of all its physical content and their states, activities, and attributes. It will also include a description of <u>persons just like those who actually exist,</u> their histories, memories, thoughts, sensations, perceptions, intentions, and so forth. I can thus describe <u>without using a rigid designator for people</u> the entire world and everything that is happening in it—and this will include a description of <u>a person precisely like me</u> and what he is thinking and feeling. But there seems to remain one thing which I cannot say in this fashion—namely, which of the various persons <u>(so described)</u> in the world *I* am. Even when everything that can be said in the specified manner has been said, and the world has in a sense been completely described, there seems to remain one fact which has not been expressed, and that is the fact that I am <u>the person who is precisely like me</u> .... It is ... the fact that *I* am the subject of *these* experiences; this body is my body; the subject or center of my world is <u>the person having this body</u>, the one who is precisely like me. (modification of the above citation)[18]

This variation of Thomas Nagel's passage expresses, in my view, an interesting insight: upon reflection we can realize that we are under the impression that a fact about the real world is left out when we describe the real world without using any rigid designator 'for me' (for the one who thinks about the issue). It appears as if such a description of the world leaves it open 'which of the various persons in the world I am'.

How can we explain that cognitive appearance? I propose to explain that cognitive appearance by reference to what we are able to conceive of in a positive way. The following feature of first person thought is 'behind' that cognitive appearance: a thinker who considers a description of the real world which makes no use of any rigid designator of the thinking subject himself but is otherwise maximally complete can still positively conceive of many different counterfactual possibilities satisfying that description. The thinker can specify different counterfactual possibilities satisfying the description, picking out some experiencing subject existing according to the description and stipulating that he* is—in the situation thus specified—the subject satisfying

---

[18] All changes to the original citation are underlined. The motivation for each change will be clear on the basis of the remarks following in the text. The description 'the person having this body' towards the end of the modified passage needs to be understood in a particular way: 'this body' may refer to the actual body of Thomas Nagel and may be understood as rigidly referring to it. The whole definite description 'the person having this body', however, must be understood as a non-rigid designator.

that description.[19] The thinker has a positive understanding of the feature of a counterfactual situation which would make that additional stipulation true. In that manner he can positively conceive of possibilities that at least appear to be genuinely different. Thomas Nagel makes it quite clear how we manage to conceive of the different counterfactual possibilities compatible with the otherwise maximally complete description of the real world: a world satisfying that description might be such that I have the body I actually have (I experience the world 'from the perspective' of someone having that particular body); a counterfactual world satisfying the description might be such that I have a different human body or it might be such that I do not exist at all ('there is no world from my perspective'). All these possibilities (which can be further subdivided) appear to be left open since we have a positive understanding of the additional feature of the world which would render them actual respectively. In conceiving of these different possibilities, we consider the case from the first person perspective; thinking of them in this particular way we appear to grasp a genuine difference existing between them.

Nagel seems to have thought when writing the passage that we need the first person pronoun to complete the description of the real world in a way that the gap appears to be filled and the relevant fact about my identity included. I disagree. We can complete the description in the relevant way using some rigid designator or other referring to me (my name, for instance, does the job equally well). The first person pronoun is not needed to complete the description but it enters the picture in a different way: to conceive of the feature responsible for the fact that the real world satisfies the description thus completed we need to engage in first person thought; and we need to engage in first person thought when we contrast the real situation with relevant alternatives (where I have, for instance, a different human body). According to this diagnosis Nagel conflated two questions in the cited passage: what are the *linguistic* tools necessary to complete the description of the world such that it contains the relevant fact about my identity (or more cautiously: such that the appearance of incompleteness vanishes)? What are the *conceptual* tools required to fully understand a description of the world which is completed in the relevant way (in other words: what are the conceptual tools employed in conceiving of the feature apparently left out in the description at issue)? The answer to the first question is (in my view): we need a rigid designator referring to me (to the thinker at issue). A partial answer to the second question is: we need to engage in first person thought.

The above citation in its modified version may help to uncover the following feature of counterfactual first person thought: when a rational thinker considers a description of how the world could have developed which contains the description of a person who resembles him or her physically and psychologically in every detail, then the thinker will still be able to conceive of the possibility that he or she is not the person

---

[19] Following Hector-Neri Castañeda, I use stars attached to personal pronouns in order to mark *de se* beliefs in belief reports (cf., for instance, H. N. Castañeda 1968).

thus described. Both possibilities, 'I am that person' and 'I am not the person', remain positively conceivable. The thinker has the conceptual capacity to grasp what would have to be the case if the person described were a different experiencing subject not identical to the thinker. A rational thinker can grasp that possibility by considering the case from the first person perspective, by employing the tools of first person thought. The thinker will understand what would make the assumption of non-identity true by entertaining the thought that he or she—in the circumstances described—does not have the relevant human body (by thinking thoughts like 'I do not see the world from the perspective of that body, it is not me who is active when that body moves in an action, it is not me who feels pain when that body is injured', etc.).

8. Counterfactual thought about oneself (part 3: general formulation of the result)

We can now summarize what has been said in the last two sections about counterfactual first person thought by two conceptual observations. The following observation CO3 has been illustrated above using the example of a child born a month earlier.

Conceptual Observation 3 (CO3):

X is a person existing in the real world. L is a language containing no expression which can be used to rigidly refer to X.

X is rational and capable of first person thought and X is maximally informed about her own properties.

For all non-trivial conditions C which can be formulated using L, X can still positively conceive of the possibility that (a) the conditions C are met and yet (b) he★ (or she★) exists (under those circumstances).

A way to trivially exclude the existence of P would be to include the assumption that there are no experiencing subjects at all under the circumstances described: we cannot positively conceive of our own existence in circumstances where there are no experiencing subjects (we cannot positively conceive of being identical to a stone, for instance, if we presuppose as we should that stones are not endowed with consciousness). Another way to trivially exclude P's existence is to stipulate for each candidate for identity with P that it is identical with some *other* subject existing in the real world.[20] We cannot positively conceive of counterfactual circumstances where two subjects existing in the real world are identical to one another.[21] To exclude these trivial ways to falsify the above observation 'non-trivial conditions' have to be specified

---

[20] I would like to thank Stephan Leuenberger for pointing this difficulty out to me in conversation.
[21] One might argue for the conceivability of a counterfactual situation where you and I have the same body. This is not, however, a case where we are one and the same subject. There is no argument needed though in the present context for the inconceivability of cases of this kind. The point is that the observation I wish to propose should not depend on the conceivability of such cases. So they must be excluded by defining 'non-trivial conditions' accordingly.

accordingly: (a) their description does not imply that there are no subjects of experience; (b) their description does not imply that each subject of experience is identical to some person or subject in the real world different from the person X at issue.

Note that the above specification of 'non-trivial conditions' does not exclude descriptions of counterfactual circumstances as trivial which imply that there are only nonhuman animals in the situation described. As a consequence, the observation so formulated states that each of us can positively conceive of his or her identity with some non-human animal. Many readers will find this doubtful (to say the least), but I think it is correct when understood in the way intended. Let us take as an example the description of a world where a dolphin, let us call her Delfina, swims around near the coast of Costa Rica ('Delfina' does not refer to a dolphin in the real world). I do not know what it is like to be Delfina. I can only vaguely imagine how it might be for her to jump out of the water with a group of others. But I do have a clear understanding of the feature of the world that would render it true that I am Delfina. I am Delfina (in these circumstances) if and only if it is me who has the relevant dolphin body: it is me whose experiences depend in the right way on that body and it is me who does the jumping when Delfina jumps. I do *not* know what it is like to have that dolphin body (I can only vaguely imagine, for instance, what it is like for Delfina to hear her friends' voices), but I do understand in the way described what has to be the case for it to be true that I have that dolphin body. In order to understand what it takes for me to have a specific body I need not know what it is like to have that body.

A less radical version of observation CO3 results from a different characterization of 'non-trivial' conditions: (a′) their description does not imply that there are no human beings (b′) Their description does not imply that each human being is identical to some person or subject in the real world different from the person X at issue. This version is implied by the stronger version where (a) and (b) characterize 'non-trivial conditions'. I do not see any good reason to accept the weaker version while rejecting the stronger one. The conceptual capacities involved in conceiving of the relevant identities are the same. In conceiving of those identities, we do not 'project' any of our present properties upon the relevant individual existing in different circumstances. We do not 'hold constant' any of our physical or psychological properties in this conception. The only fact about ourselves 'held constant' in that conception is that we are a subject of experience capable of having some biological body or other. If this is correct, then the weaker and the stronger version of CO3 are supported by the same reasons and therefore stand or fall together.

Observation CO3 is in contrast with CO1. In the case of the table Tavola we *can* formulate conditions which conceptually 'exclude' the existence of Tavola: it is not positively conceivable what would have to be the case if Tavola existed under the conditions specified. We can formulate conditions of this kind without using a rigid designator for Tavola and without excluding the existence of Tavola in a trivial manner. (A trivial manner to exclude the existence of Tavola would be, for instance, to include the assumption that there are no tables at all under the circumstances described). Contrary to this, using a language which does not contain any rigid designator for the person P existing in the real world, we are unable to describe counterfactual circumstances in such a way that the existence of P is excluded in a non-trivial manner (in P's own conception of the case). The person P, if rational and capable of first person thought, will still be able to positively conceive of the possibility that she★ exists under the specified conditions, even if the description of these conditions entails that there is no person in these conditions who remotely resembles her★ (as she is in the real world). The conceptual capacity to conceive of the way a counterfactual situation has to be in order to fulfil the relevant description is not based on the thinker's ignorance about her own properties. The claim remains true if we assume that X knows as much about her own properties as is in principle possible to know about oneself.

The above claim CO3 states that a rational thinker capable of first person thought need not assume any similarity with a conscious individual in counterfactual circumstances in order to be able to positively conceive of the possibility that he★ or she★ is that individual. The following claim CO4 states that even in an extreme case of similarity with a person in counterfactual circumstances, non-identity with that person remains positively conceivable in the first person mode.

Conceptual Observation 4 (CO4):

X is a person existing in the real world. L is a language containing no expression which can be used to rigidly refer to X. X is rational and capable of first person thought and X is maximally informed about her own properties.

For any conditions that can be described using L, X can still positively conceive of the possibility that (a) these conditions are met and yet (b) *he★* or *she★* does *not* exist under those conditions.

According to CO4, no matter how similar a person existing in counterfactual circumstances described might be to the thinker X, X can still conceive of the possibility that he★ or she★ is not that person. This observation is in contrast to CO2. We *can* describe circumstances such that Tavola's existence under those circumstances is conceptually implied by the description in the relevant sense: we cannot positively conceive of what would have to be the case for Tavola *not* to exist in circumstances where there is a table precisely like Tavola in all relevant respects. Without using any rigid designator referring to Tavola we thus can specify conditions that 'conceptually imply' (in the relevant sense) Tavola's existence. Contrary to this, even when we describe circumstances where there is a person perfectly similar to X, a person sharing all her relevant psychological and physical properties and even sharing her biological origin, X can still positively conceive of the possibility that he★ (or she★) is not that person, that he★ or she★ does not exist under the circumstances described. X's capacity to positively conceive of that possibility does not rely on ignorance: we may assume that X knows everything there is to know (as far as this is possible) about her own physical and psychological properties.

9. The relation to other features of first person thought (first part: incorrigibility and immunity to error through misidentification)

It is well known in the philosophical literature that first person thoughts—thoughts that are to be verbalized using the first person pronoun—have quite special features. It has been argued that (a) certain judgements about one's own present mental properties cannot possibly go wrong (incorrigibility theses) and that (b) certain first person judgements are immune against any error through misidentification. The second feature of first person thought has been explained by pointing out that (c) the relevant judgements do not involve any identification in the first place. One might suspect that the feature of first person thought the present paper focuses on is closely related or even a consequence of some of these well-known peculiarities of first person thought. It can be seen, however, that the special features of counterfactual first person thought formulated in CO3 and CO4 are independent of all these other characteristics of first person thought.

Let us turn to the incorrigibility thesis first. In its best version the thesis says, roughly, the following: when a person judges on the basis of having a specific kind of experience and using a phenomenal concept of that kind of experience that she is now having that kind of experience, then she is having that kind of experience at the moment at issue.[22] We need not go into the discussion of potential counterexamples and possible modifications of the incorrigibility thesis in order to see that it is about a phenomenon different and independent of the two claims here discussed about counterfactual first person thought. The incorrigibility thesis is based on the idea that we have direct access to the phenomenal character of our own present states in a way that excludes certain kinds of error. Contrary to this, our special access to present phenomenal states does not play any role in our capacity to conceive of our own identity with an individual quite different from us and of our non-identity with an individual just like us in counterfactual circumstances. One may subscribe to some version of the incorrigibility thesis and yet reject CO3 and CO4, and one may accept CO3 and CO4 and yet maintain that error about one's own present state is always possible.

Let us now turn to the claim that certain first person judgements cannot go wrong by misidentification. What it is for a first person judgement 'I am F' to go wrong through misidentification may be explained as follows: (a) the judgement 'I am F' is false and (b) it is based on the correct and justified judgement that some individual X has F and on a mistaken self-identification with that individual X. When Peter judges incorrectly that he★ is embarrassed on the basis of the expression of what he takes to be his★ face in a mirror while in reality he is looking into the face of his embarrassed twin brother, then Peter's judgement is false through misidentification in the sense just

---

[22] For a sophisticated version of the claim, see T. Horgan and U. Kriegel (2007).

explained: it is based on his correct and justified judgement that the one he★ sees in the mirror is embarrassed and on the mistaken assumption that he★ is the one he★ sees in the mirror. Whether a first person judgement can or cannot go wrong through misidentification depends on the evidential basis of the judgement. If, for instance, Peter judges that he★ is embarrassed on the basis of how he feels, then he may still be wrong, but he cannot go wrong through misidentification. In that case, his judgement is not based on any mistaken self-identification.

Since the thesis of immunity against error though misidentification has to do with judgements about our own identity, one may be led to suspect a close relation between that thesis and the claims CO3 and CO4 about counterfactual first person thought. I will argue, however, that the claims about counterfactual first person thought here proposed are neither a variant nor a consequence of the thesis at issue, and that they have a different conceptual origin. First person judgements which are immune against any error through misidentification are characterized by their specific basis: when we judge, for instance, that our body is in a specific position on the basis of proprioception, then we attribute the property of having a body so positioned directly to ourselves without basing that judgement on some identification of ourselves with an individual given in a specific manner.[23] It is for that reason (no self-identification is involved) that no error through misidentification can be committed. Contrary to this, when someone conceives using the tools of first person thought of a counterfactual situation where he★ or she★ is a person with a different biological origin and different physical and psychological properties, the judgement involves an identification—in fact it *is* an identification: the thinker first refers to a person in counterfactual circumstances given in a specific way by description, and then thinks of herself as being that person. In this case, the thought involves identifying oneself with an individual given in a specific way. As a consequence, error through misidentification is not excluded in thoughts about oneself that could be based on the relevant identity judgement. For instance, a child might believe that she★ would have lived with her parents if her★ mother had got pregnant a month earlier based on the belief that she would have been the child born in those circumstances. But the latter, and so the former belief would be (I suppose) mistaken. So the conceptual capacity described in CO3 and CO4 cannot be explained by the lack of any self-identification; the thoughts at issue do involve identifying oneself with an individual given in a specific manner. It follows that the feature of first person thought captured by the thesis of immunity against an error through misidentification is different from the feature of first person thought captured by CO3 and CO4.

Even though the phenomena at issue are different, one might still try to establish a deeper connection between the well-known feature of first person thought mentioned

---

[23] I owe the example to G. Evans, 1982, pp. 220–4. For discussions of the immunity against error through misidentification, see Shoemaker's seminal article (Shoemaker, 1968) in which the term is introduced, and see Pryor (1999).

above and the feature of counterfactual first person thought described by CO3 and CO4. One might try to do so along the following lines. When we conceive of the possibility of being the person who would have come into existence with a different biological origin in counterfactual circumstances from the first person perspective (using the tools of first person thought), then we conceive of that possibility by considering the possibility of having certain properties under those circumstances: a thinker can conceive of that possibility by conceiving of a situation where he★ or she★ has a particular human body; and a thinker conceives of the possibility of having a human body given by some description by considering that he★ or she★ would have certain properties under those conditions (e.g. the property of being hurt when that body is injured etc.). If this is correct, then the capacity of a thinker to grasp the feature which would make it true that he★ or she★ is the child born a month earlier (for instance) is based on the capacity to grasp what would make it true that he★ or she★ has certain properties in the circumstances considered. In other words: counterfactual self-attribution of properties is conceptually prior to counterfactual self-identification: we conceive of what renders counterfactual self-identifications true by conceiving of what renders counterfactual self-attributions true.[24] This result implies that we need to investigate the conceptual features of counterfactual self-attribution of properties in order to understand the conceptual origin of the phenomenon described by CO3 and CO4. The idea to pursue in what follows is this: maybe the deeper relation between CO3 and CO4 on the one hand and the thesis of immunity against error through misidentification lies in some commonality between judgements that are immune against error through misidentification on the one hand, and the way a thinker conceives of what would make it true that he★ or she★ has certain properties in counterfactual circumstances on the other.

To avoid confusion it might be useful to note that the commonality at issue is *not* the immunity against error through misidentification itself. In a case where someone judges that a particular thought about his★ or her★ properties in counterfactual circumstances is true, the thinker may go wrong and he★ or she★ may go wrong precisely because he★ or she★ has an incorrect belief about who she would be in those circumstances. There is no incompatibility between the following two description of someone's counterfactual thought: (a) a thinker believes that she would have property F in certain counterfactual circumstances because the thinker believes that he★ or she★ would be the individual X in these circumstances and (b) the thinker grasps what would make it the case that he★ or she★ is the individual X in those circumstances by grasping what would make it the case that he or she★ would have certain properties in these circumstances. In other words: the belief that a certain thought

---

[24] For more on this claim of conceptual priority with respect to transtemporal first person thought compare M. Nida-Rümelin (1997, 2001, 2006a, 2008).

'I would have property F' is true may be based on the belief 'I would be the individual I' although the capacity to understand what renders 'I would be the individual I' true is based on the capacity to understand what renders thoughts like 'I would have property G' true. In order to avoid confusion one has to clearly distinguish questions about the epistemic basis of a judgement from questions about conceptual priority. First person judgements that are immune against error through misidentification are not epistemically based on self-identification. First person thoughts that are covered by CO3 and CO4 may well be epistemically based on self-identifications. It is this disanalogy which led to the conclusion that we are dealing with different features of first person thought. Still, there is the following analogy: both kinds of thoughts do not involve any *conceptual* priority of first person identification. My understanding of what makes it true that my legs are crossed is not based on any prior understanding of what makes it true that I am a certain individual given in a specific way. The same applies to the relevant kind of counterfactual thought about oneself: my understanding of what makes it true that I would have certain properties in a given counterfactual situation is not based on my understanding of what makes it true that I am a certain individual existing in those circumstances. Can this commonality justify the claim that the two phenomena are one and the same after all?

The answer to this question, or so I claim, should be negative. The feature of certain thoughts in the first person mode described by the thesis of immunity against error through misidentification cannot be explained by the feature these thoughts have in common with counterfactual thoughts covered by CO3 and CO4. In order to explain why certain first person thoughts are immune against this kind of mistake we need to refer to the fact that these thoughts do not involve identity judgements in their *epistemic* basis. The *conceptual* feature at issue cannot serve to explain that kind of immunity which is easy to see: first person judgements which are *not* immune against error through misidentification share the relevant conceptual feature. Even in a case where a thinker judges that he★ or she★ is embarrassed by apparently looking into her own face in a mirror (and so by making a judgement that may well be false through misidentification), the thinker's understanding of what would make it the case that her judgement is true is in no way based on her understanding of some identity judgement. The thinker does not understand what it takes for her★ to be embarrassed by understanding what it takes for her★ to be identical with the person in the mirror. It is a fact about the *epistemic* basis which explains immunity against error through misidentification and *not* a fact about *conceptual* priority. Therefore, the feature which explains immunity against error through misidentification is not a feature the relevant thoughts share with counterfactual first person thoughts. So far we have not been able to find a deeper link between the special features of first person thought which have been discussed in the literature and the feature described by CO3 and CO4.

10. The relation to other features of first person thought (second part: non-descriptive reference)

To find such a deeper connection one might, however, have to approach the question in a different manner. Maybe the deeper connection lies in the way in which we refer to ourselves in both kinds of thoughts. In both kinds of thoughts we refer to ourselves directly and without using any description. As has often been noted, in both kinds of thoughts our act of reference cannot go wrong. Let me note in passing: this feature of first person thought is common to first person judgements that are immune to error through misidentification, and to judgements that are not immune to errors of that kind. Even when Peter judges 'I am embarrassed' on the basis of what he takes to be his* face in the mirror, Peter refers to himself in the same non-descriptive and direct way using the word 'I' as he does when he makes the same judgement based on his emotional feeling. It is misleading to describe first person judgements going wrong through misidentification as cases of failed reference. When Peter judges 'I am embarrassed' on the basis of his visual experience of someone's face in the mirror, then he successfully refers to himself using the word 'I'; the predication goes wrong since he incorrectly believes what he could express saying 'I am the person in the mirror' using, again, the word 'I' to directly refer to himself. Our question now is this: can we explain the conceptual feature described by CO3 and CO4 by the fact of direct and non-descriptive reference in normal I-thoughts?

It may look as if this is the right thing to say. A person who thinks a counterfactual first person thought like 'Under those conditions I would be happy' refers directly to herself (in a way which does not involve any descriptive content), and then goes on to attribute a property to her under counterfactual circumstances. A person who judges 'I would be that individual' with respect to certain counterfactual circumstances understands that judgement—as we have seen—on the basis of counterfactual self-attributions of properties like 'I would be hurt if that body were injured'. In these self-attributions she directly refers to herself and then goes on to attribute those properties to her. One may thus be led to the following idea: the fact that reference to oneself is achieved in a non-descriptive 'direct' manner explains why we can understand (or seem to understand) what it is for me to be a particular individual in counterfactual circumstances in a way which does not involve any description. This is why—so someone might think—I seem to be able to conceive of my own identity with a subject who has nothing in common with me as I am in the actual world.

The explanation just given is, however, unconvincing as I will argue in a moment. Before I start, a remark about 'direct reference' or 'non-descriptive reference' might be necessary. In the literature these locutions have been used mainly in theories about the linguistic meaning of utterances containing indexicals. According to Kaplan, for instance, 'I', 'here' and 'now' directly refer in the following sense: the referent itself enters the proposition expressed (cf. Kaplan 1989a). According to a widely held view, so-called pure indexicals (like 'I', 'here' and 'now') refer 'non-descriptively': no description of the referent enters the content expressed by the whole utterance in which they occur. In the present context, however, we are not primarily interested in linguistic meaning, but rather in *cognitive* content: we are interested in the way in which a thinker conceives of the content of a thought which can be expressed using the indexical 'I'. With respect to reference, we are interested in the way in which the thinker conceives of the individual he or she refers to using the word 'I'. In a first approximation one might be willing to say that the thinker refers to him or herself using the first person pronoun in a non-descriptive and in that sense direct manner. As has been pointed out in the literature about *de-se*-belief, a thinker may entertain I-thoughts even in complete amnesia when she cannot remember any property he or she might use to single him or herself out (let us put apart descriptions like 'the thinker of that thought' for the moment). The proposal I now wish to address and to reject explains the special feature of counterfactual first person thought formulated in CO3 and CO4 by that well-known insight about first person thought. The explanation to address may be formulated along the following lines: there is no descriptive content associated to the way the thinker conceives of him or herself when referring to him or herself in a thought using the first person pronoun. Therefore, no descriptive content cognitively associated with the individual referred to using the word 'I' can possibly conflict with what is assumed about the counterfactual individual the thinker identifies him or herself with when thinking the thought that he* or she* might be a radically different person (compare CO3). Furthermore, since no descriptive content is cognitively associated with the individual referred to, the assumption that a counterfactual individual shares all relevant actual properties with the thinker cannot conceptually exclude non-identity of the thinker (conceived of in the first person mode) with that counterfactual individual (compare CO4).

If this were the correct explanation, however, then CO3 and CO4 should generalize to other cases where we still succeed to refer to an individual even when we have no knowledge that distinguishes the individual from others of its kind. When—in the sense just given—we non-descriptively refer to an apple, for instance, then we should be able to distinguish in thought, analogous subcases of counterfactual situations. To test this hypothesis let us consider a case where a thinker has an apple in his hands and is thus in a position to demonstratively refer to that apple. Reference is achieved in a non-descriptive manner. The following story about the case will render it analogous to the example of the child born a month earlier: The thinker, Paolo, planted an apple tree when he was a child. Unfortunately the small plant was destroyed by mistake. It never evolved into the beautiful tree it could have become. Years later, Paolo planted another apple tree in the same place. This time he protected the evolving plant more carefully and he succeeded. He now holds an apple of that tree in his hands. To discuss the case we still need a way to refer to one of the apples that would have developed had the first tree not been destroyed. Let us suppose, for that purpose, that the trees Paolo has planted belong to a kind with a particular feature: these trees produce their first apples one after the other with a considerable time distance in-between; so there would have been a particular first apple on the tree which has been destroyed.

In the case of the child born a month earlier, the thinker can positively conceive of two subcases of the counterfactual situation considered—one in which she★ is the child born earlier and one in which she★ is not. Our question now is this: can Paolo, referring demonstratively to the apple in his hands, positively conceive of the following subcases (a) and (b)?

(a) *This* apple is the first apple that would have grown on the tree had the small plant not been destroyed and
(b) *This* apple is not the first apple that would have grown on that tree.

If Paolo (or rather an ideally rational person in his situation) does not have that conceptual capacity, then the explanation of CO3 and CO4 by the mere fact of non-descriptive reference is falsified. Paolo will not have any difficulty in conceiving of the second possibility (b) and it will appear obvious to him—like in the case of the child born earlier—that (b) is correct. Unlike in the case of the child born a month earlier, however, Paolo cannot make sense of the first description. We assume that Paolo is not a panpsychist: he is convinced that apples are not endowed with consciousness, that there is no world 'from the apple's perspective', no subject having the apple as its body. So there is no way to make sense of the first possibility by the assumption that *this* apple would have experienced the world from the perspective of the first apple on the tree which would have evolved had the plant not been destroyed; and there does not appear to be any other way to make sense of (a). If this is so, then we do not have any way to positively conceive of some feature of the counterfactual situation which could make it true that *this* apple (referring to the real apple in Paolo's hands) would have grown as the first apple on the counterfactual tree which actually has been destroyed. One may, of course, describe the alleged difference saying: the first apple that would have grown on the tree which has been destroyed would have been *this* one in the first case and a different one in the second. But what about the first apple on the counterfactual tree could possibly make it the case that it is *this one* in the real world? As observed earlier for the table Tavola, we are unable to switch in thought between two positively conceived possibilities (a) and (b). Contrary to this, in the case of the child born a month earlier we realize upon reflection that there is a particular way we can conceive of the difference from the first person perspective. Reflecting upon the difference in the first person perspective we appear to grasp a substantial difference between two genuinely different possibilities. Assuming that the apple is not endowed with consciousness, there is no way to do the parallel cognitive switch with respect to the apple.

The apple example can be used to argue for the following conclusion: the fact that references using 'I' in the normal way are cases of non-descriptive reference (no properties of the referent are used to fix the reference) cannot explain the conceptual features of counterfactual first person thought in question. Demonstrative reference shares this feature with first person reference, but counterfactual demonstrative thought does not share the special features of counterfactual first person thought.

The rejection by an intuitive counterexample, however, is not yet satisfying as a reply to the proposed explanation. One would like to see the mistake in the idea that non-descriptive first person reference might explain the feature of counterfactual first person thought. The mistake is, as I will argue, (a) an implicit conflation of properties used to fix the reference of some object with properties we take to be necessary or essential for the thing referred to and (b) a misunderstanding of the explanandum: what has to be explained is taken to be the absence of a conceptual conflict in the description of counterfactual cases where, in reality, we have to explain the absence of the capacity for any positive conception of the cases thus described. This diagnosis emerges when one tries to understand how the proposed explanation might possibly work.

To explain the features of counterfactual first person thought by the lack of any descriptive element involves, I suppose, the following ideas: in other cases of counterfactual thought which do not share the special features of counterfactual first person thought, reference is achieved using some 'descriptive element', using some knowledge about the relevant object which then can get into conflict with the properties stipulated for the object at issue in a counterfactual situation. As a consequence of that conflict, identity of the object referred to with the relevant object in counterfactual circumstances is no longer conceivable. No such conflict can occur in the case of first person reference since there is no descriptive element involved in the act of reference.[25]

An explanation along these lines takes for granted that the relevant features of counterfactual first person thought would be explained if we had an explanation for the lack of any hidden contradiction in the assumption that I might be a person with different properties, and origin, and with a body of different material constitution (supposed explanation of CO3), and of the lack of any contradiction in the assumption that I might not exist although there is someone who has all my relevant actual properties (supposed explanation of CO4). What has to be explained, however, is not the lack of a hidden contradiction in these descriptions: it is our conceptual capacity to *positively conceive of* the corresponding possibilities. So even if the explanation were successful in explaining the lack of hidden contradictions in the relevant descriptions of counterfactual possibilities, it would not have shown enough.

The explanation, however, is unsuccessful, even as an explanation for the lack of a hidden contradiction in the relevant descriptions. There are only two ways in which the attribution of a property P to the real individual X, and the ascription of properties to Y in counterfactual circumstances can explain a hidden contradiction in the assumption that X would be Y (or that X would not be Y) in the relevant counterfactual situation: a hidden conflict may occur if (1) P is taken to be a necessary property of

---

[25] This explanation if adapted to CO3; it is not quite clear what a parallel attempt at explaining CO4 might look like.

X (a property X has under all metaphysically possible circumstances), and if Y is supposed to lack that property (this is the part relevant for the supposed explanation of CO3), and it may occur if (2) P is taken to be an essential property of X (a property such that each individual having P is necessarily identical to X), and if Y is supposed to have that property (this is the part relevant for the explanation of CO4). In the first case, the assumption that X is Y in counterfactual circumstances involves a hidden contradiction in the light of the thinker's implicit assumptions; in the second case, the assumption of non-identity between X and Y involves a hidden contradiction. Both explanatory schemata are however unavailable to someone who wishes to explain the features of counterfactual first person thought on the basis of non-descriptive first person reference. Following the above schema, CO3 has to be explained by the assumption that there are no properties that we take to be necessary properties of ourselves (with the exception of being a potentially experiencing subject). This assumption is not to be conflated with the fact that we do not need any descriptive cognitive element to successfully refer to ourselves in first person thought. CO4 would have to be explained—according to the above schema—by the assumption that there are no properties that we take to be essential properties of ourselves; again it is a bad mistake to conflate this assumption with the claim of non-descriptive first person reference.

According to the present diagnosis, the idea that the special conceptual features of counterfactual first person thought can be explained by the non-descriptive nature of first person reference is ill-founded in multiple ways, and the mistakes involved may appear so obvious that the idea should have no plausibility in the first place. But the idea does have some plausibility, and might not loose its intuitive attraction even when criticized in the preceding manner. The diagnosis just given should therefore be supplemented with some explanation for that resilient intuition. I will address that challenge in what follows.

11. A deeper connection between non-descriptive first person reference and the special features of counterfactual first person thought

It is a simple linguistic fact established by linguistic convention that whoever utters the first person pronoun in some given language—independently of what he knows about himself—thereby refers to himself. The same rule could exist in a language programmed into robots without consciousness. The capacity to refer to oneself non-descriptively, therefore, does not appear to have any interesting cognitive counterpart. Since the capacity to successfully refer to oneself is due to a simple convention about the reference of the word 'I', there does not appear to be any motivation for the introduction of some non-descriptive concept of ourselves to explain that capacity. One might even be led into an apparently plausible illusion theory: the idea that we do have a substantial non-descriptive concept of ourselves is created by the simple fact that we are able to successfully refer to ourselves without thereby thinking of ourselves under any description. We have that capacity thanks to a simple reference rule. The capacity does not require any cognitive achievement. Having the capacity creates the illusion that we have some non-descriptive substantial cognitive grasp of ourselves. In reality we lack any such substantial cognitive grasp of ourselves as subjects of experience.

The illusion theory just sketched may appear plausible at first sight. Upon reflection, however, one will not get rid of the impression that each of us has some substantial cognitive and non-descriptive grasp of himself as a particular subject of experience, as a 'particular centre of the world'. To have a substantial *non-descriptive* cognitive grasp of oneself in the sense here at issue, which is not easy to explain, must not be conflated with the substantial *descriptive* self-conception each of us develops in the course of his or her life. We self-attribute properties to ourselves which we take to be constitutive of our specific and unique personality. But upon reflection we realize that we might lose all these important and often highly valued properties under unfortunate circumstances, for example in an accident involving serious brain damage. When we think of the possibility of continuing to exist while having lost all psychological properties that we took to be constitutive of our specific and unique personality, then we think of ourselves using the substantial non-descriptive concept each of us has of him or herself.[26] Using the non-descriptive substantial I-concept we can think of ourselves as an individual that could change all its psychological and physical properties while remaining the same individual experiencing subject. It is the non-descriptive substantial I-concept which is involved when we understand Nagel's point in its modified version formulated above.

What is it to have the 'non-descriptive substantial I concept'? What is it to master that concept? I would like to propose the following partial explanation: mastery of the non-descriptive substantial I-concept shows itself in the capacity to counterfactual first person thought which exhibits the features described by CO3 and CO4. A thinker who has the concept, or rather a full mastery of the concept, thereby has the capacity to positively conceive of the relevant counterfactual cases. The proposal does not imply that we use that non-descriptive I-concept only when engaged in counterfactual thinking. The idea is rather that this is the concept used in normal everyday first person thought, the special status of which becomes obvious when we use it in counterfactual first person thought.

If this brief sketch goes in the right direction, then there *is* a deeper connection between first person reference in normal first person thoughts and the special features of counterfactual first person thought described by CO3 and CO4: in normal first person reference we use a concept of ourselves—a 'non-descriptive substantial

---

[26] Compare ch. 3 of M. Nida-Rümelin (2006a) and M. Nida-Rümelin (2008).

'I-concept'—which has a remarkable conceptual status. A partial description of that remarkable status is given by CO3 and CO4. The concept used quite generally in first person thought is partially characterized by its specific contribution to the content of counterfactual thoughts in which it occurs; this specific contribution is described by CO3 and CO4.

We now can provide an error theory for the mistaken idea that CO3 and CO4 can be explained by reference to the simple fact of non-descriptive self-reference. The special features of counterfactual I-thoughts partially describe the special status of the I-concept involved in normal first person reference. The error of a theorist who tends to explain (and thereby trivialize) CO3 and CO4 by reference to the non-descriptive nature of first person reference may therefore be said to consist in a subtle conflation: the non-descriptive nature of the substantial I-concept involved in normal first person reference and the rather trivial non-descriptive nature of first person reference are not clearly kept apart.[27]

12. Other-directed thought

We can run exactly the same thought experiments that have been used to support CO3 and CO4 with respect to another person, or more generally with respect to another experiencing subject. The counterfactual features of first person thought might be more obvious in the first person case, but upon reflection the reader will be able to rediscover the same peculiarities of counterfactual thought in examples concerning some other person or some other sentient being. Think of some individual animal, A, that you believe to be conscious. Consider some counterfactual possibility where the parents of that individual animal never met and the actual mother of that animal had a child with a different father. Again, you will be convinced that under those circumstances A would never have come into existence: this particular subject of experience would never have felt the sun or the feeling of hunger. No 'world' would have been given to A, to say it in a telling metaphorical manner. Still, you will be able to realize that you do understand the opposite hypothesis, the hypothesis that it would have been A who would have been born as the offspring of a different father, looking different and behaving in a different manner. In order to understand the hypothesis you take the perspective of the actually existing individual A: you consider the possibility from its 'first person perspective'. You can do so even if the subject you consider is not a person, and even if the subject you consider is unable to think first person thoughts. You then use your own capacity to think of that individual as of a subject of experience. You are able to think of another individual as of a subject of experience independently of whether the individual itself is capable of thinking of itself in that particular way. The example just mentioned concerning a counterfactual offspring of a different father can

---

[27] I leave it to another occasion to develop an account of the relation between these two facts.

be used to intuitively test the claim about other-directed thought which is parallel to CO3. I will leave it to the reader to imagine a case of the kind that can be used to support the claim analogous to CO4. If I am right that the features described of counterfactual first person thought can be found as well in other-directed thought, then the following two claims hold:

Conceptual observation 5 (CO5)

X is a conscious individual existing in the real world. L is a language containing no expression which can be used to rigidly refer to X.

For all non-trivial conditions C which can be formulated using L, we can still positively conceive of the possibility that (a) the conditions C are met and yet (b) X exists (under those circumstances).

By adding 'non-trivial' above, trivial counterexamples are excluded: we thereby exclude a description implying that there are no conscious individuals, and we exclude a description implying that each conscious individual existing under the circumstances described is identical to some other sentient being in the actual world. Even if according to a given description of a counterfactual situation there is no sentient being resembling X in any relevant manner, we still have the capacity to conceive of what would have to be the case for X to exist under the circumstances described. This is what CO5 states. We conceive of that possibility by 'taking the perspective' of the actual individual X; we conceive of that possibility by conceiving of it as having the feature that X is one of the subjects existing under those circumstances, in other words: we conceive of it by thinking that X is the subject who has a particular body existing under the circumstances described.

Conceptual observation 6 (CO6)

X is a conscious individual existing in the real world. L is a language containing no expression which can be used to rigidly refer to X.

For *all* conditions C that can be formulated using language L we have a positive conception of how the world would have to be if (a) those conditions are satisfied and (b) X does not exist.

According to CO6 we have the capacity to positively conceive of a counterfactual situation where some subject is just like X in all its relevant physical and psychological properties and where that subject has a body built up of the material constituting X's body in the real world and yet under those circumstances X does not exist. We conceive of that possibility by 'taking the perspective' of the actual individual X existing in the real world. We think of that possibility by thinking of it as a situation where 'there would be nothing from X's perspective'.

The special features of counterfactual thought with respect to other sentient beings are, as I would like to put it, a symptom of our capacity to think of another being as a subject of experience. To conceive of another being as potentially conscious, as being, 'a centre of a world' involves 'taking its perspective' when thinking about what could have happened to that being under different circumstances. If this is correct then CO5 and CO6 partially describe what it is to master the concept of an experiencing subject.

To sum up, according to the view here developed, the special features of counterfactual I-thought captured by CO3 and CO4 partially describe what it is to have a substantial non-descriptive I-concept which I claimed to be used in any normal first person thought. The special features of counterfactual thought with respect to others captured by CO5 and CO6 partially describe what it is to have the general concept of a subject of experience. One might now wonder about the relation between the two—the relation between having a substantial non-descriptive I-concept and having the concept of a subject of experience. One may ask (in other words): what is the relation between CO3 and CO4 on the one hand and CO5 and CO6 on the other? It is natural to think of the features of first person thought described by CO3 and CO4 as more basic. One will then say that these features take over—by way of conceptually taking the perspective of another actually existing subject—to other-directed thought. According to this picture, our capacity to think of another being as a subject of experience is the capacity to use conceptual resources of first person thought when thinking about others. If this is a good picture then we may say: the non-descriptive I-concept is more basic than the general concept of a subject of experience.[28] But this might be a mistake. One will readily admit that in cognitive development of a human thinker the acquisition of the two concepts might go hand and hand; the concept of another subject might even emerge first. This empirical issue is, however, not at stake. The question I am raising is rather about conceptual priority: is the substantial non-descriptive I-concept conceptually prior to the concept of a subject of experience as the remarks just made make it appear? On the background of the present analysis we might ask the question in a different manner: Is the capacity described in CO5 and CO6 (concerning other-directed counterfactual thought) based on the capacity described in CO3 and CO4 (concerning counterfactual first person thought)? It is not clear to me what one should say about this issue. There is some plausibility to the idea that a thinker who has the full mastery of the non-descriptive I-concept thereby conceives of himself as of a subject of experience, as of 'a centre of a world' among others. If so, then using the substantial non-descriptive I-concept appears to involve using the general concept of a subject of experience which casts doubt on the conceptual priority thesis sketched above. Maybe the two concepts conceptually presuppose each other and none of them can be said to be conceptually prior to the other.[29]

---

[28] This is the way I described the parallel relation for transtemporal thought in earlier publications (compare M. Nida-Rümelin 1997, 2001, 2006a, 2008).

[29] The way in which we positively conceive of the relevant possibilities essentially involves 'taking perspectives' in the sense sketched in the text. There is no way to take the perspective, in that sense, of a piece of inanimate matter (like a stone). This explains why we do not have an analogous positive understanding of a world in which a subject (a dog or a person) turns into a stone. One might ask, on the other hand, if we do have a positive understanding of a world in which a subject exists *without* a body. In this paper I do not address this issue. For the purpose of the paper (which is to show that we conceive of ourselves as

13. Perfect individuals and subject–body dualism

If the view about our conceptual architecture here developed is correct, then conscious individuals are—according to our natural understanding—what one might call 'perfect individuals'. Perfect individuals are characterized in the following way: their individuality is not constituted by any of their properties, nor is it constituted by being composed of a specific concrete stuff, nor is it constituted by a combination of having certain properties and being composed of a specific stuff. Perfect individuals can be characterized in a more precise manner, saying that the metaphysical claims corresponding to the conceptual claims CO5 and CO6 apply to them. This characterization is captured by the following definition:

Perfect individuals (definition)

An individual X existing in the real world is a perfect individual iff the following claim holds:

If L is a language containing no expression which can be used to rigidly refer to X, then

(1) for all non-trivial conditions that we can formulate using L, it is metaphysically possible that
    (a) none of these conditions is met and yet (b) X exists,

and,

(2) using L we cannot formulate any conditions such that the fulfilment of these conditions metaphysically necessitates the existence of X.

Part (1) is the metaphysical counterpart of CO5, part (2) is the metaphysical counterpart of CO6. The way we conceive of sentient beings according to CO5 and CO6 would be appropriate if and only if the 'possibilities' we are able to positively conceive of according to CO5 and CO6 are genuine metaphysical possibilities.[30] In other words: our concept of a subject of experience (which is partially characterized by CO5 and CO6) is adequate only if experiencing subjects are perfect individuals in the sense just defined. We can now summarize the results obtained as follows: we conceive of conscious beings as perfect individuals; our conception of conscious beings is adequate only if conscious beings *are* perfect individuals.

This result may be used for an argument in favour of subject–body dualism: we assume as a first premise that our concept of experiencing subjects is adequate. It follows that we are perfect individuals. We assume as a second premise that no material thing is a perfect individual. It follows that experiencing subjects are numerically

'perfect individuals' in the sense of Section 13) there is no need to discuss this further question about whether or not being embodied is somehow incorporated into our I-concept.

[30] I wish to use the term 'metaphysical possibility' roughly in the following sense: a case is metaphysically possible if its realization is compatible with the nature of the things, properties, and relations involved.

distinct from their bodies, their brains, and any parts of their brains. Other alternatives to subject–body dualism are excluded in a similar manner: entities constituted by their functional properties, for instance, are no perfect individuals either. Certain dualist alternatives to subject–body dualism are excluded as well: 'bundles' of non-physical mental properties are no perfect individuals either.

The weakest point in the argument is its first premise. The obvious alternative is to suppose that our concept of a subject of experience is inadequate.[31] One way to defend the premise is to attract attention to the way in which we would have to be the victims of a fundamental and ubiquitous illusion if the first premise were false. Arguably the concept of a subject of experience is deeply incorporated in the way we think, in the way we perceive, and into the content of emotional experience. Another way to defend the premise is to show that there are epistemic reasons to accept it: the concept is formed on the basis of what we know about subjects by being a subject. The argument would have to explain why and in what way this is a reliable basis for the acquisition of an adequate concept. A third line of argument supports the crucial premise showing that its direct consequence—subject–body dualism—can be developed in a way which avoids absurdities and is compatible with available empirical data.[32]

References

Adams, R. M. 1979 "Primitive Thisness and Primitive Identity", *The Journal of Philosophy* 76, 5–26.

—— 1981 "Actualism and Thisness", *Synthese* 49/1, 3–41.

Castañeda, H. N. 1968 "On the Logic of Attribution of Self-Knowledge to Others", *The Journal of Philosophy* 65, 439–456.

Chalmers, D. 1996 *The Conscious Mind: In Search of a Fundamental Theory*, Oxford, Oxford University Press.

---

[31] Inadequate concepts in the sense here at issue can nonetheless refer. A concept C of an entity E is inadequate iff having that concept C of E involves attributing a certain feature F to E (or taking E to be of a certain kind) which E actually does not have (or to which E actually does not belong). For instance, according to the view here presented, having a concept of subjects of experience involves taking them to be perfect individuals; so that concept of experiencing subjects would be inadequate if the metaphysical thesis that subjects actually are perfect individuals were false. One should admit, however, that the concept would refer (to people and other conscious beings) even if it were inadequate for that reason.

[32] Since David Chalmers' seminal book, *The Conscious Mind*, there has been a lot of discussion about so-called conceivability arguments. Conceivability arguments start with the claim that some proposition p is conceivable and—introducing further premises—conclude that p is metaphysically possible. The argument sketched in the last section shares this general feature with conceivability argument but the additional premise is of a quite different kind. The additional premise could not be captured, for instance, by the identity of primary and secondary intensions, since the relevant concepts are themselves characterized by alleged modal properties of the individuals referred to. Furthermore, the defence—at least when the first strategy mentioned is chosen—of that additional premise is quite different from the corresponding defence of the additional premise in conceivability arguments. A detailed comparison would be worthwhile but goes far beyond the scope of the present chapter.

Evans, G. 1982 *The Varieties of Reference*, Oxford, Oxford University Press.
Horgan, T. and Kriegel, U. 2007 "Phenomenal Epistemology: What is Consciousness that We May Know it so Well?" *Philosophical Issues* 17, 123–44.
Kaplan, D. 1989a, "Demonstratives", in J. Almog, J. Perry, and H. Wettstein (eds.) *Themes from Kaplan*, Oxford, Oxford University Press, 481–564.
——1989b "Afterthoughts", in J. Almog, J. Perry, and H. Wettstein (eds.) *Themes from Kaplan*, Oxford, Oxford University Press, 565–614.
Kripke, S. 1980 *Naming and Necessity*, Oxford, Basil Blackwell.
Lewis, D. 1971 "Counterparts of Persons and their Bodies", *The Journal of Philosophy* 65, 113–26; repr. with 'postsripts' in Lewis 1983.
——1983 *Philosophical Papers*, vol. 1, Oxford, Oxford University Press.
——1986 *On the Plurality of Worlds*, Oxford, Blackwell.
Nagel, T. 1965 "Physicalism", *Philosophical Review* 74/3, 339–56.
Nida-Rümelin, M. 1997 "Chisholm on Personal Identity and the Attribution of Experiences", in E. H. Lewis (ed.) *The Philosophy of Roderick M. Chisholm (Library of Living Philosophers)*, Chicago (Ill.), Open-Court, 1997, 565–85.
——2001 "Identité transtemporelle et attribution de propriétés futures", *Studia Philosophica*.
——2006a *Der Blick von innen: Zur transtemporalen Identität bewusstseinsfähiger Wesen*, Suhrkamp, Frankfurt am Main (English translation in preparation).
——2006b "Dualist Emergentism", in B. McLaughlin and J. Cohen (eds.), *Contemporary Debates in Philosophy of Mind*, Oxford, Blackwell, 2006, 269–86.
——2007 "Doings and Subject Causation", in A. Newen, V. Hoffmann, and M. Esfeld (eds.), *Mental Causation, Externalism, and Self-Knowledge*, Special Issue of *Erkenntnis* 67/2, 147–372.
——2008 "An Argument from Transtemporal Identity for Subject–Body Dualism", in G. Bealer and R. Koons (eds.) *The Waning of Materialism*, Oxford, Oxford University Press, 191–211.
—— 2010 "What About the Emergence of Consciousness Deserves Puzzlement?", in A. Corradini and T. O'Connor (eds.) *Emergence in Science and Philosophy*, Routledge Studies in the Philosophy of Science, London, Routledge, 149–162.
Pryor, J. 1999 "Immunity to Error Through Misidentification", *Philosophical Topics* 26/1, 271–304.
Shoemaker, S. 1968 "Self-Reference and Self-Awareness", *The Journal of Philosophy* 65, 555–67.

3

Subjects and Consciousness

Christopher Peacocke

What is it to represent oneself as oneself? And what is the nature of the entity, if any, so represented? These are the two questions to be addressed in this chapter. The first is a question about the nature of intentional content; the second concerns the metaphysics of the self. We should aim for an integrated pair of answers to these questions, an integration that makes it clear why the content elucidated in answering the first question is a way of representing an entity of the sort characterized in answering the second question. In this particular area, I believe that reflection on the question about content yields some important resources for answering the second question. So I will begin with the question about content.

I

A creature may see something as coming towards it. It may have an apparent memory of being involved in an earlier encounter at a particular location. It may have an apparent action-awareness of moving its head. All these conscious events have a content concerning a subject. The content in question has an intermediate status. The content is more than merely one which concerns the object that is in fact the subject. The content involves less than the full conceptual first person content. Merely seeing something that is in fact the subject includes the case of seeing something that is in fact oneself, say in a mirror, without one's realizing that it is oneself. That can occur without the object being in any way represented as oneself in the perceptual experience. Seeing something as coming towards one involves much more than merely reference to something that is in fact oneself. Yet seeing something as coming towards one is something that can occur in subjects who lack concepts. Concepts are constituents of the intentional contents of states that subject can enter for reasons; concepts are constituents of the contents of judgements; it is in the nature of concepts that they are constituents of the states and events in which a subject displays a sensitivity to reasons. It seems that first person perceptual events, memories, and action-awarenesses of the sort we have just mentioned can be present in creatures that have only a more primitive system of nonconceptual representations of the world, and who do not operate at the level of reasons at all. So the question arises: what is the nature of the self-representation in the content of these conscious events?

It is in the nature of the type of content of each of the events of this sort that their correctness conditions concern the subject of the event. A particular token perceptual experience of an object as coming towards one has a correct content only if the object in question really is coming towards the subject of the experience. A subject who has an apparent memory of an encounter with a certain kind of animal at a certain location has a correct memory only if the subject enjoying the apparent memory really did have such an encounter. A subject's apparent action-awareness of moving his head is correct only if the subject enjoying the apparent awareness really is moving his head. As is well known, in all three cases, causal materials must be added if these necessary conditions are to be strengthened to reach the status of genuine perception, memory, and action-awareness.

When I say that "it is in the nature of the type of content" that the correctness condition concerns the subject of the events, I mean at least the following: that no further information about the reference of the ways things, events, and properties and relations are given in the intentional content of these events is needed to settle whether or not the content refers to the subject of the event. The way in which the subject is given in the awareness entirely settles that it is the subject of the awareness that the content concerns. In this it differs from any perception that presents a person, and which happens to refer to the subject who enjoys the perception. The fundamental reference rule for any instance of the perceptual-demonstrative type *that F* (such as *that man*), where the demonstrative is tied to an experience in which something is apparently presented in a given way W, is this: the demonstrative refers to the man that is perceived in way W. This fundamental reference condition implies that the reference of the perceptual demonstrative is not necessarily the subject who is enjoying the perceptual experience in question.

Actually we need a stronger formulation of the point. In the contrasting conceptual case, we can conceive of a mixed descriptive-demonstrative content such as *the agent of this thinking*, or *the owner of this experience*. There is clearly a sense in which it is in the nature of the type of these contents too that they refer to the agent of the thinking and to the owner of the experience respectively. At the conceptual level, neither of these is equivalent to the first person concept. Although the referents of these complex descriptive-demonstrative concepts are guaranteed to be, respectively, the subjects of the thinking and of the experience, the determination of this reference goes via a component *the agent of* and *the owner of* that features in the content itself. For the genuine first person, by contrast, the determination of the reference as the subject does not go via such a descriptive component in the content itself.

We must respect the distinction between complex descriptive-demonstrative notions and the genuine first person if we are to characterize properly such states as the phenomenology of ownership. In his paper "Self-Consciousness and the Unity of Consciousness", Tim Bayne writes, "I take the sense of ownership to be an experience whose representational content is roughly: this (target) experience is had by the subject of this (reflexive) experience" (Bayne 2004, p. 231).[1] It seems to me that this understates the sense of ownership, which involves the sense that the experience in question is *mine*, and not merely something had by whoever may be the subject of this experience. We cannot properly capture the sense of ownership without mentioning the first person notion as part of the (nonconceptual) content of the subject's consciousness. Any syndrome in which someone experiences a pain but does not experience it as meeting the condition *This is mine*, is a syndrome in which the subject lacks a sense of ownership of that particular pain, whatever else she may represent about whoever is the subject of the experience.

So in the requirement that it be in "in the nature of the type of content" of the event or state in question that it refer to the subject of the state or event possessing the content, the following should be understood: that the determination of the subject as the reference does not proceed via satisfaction of some other condition that is involved in the nonconceptual content. It may help to point out that the distinction being invoked here is an analogue for these contents of Saul Kripke's distinction at the linguistic level between *de jure* and de facto rigid designation.[2] The first person nonconceptual content of a mental event is of a type whose instances refer *de jure* to the subject of the mental event in question.

These points are at the level of type of content, rather than the contents themselves. The fact that they are at the level of the type permits us to sidestep an objection. We can imagine an objector who believes in *de re* senses, and in their analogues at the nonconceptual level.[3] This objector might take a case like the one mentioned by Ernst Mach in which he sees a reflection—in fact of himself—in the window of a bus, and represents the object using the perceptual-demonstrative "that shabby pedagogue" (Mach 1914, p. 4). The believer in *de re* contents might develop his position in such a way that he insists both that: this particular *de re* content "that shabby pedagogue", as employed in thought on this occasion, has Ernst Mach as its reference essentially; and that only Ernst Mach could be the subject who enjoys the particular token perceptual visual experience that makes the perceptual demonstrative available. We need not for present purposes enter discussion of the former (contentious) claim, because at the level of types, nothing analogous can be said of the perceptual-demonstrative type *that shabby pedagogue*. That is, it is not in general true that any intentional content of the perceptual demonstrative *type* "that shabby pedagogue" will also refer to the subject who enjoys the relevant perception of the shabby pedagogue. By contrast, it is in the nature of the first person type, as it occurs in the intentional content of some mental event, that the

---

[1] Bayne could certainly change his formulation in the way I will be recommending consistently with (and arguably strengthening) the rest of the arguments in his paper, whose main points seem to me very well taken.

[2] See his introduction to the book version of *Naming and Necessity* (1980).

[3] On *de re* or "object-involving" senses, see G. Evans (1982); J. McDowell (1984); and on the relation between types and instances of types in the realm of the senses, see C. Peacocke (1981).

instance so occurring refers to the subject of that same mental event. The points I am making about the first person type, whether conceptual or nonconceptual, are then orthogonal to the issue of whether or not there are *de re* contents.

De jure truths about the nonconceptual first person must have a source or explanation. What is it? One natural answer to this question is this:

> what makes a component of nonconceptual content something of the first person type is that the fundamental condition for an instance of the type to refer to something, when it is in the content of mental state or event M, is simply that it refers to the subject of M (M's owner).

We can call this *the subject-constitutive hypothesis* about the nature of the nonconceptual first person.

The subject-constitutive hypothesis does not imply that the nonconceptual first person is some disguised complex descriptive-demonstrative content. We must always distinguish the material involved in the reference rule for a concept (or nonconceptual content) from the concept (or content) itself. The conceptual content *now* is individuated by the rule that in any thinking, it refers to the time at which that thinking occurs. But concept *now* itself is not structured. It should not be identified with the complex descriptive-demonstrative *the time of this thinking*. Nor should the nonconceptual first person—*i* as I will label it—be regarded as identical with some complex content *the subject of this state*. The nonconceptual content *i* itself is unstructured.

There is a consequence of the fact that an instance of *i* refers *de jure* to the subject of any state in whose content it features. Suppose a particular conscious subject *s* is in a mental state with the nonconceptual first person content. (My apologies for the use of the variable, but we need it to make the point sharply.) Then our subject *s* is in a mental state that *de jure* represents something about *s*. Our subject is a self-representer. Our subject has the property

λy [y represents something about y];

and our subject has this property in virtue of the nature of the type of content of his mental state. (Here I follow standard notation: $\lambda x[Fx]$ is the property of being F; $\lambda x \lambda y [Rxy]$ is the relation R; and so forth).

In his important discussion of Elizabeth Anscombe's view that "I" does not refer at all, Gareth Evans notes that some of her points can be met by observing that the word "I" is a device that each person knowingly and intentionally uses to refer to himself. That is, each person knowingly and intentionally has the property

λz [In using "I", z refers to z],

the property of being a self-referrer.[4] This distinguishes "I" from any proper name, or, I would say, any other expression or concept other than the first person. Now we have

---

[4] See the appendix to ch. 7 of G. Evans (1982).

just observed in the preceding paragraph that our subject in a nonconceptual first person state has the property λy [y represents something about y], and does so as a result of the very nature of the content. This shows that a form of Evans's point applies equally at the nonconceptual level, at a level below that at which we can properly speak of the intentional and knowing use of either words or concepts.

Whatever may be the explanation of the *de jure* truths about *i*, we can say that the (nonconceptual) content of the events and states in the intermediate cases in which we are interested is *intrinsically subject-referring*. It will be very convenient to have a label for this phenomenon. Suppose a particular subject *s* and one of its mental events *e* stand in the following relation, and do so as a result of the nature of the type of content *e* in the way we have been discussing: λx λy [x is the subject of y & the content of y refers to x].

Then when that condition is met, I will say *e* stands in the relation of *subject-reflexivity* to the subject *s*. The same applies to states as well as to events. More briefly, I will often speak of the mental event *e having the property of subject-reflexivity* if there is some subject to which *e* stands in the relation of subject-reflexivity.

In the most recently displayed formula, within the square brackets, the variable 'x' occurs twice in the characterization of subject-reflexivity. That is an initial identification of a respect in which these contents involve a kind of subject-reference in the subject's mental event. It is at the very least an open question whether or not the subject of any such event must thereby be employing a first person concept of the subject. I will be arguing that the subject can enjoy such an event without possessing the first person concept. The property of being subject-reflexive in the sense characterized is a generic notion of an event or a state's having a *de se* content. It can apply both when an event or state's content is conceptual, and when it is nonconceptual.

A subject-reflexive state or event can have a content that refers to the subject of that state or event without the subject also being given at the same time in some other, further way—be it perceptually, or in some other demonstrative fashion made available by some conscious state. To be a subject-reflexive state or event, it suffices that the state or event's content be of a type whose instances refer *de jure* to its subject. Whether a subject enjoying mental states with *de se* contents also has to have other background capacities or representations of the world, or must conceive of the world as being of a certain kind, are questions to which I will return.

It is the subject-reflexivity of the state involved that we need to highlight if we are to characterize adequately what is distinctively required by the English locutions "remembering being F", "remembering doing so-and-so", as distinct from "remembering my being F", "remembering my doing so-and-so". As James Higginbotham and Michael Martin have remarked to me, the latter pair of locutions can apply even when remembered from the third-person point of view—for instance, you see oneself in the mirror or on closed circuit TV in the memory. The former pair, "remembering being F" and "remembering doing so-and-so", can be applied correctly only when the subject has a memory with the property of subject-reflexivity. You may remember your conducting the orchestra if you remember seeing the then-live video feed of your doing the conducting. But you remember conducting the orchestra only if you remember the conducting from the point of view of the conductor, with the orchestra in front of you. The utility of the linguistic form "remembering ϕ-ing" is precisely that it allows us to pick out exclusively memories that are subject-reflexive in respect of the ϕ-ing, in a way the locution "remembering my ϕ-ing" does not.[5]

We could give an entirely parallel explication of the similar intermediate case of a present tense but nonconceptual analogue of *now*, one that features in the contents of apparent perceptions and action-awarenesses. For events with such an intermediate kind of present-tense content, the following relation holds between the time *t* such an event *e* occurs, and the event *e* itself, and the relation holds as a result of the nature of the type of content, without reliance on further information about the case:

$\lambda x \lambda y$ [x is the time of occurrence of y & the content of y refers to x].

This can equally be part of an initial identification of a respect in which these events can have a distinctively present-tense content without apparently requiring the subject to have a conceptual constituent *now*. We could similarly call the relation and property in question in this temporal case that of *time-reflexivity*.

In central cases, when a subject has an experience of, say, having a pond to his left and also has an action-awareness of running straight ahead, the subject represents himself as instantiating the conjunction of these two properties. This raises a question. Under the characterization I have given, the fact that the subject is in a position to represent himself as having the conjunctive property does not immediately follow from his being in a subject-reflexive state that he has a pond to his left and is in a subject-reflexive state that he is running straight ahead. From the fact that someone is in a subject-reflexive state that concerns object x, and is at the same time in a subject-reflexive state that concerns y, where in fact $x = y$, it by no means follows that the subject is in a position to appreciate that it is one and the same thing that is in both states. Though a creature can be in a subject-reflexive state that represents it as F and also be in a subject-reflexive state that represents it as G, nothing in what I have said so far has explained how the subject is in a position to register that he is in a subject-reflexive state of being both F and G.

Now subjects must in fact be capable of integrating the contents of those of their conscious states that exhibit subject-reflexivity into such conjunctive representations. For a subject who possesses and exercises the first-person concept, it is unproblematic how this could be done. A perceptual experience which represents the subject as having a pond to his left entitles the subject, other things equal, to judge a conceptual content of the form *that pond is to the left of me*. This content contains the first-person concept, with 'me' as the accusative form of the English expression of the first person

---

[5] The false claim that "I remember being at the meeting" is equivalent to "I remember that I was at the meeting" is implied in A. Prior (2003, p. 225).

concept. The judged content *that pond is to the left of me* is then suitable for inferential integration with other first-person contents, such as *I am running quickly straight ahead*. A thinker who accepts these two conceptual contents will, as a result of an inference of conjunction-introduction, be in a position to self-ascribe the property of both having a pond to the left of him, and of running quickly straight ahead. This solution is evidently not available for subjects who do not have the first-person concept, yet who nevertheless succeed in integrating representations about themselves. It is quite implausible that the integration of the contents of such representational states is restricted to creatures who possess concepts (if we admit a conceptual/nonconceptual distinction at all). So we need a different explanation of this phenomenon.

When a subject has a perceptual experience of being *F* and, say, an action-awareness of being *G*, normally representations of those two properties each enter an object file on the subject. An object file is a store of mental representations whose contents are all taken, in one way or another, to apply to the same thing. The idea of an object-file has been used in the explanation of propositional-attitude phenomena by a series of writers including Paul Grice, Michael Lockwood, Peter Strawson, and Robin Jeshion (cf. Grice 1969; Lockwood 1971; Strawson 1974; Jeshion 2002). It has also been used in the explanation of perceptual phenomena by Daniel Kahneman (cf. Kahneman et al. 1992). In the propositional-attitude case, the taking to apply to the same thing is at the level of belief and judgement. In the perceptual case, it is a matter of the perceptual system representing to the subject one and the same thing as having several current properties, including relational properties. Some apparatus takes information from the subject's various sensory, perceptual, and action systems, and integrates that information by placing predicative materials drawn from various sources into the subject's file on itself. That will determine the subject's present-tense awareness, his experience of how things are with him now.

There is, however, a fundamental difference between the operation of a subject's file on itself and perceptual object files, even if we consider only the nonconceptual level. To articulate the difference, I consider first perceptual object files.

A file on a perceived object is indexed by where, egocentrically, the object is perceptually given. It contains information about the object's currently perceived properties. Human perceptual systems also have the ability to keep track of where the object has been recently, the location from which it has travelled to its current position. Humans can do this for several objects simultaneously, as one of Zenon Pylyshyn's well-known demonstrations shows.[6] So as time passes from t_1 to t_2, in the case of perceptual object files, the system has to accomplish two tasks. One task is to form new object files, with information about the current properties of the object at a given location is at the new time t_2. The other task is to achieve representations of identities over time between the objects currently perceived at this later time t_2, and the objects as perceived as being at particular places at the earlier time t_1. Which of these identities hold is an entirely

---

[6] See the demonstration online at http://ruccs.rutgers.edu/finstlab/MOT-movies/MOT-Occ-baseline.mov (accessed 1 August 2010).

empirical and contingent matter. The object that is at a particular location at the later time might earlier have been at any one of many other locations.

By contrast, as time passes in the first person case, nothing of quite the same kind is required as is needed for the second task in the perceptual case. If a subject at t_1 has a nonconceptual representation of itself as f, by means of a file on itself, it suffices to update this at t_2 to a representation that at the earlier time, it was f. (I continue to use lower case italics for nonconceptual contents.) This past tense predicate can be combined with other present tense predicates in the subject's file on itself to yield representations to the effect that the subject was f and is g. In contrast to the perceptual case, here there is no empirical, contingent identity over time that needs further determination. If the earlier representation of itself as f was correct, then when the later representation is updated by the appropriate change of tense, so will the representation updated at t_2 also be correct. This holds unconditionally, and not merely in normal circumstances. It holds unconditionally because the later representation is a representation by, and about, the same subject as the earlier representation is about.

This contrasts sharply with the effect of similarly pure temporal updating of the object file labelled "the thing at egocentrically identified location p at t_1". Suppose a predicate with the meaning f is in the perceptual object file so labelled. (Actually it would be labelled using a form of the present tense.) Simply changing, as time passes from t_1 to t_2, the temporal parameter from *now* at t_1 to *a moment ago* at t_2 in no way ensures the preservation of truth-value. It may be a different object at the location p at the later time t_2 than was there at the earlier time t_1. That different object may not at t_2 have been f a moment ago. That is why a tracking mechanism is also needed in the perceptual case. It performs the second of the two tasks we mentioned.

In the case of perceptual object files, Pylyshyn has a theory of what he calls 'FINSTS', 'fingers of instantiation', subpersonal pointers that keep track of a perceived object over time.[7] When the same subpersonal finger of instantiation points to an object over time, it is experienced as the same object over time. On Pylyshyn's account, the explanation of our ability to keep track of an object over time involves these FINSTS. Perceptual object files must be supplemented with FINSTS if we are to explain our abilities to keep track of a particular object over time. My point is that in the first person case, there is no need for an analogue of FINSTS. Pure temporal updating of the subject's file on himself suffices in a way in which it cannot suffice in the perceptual case.

The argument developed in the preceding three paragraphs is essentially an adaptation, both to the nonconceptual case and to the level of mental representations, of points made about the updating of conceptual first person beliefs by Evans. In *The Varieties of Reference*, Evans discussed the relation between a later disposition to judge "I was previously F" and its relation to a present tense judgement "I am F" made at an

---

[7] For an overview of much previous work, see Z. Pylyshyn (2007, ch. 1).

earlier time. He wrote, "as far as the 'I'-idea is concerned, the later dispositions to judge flow out of the earlier dispositions to judge, without the need for any *skill* or *care* (not to lose track of something) on the part of the subject" (Evans 1982, p. 237). I suggest that the explanation of the 'flowing out of the earlier dispositions' that Evans mentions here is the phenomenon of pure temporal updating of the subject file, together with the constitutive links between the nonconceptual first person and conceptual "'I'-idea".

Whenever an animal or a human has the ability to distinguish in one way or another between the case in which it is the same and the case in which it is a different object which is now *F* and was *G*, there must be an explanation of how the animal or human has this ability. In the case of the perceptual distinction, Pylyshyn's FINSTS provide us with a possible and plausible explanation. In the case of distinguishing from the first person point of view whether it was oneself who was recently *F*, pure temporal updating of the subject file, as part of the mechanism that places past tense contents in the subject file, explains the capacity.

In each of these two very different kinds of case, the underlying explanation of the ability in question involves a sensitivity to identity without requiring at the explaining level a further representation of identity. We do not have to check, at the conscious personal level, whether or not it's the same FINST as earlier that's doing the pointing. That way infinite regress lies: for how would the system determine sameness of FINST? That itself is another identity question, and it is a mistake to think that it is a question the system must somehow address. These questions must come to an end at some point if they are ever to be answered by the system, and it is sensitivity without further representation that makes this possible.

The same applies to the operation of entry mechanisms for past tense predicates into the subject's file on himself. There is no question of the subject, at the personal and conscious level, checking whether the pure temporal updating is being done correctly, or is being done on the file with the right labelling. Again, that way regress lies, a regress that is entirely avoidable. And once again, a mechanism that is sensitive to identity does not need to have some independent test or criterion for identity.

None of these mechanisms is infallible. They may all fail or misfire in various circumstances, in which cases they respectively fail to represent, or misrepresent.

In an effort to make clear the central difference between the updating of the subject file on the one hand and perceptual object files on the other, I have used the simple notation '*f*' for the predicative component of a nonconceptual content. The simplicity of the notation should not mislead. In a wide range of cases, the representations that enter the subject's file on itself will be those appropriate to the distinctive rich spatial contents of perception and action-awareness. Just as these states and events have spatial content (that I tried in earlier writing to capture by the notion of scenario content), so do autobiographical memories of these very states. So a subject's file on itself should not be thought of as some subpersonal analogue merely of a set of predicates, some with past-tense parameters. It should be thought of as including a rich array of imagistic representations. They will be prime candidates for representations that enjoy what

Roger Shepard and Susan Chipman describe as standing in second-order isomorphisms with the reality they represent (cf. Shepard and Chipman 1970).

We can distinguish various categories of object file by what explains how a representation enters an object file of that category. For belief files associated with names (in a given connection), what explains a sentence entering that file is the thinker's acceptance of some sentence containing the name (in that connection). The sentence might be "Paderewski played Chopin rather fast". Such acceptance is something potentially under the subject's rational control, as the agent of his thinking; it is at the personal level; and it can be conscious.

By contrast, the conditions for entry of information into an object file in perception—as when information reaches it via one of Pylyshyn's FINSTS—are entirely unconscious, at the subpersonal level, and explain facts about perception, something that simply happens to the subject at the personal level. The conditions for entry of information into the perceptual object file require that it be information from the FINST-tracked object, when all is functioning properly, and this concerns an unconscious, computational level of representation.

A subject's phenomenological file on itself is equally constructed below the level of conscious mental action, and below the level of consciousness altogether. The seemings of perception, memory, emotion, and the rest are things that, at the conscious level, just happen to the thinker. Subject-reflexive perceptual seemings whose content concerns *de jure* the thinker himself are just a special case of this more general fact.

An account somewhat analogous to that given here for the first person can also be given for the case of conscious events and states with present-tense contents. The account would refer to a 'now' file on a time. The same applies again to conscious states and events that represent something as happening or being the case *here*. Representations of these states and events would be collected in a 'here' file.

There is a further respect in which a subject's file on itself has a distinctive status. A time can exist without representing itself and having a file on itself, the idea makes no sense. The same applies to places. By contrast, a subject may represent itself, and when it does, it must have a file on itself, a subject file.

A subject's primitive file on itself should not be regarded as integrating representations that already exist as the basis of conscious phenomenal events. You may be aware of your having both the properties of having a pond to your left and of walking straight ahead; but this should not be described as your operating, at the conscious personal level, on two already existing conscious events to somehow make them co-conscious. Your total state of integrated awareness is not a result of your conscious mental action upon some more primitive, already-conscious events and states. Your total state of subjective consciousness is not generated by your conscious mental action at all (though of course it may have mental actions as a component). The subject's file on itself, if it is to contribute to the explanation of subjectivity, must be regarded as operating on representations which are precursors of the representations that underlie conscious events and states, on pain of misrepresenting consciousness and phenomenology.

In this respect what is integrated in the subject's file on itself is very different from the case in which we have inferential integration that moves at the personal level from the two judgements *I am F* and *I am G* to the conjunctive *I am both F and G*. That inferential integration operates on conscious judgements at the personal level; the subject's file on itself does not. This means that we have to distinguish two kinds of subject file. There is the more primitive one I have recently been discussing, a file which helps to explain how things seem, nonconceptually, to the subject. But there is also, at the level of judgement, something that can still fairly be described as the subject's file on himself, that functions to integrate the contents of conceptual judgements. In cases in which a subject rejects the content of his more primitive, pre-judgemental phenomenology—for example, in the case in which he knows that he is looking at a perfect *trompe l'œil* or hologram—the contents of the more primitive subject file and the personal-level file at the level of judgement will not be in accord with one another. The more primitive one will contain some representation of the content of the illusion. The subject file at the level of judgement will overrule the illusion.

The operation of taking materials from precursors of conscious mental events and integrating them to form the contents of a subject's file on itself may seem in certain respects to resemble the operation of transcendental apperception in Kant's critical philosophy. Some of the resemblances are real, and could be pursued as an independent (and complex) topic. But there are also important differences. Precisely because the operations inserting material into the subject's file on itself are applied to non-conscious precursors of conscious event, they should not be regarded as operating on Kantian intuitions, if those intuitions are regarded as involving even a primitive form of consciousness. Mechanisms that insert something into a subject's file on itself are also open to purely empirical investigation. We could learn more about them by further investigations in empirical psychology.

Despite these differences (and others), there is an undeniable Kantian streak in the position I am outlining. I am concerned to formulate the constitutive conditions of subjecthood. That is a goal that overlaps with Kant's. The goal is partly realized in the same way. The idea of a subject's file on itself, though very differently elaborated in these very different approaches, needs to play a role in both accounts.

The characteristic of a conscious subject-reflexive state or event, that its predicative content is carried through, in central cases, to a subject's file on itself, seems to me to be a resource on which we should draw in addressing two closely related constitutive philosophical questions.

First, we can cite this characteristic in answering the question "What is it for a conscious state or event, such as an experience, to have a content concerning a subject that is also capable of enjoying other conscious states and events?" Without the psychologically real possibility of predicative integration with the contents of other subject-reflexive events and states, it would be hard to answer this question. It is because the content of an experience enters the subject's file on itself that it can concern a subject capable of being in other mental states too.

Second, I suggest that having a nonconceptual self-representation involves having an object file for oneself into which representations of the predicative contents of subject-reflexive conscious states and events are normally placed. At this level, these three properties are all instantiated:

> having an object-file on oneself that takes in the relevant predicative contents;
> being capable of subject-reflexive mental events and states; and
> having a nonconceptual self-representation.

With these interconnections and their grounds, we begin to move from a mere description of subject-reflexivity, as given in the earlier characterizations, to the beginnings of an explanation of its possibility and its nature.

One apparent attraction of this approach to primitive self-representation is that it gives priority neither to perception, nor to thought, nor to action, nor to sensation, in an account of primitive self-representation. A subject that has perception, but no action-awareness, can meet this condition. So can a Helen Keller. Provided the subject can enjoy states and events with subject-reflexivity, and the predicative content of those states is transmitted to an object-file on the subject, then the conditions for having this primitive nonconceptual representation of the subject are fulfilled.

It is natural to compare this with the attractions of an account of the full-fledged first person concept, according to which its reference is fundamentally determined by the rule that any use of the concept *I* in thinking refers to the thinker, the agent of that thinking. This rule gives priority neither to perceptual input (as Evans did) nor to intention and action (as Brandom does), but rather sees these connections as consequential of a fundamental reference rule for *I* that in itself gives priority to neither (cf. Evans 1982, ch. 7; Brandom 1994, ch. 8, section V.2; Peacocke 2008, ch. 3).

It is reasonable to expect that the subpersonal mental representations involved in enjoying a subject-reflexive state or event contain, or have some functional analogue of, a symbol indicating the self-representation. It could be the presence of this symbol that normally pulls the predicative content of the subject-reflexive representation into the subject file. It then becomes reasonable to ask how this subpersonal symbol, or functional analogue thereof, differs from a subpersonal representation for the first-person concept itself. The distinction between the conceptual and the nonconceptual demands a separate chapter, but there are still some brief answers to this reasonable question.

First, the phenomena and the states and events I have been discussing so far, at the level of perception, memory, and action-awareness, and registration of the contents thereof, can all be present below the level of judgement, a rational and potentially reflective mental activity. The notion of a concept is essentially that of something that features in the contents of judgements. Different current substantive theories of concepts vary in their account of the general form that the individuation of a concept must take, but they commonly respect this constitutive connection between concepts and judgement. If this connection does exist, then the primitive subject-reflexive states and events that I have been discussing so far need not involve concepts so conceived at all. The integration of the contents of subject-reflexive states, the proper updating of object-files, and the rest, can all be present in the mental states of a being that does not make judgements that are made reasonable, but not forced, by these various non-judgemental states. Similarly, if you hold that critical thinking is essential to possession of a concept, that too is a capacity additional to anything so far cited in this discussion of subjects and subject-reflexive states and events. Finally, many of the contents in which a primitive form of subject representation is involved may be scenario contents of the sort I discussed in *A Study of Concepts*, the wrong sort of content to be conceptual content (cf. Peacocke 1992). In short, we have been operating so far at a level below the kind of rationality and reasons involved in making judgements. In fact, it is precisely because we are below that level that we can use this material in elucidation of the first-person representation that is genuinely conceptual.

There is an argument that we need not two, but three degrees of self-representation to accommodate the phenomena. We can conceive of a creature with perceptions of the world, and whose location in the spatial world changes, but who uses no notion of itself as having a location in the world, neither at the conceptual nor at the nonconceptual level. This creature will use, at the nonconceptual level, and perhaps even at the conceptual level, versions of demonstratives about perceived objects and events. It may represent these objects and events as being at various locations identified in relation to a 'here'. It may represent observable properties and relations as holding between the perceived objects and events. All this can be done without using the notion of these objects as being related to itself. Yet this creature has perceptual states, and there is certainly a subject who has these perceptual states, and experiences the changing objective world. This subject will, like other subjects, have apparent memories of some features of the way the world was at earlier times. But at no point does this subject represent itself as having a location in the spatial world. A fortiori, it does not represent itself as tracing a route through the spatial world as time passes. It has neither states with the content "I am here now", nor states with contents of the form "I was there then".

In imagining this case in more detail, it may help to consider underwater worlds, in which a perceiving subject without an intentionally active body is passively moved around. The underwater subject can still represent things and events that occur in what is in fact its environment, though of course it is not represented by the creature as *its* environment. Someone might doubt that this case is possible on the grounds that the contents of perceptual experience concerning distance and direction are possible only for a creature enjoying bodily agency, and which can act by moving in certain directions and distances, in accordance with its representations of those distances and directions. I suggest, however, that the connections between perception and action are not so tight. I agree that true statements about the representational content of a creature's perceptions, including those about distance and direction, must have explanatory repercussions for the creature's actions in some possible circumstances. But it does not seem to me that that general constraint implies that spatial perceptual content is possible only where there is spatial action. The kind of creatures envisaged who do not self-represent may act differently according as they are in one part of the world, rather than another, as represented on their map of their environment. The map may distinguish qualitatively similar environments. The creature may act by changing its colour, or its acidity level, or the noise it emits, or its electric charge, accordingly. Perceptions with specific spatial contents will be essential in building up its cognitive map of the world as it changes location over time. Prima facie, all this can be present without the capacity for spatial bodily action on the part of the creature.

It follows that we do need to acknowledge three degrees of involvement of subjects in the representation of the objective world. Since the creature we have just described does not represent itself as an element of the objective spatial world at all, its degree of involvement in such objective representations is zero. This is a limitation on the content of the subject's representations, not the nature of the subject itself. The subject itself really is an element of reality. The states enjoyed by creatures with this Degree 0 involvement of subject-representation in the objective world are states that make possible all the richer degrees of subject-representation.

Are these cases of Degree 0 merely ones in which the reference to the self is implicit? The implicit/explicit distinction is an important one, but it cuts across the distinction in question here. A subject at this Degree 0 may employ a representation with the content *pond to the left*, and that may indeed involve implicit elements. But the implicit reference is, in this case, to a place—the location of what is in fact the perceiving subject—rather than being a reference to a subject or person. The implicit/explicit distinction classifies representations, be they mental representations, or sentences, or utterances, rather than what is represented. The difference between Degree 0 cases and others concerns what is represented, not the vehicle of representation.

The existence of cases in which there is Degree 0 of subject-involvement in the representation of the objective world offers support for an even more radical version of the claim that, way back in *A Study of Concepts*, I called 'the Autonomy Thesis'. The Autonomy Thesis states that a subject might enjoy a set of events and states with nonconceptual contents without possessing a set of genuine concepts at all. This Autonomy Thesis is denied by those—including me in an erroneous past—who think that any content at all, even the nonconceptual kind, must have connections with states with first-personal conceptual contents. The denial of the Autonomy Thesis sometimes rests on a failure to recognize that supposed connections with the first person can be connections, not with the first person concept, but rather with a nonconceptual analogue that has the sort of links we have been discussing with a subject's file on itself, and with subject-reflexive events. But if these Degree 0 cases exist, then the idea of a constitutively autonomous level of nonconceptual content operative in the minds of animals and in our less sophisticated representations understates the position. If Degree 0 cases exist, then the sort of sensitivity to changing relations as one moves (or is moved) in the spatial world may be a sensitivity that does not require that one represent what is in fact one's current location as one's current location. The location may be represented simply as *here*. Not even a nonconceptual first person is required for representation of an objective spatial world.

The representations involved when there is Degree 0 of subject-representation are in the literal sense, and in respect of the subject itself, 'nonpositional', a word that occurs in the natural translation of Sartre's phrase 'conscience non positionelle de soi'. Sartre also held that 'Toute conscience positionelle d'objet est nécessairement conscience non positionelle de soi' (Sartre 1936, p. 136).[8]

In a popular lecture, Vilayanur Ramachandran writes, "the self, almost by its very nature, is capable of reflection–being aware of itself. A self that's unaware of itself is an oxymoron" (Ramachandran 2003, p. 114).[9] If there are cases of Degree 0, as I have argued, then there are conscious subjects who do not self-represent. A fortiori, such subjects are unaware of themselves. One can restrict the term 'self' stipulatively to subjects who do self-represent, and then drain Ramachandran's claim of any substance. The phrase "almost by its very nature" shows that this was not at all Ramachandran's intention, otherwise the "almost" would not be there. So I am in disagreement with him on this issue.

The next degree of subject involvement in representation of the world, Degree 1, is exhibited by a subject who enjoys states with nonconceptual content that is objective, and which represent the subject has having a location, and as standing in other relations, in the spatial world.

At Degree 2 of subject involvement in the representation of the objective world we have use by the subject of the conceptual first person, as expressed in English by 'I', and the enjoyment of conceptual states that represent the subject as located in the spatial world. Just as the states enjoyed by a creature at Degree 0 make possible the nonconceptual first person states enjoyed at Degree 1, so similarly the states at Degree 1 make possible the conceptual states enjoyed at Degree 2.

If there can be subjects with only Degree 0 of involvement of self-representation in its representations of the objective world, there are some important conclusions to be drawn about the most basic structures underlying the existence of a subject. It is not correct to speak of the existence of a subject file in cases of Degree 0, because the file is meant to include predicates the subject represents as holding of himself; but the subject at Degree 0 does not represent himself at all. Instead of a file at Degree 0, we have just the even more primitive binding of representations (such as the perceptual representation of something heard on the right with something seen straight ahead). These more

---

[8] I am not, however, at all in agreement with Sartre's other theses about nonpositional consciousness, which seem to involve a form of no-ownership thesis about mental states and events. There is further discussion of this in Part II below.

[9] Published in the US as *A Brief Tour of Human Consciousness* (New York, NY: Pearson, 2004), in which the quoted passage is on p. 97.

primitive states and their binding must exist if there is to be a subject at all. At Degree 1, the binding function and the realization of a simple kind of *de se* representation are intertwined. But the binding and the representational functions can in principle come apart, if cases of Degree 0 are possible. There can be subjects without *de se* representation of the subject by the subject.

The points I have been making about nonconceptual self-representation are neutral on the question of whether subjects must, in some central or fundamental case, be embodied. Those who think that subjects must, in the fundamental and explanatorily central cases, have a body can consistently endorse the legitimacy, interest, and importance of the notion of subject-reflexive events and states. Those theorists could consistently insist that embodied subjects may enjoy subject-reflexive states as characterized here. So could those who deny that subjects must, in some central cases, be embodied. The notion of a subject-reflexive state can by itself serve several radically different ontological views.

II

I turn to the second of the questions identified at the outset, that of the metaphysics of subjects, the nature of the entity referred to in self-representation.

The nature of subjects and the nature of conscious states and events are ontologically interdependent. In one direction, there is a dependence because:

> what makes something a conscious state or event is that there is something it is like for the subject of that state or event to be in that state, or to be the subject of that event.

This is a statement of the classical characterization of Thomas Nagel, and the characterization entails that conscious mental events and states have subjects (cf. Nagel 1974). The characterization does not in itself say anything about what it is for a mental event or state to have a subject. What I recommend is that we look at this intuitive characterization of consciousness as one part of an account of the ontological interdependence of mental events and their subjects. As Frege said, "It seems absurd to us that a pain, a mood, a wish should go around the world without an owner, independently. A sensation is impossible without a sentient being. The inner world presupposes somebody whose inner world it is" (Frege 1977, p. 14). In contrast, "Things of the outer world are on the contrary independent" (ibid.), and do not need any bearer. The claim of ontological interdependence disputes the view Hume formulates when he says of "particular perceptions" that "All these ... may exist separately, and have no need of anything else to support their existence" (Hume 1739–40, Book 1, Part IV, sect. 6, par. III).

The principle I am defending—that what makes something a conscious state or event is that there is something it is like for the subject of that state or event to be in that state—is a metaphysical principle about the nature of the property of being conscious.

It makes a claim about a certain type of event or state. Using the very helpful apparatus of Kit Fine, we would formulate the claim thus: it is in the nature of the property of being a conscious occurrence that for anything with that property, there is some subject who enjoys (or suffers) that occurrence. In the Appendix to this chapter, I give a formalization of this claim and some further distinctions using Fine's notation (cf. Fine 1995).

There is an equally plausible dependence in the other direction, a dependence of the nature of subjects on conscious states. The dependence is captured in this principle:

> what makes something a subject is that it is capable of being in conscious states and of being the subject of conscious events.

Here, despite some other disagreements with him, I am in agreement with Sartre (or at least with the spirit of his claim) when he writes that consciousness is the subject's dimension of being: 'la conscience', he says, is 'la dimension d'être du sujet' (Sartre 1948, p. 136).

It is also plausible that the property of being a subject is a subject's most fundamental substantive kind. Anything that is a subject is essentially a subject.

Such a conception of ontological interdependence between subjects and the capacity for being in conscious states is not intrinsically a Cartesian conception. It is entirely consistent with this ontological interdependence that both subjects and their conscious states require some material realization.

The ontological interdependence does not, or at least does not obviously, imply that subjects are essentially or fundamentally embodied. The interdependence does not, or at least does not obviously, imply that subjects are essentially or fundamentally living animals. If embodiment is in some fundamental way necessary to being a conscious subject, that necessity would need to be shown by further arguments. So too would the claim of mere contingency of embodiment.

It may be asked why a particular pain or other mental event isn't individuated in the same way as any other particular event, by (perhaps) its particular causes and effects, as in Donald Davidson, or by some other account of particular events (cf. Davidson 1969). I answer that there is no incompatibility between such view of the individuation of particular, token events and the claim I am making of the interdependence of conscious events and their subjects. The claim of interdependence is a claim about types or kinds: what makes something a pain, for example, is that it bears a certain relation to a subject that suffers it. That is something concerning its kind (and no doubt its most fundamental kind), rather than its identity as a particular, for which some other account may be correct. The distinction between the nature of the kind and the individuation of the particular member of the kind applies to events quite generally, whether conscious or not, whether mental or not. Consider, for instance, explosions. What makes an event a member of that kind is that it is, roughly, a flying apart of some object or mass of material caused by forces acting from within that object or mass. That account of the nature of the kind is entirely consistent with there being some other account of the individuation of any particular explosion occurring at a particular time.

The interdependent conception I am offering is, by contrast, opposed to 'no-ownership' views of mental states and events. On the approach I am advocating, it is not only essential to conscious states and events that they have subjects, but this possession by a subject is also involved in what makes them conscious events and states. It is this notion of a subject, distinct from all three of Cartesian conceptions, from conceptions of essential embodiment, and from the constructed subjects of no-ownership views, that I would argue is also crucial for the philosophical elucidation of such matters as self-consciousness and the nature of first-person thought.

Subjects can sense, perceive, and think. They can act physically and act mentally. These sensings, perceptions, thinkings, and actions are conscious states and events of the subject. Subjects persist through time. Some conscious states are experienced by their subjects as continuing conscious states. Subjects can remember some of their previous conscious states and events; and some subjects are capable of thinking about their future states and events. Many of these mental states and events each have correctness conditions concerning the subject of that very state or event.

Hume famously remarked, "when I enter most intimately into what I call *myself*, I always stumble on some particular perception or other, of heat or cold, light or shade, love or hatred, pain or pleasure. I never can catch *myself* at any time without a perception, and never can observe anything but the perception" (Hume 1739–40, Book I, sect. VI). What is right in Hume's remark does not, as he thought, tell against an ontology of subjects of the sort I am advocating. What Hume's remark highlights is something quite different. It highlights rather the fact that what G. E. Moore called the diaphanous character of conscious events and states applies equally to the subject itself, as it can be given in conscious states and events. Moore described the diaphanous character of consciousness thus: "the moment we try to fix our attention upon consciousness and to see *what*, distinctly, it is, it seems to vanish: it seems as if we had before us a mere emptiness. When we try to introspect the sensation of blue, all we can see is the blue: the other element is as if it were diaphanous" (Moore 1903, p. 41). In conscious states and events, the subject is diaphanous in the way in which Moore rightly says the consciousness or awareness is diaphanous. In enjoying an experience or any other conscious event, we can equally say of the subject of the conscious event that "the moment we try to fix our attention upon the subject and to see *what*, distinctly, it is, it seems to vanish". The correct response to Hume's position is that he, the subject, no more needs to be an object of awareness and attention to exist and to be involved in his current conscious states and events than consciousness itself needs to be an object of awareness to be involved in his current conscious states and events. The ontological status of the subject is no more impugned by the phenomenon of diaphanousness than is consciousness itself.

Hume did not draw the same conclusion about consciousness itself that he drew about the subject of experience. Almost everyone would regard it as a *reductio ad absurdum* of his form of reasoning if he were to have done so. So we have to avoid a double standard that accords to subjects a treatment that it does not apply to consciousness. Hume's line of thought gives no reason to dismiss an ontology of subjects that would not apparently equally apply to consciousness itself. Suppose we write (very crudely, and ignoring distinctions important for other purposes) the basic form of attribution of a conscious state as

(1) Subject x enjoys event e of conscious kind K with intentional content C.

What we are aware of in enjoying a conscious state or event is what is given in the content C in the mental event or state of kind K. The four elements—x, the subject of the awareness, the conscious state or event e, the intentional content C, and what at the level of reference is given in C—are equally and essentially involved in this state of affairs. Neither the subject nor the consciousness is involved by being something on which the subject can fix his attention. The consciousness is of what is given in a certain content, in a state of kind K. It is equally a consciousness belonging to the subject.

I do not mean to imply that whenever a subject is in a conscious state, the subject has some awareness of himself as being in that state. That would collapse the distinction between consciousness and self-consciousness. We are concerned here with a subject's having a mental event or being in a mental state, rather than with the subject representing something as being his own in enjoying that event or state. The thesis is only that in any case of a conscious event or state, there is a subject who enjoys that state or event, and that it is a nonsequitur to argue from the fact that one cannot attend to or be aware of the subject in a certain way to the conclusion that the subject is not so involved. But I do add that even when a subject is aware of his being in a conscious state, as when you are aware of your seeing a red traffic light, you need not be given to yourself in a way which allows you to attend to yourself.

Still, it may be objected, are you not attending to yourself when you look at yourself in a mirror, or when you look at your hand to examine a cut? Isn't there an entirely unobjectionable and commonplace phenomenon of attending to yourself? I agree that there is; but I also want to distinguish. There is a distinction, in examples of attending, between what we can call *derivative* and *original* attention. When you attend to yourself by attending to yourself in a mirror, you attend to yourself by attending to something not given in a first person way, but rather to something given as your body. The same applies when you are attending to your hand. In these cases, you are attending to yourself by attending to something given in a way distinct from the first person way. By contrast, when you attend to the road in driving, or to the traffic light, you do not do that by attending to something given as anything other than the road, or as the traffic light. When you attend to one of your throbbing pains, you do not do that by attending to something given in some way other than as that very pain. When you attend to the road, or the pain, or the light, these are cases of original attention. The thesis that you cannot attend to yourself should more properly be formulated as the thesis that a case of attending to yourself cannot be a case of original attention. It can be only a case of derivative attention.

Hume was surely well aware that he could attend to his own body. It is very unlikely that he would have taken this obvious fact as a counterexample to what he meant when he wrote that he could never catch himself when he enters most intimately into himself. If this is right, then Hume could have used the notion of original attention. He could have said: any example of attending to yourself is an example of derivative attention. In my view, Hume would be right in elaborating his position in that way. He was wrong to presume that everything that is essentially involved in consciousness must be something to which one can attend in a case of original attention.

Attending is a relation between a subject and an object, but when we speak, as I have, of "attending to something given in a different way", the basic relation from which that concept is built is this: attending to x as given in way m. Consider the example, familiar from discussions of identity, of an aircraft carrier seen through one window, and an aircraft carrier seen through a second window, where in fact the same carrier is seen through both windows. It makes sense to say that someone is attending to the aircraft carrier as seen in the window to the left, as opposed to the attending to the aircraft carrier as seen in the window to the right. When we use the intuitive locution "attending to one thing by attending to something given in a different way", this means: attending to an object given in one way m by attending to an object given in a distinct *way* m'. So attending to an object given in a different way does not necessarily mean attending to a different object (it would not be a different object in the example of the aircraft carrier). What matters is that the ways are distinct, not that the objects given in the two ways are distinct. The ways *that person* and *I* are certainly distinct. That suffices for correct application of the distinction between original and derivative attention, and its use in discussing Hume's point. The distinction between the two cases of attention leaves open the question of whether the entity given in the first person way is the same thing as the entity given as *that person*. It follows that these points can be endorsed even by someone who thinks that you are identical with your body, or holds that you are in some way individuated by your body.

The distinction between derivative and original attention takes us a certain distance. We should, however, demand much more by way of explanation of why some cases of attention fall on one side of the distinction, and others fall differently. Why is there apparently no such thing as attending to oneself originally? An immediate answer is that to be an object of attention, the object or event must be given in perception, sensation, or perhaps in certain kinds of sensory imagination, and to be given in one of those ways is not to be given as oneself. Again, this seems fine as far as it goes. The explanatory question, however, is just pushed back. Why is there no such thing as being given as oneself in perception, sensation, or certain kinds of sensory imagination? To ask the question in compressed form: why can't the subject be an object of perception?

In the previous section, I suggested that the first person nonconceptual notion is individuated at least in part, if not wholly, by the condition that in any mental state, event or process in whose content it features, it refers *de jure* to the subject (the possessor) of that state, event, or process. To be given in perception, sensation, or sensory imagination is always and necessarily different from being given as the subject of a state, event or process. There is such a thing as being given as the subject of an event. If, for instance, you are aware that you are seeing the phone, or are aware that you are in pain, in your awareness you are given as the subject of the seeing, and of the pain, respectively. But in neither case, nor in any other, are you given as yourself in the scene perceived, or in the sensed state of affairs. One cannot be given as the subject of a mental event in the state of affairs as perceptually presented in the event.

The source of this incompatibility is the very nature of the nonconceptual notions involved. To be given as the subject of an event is one thing; to be given in a perceptual, sensational, or imagistic way is a different thing. It is neither a contingent nor a merely a posteriori fact that Hume could not find himself in any of his impressions. Hume says, no doubt ironically, that another person "may, perhaps, perceive something simple and continu'd, which he calls himself; tho' I am certain there is no such principle in me" (Hume 1739–40, Book I, sect. IV, part 6). We need to be explicit about what would justify the irony, to establish that Hume's observation is not merely one about some individual's empirical psychology. I suggest that an explicit statement needs to appeal to the different natures of the first person notion and perceptual and other notions that are not first personal. This explanation of why there is no such thing as attending originally to oneself appeals not to the nature of the objects of attention, but to the distinctions between the various ways in which things are given when one is perceiving and attending.

It may be helpful here to compare the first person in this respect with the nonconceptual present tense notion *now*. It displays some relevantly parallel phenomena. When it features in the content of any perception or other mental state, event, or process, *now* refers to the time of occurrence of that state, event, or process. (It does so non-descriptively, of course, just as the first person is non-descriptive.) Now a perception may also involve the representation of other events, as for instance when a television producer sees many screens simultaneously. Some of the events on the screens may be of past events, some may be of present events. But none of them is given, in the experience, as happening now (as opposed to the displayed images being given as occurring now, which of course they are). The time of occurrence of an event represented on one of the screens is given as "the time of this screened event", if we may allow demonstrative reference to events presented on TV. That is, in its nature, a different way of being given than as the time of the perception in which the TV screens are perceived. Correspondingly, at a higher, conceptual level, "that event (as presented on a particular TV screen) is happening now" is always potentially informative.

Because nothing given in perception is thereby given as the subject, and because this holds whatever perception may be in question, a temptation may exist to say that the subject is not in the world, or that the subject is merely the limit of the world. Neither proposition follows. The fact that the subject is not given in perception as being in the world does not imply that it is not in the world. The fact about the impossibility of perceiving something as the subject is a fact about the way in which something is given. This should not be confused with a fact about the entity so given.

Wittgenstein did succumb to the temptation when, in a much-discussed passage of the *Tractatus*, he wrote:

5.632 The subject does not belong to the world: rather, it is a limit of the world.

5.633 Where *in* the world is a metaphysical subject to be found?

You will say that this is exactly like the case of the eye and the visual field. But really you do *not* see the eye. (cf. Wittgenstein 1921)

Anything one perceives or senses would be in the world, mental or non-mental. This and the preceding section supply a reading of Wittgenstein's remarks as based on a genuine insight (also in Schopenhauer) about a distinctive way of representing themselves that is available to subjects. But really nothing follows from these insights about subjects not being in the world. This is one of many points at which the insights of the *Tractatus* would have been formulated very differently if Wittgenstein had made use of Frege's distinction between sense and reference, and had applied it at every level of representation, both conceptual and nonconceptual.

On the position I am developing here, subjects and conscious events are ontologically coeval. Specifying the nature of either one involves mention of the other. So mental events already involve subjects, and not just as a way of talking. The position I am advocating is not consistent with the view that the existence of a subject consists in the existence of various mental events and other entities. I am taking it that in that neo-Humean view, 'consists in' is supposed to be an asymmetrical relation. If 'consists in' is an asymmetrical relation, my position is incompatible with the neo-Humean thesis that the existence of a subject consists in the existence of mental events and other entities that allegedly do not involve subjects.

Derek Parfit formulates his famous view of these matters as the thesis that a subject is not a 'separately existing entity, distinct from a brain and a body, and a series of physical and mental events' (Parfit 1987, p. 223). Suppose '*A* exists separately from the *B*s' is understood to imply 'The existence of *A* is not settled by or determined by the existence of *B*s'. Then of course I would have to agree that in that sense a subject of experience is not an entity existing separately from mental events. But this agreement is not an agreement to a form of reductionism or constructionism about subjects. A subject does not 'separately exist' on this understanding of the phrase 'separate existence', because mental events, on the present view, already involve subjects. So the existence of the subject *is* in one sense settled by the existence of mental events and states.

It follows that the formulation in the quotation I gave from Parfit does not fully capture his intention, the intention to formulate a species of moderate reductionism about subjects of experience. The issue of reductionism should really be formulated in terms of individuation and the ontological priority, or otherwise, of mental events and states vis à vis the subjects that enjoy them. The issue at stake in the reductionism in which Parfit is interested is that of whether mental events and states are ontologically prior to the subjects who enjoy them.

Since the fundamental issues are metaphysical, it also follows that we should be careful not to formulate the issues in terms of what is describable without explicitly mentioning subjects. We can conceive of what Derek Parfit calls an 'impersonal' description of mental events, bodily events, and physical objects and events, and their properties and relations, a description that does not explicitly mention subjects (Parfit 1987, p. 225). This does not at all mean that there is no commitment in such a description to the existence of subjects. As a comparison: we cannot establish relationism about space simply by giving a description of everything we want to say in terms of spatial relations between material things and events. If a case in metaphysics can be made that spatial relations between material things themselves consist in relations between the places at which the things are located, then the availability of the place-free description fails to establish relationism about space. The same applies to the impersonal description. If the events and the properties of events mentioned in the description cannot be elucidated without mentioning subjects, then all we have in such a description is something that does not make explicit the full ontology to which it is committed.

That any such philosophical elucidation of mental events and their properties, in particular the property of being a conscious event, must involve subjects is precisely what I have been arguing. For someone who thinks that talk of subjects is a mere *façon de parler*, there must be some replacement for the characterization of a conscious state as one such that there is something it is like to be in it for the subject of that state. I have no idea what this replacement could be.

There is, not at all surprisingly, an analogous problem for a view of action that parallels Hume's view about conscious events. We can imagine a theorist who holds that there is no subject who is the agent of actions, 'existing separately' from the actions themselves and other events and entities. Actually we do not have to imagine such a theorist, for Nietzsche held precisely this view of agents. He wrote, "For just as the popular mind separates the lightning from the flash and takes the latter for an *action*, for the operation of a subject called lightning, so popular morality also separates strength from expression of strength, as if there were a neutral substratum behind the strong man, which was *free* to express strength or not to do so. But there is no such substratum; there is no 'being' behind doing, effecting, becoming; 'the doer' is merely a fiction added to the deed—the deed is everything" (Nietzsche 1887, p. 481). A few lines later he adds, "our entire science still lies under the misleading influence of language and has not disposed of that little changeling, the 'subject' (the atom, for example, is such a changeling, as is the Kantian 'thing-in-itself')".

The problem for this view is that what makes something an action is that some subject does it; just as what makes something a conscious mental event is that there's a subject for which there is something it's like to experience (or enjoy) the event.

I equally have no idea what Nietzsche's replacement account of what makes an event an action could possibly be.

I now turn to some wider issues in the ontology of subjects. To say that the ontology of subjects and the ontology of mental states and events are interdependent is not at all to imply that subjects are immaterial things. On the contrary, such interdependence may imply just the opposite. If various aspects of the mental states and events with which the ontology of subjects is interdependent themselves require certain relations to the nonmental world, that fact will have implications for the material status of subjects too. Just that seems to be the case. The mental states and events have multifarious constitutive connections with the material world. A sensation of pain must be experienced as in some part of some apparent body. What it is for it to be experienced as in some part of an apparent body cannot be elucidated independently of relation of the pain-event to such a body part, when the subject has a body with such a part. What it is for a visual experience to represent something as being a certain distance and direction from the subject cannot be elucidated independently of the causal powers of things at certain distances and directions from the subject, when the subject is properly connected to the world—and so forth, for myriad other examples.

If something is in states that are individuated in part by their relations to material objects, properties, and relations, it seems as a matter of general metaphysics that it must have some realization in material objects and events. This is true of domains at some distance from our present subject matter. It is true of a financial institution such as a bank, of which it is constitutive that it can stand in loan, credit, and debit relations. The transactions of a bank must be materially realized, even those of an internet bank. We have, apparently, no conception of how something could stand in these material relations without itself having a material realization. The same seems to me to be true of subjects of conscious states and events. So Cartesian immateriality not only need not be, but also should not be, any part of the conception of subjects for which I am arguing. For this reason, I also think that the conception of subjects for which I am arguing is consistent with Kripke's famous views on the essence of origin for persons and, by extension, subjects (cf. Kripke 1980).

The identity of a subject over time is something to be explained partly in material terms. That a subject has some material realization plausibly follows from these considerations about the material realization of states that are themselves individuated by their relations to material things and events. More specifically, I suggest that the identity of a subject over time consists in the identity of the apparatus that integrates states and events in such a way that a single subject has, or may have, perceptions, sensations, thoughts, action-awareness, and the rest, both at a time and over time. What matters is the identity of the integrating apparatus, not the identity of the particular pieces of apparatus whose states are integrated to yield states of the subject. Your perceptual apparatus may be entirely replaced consistently with your continued existence, provided that the states produced by the new apparatus are properly integrated by some continuing apparatus with your other conscious states and events.

Like any other material object, the matter constituting the integrating apparatus may also change over time. This partial account of identity of subjects over time provides a connection between what makes something a subject—its ability to enjoy a range of kinds of conscious states and events—and the role of the material integrating apparatus in which the identity of a given subject consists.

Some thinkers hold that a subject does not persist if all its memories and beliefs are destroyed. For these thinkers, continued existence of the integrating apparatus in which a subject's existence is partially realized does not amount to continued existence of the subject itself. I myself do not share this intuition about the case. But for those who do, all that matters for present purposes is that identity of integrating apparatus is a necessary condition for continued existence of a subject, even if it is not sufficient. Further conditions can be added to reach sufficiency if such conditions are thought to be needed.

The integrating apparatus provides the realization of the subject's file on itself, the file discussed in the preceding section on primitive self-representation. This is one of several connections between the theses on representation in that section and the metaphysics of subjects outlined here.

There is also a connection between the metaphysical interdependence of conscious events and subjects, on the one hand, and the correct description of the operation of the subject's file on itself. I emphasized that the file should not be regarded as collecting together predicates in the contents of events that are already conscious. If they were already conscious, it certainly seems that there could be conscious events that could exist both temporally and ontologically prior to there being a subject who enjoys them (since the subject file is the causal basis of the subject's being in a number of co-conscious states). On the present view, the correct conception of the subject file and the ontological interdependence of conscious states and events go hand-in-hand.

Kant famously, and as it seems to me correctly, objected to one conception of conscious subjects for the reason that it fails to distinguish between the existence of one continuing subject on the one hand, and a succession of distinct shorter-lived subjects which pass memories of their states on to their immediate successors, which in turn are ignorant of the change in identity (cf. Kant 1787, p. 423). Kant's point need not be construed as verificationist. It can be regarded as a constitutive challenge to conception of subjects in question. If the ontology of subjects is legitimate, what is the difference between being sensitive to genuine identity over time, as opposed to apparent identity realized in a succession of subjects? The question is analogous to nonverificationist objections to classical Newtonian absolute space (cf. Peacocke 1988).

I think the constitutive question is well posed against any position that makes genuine identity consist in seeming-identity. But the present account is not such a position. Genuine identity of subject consists in real identity of the material, integrating apparatus in which a subject is realized. There could in extreme, distant counterfactual cases be transmissions of memories through a succession of distinct underlying physical pieces of integrating apparatus. That really would involve an illusion of identity over time on the part of the subjects in the later parts of the series. So apparent identity by no means ensures genuine identity on the present view. It meets Kant's justified demand.

III

The agenda of this chapter is just a first step towards a fuller account of subjects of consciousness and first person representation. A fuller account must deal with a variety of richer and important notions of self-consciousness that go beyond mere first person representation, and it must account for the epistemological and psychological significance of those notions of self-consciousness.

That fuller account should also apply the conception I have developed here to the classical dispute between Descartes and Kant on rational psychology, and to more recent treatments of the first person and the self. It is striking that, in contrast to many other recent theories of subjects and the first person, a subject's body seemingly plays no fundamental role in the account I have offered of subjects and of first person representation. Yet we still have to give a constitutive account of the distinctive phenomenon of embodiment, and we have to explain its ramifications. This all has to be done whilst also respecting the important role the first person plays in the individuation of many notions and concepts. We need a general reorientation and restructuring of our thought about the self and self-representation.[10]

★★★

Appendix: Natures, Properties, Occurrences, and Subjects

I said in Section I that it is in the nature of the property of being a conscious occurrence that for anything with that property, there is some subject who enjoys (or suffers) that occurrence. We can formalize this claim, and make its commitments more explicit, by using the notation in Kit Fine's paper 'The Logic of Essence'. Fine there introduces the notation $\Box_F A$, which is to be read as: A is true in virtue of the nature of the objects which F. Let C be the property of being a conscious event or occurrence. Then the claim I am making about that property is that:

(i) $\Box_{\lambda P(P=C)} \forall x(Cx \rightarrow \exists y(y$ is the subject who enjoys (suffers) $x))$.

---

[10] Material overlapping with this chapter was presented in 2008 at Syracuse University, at a Special Lecture at Oxford University, and at the Conference 'Self and Self-Knowledge' at the Institute of Philosophy in London. Versions were also presented to my seminars at Columbia University and University College London, and at the Brown University conference on perception in 2009. I thank Andre Gallois, John Hawthorne, James Higginbotham, Patricia Kitcher, Rory Madden, Michael Martin, Lucy O'Brien, Ian Rumfitt, Paul Snowdon, and Ralph Walker for comments; and Ned Block and Jesse Prinz for their extended remarks on a presentation of this material at the NYU Language and Mind Seminar in Spring 2010. Some of this material was also covered in the first of my 'Context and Content' Lectures at the Institut Jean Nicod, Ecole Normale Supérieure in Paris in October 2010. The text has benefited from my discussions there with Jérôme Dokic, Pierre Jacob, Joëlle Proust, François Recanati, and Georges Rey. The penultimate draft was improved by comments from Antonia Peacocke.

For a range of individual (nonsocial) mental events, it may be in the nature of any such event e that it has its particular subject essentially. That further claim, using Fine's notation, is that for any such event e,

(ii) If s is the subject of e, then $\Box_{\lambda x(x=e)}$ (s is the subject of e).

The proposition with the converse relation embedded in the 'nature of' operator is false. It is not in the nature of s that e be one of its mental events. The conscious subject s could have existed and had a different mental life, one in which e does not exist at all. So,

(iii) If s is the subject of e, then $\sim\Box_{\lambda x(x=s)}$ (s is the subject of e).

References

Bayne, T. 2004 "Self-Consciousness and the Unity of Consciousness", *The Monist* 87/2, 219–236.
Brandom, R. 1994 *Making It Explicit: Reasoning, Representing, and Discursive Commitment*, Cambridge (Mass.), Harvard University Press.
Davidson, D. 1969 "The Individuation of Events", in N. Resche and D. Reidel (eds.) *Essays in honor of Carl G. Hempel*, Dordrecht, Reidel, 1969, 216–34; repr. in D. Davidson *Essays on Action and Events*, Oxford, Oxford University Press, 2001, 163–81.
Evans, G. 1982 *The Varieties of Reference*, Oxford, Oxford University Press.
Fine, K. 1995 "The Logic of Essence", *Journal of Philosophical Logic* 24, 241–73.
Frege, G. 1977 "Thoughts", in G. Frege (ed.) *Logical Investigations*, tr. P. Geach, R. Stoothof, Oxford, Blackwell, 1–30.
Grice, H. P. 1969 "Vacuous Names", in D. Davidson and J. Hintikka (eds.) *Words and Objections: Essays on the Philosophy of W. V. Quine*, Dordrecht, Reidel, 118–45.
Hume, D. 1739–40 [2000] *A Treatise of Human Nature*, D. F. Norton and M. J. Norton (eds.), Oxford, Oxford University Press.
Jeshion, R. 2002 "Acquaintanceless De Re Belief", in J. Campbell, M. O'Rourke, and D. Shier (eds.) *Meaning and Truth: Investigations in Philosophical Semantics*, New York, Seven Bridges Press, 53–78.
Kahneman, D., Treisman A., and Gibbs B. J. 1992 "The reviewing of object files: Object-specific integration of information", *Cognitive Psychology* 24, 175–219.
Kant, I. 1787 [1998] *Critique of Pure Reason*, tr. P. Guyer and A. Wood, Cambridge, Cambridge University Press.
Kripke, S. 1980 *Naming and Necessity*, Oxford, Basil Blackwell.
Lockwood, M. 1971 "Identity and Reference", in M. Munitz (ed.) *Identity and Individuation*, New York, NYU Press, 1971, 199–211.
McDowell, J. 1984 "*De Re* Senses", *The Philosophical Quarterly* 34, 283–94.
Mach, E. 1914 *The Analysis of Sensations*, tr. C. Williams and S. Waterlow, Chicago (Ill.), Open Court.
Moore, G. E. 1903 "The Refutation of Idealism", *Mind* 12/48, 433–53; repr. in T. Baldwin (ed.) 1993 *G. E. Moore: Selected Writings*, London, Routledge, 23–44.

Nagel, T. 1974 "What Is It Like to be a Bat?", *Philosophical Review* 83, 435–50.
Nietzsche, F. 1887 [2000] "The Genealogy of Morals", *Basic Writings of Nietzsche*, tr. W. Kaufmann, New York, Random House.
Parfit, D. 1987 *Reasons and Persons*, Oxford, Oxford University Press.
Peacocke, C. 1981 "Demonstrative Thought and Psychological Explanation", *Synthese* 49, 187–217.
—— 1988 "The Limits of Intelligibility: A Post-Verificationist Proposal", *Philosophical Review* 97, 463–96.
—— 1992 *A Study of Concepts*, Cambridge (Mass.), MIT Press.
—— 2008 *Truly Understood*, Oxford, Oxford University Press.
Prior, A. 2003 *Papers on Time and Tense* (New Edition) P. Hasle, P. Øhrstrøm, T. Braüner, and J. Copeland (eds.), Oxford, Oxford University Press.
Pylyshyn, Z. 2007 *Things and Places: How the Mind Connects with the World*, Cambridge (Mass.), MIT Press.
Ramachandran V. S. 2003 *The Emerging Mind: The Reith Lectures 2003*, London, Profile Books.
Sartre, J. P. 1936 [2003] *La Transcendance de l'Ego et autres textes phénoménologiques*, V. de Coorebyter (ed.), Paris, Librairie Philosophique J. Vrin.
—— 1948 "Conscience et connaissance de soi", repr. in de Coorebyter (ed.).
Shepard R. and Chipman S. 1970 "Second-Order Isomorphism of Internal Representations: Shapes of States", *Cognitive Psychology* 1, 1–17.
Strawson, P. 1974 *Subject and Predicate in Logic and Grammar*, London, Methuen.
Wittgenstein, L. 1921 [2001] *Tractatus Logico-Philosophicus*, tr. D. Pears and B. McGuinness, London, Routledge.

4

Does Perception Do Any Work in an Understanding of the First Person?

John Campbell

One argument for the role of perception in an understanding of the first person is that it is only through the use of perception that one can plot one's route through the world. And, the argument runs, this capacity to plot one's route through the world is constitutive of a grasp of the first person. This is a natural way of developing Lichtenberg's point that Descartes, in the absence of an appeal to veridical perception, could not think first-personally at all, but had the right only to 'there is thinking', rather than 'I think' (cf. Strawson 1966; Williams 1978).

In this chapter I want to consider an alternative line of argument. Knowledge of what it is for one of one's psychological states to be causing another depends on one's having an understanding of what happens when there is an external intervention on one's mental life. I will argue that it is our understanding of perception that provides us with our grasp of the prototypical interventions on one's mental life.

From a Cartesian perspective, it is natural to have the idea that even if one is, so to speak, alone with one's thoughts, and not relying on perception in any way, one can still identify which thoughts one is having and ask which of one's thoughts are grounded on which. Even from the purely solipsistic standpoint, one can still ask which of one's beliefs are grounding others of one's beliefs or desires, for example. And having asked the causal question, one can assess the situation and ask whether this is normatively correct. That is one aspect of the Cartesian project. My point in this chapter is that one cannot even raise the causal question, the question about the causal relations between one's thoughts, from a solipsistic standpoint. There has to be a background appeal to veridical perception, in which the world intervenes on one's beliefs, for these causal questions to be so much as formulated.

1. Knowing the causes and effects of one's own psychological states

We ordinarily take it that an understanding of the first person carries with it an ability to say what are the causes and effects of one's own beliefs and desires. Of course, we accept that there are limits on our insight into what causes what in our own minds. We accept that knowledge of one's own motivations is liable to self-deception and incompleteness. But still we take it for granted that in ordinary cases we do have some limited insight here. And it is hard to see how you could have the idea of yourself as a single person if you did not have the idea that your psychological states causally impact on one another. For instance, you might say, 'I opened the letter because I thought it was addressed to me', or 'I used the route past your house because I thought the lamp was on'. When we make such remarks we are not just saying, for example, that both:

(a) I opened the letter; and
(b) I thought the letter was addressed to me.

For both of those might be true and it might still be the case that I opened the letter simply because I thought there was money inside it. My belief about who it was addressed to might have been causally irrelevant.

If epiphenomenalism is true, of course, then our mental states characteristically do not have mental causes and they have no effects at all. Epiphenomenalism is a radical and subversive doctrine. Those who advocate it, however, do not always explain what all the consequences would be of accepting it. One consequence is that we would lose our ordinary grasp of the first person as a referring term. We could, of course, still have terms that referred to physical bodies. We could even have a token-reflexive term that referred to the physical body that produced it; or to the brain that was involved in its production. In our ordinary use of the first person, however, we take it that the term refers to the person whose underlying mental states—knowledge, memories, interests, and so on—were causally implicated in the production of this particular use of the first person. If it seems to you that the uses of the first person generated by your body have someone else's, rather than your own, underlying mental states causally implicated in their production, then it will seem to you that your body has been taken over by this other person, and that the uses of 'I' produced by your body are referring to that person rather than to you. (cf. Campbell 1999, 2004). Similarly, if the uses of 'I' generated by your body have not been caused by any ongoing mental life at all, then they will not refer to any person.

A grasp of the causal structure of the self seems to be needed if one is to have self-reference at all: it is only because we grasp the causal structure of the self that we can be said to think of the self as an object (Campbell 1995). Without any grasp of the grasp of the causal structure of the self, we could still express our possession of thoughts in the way that Lichtenberg suggested, by saying 'There is thinking', for example—a cry with which one greets one's thoughts. But in the absence of any grasp of the causal structure of one's mental states, it is hard to see how one could make out a claim to be using 'I' to refer to a person.

Of course, we do often get it wrong about what the causes and effects are of particular mental states that we have. This is so especially when we consider unreflective or immediate judgements about the causes and effect of a particular mental state. But the extent of our errors should not be exaggerated. Of a variety of current mental states that you have, you might choose the wrong one as specifying the cause of a particular belief or desire or action. But typically, you are not radically mistaken, in the following sense: you know what kind of causal architecture you are dealing with, even if you sometimes go off track in execution. You typically know what the candidate causes and effects are, even if you go wrong in which one you choose. In practice, where it matters, you are able to discuss what caused the formation of a particular belief or desire that you have: was it prejudice or malice or misinformation that led you to this, for example? And in many commonplace cases it can be quite obvious what caused a particular belief or desire or action. We do not come close to the kind of radical error that would undermine your grasp of the first person.

What does it mean to say that you grasp the causal connections between your own mental states? When I say, 'I opened the letter because I thought it was addressed to me', I am not saying either that in general, my opening a letter is correlated with my thinking that the letter is addressed to me. It might be that I am the only person in the house who still gets letters rather than emails and texts and so on. So when a letter falls though the mailbox I both open the letter and assume that the letter is addressed to me. But the fact is that I open every letter in the mailbox and whether I think it is addressed to me is causally irrelevant to whether I open it.

So when I say, 'I opened the letter because I thought it was addressed to me', what is the content of my causal claim? And how do I know that it is true? You might say that the causal role of the belief here can only be understood by reference to the causal role of an associated desire. For example, when I open the letter, it might be that there are two candidate desires:

(c) I wanted to open letters addressed to me; and
(d) I wanted to open every letter in the mailbox.

You might argue that the question what belief was causally operative depends on what desire was causally operative. If desire (c) was causally operative, that suggests that the belief that mattered was my belief that the letter was addressed to me. If desire (d) was casually operative, that suggests that the belief that mattered was my belief that the letter was in the mailbox. There are two problems with this, though. One is that it presupposes a certain rationality on the part of our subject; it is only the presumption of rationality that is allowing us to pair up the beliefs with the desires. The other is that we are simply pushing the problem back to the question what it means to say that one desire rather than another was causally operative.

If we keep our focus on the causal role of the belief, then we might say that what is at issue here is a counterfactual claim. When I say, 'I opened the letter because I thought it was addressed to me', the claim I am making is that had I thought the letter was not addressed to me, I would not have opened it. The basic problem for this simple appeal to counterfactuals is that the counterfactual may be 'backtracking'. Let me give a simple parallel. Suppose that, encountering a barometer for the first time, after many months of observation I say: 'I wonder whether the position of the barometer needle causes the storm.' You might say that for the position of the barometer needle to be causing the storm is for the counterfactual to hold: if the needle hadn't pointed to 'Stormy', there wouldn't have been a storm. The trouble is that this counterfactual might be true even though there isn't a causal connection. It might be that the following holds: if the barometer needle hadn't pointed to 'Stormy', that would have been because of a rise in atmospheric pressure, and in that case there wouldn't have been a storm. Had I not thought the letter was addressed to me, that would have been because it didn't come through the mailbox at all; and in that case I might well not have opened it.

We need a way of distinguishing between forward-tracking and backward-tracking counterfactuals. And here it is very natural to find a role for agency. Part of the appeal of an 'agentive' or action-based approach to causation is that it provides a way of drawing this distinction. The point about the barometer needle and the storm is that manipulating the needle is not a way of affecting whether or not there is a storm. Were I to manipulate the needle, that would make no difference to whether or not there is a storm. The 'forward-looking' counterfactuals are those that have to do with what would happen were I to act on the needle in various ways. This 'agentive' approach to causation has been vigorously advocated by, for example, Huw Price and Peter Menzies in a series of papers and books. In this essay I want to look at whether we can apply it to one's knowledge of the causal relations among one's own mental states. I will argue that we can't think of knowledge of the causal relations among one's own mental states in these agentive terms.

2. An agency-based approach to causation

I begin by restating the appeal of an agency-based approach to causation. Suppose you are put into a room full of gadgets and switches, wires and pulleys, levers and lightbulbs. Your task is to find out what causes what to happen in here. Does that lever cause the light to go on? Does the rotation of this cog ultimately cause that axle to move? And so on. How would you go about establishing what causes what? One possibility is that you could simply observe what happens in the room. You could see what is correlated with what. Is the position of this lever correlated with the light being on? Is the rotation of that cog correlated with the movement of the axle? However, there is a fundamental problem that you face if that is your method. You may not be able to distinguish between two cases:

(a) You observe a correlation between X and Y because X causes Y; and
(b) You observe a correlation between X and Y because there is a third factor, Z that is a common cause of both X and Y.

In drawing this distinction it is natural to appeal to agency. So for example, suppose the rotation of the cog is correlated with the turning of the axle. That might be because the movement of the cog causes the movement of the axle. Or it might be because there is some third gear that turns both of them. How are you to make the distinction between these two cases? Here is how to make the distinction. Seize hold of the cog, suspending it from the influence of its usual causes, but keeping everything else the same. Now turn the cog yourself. If the turning of the cog causes the turning of the axle, then the axle will turn too. Suppose, on the other hand, that there is some third gear that drives both the cog and the axle. In that case you can turn the cog as much as you like and it will make no difference to the turning of the axle. So an appeal to agency seems to explain how to make the distinction between a causal connection and a mere correlation between two phenomena. Why do we say that the position of the barometer needle is merely correlated with the presence of an upcoming storm, rather than being the cause of the upcoming storm? Because were you to seize the barometer needle and turn it yourself, that would make no difference to whether the storm happens.

The question I am raising in this chapter is whether this gives a persuasive model of one's relation to one's own mind. Here you are, in introspection, confronted with the gadgets and switches, wires and pulleys, levers and light-bulbs, of your own mental apparatus. Can we think in similarly experimental terms of your perspective on the causal relations between your own mental states?

I will address that question in the next section. First, let me fill out a little what the agency-based model is saying. The point is that one way to tell whether X is a cause of Y is to manipulate X and see what happens to Y. But the point can be pressed further than that, in two ways. First, you might point out that similarly, someone who has formed a judgement that X causes Y, and then wants to change Y, has the potential to do so by manipulating X. Secondly, you might say that your understanding of what it is for X to be causally connected to Y depends on your practical grasp of this link to the potentialities of your own agency.

When I say a 'practical' grasp, the point here is that an understanding of what causation is might be thought to reside in a procedural, or tacit, or implicit understanding of the potentialities for manipulation provided by a causal relation, and the role of manipulation in verifying the existence of a causal connection. So we might say that the canonical way of verifying that X causes Y is specified by a procedural rule, namely:

<u>Manipulations of X are correlated with changes in Y</u>
Form the judgement: X causes Y

And the canonical conclusion one can draw from the existence of a causal connection between X and Y is this:

Judgment: X causes Y.

Manipulations of X are correlated with changes in Y.

One's grasp of these connections between causation and manipulation need not consist in an ability to make the connections explicit. Rather, from the fact that in practice your manipulations of X are correlated with changes in Y, you move straight to the judgement, 'X causes Y'. You do not go via some explicit judgement to the effect that manipulations of X are correlated with changes in Y. Rather, you are in practice manipulating X and concomitantly observing changes in Y, and you move straight to the judgement that X causes Y. Similarly, if you have made the judgement that X causes Y, the canonical implication of that judgement is not some further explicit reflection to the effect that manipulations of X are correlated with changes in Y. Rather, you simply move from the judgement that X causes Y to having the potential to in practice manipulate X to change Y. This is a matter of your potential for action, not reflective judgement. This proposal is mapping both normative and causal relations between:

(a) grasp of the concept of cause, as exercised in the judgement, 'X causes Y'; and
(b) states involving manipulation of aspects of your environment, and these are states that do not involve an explicit grasp of the concept of cause.

The normative aspect of these claims is that transitions from facts about correlations under manipulations to judgements of causation are normatively correct, and that transitions from judgements about causation to attempts to manipulate one property by manipulating another are also normatively correct. The causal aspect of the proposals is that someone who grasps the concept of cause will characteristically be caused to form causal judgements by these facts about manipulations, and that someone who grasps the concept of cause will typically be caused to have the potential to engage in manipulations by forming causal judgements. Finally, the proposal says that describing these causal and normative transitions says all that there is to say about an understanding of the concept of cause. These transitions exhaust the concept of cause.

This last claim is maybe a bit overstated, even by the lights of someone who thinks this proposal is correct in spirit. I am here characterizing only the most generic concept of cause, and ignoring many important and often subtle distinctions that we often make, between, for example, causes and standing conditions, or between component causes and net causes, and so on. However, so far as I can see, these distinctions could generally be given some analysis within the kind of framework I am describing, and the problems I want to discuss are problems for the whole approach, rather than difficulties about implementing it fully. So I will not go into these subtler classifications, beyond warning you here that I might be wrong about this, and that it's possible that what I am here regarding as mere complications may actually be central for the problems I want to discuss.

To sum up, there are two ways in which a capacity for action might be related to your ability to make judgements about causation. First, your capacity to make judgements about causation might be thought to depend on your capacity to manipulate aspects of the world around you so as to verify judgements about cause. And your ability to draw implications from judgements about causation might centrally feature your actions, manipulating causes to as to make changes in the phenomena they cause. Secondly, those links between causal judgements and agency might be thought to constitute your understanding of the notion of cause. When we are asking whether a child has the concept of causation, we naturally look for an understanding that consists in an ability to think and reason in accordance with these transition rules. The child who has understood the contrast between causation and correlation is a child who has grasped the significance of causation for action.

3. An agentive approach to knowledge of causal relations among one's own psychological states?

3.1 The interventionist analysis of the importance of agency

Why does an appeal to agency serve so effectively to distinguish between causal connections and mere correlations? One analysis is that actions often have the structure of what Pearl (2000) calls 'surgical' interventions. The idea here is that an intervention on X with respect to Y suspends X from the influence of all other variables; the intervention is 'surgical' in that causal arrows into X from any other variables are cut. Then, having seized control of the value of X, we can vary it to see what happens to the value of Y. If the values of X and Y are correlated under interventions, that is what it is for X to be a cause of Y.

On the interventionist analysis, talk about causation comes into play only when we have a distinction between variables characterizing the system we are studying, and other, 'exogenous' variables. Suppose for example we have a collection of wires and pulleys and so on. Suppose X and Y are variable endogenous to our system—say, X is the position of a lever and Y is whether the light bulb is on or off. Then an intervention on X with respect to Y will be something that comes from outside the system and seizes control of X. For X to be a cause of Y is for X and Y to be correlated under such interventions on X. So for example, if the position of the lever is correlated with whether the light bulb is on, under interventions on the position of the lever, that is what it is for the lever to be a cause of the light bulb's being on (cf. Woodward and Hitchcock 2003).

You can see the appeal of the idea that your own actions are the prototypical interventions. You yourself are not typically an element in the system you are studying; your own actions are exogenous variables. But very often you do have the power to reach in and seize control of the value of some variable in the system, as when you grasp the lever and take control of its position.

The importance of the interventions being 'surgical' is that, since the intervention has taken complete control of the value of X, a correlation between X and Y under interventions on X cannot reflect the operation of some common cause of X and Y. In the case of the barometer and the storm, when you reach in and move the needle, atmospheric pressure no longer affects where the needle is. So any correlations now observed between the position of the needle and subsequent storms could only reflect a causal connection between the position of the needle and the storm, not the operation of a background common cause.

3.2 Silencing vs. surgical interventions

It is important to distinguish between what I will call 'silencing' interventions, and 'surgical' interventions in Pearl's sense. Consider again the case of the barometer and the storm. What determines whether the position of the needle causes the storm is what happens when there is an intervention on the position of the needle. The point of demanding 'intervention' is that action on the needle has to suspend the influence of any other cause on its position. And the point of the suspension is that if some other cause, such as atmospheric pressure, is left as operative, then we may find a correlation between the position of the needle and the storm that is explained by this factor being a common cause of the position of the needle and the storm.

At first sight, there are two different ways in which you might achieve 'suspension of the influence of any other cause' on the position of the needle. One is to rip out the mechanism in the barometer that connects the position of the needle to atmospheric pressure. Then, on reasonable assumptions, we have ensured that the only factor affecting the position of the needle is the way we push it. The need for a step like this is easy to miss because in practice the impact of a hand on the barometer needle is so much greater than the impact of atmospheric pressure. To make the point more vivid, you might suppose that you have very weak hands, so that the needle is turned only with great effort and where it goes is always jointly caused by your hand and by the atmospheric pressure. In fact, some positions of the needle may be attainable only with the help of atmospheric pressure, rather than with the action of your hand alone. Then the point of ripping out the mechanism connecting the needle to the atmospheric pressure would be to make it that your hand is the only factor affecting the position of the needle, so a common cause for the position of the needle and whether there is a storm has been ruled out. This is what I mean by a 'silencing' intervention. For each barometer we are considering, we shut off every mechanism, other than the intervention itself, that might affect the value of our candidate cause variable.

The other approach, which at first sight looks different to silencing in this sense, is commonly used in randomized controlled trials. Suppose we are trying to determine whether the level of some drug in the blood causes recovery from epilepsy. There may actually be many factors, other than direct administration of the drug by the experimenter, that determine how much of the drug is in an individual's blood. If we were trying to achieve a silencing intervention, then for each subject in the trial we would have to shut off all the mechanisms, other than the direct action of the experimenter, that affect the level of that drug in the subject's blood. There typically will be no way of doing this in practice. The point of the randomization is to rule out the operation of common causes in a different way. If the design of the experiment is successful, then each of the cohorts assigned a particular level of drug administered will contain a population across which there is wide variation in the other factors that could possibly contribute, positively or negatively, to the level of drug in the blood. So when we look at the average outcomes in each cohort, the only factor that is systematically affecting the level of drug in the blood will be the administration of the drug by the experimenter. This will be a 'surgical' intervention on the level of drug in the blood, in that the only factor systematically affecting the level is the intervention by the experimenter. For the case of the barometers, a parallel approach would be to leave intact mechanisms connecting position of the needle to atmospheric pressure, where they exist in the barometer, but to look at whether storminess is correlated with position of the needle across a wide population of barometers, in some of which there is a mechanism by which atmospheric pressure affects position of the needle in one way, in others of which there is a mechanism by which atmospheric pressure affects position of the needle in another way, and in fact many different sorts of case here, including cases in which atmospheric pressure has no impact on position of the needle. If we do achieve a randomized sample here, then the impact of the hand on where the needle goes will be the only systematic factor affecting the position of the needle. So if we do now find a correlation between storminess and the position of the needle, across our randomized cohorts, that can only reflect a causal connection between the two.

I said that at first sight there is a difference between silencing and surgical interventions. You might reasonably point out that silencing interventions are merely one type of surgical intervention. Still, I want to propose that the distinction between interventions that are silencing, and those that are, as it were, merely surgical, has a lot of interest in the case of mental causation. To anticipate, I will suggest that the special impact of perceptual experience on belief has to be explained in terms of the notion that perceptual experience is typically a silencing intervention on belief. Now the reason why it is natural to think of the actions of an agent as constituting interventions is that the agent is typically external to the system acted on, and the agent can be in a position to seize control of one variable while suspending the influence of other variables on it. But this picture of agency does not apply to one's relation to one's own mental states.

3.3 Interventions on the psychological lives of other people

Our target is knowledge of the causal relations among one's own mental states. But some of the issues here are easier to see if we start by looking at one's knowledge of the causal relations among someone else's mental states. Suppose we ask how the agency-based approach applies to your understanding of what is caused by someone else's particular belief. Suppose we take, for instance, the question whether Sally's belief that there is mud in the water caused her to throw it away. Maybe she also believed that the water was no longer needed. Which was the cause of her action? On the interventionist analysis, the question has to do with what would happen under interventions on Sally's belief that there is mud in the water. That belief has to be moved as one would a lever, so that we can find the upshot. If whether she throws the water away is correlated with whether she believes that there is mud in the water, under interventions on that belief, that is what it is for there to be a causal connection between the belief and the action.

Yet what would it be for you to seize control of Sally's belief that there is mud in the water? We can take it that there is in place a distinction between the variables endogenous to the system we are studying—Sally's psychology—and the exogenous variables, such as your actions on Sally. And the intervention must come from outside, and seize control of whether Sally has the belief. As I said the intervention has to be surgical, because we have to rule out the possibility that there is a background common cause of Sally's belief and her action that explains a co-variation between them. Whether Sally has the belief must be suspended from the influence of its usual causes, such as her background reasoning from other beliefs she has.

This would obviously be an unusual situation. It does not happen very often that one person is able to reach into another's mind and take control of their belief. Moreover, when we act on a belief, we typically keep the belief under review while executing the action. Suppose I think the big box will be relatively easy to lift, and on that basis try to pick it up. If I have difficulty executing the action, I may revise my belief. However, if someone else has reached in and seized control of the belief, I will be unable to do that. In that sense at least, my acting on the belief will no longer be an exercise of rationality on my part. In fact the belief has so far parted company from my reasons for it that we would naturally say that it is not 'my' belief at all, but something implanted in me by the intervener.

It is difficult to take seriously the idea that our interest in whether one belief rather than another is causing a particular outcome is an interest in what would happen in this unusual scenario. When we are concerned with psychological causation one topic that is of importance is causal connections among propositional attitudes that reflect the rationality of the subject. But, on the face of it, on this third-person agentive approach to mental causation, we seem to lose sight of anything but scenarios in which the rationality of the subject has been short-circuited.

You might point out that these points apply only on the supposition that interventions on the mental life of another person are to be silencing interventions. If we think of intervention on another's mental life as silencing, then the above comments are entirely correct. If, however, we ask only that interventions on the mental life should be surgical, then we can leave in place all the usual causes of each individual's belief formation. We can still consider what happens under a particular type of intervention from our experimenter, across a population that varies widely with respect to the factors that are the usual causes of belief. If, across this population, we still find a systematic relationship between an intervention on (say) the belief that there is mud in the water and throwing away the water, then that will reflect a causal connection between the belief and the action. The interventions in question here will, though, be surgical rather than silencing.

The problem reappears, though, when we are considering a population consisting of Sally alone—a population of one. In this special case, there is no possibility of 'randomization across the population', and there is no difference between silencing and surgical interventions, at any one time. If we are considering a population of only one, then it is difficult to see how the agentive version of an interventionist approach to mental causation can be correct; we are being forced to consider only what happens under silencing interventions by one agent on another's beliefs, and as we saw earlier, what happens under such an alien scenario seems to have little to do with our ordinary concerns in thinking about mental causation. (To pursue the issues here we have to look further at the relation between type-causation and token-causation in the mentalistic case, for which see Campbell 2010.)

You might point out that there is a way in which one can engineer a silencing intervention on someone else's beliefs: namely, by arranging the scene so as to make it so that p, so that when the other person looks at it, she will see that p. I will suggest below that this would indeed be a true silencing intervention on belief. But notice that the fact that an agent was involved in setting the scene, so to speak, had nothing to do with whether the intervention was silencing. What has happened is rather than the world itself, through perception, has exerted a silencing intervention on belief. That would have happened whether or not the agent had acted to affect the scene. Whichever way the scene was, it would have exerted a silencing intervention on belief, through the subject's perceptual experience. But the whole point of the agentive approach to causation was to suggest that it is special features of agency that explain the characteristic marks of intervention.

3.4 Interventions on one's own psychological life

You might conclude from this that if we are interested in an agentive approach to mental causation, we should think in terms of what happens under one's own interventions on one's own psychological life. (Another response would be to consider what happens under non-surgical interventions; I pursue this in Campbell (2007) but will not go down that path here.)

What does it come to, that you grasp the causal role of your own belief? In particular, what does it come to that you grasp the possibility that one of your beliefs may cause you to have further beliefs, to act in particular ways, and so on? On the interventionist account, what it comes to is this: you grasp that interventions on your belief would be correlated with changes in your further beliefs, and with changes in your actions. An exogenous cause tweaking your belief would be correlated with changes in your further beliefs and your actions.

The agentive version of interventionism takes your own actions to be the paradigmatic exogenous manipulations. So on this approach, the way to understand the significance of a proposition, 'the belief that this letter is addressed to me causes me to open it', is something like this:

My own manipulation of my belief, 'this letter is addressed to me' is correlated with changes in whether I open it.

For that to work you would have to be capable of manipulation of your own beliefs. You have to reach into the system of mental wires and pulleys and levers. You would have to be able to manipulate your own belief to see what happened next. But that is not possible. You can't decide what to believe. There is, as Bernard Williams once pointed out (Williams 1973a), arguably an in principle impossibility about this. Belief intrinsically aims at the truth. For that reason, beliefs can't simply be manipulated at the will of the agent. Any state that could simply be manipulated at the will of the agent would, for that reason, not be a belief. But this means that we can't explain an understanding of the causal significance of one's own beliefs in terms of agentive version of interventionism.

Of course, there is some discussion about the possibility of deliberation as to what to believe (cf. Shah and Velleman 2005). Whatever we say about the extent of deliberation as to what to believe, this deliberation cannot amount to an intervention on one's own belief. An intervention on one's own belief would have to suspend the usual causes of the belief from affecting it; but of course what one does in deliberation is to weigh the usual reasons for belief, not to somehow set them aside.

You can manipulate the distal causes of your belief (the world itself about which you have beliefs), but that isn't the same thing as you intervening on the belief itself. Manipulating the outside world itself might well result in changes in your beliefs. If you change whether there's mud in the water, that will typically change your beliefs on that point. But what the interventionist analysis of causation requires us to consider is a manipulation that directly affects the target variable itself. Manipulating an aspect of the world itself leaves open the possibility that the aspect of the world you are manipulating might be a common cause of both the belief itself and the outcome variable. We need to know what in principle would happen to the outcome variable under manipulations of the target variable itself. The role of the agent in manipulating the outside world rather than the target variable, belief, directly, is not relevant to the question of what constitutes a causal connection between the target variable (belief) and the outcome variable (further beliefs or action). So again, the agentive version of interventionism does not explain what grasp of the concept of cause comes to in this case.

The agent himself/herself can't manipulate the target variable, in this case. That is not to say that there can't in principle be interventions on the belief variable. And it's not to say that the agent can't have the conception of what would happen under interventions on the belief variable. It's just that these interventions won't, typically at any rate, be exercises of the believer's own agency. The believer has to have a more abstract or objective conception of 'intervention', so as to be able to form the conception of the world intervening on his own beliefs. We have to conclude that one's understanding of the causal relations among one's own mental states can't be explained in agentive terms. Rather, one has a more 'objective' or 'impersonal' conception of intervention that is merely exemplified by one's own actions, rather than being constituted by one's capacity for action. And this objective conception of intervention that is merely exemplified by one's own actions, is also exemplified by the way in which, in perception, the world intervenes on one's beliefs.

4. Perception as the world intervening on belief

To understand causal relations among one's own mental states, one has to grasp the possibility of interventions on them. But the prototypical interventions here are not provided by one's own actions on one's mental states. Rather, there seems to be something fundamental about the role of perception as making possible exogenous impacts in which the world intervenes on one's belief, without there being any involvement of agency.

Suppose you are sitting in a chemistry class. You are watching an experiment and you are going to write down a report. You have it on the authority of textbook and teacher that the liquid in the test-tube will turn yellow. You believe that the contents of the test-tube will turn yellow. When you write down your report, what is the cause of your action, reporting the liquid to be one color rather than another? Are you a mere mouthpiece of the official view, writing down whatever color text and teacher specified? Or did you write down the color you did because that was the color you believed the liquid to be? So long as the values of all three variables are correlated there is no way of applying the distinction.

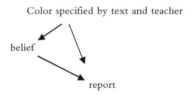

You might claim to have some insight into your own motivation here. You might protest that you are not a mouthpiece. What you write down causally depends on what you believe. Text and teacher enter into the proceedings only because you believe them. You are not merely writing down whatever they say, whether you believe it or not. Well, what is the difference between these two hypotheses? The difference shows up when there is an intervention on belief. Some external factor has to take control of your belief, suspending it from the influence of these other factors. In this situation, we can look at whether your belief and action are correlated. The holding of the causal relation consists of them being correlated under such an intervention.

In perception, ordinarily, the world itself intervenes on your belief, suspending it from the influence of those prior expectations. The critical point comes when the test-tube itself is displayed and you see that it is, for example, bright blue. What then do you write down? Does your action vary with the belief? Or does it vary rather only with the specification of color by text and teacher? If, under the intervention on belief provided by the world in the case of perception, your report is correlated with what you believe, then the belief is causing the report.

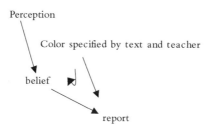

I am suggesting that our ordinary understanding of the causal relations between our own mental states depends on grasp of this role for perception as providing for interventions on belief. Our grasp of the role of perception shows up in what we would ordinarily say, in the situation I have envisaged, about a classroom full of people who wrote down 'yellow' in the situation I have described. We would say that they are not writing this down because they believe the contents of the test-tube are yellow. We would say: they are writing this down because that is what the officials say they should write down. If I recall that I myself wrote down 'yellow', I would have to acknowledge that this was not because of my belief about the contents of the test-tube. (For discussion of the implications of the status of perception as an intervention for belief updating in a Bayesian framework, see Glymour and Danks 2007.)

It is not just that perceptual experience provides us with surgical interventions on our beliefs; arguably, perceptual experience provides us with interventions on our beliefs that are, in the terms I explained earlier, 'silencing'. To take an old example of Austin's, suppose that I am wondering whether there is a pig in the clearing. There are various considerations I might marshal for and against: whether there is a pig farm nearby, whether one is likely to have escaped, and so on. So I might form a provisional, probabilistic belief on that basis. Suppose now that I come across the pig. I see it in plain sight. I walk all around it. I prod it with a stick. It grunts as I do so. Here it is not that the perceptual experience merely provides us with one reason to be weighed in the scales along with other reasons for and against the belief that there is a pig here. The perceptual experience reaches right in and silences all other considerations, taking charge of the formation of the belief.

I take the term 'silencing' from a discussion by John McDowell of the decisive role that moral considerations play in the mental life of the virtuous agent. McDowell cast his point in normative terms; but it has a clear causal reading too. According to McDowell, when a virtuous agent grasps a conclusive reason for acting, even in the face of danger, what happens is not that one motivation is balanced against another. Rather:

> some aspect of the situation is seen as constituting a reason for acting in some way; this reason is apprehended, not as outweighing or overriding any reasons for acting in other ways, which would otherwise be constituted by other aspects of the situation (the present danger, say), but as silencing them. (McDowell 1979, pp. 55–6)

In our terms, the causal reading of this idea is that in the virtuous individual, the decisive reason shuts off the causal connection between other possible motives the individual might have and action. Whatever the merits of McDowell's picture of the virtuous agent, I am proposing that this kind of picture does apply to the role of perceptual experience in cognition. In fact, it seems to me arguable that this silencing role for perceptual experience is foundational for our distinction between probable opinion about our surroundings, and knowledge of our surroundings. This account contrasts with a Quinean picture on which the sensory irritations at the periphery are merely one input among many to the formation of beliefs in the great web, and the interventions from the periphery are never silencing (Quine 1952). On Quine's picture of the formation of beliefs in response jointly to impingements from the periphery and centripetal forces in the web of belief, it really is puzzling why we should have any distinction between perceptual knowledge and merely probably opinion. What makes Quine's view seem compulsory is that we do, in some unusual cases, faced with extraordinary evidence, say: 'Well, maybe there wasn't a pig there after all'. You can in special cases, where you have a case to make, appeal the decisions of the tribunal of experience. Nonetheless, in the absence of grounds for appeal, the judgement of the tribunal is decisive, and silences other considerations. This point seems to me central to an understanding of our concept of perceptual knowledge, and, I am suggesting, it is also central to our understanding of mental causation. It typifies a non-agentive intervention on one's psychological states that is at the core of our understanding of how mental states causally affect one another.

5. Two ways perception does work in self-consciousness

I began by remarking that one basic aspect of self-consciousness is one's knowledge of the causal relations among one's propositional states, one's beliefs and desires and so on. To be self-aware is, in part, to be able to explain why one has various particular beliefs and desires. I am suggesting that this is a matter of knowing what the upshot would be of one or another intervention on one's propositional states. And I am suggesting that the fundamental intervention on one's propositional states is provided by ordinary perception. In perception, the world intervenes on one's beliefs. Knowledge of the causal relations among one's propositional states is ultimately based on knowledge of what would happen under various perceptual interventions on one's beliefs.

This kind of knowledge is not available so long as one confines oneself to a solipsistic awareness of one's thoughts, as Descartes' project required him to. If my line of argument has been correct, Descartes was not in a position to reflect on the bases and consequences of his propositional states. He could not locate his beliefs and desires in a pattern of causes and effects. Arguably, he would therefore lose his claim to have any fix on which particular thoughts he was thinking, for thoughts are identified by their places in such a pattern of causes and effects. He could no longer engage in sustained discussion of whether the basis of any particular belief or desire was good, for he has lost his grasp of the very idea of the basis on which he holds any particular belief or desire. Lichtenberg's objection was that without an appeal to perceptual experience, Descartes could say only, 'There is thinking'. The idea is that perceptual experience plays some critical role in identifying the 'I'. My present point is that perceptual experience also plays a critical role in defining what mental causation is, and that without it, one loses one's grasp of the pattern of causes and effects within which one could so much as identify a particular thought, and say, 'there is thinking that p'.

You might argue that perceptual experience can be present whether or not it is veridical, and that even if it is not veridical, perceptual experience may still be playing a role as an intervention on one's beliefs. This way of thinking of perceptual experience runs into trouble, however, when we consider the normative status of the silencing role of perceptual experience in producing knowledge. Why should perceptual experience have that silencing role? Why isn't it just one source of evidence among many, to be put in the scales with other considerations of prior plausibility? If you think of perceptual experience as a state that can be present whether it is veridical or not, then you have no reason to suppose that it should be silencing. You have no reason to think that it can ground a distinction between perceptual knowledge and merely probable opinion. To understand why it is normatively correct for perceptual experience to have its silencing role, we have to think of it not as a state that can be there whether or not the external scene is there. We have to think of perceptual experience as a relation that one stands in to the external scene, whereby the external scene itself can exert a silencing intervention on one's cognition of the scene.

I began by saying that one way in which perception has been thought to do work in grasp of the first person is this: perception provides you with your knowledge of your route through the world, and that is what provides you with your knowledge of which person you are. I have said there is another way in which perception contributes to self-knowledge. In perception, the world intervenes on your beliefs. Your knowledge of what happens when the world intervenes on your beliefs is one aspect of your knowledge of the causal relations among your psychological states.

You can see how these two roles for perception come apart if you consider a subject who has quite an unusual take on his own perceptions. There is an analogy between the way in which this subject regards her own perceptions and the way in which we usually regard the scenes shown in a film. When you watch a film, it can happen that what you are seeing is the world from the viewpoint of one of the characters in the film. But that is not ordinarily what happens. As Bernard Williams once pointed out, it would wreck the point of many film scenes if you find yourself constantly asking, 'Who is it that is tiptoeing around these lovers / watching this shipwrecked mariner / listening to this soliloquy' and so on. Typically, when you are watching a film you are not raising or answering the question, 'From whose viewpoint are these scenes being shown?'. In particular, we can say that when you are watching a film you typically do not take it that you are yourself spatially related to the scenes being shown. Indeed, you may not know about your temporal relation to the scenes being shown. This point does not apply only to fictional films. It also applies to documentaries. You can watch a documentary and be quite sure that you are building up an accurate picture of the events shown, without asking or answering any question about your own spatial or temporal relations to those events.

Consider a subject who regards her own perceptions in something like this way. That is, the subject is untouched by Cartesian scepticism, and assumes she is building up an accurate picture of the events she perceives. But it does not occur to her to ask or answer the question: 'And where am I in relation to all this?'. This subject is not using perception to build up a picture of the path she is taking through the world. But she may nonetheless have the conception that in perception, the world intervenes on her beliefs, and that may be a basic element in her understanding of the causal relations among her own psychological states. This role for perception contrasts with the idea that the role of perception, in an understanding of the first person, is to allow one to identify the substantial self. For all that I have said, one could understand the first person perfectly well, and use it to express self-conscious thought about one's propositional states, even though one has not yet achieved an identification of the substantial self. Our 'film' subject may be just such a person. At the end of the day, there must of course be such a thing as identification of the referent of one's uses of 'I', and I am not suggesting that this is anything other than the identification of a perceptible person. But the pattern of use that we make of the first person, in expressing and reflecting upon the bases of our own propositional states, may be prior to identification of the reference of the term.

Acknowledgement

An earlier version of this chapter was presented to the conference on 'The Self and Self-Knowledge' conference in London in 2007, and I am indebted to participants for their comments. Thanks also to two anonymous referees for excellent sets of comments, and to Annalisa Coliva for much support.

References

Campbell, J. 1995 "Self-Consciousness and the Body Image", in N. Eilan, A. J. Marcel, and J. Bermudez (eds.), *The Body and the Self*, Cambridge (Mass.), MIT Press, 29–42.

——1999 "Schizophrenia, the Space of Reasons and Thinking as a Motor Process", *The Monist* 82, 609–25.
——2004 "The First Person, Embodiment, and the Certainty that One Exists", *The Monist* 87, 475–88.
——2007 "An Interventionist Approach to Causation in Psychology", in A. Gopnik and L. Schulz (eds.) *Causal Learning: Psychology, Philosophy and Computation*, Oxford, Oxford University Press, 58–66.
——2010 "Independence of Variables in Mental Causation", in E. Sosa and E. Villanueva (eds.) *Philosophy of Mind: Philosophical Issues* 20, 64–79.
Descartes, R. 1641 *Meditations on First Philosophy*, tr. J. Cottingham, Cambridge, Cambridge University Press, 1996.
Glymour, C. and Danks, D. 2007 "Reasons as Causes in Bayesian Epistemology", *Journal of Philosophy* 104, 464–74.
McDowell, J. 1979 "Virtue and Reason", *The Monist* 62/3, 331–50; repr. in J. McDowell, *Mind, Value and Reality*, Cambridge (Mass.), Harvard University Press, 1998, 50–73.
Pearl, J. 2000 *Causation*, Cambridge, Cambridge University Press.
Price, H. 1992 "Agency and Causal Asymmetry", *Mind* 101, 501–20.
——and Menzies, P. 1993 "Causation as a Secondary Quality", *British Journal for the Philosophy of Science* 44, 187–203.
Quine, W. V. O. 1952 [1953] "Two Dogmas of Empiricism", in W.V.O. Quine, *From a Logical Point of View*, Cambridge (Mass.), Harvard University Press, 20–46.
Shah, N. and Velleman, J. D. 2005 "Doxastic Deliberation", *Philosophical Review* 114, 497–534.
Strawson, P. F. 1966 *The Bounds of Sense*, London, Methuen.
Williams, B. 1973a "Deciding to Believe", in B. Williams (ed.) *Problems of the Self*, Cambridge, Cambridge University Press, 136–51.
——1973b "Imagination and the Self", in B. Williams (ed.) *Problems of the Self*, Cambridge, Cambridge University Press, 26–45.
——1978 *Descartes: The Project of Pure Enquiry*, Harmondsworth, Penguin.
Woodward, J. 2003 *Making Things Happen: A Theory of Causal Explanation*, Oxford, Oxford University Press.
——and Hitchcock, C. 2003 "Explanatory Generalizations, Part 1: Counterfactual Account", *Noûs* 37, 1–24.

PART TWO

Consciousness, Action Awareness, and Their Role in Self-Knowledge

5
Consciousness and Self-Awareness

Jane Heal

1. Introduction

A person may sometimes have explicit, verbalizable beliefs about his or her own psychological life. For example I may believe and report that I have a headache, or I may believe and report that I have just noticed that the first primroses are out. How might the explicit self-awareness manifested in such reports be related to phenomenal consciousness? Can such explicit views about oneself be grounded in and justified by the fact that the states or events they are about are phenomenally conscious? And if so how? This chapter argues that one pleasingly simple account of the situation is not acceptable and begins a discussion of what other, more nuanced, views might be possible.[1]

I shall not consider the question of whether, and if so why, our views about ourselves should be thought of as knowledge. The focus of the paper is on possible ways of arriving at views, rather than on what sort of provenance a view needs to have to count as knowledge.

A psychological state is 'phenomenally conscious' if (in the familiar phrase) 'there is something it is like for its subject to be in it'.[2] Some accounts of this notion say that what it is for a state to be phenomenally conscious is for the subject of it to have a belief that she is in it, or for her to be disposed to acquire such a belief with great ease. Such 'higher order thought' views about phenomenal consciousness build in a link between phenomenal consciousness and explicit belief in a direct way which makes the answer

---

[1] In developing the views set out in this chapter I have benefited greatly from discussion with Annalisa Coliva and other participants in workshops organized by her, many of whom are contributors to this volume.
[2] Philosophers of mind tend to talk of 'psychological states', often ignoring other possible items such as psychological events, relations, processes, actions, activities etc. Use of the phrase 'psychological state' has risks, in that it may, without our being aware of it, make a monadic view of the nature and capacities of subjects of experience seem more inevitable than it is. So for some purposes, use of the idiom, and neglect of other logical categories of the psychological, could be distorting. But for the time being, we shall continue to talk in the familiar way.

to our question about the relation between self-awareness and phenomenal consciousness trivial and obvious.

In this chapter, however, we shall start from a conception of phenomenal consciousness which is not committed to a view of this kind. We shall take it that what is required for phenomenal consciousness is only that the 'something it is like' idea gets a grip. And (as against the higher order thought theories) it is plausible to suppose that animals and very young children, who do not have the cognitive and conceptual resources to make higher order judgements about themselves, are often in the kinds of states which are paradigms of the phenomenally conscious—they feel pain and warmth, can see, taste, etc. If this is so, then it is not the case that higher order awareness is, in any immediate or obvious way, built in to phenomenal consciousness.

But could it, all the same, be the case that, for beings who do possess the cognitive and conceptual resources to make judgements, phenomenal consciousness grounds explicit self-awareness? That is our question.

Christopher Peacocke suggests that the answer is 'yes'. He writes 'Conscious thoughts and occurrent attitudes can, like other conscious mental events, give the thinker reasons for action and judgement. They do so also in the special case in which they give the thinker a reason for self-ascribing an attitude to the content which occurs to the thinker, provided our thinker is conceptually equipped to make the self-ascription.' He adds 'To say that [making a conscious judgement] is the thinker's reason for [self-ascribing that judgement] is not to say that he infers the self-ascription from a premise that he has made such a first-order judgement. A mental event can be the thinker's reason for...making a judgement...without the case being one of inference. An experience of pain can be the thinker's reason for judging that he is in pain...The conscious pain itself, and not some alleged perception of it, is reason giving' (Peacocke 1999, pp. 214–15).[3]

In what follows I shall take off from the proposal outlined by Peacocke, namely that a phenomenally conscious state provides its subject with non-inferential justification for self-ascription of the state. But I should make clear that I am not attributing to him the further ideas discussed below, in particular the detailed spelling out of the view considered in Section 3. The project of the chapter is not to reconstruct or test Peacocke's view in detail, but rather to consider various ways of developing the attractive schematic idea he puts on the table, the idea of a link between phenomenal consciousness and explicit self-awareness.[4] I shall suggest that teasing out how it might

---

[3] A similar view is expressed in C. Peacocke (2005). Another writer sympathetic to ideas of this kind is L. O'Brien (2007). J. Pryor (2005) is also interested in the idea that there may be non-inferential justification, and he gives the example of a headache justifying its subject's belief in its existence. He does not, however, highlight the role of consciousness in the way Peacocke does. F. Dretske (1999) has interesting thoughts in this area. C. Travis (2007) also seems to be interested in the idea that experience provides non-inferential justification for belief.

[4] Peacocke's views are examined in detail by A. Coliva (2008). She lays out various interpretations of what he says, and some of the difficulties she raises for those interpretations are fuller versions of worries raised in Section 3 below.

work presents considerable challenges. When we consider the variety of states which may be phenomenally conscious, we see that a minimal notion of phenomenal consciousness does not, just by itself, intelligibly underpin the existence of some *sui generis*, inference-independent, ability to self-ascribe that conscious state. The conscious states which illustrate that negative point do not show that there is no justificatory link between phenomenal consciousness and explicit judgement. But they do suggest that the nature and complexity of phenomenal states themselves, together with the kinds of skills we have in dealing with those complexities, will need to be considered in any adequate account of the link between phenomenal consciousness and self-ascription. And when we begin to delve into the nature of the complexities and the skills, it becomes evident that a considerable range of philosophical articulations of the situation are available.

In more detail, the structure of the paper is as follows. Section 2 will comment on one aspect of the understanding of 'phenomenal consciousness' which informs the use of the notion in this paper. Section 3 considers further the idea of an occurrent thought or a pain giving its subject reason to self-ascribe it and raises a difficulty for one way of understanding the proposal. The difficulty is to explain how the account avoids being a version of views from which it wants to distance itself—namely that self-knowledge is based on a special inward directed form of perception, or that it is merely a matter of reliable causation of beliefs. This section will also outline how the invocation of phenomenal consciousness might seem an attractive answer to this difficulty. Section 4 will consider unconscious mental states (unconscious in the Freudian sense that is), and will suggest that their existence shows that the attractive answer cannot be right. Whatever the relation between phenomenal consciousness and explicit belief about oneself, it cannot be as simple as the initially attractive proposal suggests. Section 5 takes stock, examining the key notions of 'consciousness' and 'non-inferential justification', to see what ways forward a better understanding of them might offer. Section 6 offers some very sketchy thoughts about the options which open up at this point and the further issues they bring into view.

2. 'Phenomenal consciousness'

The line of thought in Sections 3 and 4 below is independent of the suggestion offered in this section. That later line of thought depends only on agreeing to classify some states as phenomenally conscious, not on the reasons for so doing. But the suggestion floated in this section may provide some reinforcement of the classification suggested and make a link with some of the discussion in Section 5. It also raises issues which, in any case, merit consideration.

Many discussions of phenomenal consciousness start out with strikingly brief accounts of the target notion. Often we have little more than what is provided in the third paragraph of this paper, namely the introduction of the idea that there are states such that 'it is like something for their subject to be in them', together with the giving of some paradigm examples, such as feeling bodily sensations (pain, nausea, warmth) or being the subject of visual, olfactory, or other extero-perception (seeing out of my window, smelling coffee). But what other elements in psychological life ought to be included beyond the agreed paradigms?

The answer to this question will depend on what meaning we attach to the somewhat gnomic phrase 'something it is like for the subject' and on what feature of the paradigm states we extrapolate. One thing these paradigm states share is that their occurrence can contribute, positively or negatively, to the enjoyment or suffering of the subject. So I propose in what follows to operate with a concept of phenomenal consciousness which gives a central role to enjoyment and suffering, to what makes a subject a potential target of moral concern of a particular kind, namely sympathy and related attitudes. I should stress that it is not part of this suggestion that the only grounds for thinking that things go well or ill with a living creature (and hence the only grounds for moral concern) have to do with what conscious states he or she is in. Partly objective accounts of well-being may, for anything said here, be correct. The claim is rather that it is in virtue of having states which are phenomenally conscious that a creature is capable of well-being which has a 'subjective dimension', that is, enjoyment or suffering, and that all and only states of this kind are capable of contributing to such well-being. A corollary of this thought is that if you want to make things more or less subjectively satisfactory for a person, to comfort or to torment, the knowledge you need is of how to affect those states of his or hers which are phenomenally conscious.

My hope is that in making this link of consciousness with enjoyment and suffering, I am not distorting the notion philosophers have been using but rather bringing out a connection present also in others' implicit understanding of it.[5] That we think of phenomenal consciousness this way supplies at least one explanation of why the topic was acknowledged to be deserving of philosophical attention when it forced its way back onto the stage in the 1970s. It did so at a point where functionalism, artificial intelligence, and the like were the major focuses of interest in philosophy of mind. But 'Where's the painfulness of the pain?' we asked. And perhaps in asking this we had the sense that the accounts then on offer provided no place for the fact that subjects rejoice or suffer, that things matter to them, in some sense which seems overlooked by saying merely that they exhibit goal directed behaviour. A further point in favour of the suggestion is that it makes sense of generally agreed extrapolations from the core cases, for example to emotions and to occurrent thoughts. These are evidently states of mind which can contribute in their distinctive ways to boredom, interest, happiness, distress, and the like.

My sense, then, is that understanding 'phenomenal consciousness' in a way which builds in a link to suffering and enjoyment is not wildly eccentric. But it is not clear that it is the only understanding manifested in the literature. Philosophers rightly stress that

---

[5] I am encouraged by finding a similar view proposed by P. Robbins and A. I. Jack (2006).

divergent extrapolations from examples are possible. Hence our agreement in accepting the paradigm cases may lull us into a false sense that we have a common concept. And the further facts that we agree in saying that consciousness is familiar but mysterious and that we happily repeat together the mantra 'a state such that there is something it is like to be in it' do not do a great deal to reassure me that this is not the case. It would be good to have more discussion of the logical shape of ascriptions of conscious states, reflection on a wider variety of putative examples, and more consideration of conceptual links the notion may have.[6]

The possibility of different understandings of 'phenomenally conscious' is one reason for setting out the ideas above. Another reason is that focusing reflection on consciousness in the context of an acknowledged connection with well-being might suggest different lines of approach to the topic from those found in a good deal of the literature. It would, for example, encourage more thought about what is required for there to be a subject of consciousness at all, a being who can enjoy or suffer. That in turn might point us in the direction of thinking more about whole organisms, their lives, and what kinds of things could matter to them, rather than about experiences conceived in an isolated way.

3. Phenomenal consciousness and self-awareness

The proposal under consideration, the one to which Peacocke draws our attention, is about our coming to have explicit and verbalizable awareness of how it is with us. It is about what is involved, not just in making an occurrent judgement or having a headache, but in thinking of ourselves as so doing. There are in the philosophical literature many accounts of how we arrive at explicit self-awareness, and two in particular—the inner-directed perception view and the simple causal view—are worth contrasting with the account we want to assess.

The inner-directed perception view says that we can turn inward on ourselves a perceptual capacity ('introspection') which yields us perceptual awareness of our psychological states. It is the awareness of the state, delivered by the introspection of it, which grounds belief in its existence. The simple causal view, by contrast, says that some psychological states just do tend to cause beliefs in their own existence. As against the perceptual view, this second view takes these beliefs to be ones which just pop up in the mind, without being based on a distinctive experience arising from perceptual contact with the states of affairs they are about. The fact that they are reliably caused by

---

[6] There is certainly much more to be said in clarification of the account I have gestured at. For example, I have skated over a great deal of complexity in the ideas of value and subjective welfare. More attention to the many different dimensions of value would be useful as would also attention to the many different ways in which things can be experienced by a person as going well or ill. Relatedly, more attention to the contrasts between phenomenal states the affective status of which is built into their description ('pain'), and those where it is not ('tasting sweetness') might be of importance. But I will leave all such complications for the time being.

the states of affairs which make them true may make them 'justified' in a sense which an epistemological externalist would be happy with. But, on this second view, they have no justification of an internalist character, such as might be supplied by perceptual experience.

The proposal under consideration is able to distance itself from some problems of both of these familiar accounts. In contrast to the first, it denies that there is some extra perceptual state with its own phenomenology, that of, for example, perceiving the judgement that the first primroses are out or of perceiving the headache. Hence it denies that any such further state is the basis for the subject's belief about her occurrent judgement or her belief about her headache. In contrast to the second it claims that the subject is, all the same, justified in taking it that she makes the judgement or that she has a headache, and not merely in the externalist's sense. So we can say not only that her first level occurrent judgement or her headache makes true her further belief—everyone will acknowledge this unexciting fact. We may say also that the occurrent judgement or the headache justifies the further belief, in a more internalist spirit.

There is, however, a prima facie difficulty in seeing how, given that there is no self-directed perceptual capacity, anything other than the simple causal view could be available. All we seem to be supplied with are, first some worldly items—the headache, the occurrent judgement—and then, second, the fact that these things have become the content of some, allegedly justified, belief that they occur. But, given that there is no self-directed perception, how do the worldly items get from existing outside any explicit belief to being inside such a belief as its content, if it is not by mere causality?

A possible answer to this supposed difficulty of course leaps to mind, and it pivots on consciousness. It is precisely the phenomenally conscious nature of the items we are dealing with which is crucial. The fact that there is 'something that it is like' to make the judgement, or to have a headache, will, it seems plausible to suggest, make that judgement or headache capable of playing a justificatory role vis-à-vis a belief in its own existence. The judgement and the headache are not items which, given their natures, are capable of existing external to the conscious mind but, on the contrary, already items in the conscious mind itself. So surely, somehow, the reflective subject must be able to exploit this fact to arrive at explicit self-awareness?

But how, exactly, does this work? Perhaps it is extremely simple and direct. Consider the following principle concerning any psychological attitude, relation, action, or state F:

(C) Whenever someone consciously Fs and also has the concept F then she will be able to judge explicitly, with non-inferential justification, that she Fs.

In assessing this principle in what follows we shall take it that 'to F consciously' requires being in a state which is phenomenally distinctive of Fing. The principle would have little attraction if two states F and G were both 'conscious', in that being in them made a difference to what things were like for their subject, but they made the same difference.

Is the truth of the principle implicit in the nature of phenomenal consciousness? We might develop an argument that it is in the following way. In saying that some state is conscious we commit ourselves to acknowledging that its presence or absence makes a distinctive difference to how it is with the thinker subjectively. In turn, that suggests two further plausible claims. The first is that the thinker does not need an extra state of some kind, for example one resulting from perception of this original, conscious state, to make some second difference to how it is with her in order that she may, through that second difference, have the original state impinge on her in such a way that she can become explicitly aware of it. We already have a relevant and adequate difference which the state has made to her, simply in virtue of its being itself a conscious state. That is why we escape any need to postulate inner-directed perception. The second claim which may seem plausible here is that all the thinker needs in order to exploit this distinctive phenomenal difference, so as to turn it into explicit awareness of her state, is possession of the concept of that state. The concept will bring with it, will be in part constituted by, sensitivity to the phenomenal difference which being in the state involves. And such sensitivity to phenomenal difference, we might add, is not a matter of performing an inference.[7]

But (C), just as it stands, is false. The proposed justification for it, although it may embody a real anti-introspectionist insight in its first plausible claim, is unwarranted in the second claim. The plausibility of this second claim is specious, and in adopting it we overlook various important complications. We shall pursue these matters in the next section.

4. The unconscious mind

It has long been realized that people may have desires, feelings, beliefs, and projects which they do not, perhaps cannot, acknowledge to themselves or others and of which they therefore lack explicit, verbalizable awareness. Moralists and novelists had made the possibilities of self-ignorance and self-deception vivid and compelling well before Freud came on the scene and gave us further examples and tools for thinking about such cases. So let us accept that there are such things as 'unconscious fears', 'unconscious desires', etc.—psychological states which are unconscious in the sense that they are unavowed and unavowable (or at least unavowable at some times) by their subjects.

But are these states unconscious in the sense that they do not manifest themselves in phenomenologically distinctive states or episodes? Let us start by considering ordinary, avowable emotions. Suppose that a person is frightened of authority figures, in the ordinary non-Freudian way. It is plain that such fear manifests itself in the person's experience, showing up in what it is like for him at many points and in distinctive ways.

---

[7] Peacocke thinks that it is built into the nature of at least some psychological concepts, e.g. 'pain', 'belief', that the possessor of those concepts is sensitive to whether or not he or she instantiates them. But (as I read him at least) he is not committed to the idea that the principle (C) holds in full generality.

It is likely to result in his experiencing some episodes of acute occurrent fear, when actually confronted with authority figures. It makes the anticipation of some situations congenial, while the anticipation of others is uncongenial. It influences when and whether he is tense or relaxed. It shows up in what kinds of thoughts or images strike him. And so on.[8] Many (though not all) of these manifestations are unpleasant to the subject and, insofar as they are, they make the fearful person a potential object of pity and sympathy. It is in the production of such unpleasant states that the bully or torturer may rejoice.

Suppose now that a person's fear of authority figures is unconscious. It is often said that attribution of unconscious attitudes is grounded in some tension between what a person says about her feelings or thoughts and what she does. And if we think of 'what a person does' as mere behaviour, then we could be tempted into a picture of the situation on which the fear, in being unconscious, has gone underground, not only in not manifesting itself in avowals, but also not showing itself in any way in conscious life, or at least not unless the person comes to perceive and pay attention to the behaviour it leads to.

But can this be right? Does the fact that our subject is unable to avow her fear do away with the kind of manifestations in consciousness noted earlier, so that the unconsciously fearful person does not undergo acute unpleasant episodes when in the presence of authority figures, does not feel tension and relaxation in certain circumstances, does not suffer from thoughts and images of distinctive kinds and so forth? Should we say that, as far as 'what it is like' is concerned, the unconscious fear has no more importance than an overlooked behavioural tic, for example, a disposition to tap one's toes while listening to music? This is deeply implausible. The difference from the normal, conscious case is not the absence of conscious experiences distinctive of fear, but rather the subject's inability to acknowledge and understand them for what they are when they occur. From the point of view of sympathy, this inability is likely to make it more difficult to offer reassurance or comfort. But it does not make the fearful person less an object of pity or less in need of comfort. From the point of view of the bully or tormentor, that the victim is unconsciously fearful may be a peculiarly satisfactory feature of the situation, because the victim's lack of self-understanding may make him or her less able to think effectively about measures of self-protection.

The implication of this is that unconscious fear is a mental state with distinctive manifestations in phenomenal consciousness. Hence a person who is the subject of such fear is both consciously afraid and unconsciously afraid. Suppose further that unconscious fear has its own distinctive phenomenology, interestingly different from that of

---

[8] Perhaps such fear also shows up phenomenologically in an even more widespread way. Perhaps there is something it is like to be timid, to have a sense of oneself as continuingly weak and vulnerable, which contributes distinctively to what it is like for the timid person all or most of the time. These kinds of unclarities about the limits of the phenomenological are ones it would be interesting to pursue. But they do not affect the argument here.

avowable fear. This seems plausible. For example, as remarked above, there will be similar kinds of distress, tension, and uneasiness in unavowable as in avowable fear, but in the case of unavowable fear, there will be no satisfactory shareable and discussable object on which the subject can focus these feelings. Hence there will be distinctive elements of loneliness and strangeness in experiencing unavowable fear. If this is so, it then follows that a person may be consciously unconsciously afraid of authority figures.

There are, of course, no paradoxes or contradictions in any of this. The notion of being avowable and the notion of contributing to phenomenal consciousness are quite different. It is an unfortunate upshot of the very tangled history of the word 'conscious' that we use the same word for both concepts and so can arrive at these odd-sounding descriptions. (Possibly our linguistic tangle with the word has contributed something to the popularity of higher order thought theories of phenomenal consciousness.)

But once we have realized that the notions are different and have realized also that their application can come apart, then Principle (C) cannot stand in the form originally envisaged. (C) says that a person who Fs in a phenomenologically distinctive way and has the concept of F will be able to make explicitly, with justification, the judgement that she Fs. But the examples just considered indicate that a person may be in a conscious (i.e. phenomenologically distinctive) state of fear and have the concept of fear, and yet be unable to judge that she fears. And, if we accept the speculation about a distinctive phenomenology of unconscious fear, they show that a person may be in a conscious (i.e. phenomenological distinctive) state of having an unconscious (i.e. unavowable) fear, and may have the concept of an unconscious (i.e. unavowable) fear, but may be unable to become explicitly aware of her own unconscious (i.e. unavowable) fear.

5. Taking stock

So F-ing consciously, together with possession of the concept of F, does not necessarily enable a person to judge explicitly that she Fs. And now that we have this possibility in focus, we can find other everyday examples. Being jealous, for example, has a distinctive effect on what things are like for the jealous person, but possession of the concept of jealousy does not guarantee ability to recognize jealousy in oneself. Some people have the sensitivity and honesty to be able to self-ascribe jealousy when they experience it, but others do not. And, for all we yet know, the same may hold for many other kinds of psychological states and characteristics.

The original proposal was that conscious states may provide non-inferential justification for their subjects to self-ascribe them. The cases described do not show that proposal to be mistaken. What the cases show, rather, is that if a conscious state is to supply justification for its self-ascription then, sometimes at least, further cognitive skill is required, in addition to possession of the concept of the state in question, namely skill to exploit the resources which the conscious state, through its phenomenological distinctiveness, makes available. The need for skill reflects the fact that exploiting these resources may present a challenge. And that in turn highlights what is in any case evident on the most cursory reflection, namely that the nature of a person's phenomenal consciousness, whether at any one time or over a period, may be very multifarious and complicated.

All this is, however, compatible with the truth of the original proposal. That skill is needed to arrive at some justified judgement does not rule out what the skill operates on having justificatory power. And whether the justification is inferential or not depends on how 'inferential' is defined. So to develop any sense of the possibilities at this point we need to do two things. We need to reflect more on what might be meant by saying that a justification is 'non-inferential'. And before that, to provide the material which this account of the non-inferential is to engage with, we need to think further about consciousness, and to remind ourselves of the various ways in which its structure and nature may be conceived.

The current literature on consciousness offers two broadly contrasted approaches to understanding its structure and nature. The first approach holds that we need to invoke qualia in our account of consciousness. By 'qualia' here I do not mean something non-committal, which any believer in 'phenomenal consciousness' will allow, namely the things, whatever they are, which are specified by answers like 'painful', 'curiously chocolatey' etc. to questions of the form 'What was X like for S?' Rather by 'quale' I mean something with a definite picture and theory attached to it, where descriptions like 'monadic', 'purely qualitative', and 'logically independent of behaviour' apply. Commitment to qualia so conceived is commitment to extra kinds of stuff, entities, or properties, over and above those recognized in physics, chemistry, zoology, physiology, and the other natural sciences. Postulation of such qualia has many familiar problems, such as tensions with natural science and our needing to countenance the possibility of zombies.

The second approach to thinking about the structure and nature of consciousness is what is often called 'representationalism', the view that the phenomenal character of a conscious state is determined by what worldly things or states of affairs the subject is conscious of, what is presented to the subject, in the conscious state.

We can make more vivid to ourselves the contrast between these two views by considering what each would say about what is at stake when the question of animal consciousness is raised. Some organisms are complex enough in their kind of life for the idea that they are conscious to get a grip. The way they advance or shrink back, become tense or relax, probe or struggle, and the way these actions and responses fit into the larger patterns of their behaviour, make it not absurd to apply consciousness-invoking descriptions to them, such as being hungry, too hot, frightened of predators, pleasantly warm, curious, etc. It is controversial what descriptions should be invoked (perhaps the familiar terms from human life are inapt), and it is controversial whether such descriptions are not merely not absurd but actually correct. But leaving all these controversies aside, how do we conceive of what is at issue? On the qualia view, what happens when or if consciousness emerges in association with some organism is that some extra kind of property or stuff comes on the scene, somehow linked to that organism. For the representational view, by contrast, the emergence of consciousness in an organism is the opening of a window (perhaps a very small and clouded one) for that organism on its world. It is the world as already existing—a world of organisms living, sometimes well and sometimes not so well, in a material environment—which is revealed by the opening of the window. It is not some extra, private, stuff on which the window opens.

There is much more to be said about these two approaches, the logical forms of statement they concentrate on, their conceptions of what it takes for a subject of experience to exist, whether just one or both of them are in tension with natural science, what scope they have for accommodating different kinds and complexities of consciousness, and so forth. My own sense is that the representational view is much more interesting and promising than the qualia view, and in what follows will assume a representational view.

Let us consider now the idea of 'non-inferential justification'. Let us say that a person's belief that p is inferentially justified if she assertively represents some premise propositions which stand in some kind of inferential relation to p, and if her belief that p is appropriately derived from her assertive representations of these premise propositions.[9] There are, given this framework definition, at least three ways of denying that a justification is inferential. We may deny that its starting point is the assertive representation of propositions; we may deny that it involves derivation from such assertive representation; or we may do both.

Within this framework both 'assertive representation' and 'derivation' could be taken in stronger and weaker senses. At the strongest end, 'assertive representation' may be construed as explicit verbal enunciation, and 'derivation' as an overt process of symbol manipulation. On these understandings, it is not controversial that the justifications of many everyday beliefs, including both self-ascriptions of headaches and also perceptually based beliefs about the environment, are not inferential. More controversial and interesting claims, however, emerge as we take 'assertive representation' and 'derivation' in weaker senses. For example, a capacious notion of assertive representation might allow that a subject S 'assertively represents a proposition' where any report of the form 'S Φs that Fa' (e.g. 'S visually registers there is light of intensity so and so in direction such and such') is correct. And a capacious notion of derivation would not require overt manipulation of symbols, but might allow for sub-personal transformation of informational states. Given these weaker notions, it now becomes much less obvious that perceptually based beliefs are not inferentially justified. To underpin the

---

[9] I have borrowed some phrases here from Pryor's Premise Principle: "The only things that can justify a belief that p are other states that assertively represent propositions and those propositions have to be ones that could be used as premises in an argument for p. They have to stand in some kind of inferential relation to p: they have to imply it or inductively support it or something like that" (Pryor 2005, p. 189). Pryor offers the Principle in clarification of a central commitment of those who think all justification is inferential.

claim that their justification was non-inferential we would need to get into much more detail about the concept of perception and the empirical workings of the perceptual system.[10]

6. Further options

With these distinctions in hand, what ways are there of spelling out the idea that the subject of a conscious state such as a headache or occurrent judgement is non-inferentially justified in explicitly attributing that state to him or herself? Let us remind ourselves that we are working on the assumption of a thorough-going representationalism. So our question is what form or forms the idea of non-inferential justification for self-attribution of a conscious state might take against this background. In what follows I sketch only two of what may be many possibilities.

The first option opens up if we accept the idea of justification of belief which is non-inferential in the sense that its starting points are not 'assertive representations of propositions' but are states of some other kind. Suppose that we allow that such justification occurs in many situations. Perhaps, for example, it occurs when ordinary beliefs about one's surroundings are justifiedly formed on the basis of perception. (How exactly any such account of perception and its non-inferential justificatory role vis-à-vis belief are to be spelled out is a difficult and controversial matter. But for our current purposes, we shall skip over all such problems.) Given this orientation, the possibility of non-inferential justification for self-ascription of conscious states might fall out as a particular case of this more widespread phenomenon.

A second possible option opens up if we consider justification of belief which is non-inferential in the sense that there is no process of derivation from premises in arriving at that belief. What this suggests is exploring ideas in the areas of 'expression' or 'avowal', understood on the lines suggested by some readings of Wittgenstein. Pursuing this line, it looks likely that this kind of 'non-inferential justification' will be intelligible only in connection with beliefs about one's own conscious states, and is linked precisely to their being conscious.

Let us spell out these options in a little more detail. Here is a way of developing the first. Let us allow that perceptual experience provides our central form of access to the world, and that the justifications it provides for the explicit beliefs to which it gives rise are non-inferential. How might we exploit this general view, within a representational approach to the nature of consciousness, to support the idea that beliefs about headaches and judgements are also non-inferentially justified? One way would be to revive the idea of inner-directed perception of headaches and judgements. But, as we saw earlier, the major benefit of the proposal we are considering is that it promises to avoid

---

[10] An example of radical thinking in this area is provided by C. Travis (2007). He argues for a non-inferential view of perceptual justification, calling explicitly on thoughts about what its logical form needs to be.

the need for such implausible, extra perceptual states. So how can self-awareness be accommodated, if no such further perceptual states occur?

An attractive and economical move here starts from the fact that the subject, the living animal or organism, is itself part of the world. This suggests the idea that what is presented to a subject in perceptual consciousness (i.e. whatever it is which provides the non-inferential justification for beliefs) may be self-specifying as well as world-specifying. To say this need not be to say that in experience a subject perceives herself. The idea is rather that the content of experience, in its phenomenal variety, provides adequate materials to underpin the application of self-specifying concepts as well as external-world-specifying concepts.

Here are the kinds of claims which might emerge on this line of thought. A subject has made available to her in visual experience, not only objects other than herself, together with their properties, but also where she is located vis-à-vis those objects. This is revealed in such phenomenally distinctive things as how large the various objects loom. She has made available to her also whether she is seeing, as opposed to hearing or touching. This is revealed, perhaps, in what properties she can detect objects to have. She may further have made available how her sight is working. This is revealed in such things as whether she sees sharply or blurrily. So when she is equipped with relevant concepts, of her own location, senses, and perceptual capacities, she is in a position to attend appropriately to what is presented in consciousness (which *ex hypothesi* provides non-inferential justifications), and thus to arrive at these judgements about herself.[11]

An account of this kind can explain, schematically at least, why consciously F-ing may sometimes not enable judgement that one Fs, even when one has the concept F. Hence it has the resources to handle the existence of Freudianly unconscious states and similar lacks of awareness. It will classify these failures instancing an evident truth, namely that it is not always a straightforward matter to bring a concept to bear on what is presented in experience, especially if what is so presented is complex and confusing, and there are also other calls on cognitive resources. Sometimes, for example, we fail to spot a tiger, amid the shifting stripey lights and shadows of the jungle, even when the tiger is, in a sense, there in full view, because we are distracted by other concerns, hampered by preconceptions, or what not. Similarly we may fail to recognize the fear which is present in our experience because we are distracted, hampered by preconceptions, or what not.

In considering whether any version of this story could work, there are various things one might wish to meditate on. One concerns whether the story can handle the familiar contrast between attitude and content. I am (often at least) able to tell whether I am judging that p or fantasizing that p. On the account sketched, which of these attitudes I have must become available to me from attention to what is presented to me in consciousness, in a way analogous to that in which relative distance from things

---

[11] For a way into recent relevant work on the representational theory of consciousness, see M. Tye (2003).

shows up in how they loom, or that I am seeing shows up in my awareness of colours. But we rightly think of the difference between judgement and fantasy as connected, in part at least, with their different functions in the causal economy of the mind, judging having a different connection with desire and action from that of fantasy. So if our story about self-knowledge is to stand up, we must make sense of these functional differences being somehow manifested, as the functional differences they are, in the content of what is presented. Does this make sense? Another issue is whether recent suggestions that experiences such as pain or itching should be thought of as representational of the body can be convincingly developed. If they can, that would be a source of strength for the account. Finally we may note that the form of representationalism envisaged in this paper is one which emphasizes, not only the material nature of the world revealed to the conscious organism, but also its value-infused nature, from the point of view of the organism. How does that thought play out in elaborating this story? In addition to negotiating these tricky issues, pursuing this approach also requires us to think seriously about how radical a version of non-inferentialism we should accept. So developing the approach convincingly presents many challenges.

I turn now to the second possible way of combining a representational theory of the nature of conscious states with the idea that such states may provide non-inferential justification for their explicit self-ascription. A corollary of conceiving the arrival of consciousness as the opening of a window on the world (as opposed to thinking of it as the appearance of qualia) is that a link of consciousness to behaviour is built into our story from the start. It is only when the life of an organism gets complex enough for some of its behaviour to be read as expression of its experience that the idea of conscious states so much as makes sense. The converse of that coin is the recognition that conscious states exist only inasmuch as such things as withdrawal, pursuit, scratching, wriggling, tensing, relaxing, etc., etc., occur.

With this idea of expression in hand, our second line of thought vis-à-vis the non-inferential becomes available, namely the one which sees justification as non-inferential where the belief arrived at is justified by some item, that is, is something to which the subject is entitled given that item, but there is no process of derivation from the justifying item in arriving at the belief. On the view sketched, the occurrence of an instance of expressive behaviour is not something separable from the state it expresses in the sense of being caused by it. The expression is to be thought of rather as an aspect of the way in which the expressed state exists at that particular time. Let us now add to this picture the familiar Wittgensteinian thought that one upshot of learning a language is the addition of ability to make avowals to the range of expressive behaviour possible for a subject in a given state. If this Wittgensteinian account is on the right lines, it supplies materials for elaborating a non-inferential view of how a conscious state may justify its subject in self-ascribing it. The conscious state, in the setting of such learnt expressive ability, entitles the subject to a belief in its existence, in that it allows the subject to arrive justifiedly at that belief, by exercising the ability to avow the state. Such self-ascription is non-inferential because there is no derivation, causal or logical, of that self-ascription from the state ascribed. Rather the spontaneous expressive self-ascription is, in some circumstances, an aspect of the particular occurrence of the state 'expressed'.[12]

How might this approach explain the existence of conscious states which are unavowable, such as Freudianly unconscious fear? It can, because we need not suppose that acquiring the ability to express is equally easy in all cases, or that all kinds of expressive manifestation are equally spontaneously possible in all circumstances. A philosopher who is attracted to the Wittgensteinian notion of avowal can acknowledge that putting oneself in a position to avow one's states may take effort or skill of various kinds. Also she need not suppose that acquiring ability to express one's states by avowals is the only element in learning to use psychological terms. Somewhere in these complexities a plausible way of handling the cases of Section 4 might well be found.

What is said above about these two ways of exploring the idea of non-inferential justification merely gestures at how things might go. Plainly a great deal more needs to be done to make either account more fully intelligible and to work out which kinds of case it might apply to. And it is worth noting that the two accounts are not incompatible. They call on different, but not rival, senses of 'non-inferential'. Perhaps the first is more appropriate for some kinds of conscious state and the second for others? Perhaps they need to be blended, even in accounts of one kind of state?

Our final conclusion, therefore is this. The claim 'a conscious state provides its subject with non-inferential justification for self-ascribing it' is extremely attractive. We may well rightly think that there is some important insight or insights encapsulated in these words. But there is still much work to do in separating out the various things which might be meant by the formulation, and articulating them in a compelling way.

References

Bar-On, D. 2005 *Speaking My Mind: Expression and Self-Knowledge*, Oxford, Oxford University Press.
Coliva, A. 2008 "Peacocke's Self-Knowledge", *Ratio* XXI, 13–27.
Dretske, F. 1999 "The Mind's Awareness of Itself", *Philosophical Studies* 95, 103–24.
O'Brien, L. 2007 *Self-Knowing Agents*, Oxford, Oxford University Press.
Peacocke, C. 1999 *Being Known*, Oxford, Oxford University Press.
———2005 "'Another I'": Representing Conscious States, Perception and Others", in J. L. Bermudez (ed.) *Thought Reference and Experience: Themes from the Philosophy of Gareth Evans*, Oxford, Oxford University Press.
Pryor, J. 2005 "Is There Immediate Justification?", in M. Steup and E. Sosa (eds.) *Contemporary Debates in Epistemology*, Oxford, Blackwell, 181–202.

---

[12] Bar-On (2005) offers a detailed working out of this thought of this kind.

Robbins, P. and Jack, A. I. (2006) "The Phenomenal Stance", *Philosophical Studies*, 127, 59–85.
Travis, C. 2007 "Reasons's Reach", *European Journal of Philosophy* 15/2, 225–48.
Tye, M. 2003 "Blurry Images, Double Vision and Other Oddities: New Problems for Representationalism?" in Q. Smith and A. Jokic (eds.), *Consciousness: New Philosophical Perspectives*, Oxford, Oxford University Press, 7–32.

6

Reasons and Self-Knowledge

Conor McHugh

1. Introduction

How do we know our own propositional attitudes? According to Christopher Peacocke (1999), certain conscious states and episodes can give their subjects *reasons* to self-ascribe corresponding propositional attitudes to their contents. They thereby constitute epistemologically internalist warrants for self-knowledge.

A major challenge facing this 'reasons account' is to explain how conscious states and episodes *can* give internalist reasons for such self-ascriptions. Annalisa Coliva (2008) has objected that any viable account of how conscious states and episodes can give genuinely *internalist* reasons will entail that subjects *already* have a kind of awareness of those states and episodes that amounts to self-knowledge, or something close to it. Thus, the reasons account is either circular, or not internalist after all.

I have two goals in this chapter: to show that Coliva's objection fails, and to offer a positive explanation of how conscious states and episodes can give genuine internalist reasons for self-ascriptions.

After setting out the reasons account (Section 2) and Coliva's objection (Section 3), I will show that the objection can be resisted if we adopt a certain conception of what is involved in a state's or episode's being conscious (Section 4). Then I will step back to consider epistemological internalism as such (Section 5). While a certain very strong version of internalism would indeed render the reasons account circular, I will show that there are two more moderate versions of internalism on which conscious states and episodes can give reasons for self-ascriptions. In the course of this I will develop an internalist conception of epistemic warrant that may have much broader application (Sections 6, 7).

2. Self-knowledge: The reasons account

The reasons account purports to explain why self-ascriptions of certain conscious attitudes, when formed in the usual way, are typically warranted.[1] The account claims that enjoying a conscious state or episode can give you a non-inferential reason to self-ascribe that very state or episode, or a constitutively related attitude (Peacocke 1999). For example, judging that it is raining can give you a reason to self-ascribe the belief that it is raining. That is partly because judgement is a conscious episode that initiates or manifests the attitude-state of belief. If you self-ascribe the belief for the reason so given, the self-ascription typically will be warranted by that reason.

Let me give an initial gloss on the central notions of a reason for belief and of believing for a reason. As I will understand it, you have a reason to believe p when some feature of your situation, accessible to you, supports the truth of p. You believe p *for* that reason if the feature in question plays an appropriate role in a certain kind of explanation of your having that belief—an explanation that shows your holding the belief to be pro tanto rational or appropriate from your own point of view. I will have more to say about these notions as we go on.

On the reasons account, first-order conscious states and episodes themselves give or constitute reasons for self-ascriptions. There is no role, in the ordinary warrant for self-knowledge of first-order states, for perception-like higher-order awareness *of* conscious states and episodes.[2] It is your judging that it is raining, and not some distinct awareness *of* that episode of judgement, that gives you a reason to believe that you believe it is raining (ibid., 214–15). In this sense, the reasons account is non-introspective.

At the same time, the account portrays the warrant for self-knowledge as internalist in character. It claims that a conscious state or episode can give a reason that is the subject's *own* reason *for* the corresponding self-ascription. It makes that particular self-ascription rational, or justified, from the subject's own point of view (Peacocke 1998, p. 96). I take it that this is an attraction of the account, for self-knowledge is surely a paradigm case of internalist warrant. When you self-ascribe a belief whose content you have just judged, for example, your self-ascription will typically be rational or justified from your own point of view. Imagine a subject whose self-ascriptions were, from her own point of view, merely spontaneous and non-justified judgements: such a subject surely would not enjoy the kind of perspective on her conscious life that *we* enjoy.

Although self-ascriptions are, on this account, made for reasons, they are not *inferred* from those reasons. You do not *infer* from your judgement that it is raining, that you have the corresponding belief. The judgement gives you a non-inferential reason to self-ascribe the belief.

---

[1] I use the term 'warrant' in the sense developed by T. Burge (1993): warrant is that general epistemic good of which justification is an internalist species. The account also explains why self-ascriptions are *knowledge*. I focus on the question of warrant.

[2] I assume here that a state's or episode's being conscious isn't itself a matter of your having higher-order perception-like awareness of it.

The notion of non-inferential reasons is familiar. On many accounts, a perceptual experience as of p's being the case gives you a reason to believe that p, but you do not *infer* that p is the case from that experience or its content. However, self-ascriptions differ in an important respect from perceptual beliefs. In the perceptual case, the subject arrives at the belief that p by accepting the *content* of the perceptual experience on which the belief is based. The subject has a reason to believe p, rather than q, because she enjoys an experience with a related, or perhaps identical, content. The situation is different in the case of self-ascriptions (according to the reasons account). When a subject judges that p, the *content* of that judgement helps explain why she has a reason to self-ascribe an attitude to p rather than q, but it does not itself explain why she has a reason to self-ascribe the *belief* that p, rather than some other attitude towards p. Rather, it is because that content occurs as the content of a conscious episode of judging, that the subject has a reason to self-ascribe the belief that p. Thus, the reasons account claims that a state's or episode's occurring consciously, and being of the type it is (a judgement rather than a wish, say), is crucial in the explanation of how it gives a reason for a particular self-ascription.[3]

I said that having a reason to believe p involves some feature of your situation supporting the truth of p. Here we have a relation of truth-conducive support. One relatum of this relation is always a content—it is the content p whose truth is (in some sense) made likely by whatever gives or constitutes the reason to believe p. But the other relatum need not be a content. Or so the defender of the reasons account says. The obvious alternative candidates are *facts* and (obtainings of) *states of affairs*. For example, the fact that there was a loud bang, or the obtaining of that state of affairs, is what supports the truth of the content that there was an explosion nearby, and gives a reason to believe it. We also talk as though constituents of states of affairs, for example events, can be relata in this relation of truth-conducive support. The occurrence of the loud bang supports the truth of the content that there was an explosion nearby. It gives or constitutes a reason to believe that content. Though a state of affairs or an event is not itself a content, and not true or false, it nevertheless makes certain contents true and certain others likely to be true, and can thus provide truth-conducive support for a content.

In the case of self-ascriptions, we can say that a conscious state or episode itself constitutes a reason for the corresponding self-ascription, just as the occurrence of the loud bang constitutes a reason for the belief that there has been an explosion. Or we can say that that it is the fact that you enjoy that state or episode that constitutes a reason for the self-ascription. The reasons account could be formulated either way. The crucial claim is that, in enjoying the state/episode, you *have* a reason, and a reason

---

[3] Lucy O'Brien (2007, ch. 6) discusses the difference between "content-based" and "non-content-based" accounts of self-knowledge. The reasons account is a non-content-based account. The distinction has roots in Peacocke's own discussion of representationally dependent and representationally independent uses of the first person (Peacocke 1999).

for which you can form a self-ascriptive belief. What the defender of the reasons account cannot accept is that having that reason is a matter of knowing or believing that you are enjoying the state/episode: this would lead to the circularity I will discuss below. The point of this paper is to work out a position on which this circularity can be avoided.

3. Coliva against the reasons account

Annalisa Coliva (2008) has argued that the reasons account cannot provide a satisfactory internalist account of self-knowledge.

Her argument turns on the point, noted above, that a genuinely internalist reason is a justifying reason *for* the subject. It is a feature in virtue of which the particular judgement or belief it justifies, with its particular content rather than any other, is rational or appropriate from the subject's own point of view. The reasons account claims that it is the conscious occurrence of a state or episode that enables it to give a reason for a particular self-ascription. So, the reasons account is committed to explaining how a state or episode can rationalize a particular self-ascription, rather than any other, from the subject's point of view, by appeal to what is involved in the conscious occurrence of that state or episode. For example, the conscious occurrence of an episode of judging that p must be sufficient to rationalize, from the subject's point of view, a self-ascription of the belief that p, rather than some other attitude to p.

Coliva says:

> Peacocke's proposal.....relies crucially on the claim that first-order mental states may be *given* to a subject in such a way as to function as reasons, from his own point of view, for the corresponding self-ascriptions. Hence, in order for the proposal to be implemented satisfactorily, he needs a notion of a *conscious* mental state that can support the claim that the corresponding self-ascription would be rationally justified merely by its occurrence. (Ibid., p. 17).

Whatever account of conscious occurrence is offered must avoid presupposing self-knowledge:

> What is precluded by Peacocke's model, however, is arrival at the self-ascription on the basis of *self-conscious consideration* of one's own first-order conscious mental states. For that would place the very self-knowledge to be accounted for at the foundation of a purported account of how such knowledge is grounded. (Ibid., pp. 16–17)

Coliva considers two accounts of consciousness that she finds in Peacocke. I want to focus on the second of these. This account claims that a state or episode is conscious when there is something it is like for the subject to enjoy it—when it has a subjective phenomenology. Given this claim, the reasons account seems to become committed to the thesis that it is in virtue of their phenomenology—of what it is like to enjoy them—that conscious states and episodes give internalist reasons for our ordinary self-ascriptions. For example, it is because of the phenomenology of a conscious episode of judging that *p* that it rationalizes, from the subject's point of view, the self-ascription of the belief that *p* rather than any other attitude to *p*.

This thesis has prima facie attraction. There is clearly a connection between phenomenology and consciousness. And it is natural to think that phenomenology is typically accessible to the subject in such a way that it could make a difference to what is rational from the subject's point of view.

Nevertheless, Coliva thinks the thesis is unsustainable. Her primary objection to the thesis[4] is based on the observation that states and episodes of different *types* are sometimes phenomenologically the same for the subject. In view of this possibility, she argues, the subjective phenomenology of a conscious state or episode will not always suffice for it to give its subject an internalist reason for the corresponding self-ascription—it will not suffice for that particular self-ascription, rather than any other, to be rational from the subject's point of view.[5] In particular, it will not always determine correctly that the subject has a reason to self-ascribe the right type of state, rather than any other type. This, Coliva claims, leads to trouble for the reasons account.

To set up the objection more explicitly: suppose there are two conscious states or episodes, S1 and S2, that have the very same propositional contents and are phenomenologically alike for a subject—there is no difference between what it is like for the subject to enjoy S1 and what it is like for the subject to enjoy S2. Suppose that everything else about the subject's situation is the same when she enjoys S1 and when she enjoys S2. The reasons account, combined with the phenomenological conception of consciousness, seems to be committed to claiming that what is rationalized for the subject by S1 and S2 depends on the subject's phenomenology when she enjoys S1 and S2 respectively, as well as, perhaps, on their contents.[6] That is, if S1 and

---

[4] She offers two other arguments against the phenomenological conception. The first is that it cannot account for self-knowledge of non-occurrent attitudes that do not have manifestations in phenomenal consciousness. This does not seem me to be a problem. *If* we know about attitudes that do not manifest themselves in phenomenal consciousness, then this knowledge requires a different account to that required for those attitudes that do so manifest themselves. Peacocke's own discussion of 'no intermediate conscious state' cases is pertinent here (Peacocke 1999): this is supposed to account for certain self-ascriptions not based on manifestations of the self-ascribed attitude in consciousness. On Peacocke's treatment, the epistemology of these cases is, in a certain way, derivative from that of the cases where there is an intervening manifestation in consciousness. The second argument against the phenomenological conception is that it cannot account for self-knowledge of attitudes that do not have representational content, because only states and episodes with representational content can rationalize and justify. This is a larger issue than I can go into. Suffice to say, I do not accept that only states and episodes with representational content can rationalize and justify, but the reader who holds that view can take the reasons account to be restricted in its scope to self-knowledge based on conscious states and episodes that *do* have representational content.

[5] I am very grateful to Annalisa for discussion that significantly clarified my understanding of her objection.

[6] I would like to remain neutral on the relation between phenomenology and content. I take it to be uncontroversial that the content of a conscious state or episode systematically makes a difference to what that state or episode rationalizes for the subject. Perhaps this is because of some close connection between phenomenology and content, but I do not wish to commit to that claim.

The question of how the type of a conscious state or episode makes a difference to what the state or episode rationalizes for the subject, and in particular how its type contributes to the subject's having a reason to make

S2 do not differ with respect to content or phenomenology, then they do not differ with respect to what they rationalize. Since, by stipulation, S1 and S2 have the same content and are phenomenologically alike, it follows that S1 and S2 rationalize the same things. In particular, they will rationalize the very same self-ascriptions, if any. But S1 and S2 might nevertheless be different in type.

Why is this a problem? When combined with the reasons account, it has two implausible consequences, according to Coliva.

First, it implies that, across the range of conscious states, episodes, and attitudes that we *do* have ordinary self-knowledge of, different types of state and episode have distinct characteristic phenomenologies, in virtue of which they rationalize the corresponding self-ascriptions. If there were no such distinct characteristic phenomenologies, then different types of state and episode would not (by the lights of this account) systematically rationalize the appropriate self-ascriptions, and so we would not as a matter of course know what type of state or episode we are enjoying, or what attitudes we have. This is implausible because many types do *not* have distinct characteristic phenomenologies in that way:

> for example, occurrent desires, hopes or wishes with the same content need hardly be different from a strictly phenomenological point of view, yet will be required somehow to rationalize different self-ascriptions. (Ibid., p. 22)

Second, it implies that if S2 has the phenomenology that is characteristic of a certain type T1, while in fact being of a distinct type T2, it will nevertheless rationalize the mistaken self-ascription of it *as* an episode of type T1. For it is the phenomenology that is doing the rationalizing work, on this suggestion. So, if an episode of hoping has the phenomenology characteristic of judging, it will rationalize a self-ascription of belief. This is implausible because such self-ascriptions are surely *not* rational:

> [C]onsider cases of wishful thinking: certain contents may manifest themselves to a subject with such an intensity and 'colouring', as it were, that, while being merely hopes, can actually be taken for beliefs. So, their phenomenology would be pretty much the same, yet only the self-ascription of the relevant hope would be *rational* on their basis (not just correct). If so, however, it is unclear how any *purely* phenomenological account of what it means for a mental state to be conscious can support the claim that a first-order state can stand in a *rational, justificatory* relation to the corresponding self-ascription. (Ibid., pp. 22–3)

Coliva concludes that the warrant for self-knowledge cannot be explained by any purported reason-giving role of conscious states and episodes, where consciousness is understood phenomenologically.

---

a specific self-ascription, is more pressing, for the reasons outlined at the end of the last section and the start of the present one.

4. Defending the phenomenological conception of access

Coliva's concern, in a nutshell, is that the *types* of conscious states and episodes, or of the attitudes they manifest, aren't always reflected in the phenomenology of the subject enjoying them; and it thus becomes unclear how the state or episode could, in virtue of its phenomenology, give the subject a reason for a self-ascription of the corresponding type.

I claim that the types of conscious states and episodes *are* reflected in phenomenology *in those cases where the subject is in a position to have ordinary self-knowledge of the corresponding type*. I claim that these phenomenological features make a difference to what is rational from the subject's point of view, in these cases. When you know that you *believe*, and do not merely *wish*, that *p*, that is because you have enjoyed an episode with phenomenology characteristic of judging and not characteristic of occurrently wishing. When the type of a conscious state or episode is *not* reflected in phenomenology, you are liable to go wrong in your self-ascription because you lack a reason to self-ascribe the correct type.

I will not try to prove that this position is correct. But I will try to show that it is plausible. If it is plausible, then Coliva's objection fails unless she can offer further arguments against the position.

Let me be clear about what the claim is. I am claiming that the conscious thoughts (etc.) that manifest propositional attitudes have a distinctive phenomenology. I am claiming that, in cases where there is self-knowledge, this phenomenology is proprietary with respect to the type of attitude being manifested, in the sense that it is a phenomenology that characteristically occurs with and only with that type.[7] I am not claiming that this phenomenology is constitutive of the type. Nor am I claiming that conscious thoughts are always accompanied by distinctive phenomenally conscious imagery, inner speech, sensations and/or feelings. The idea is that the thoughts themselves have their own non-imagistic, non-sensory, non-affective phenomenology.

This last point is important. Some philosophers conceive of phenomenology as restricted to the sensory, the quasi-sensory, and the affective—they understand it to be a matter of the presentation to the subject of instantiations of qualitative properties such as redness, loudness, painfulness, warmth, and so on, as well as, perhaps, feelings of affect.[8] Coliva seems to conceive of it this way, implicitly at least. She describes the phenomenology of an imagined instance of judging that today is a sunny day as follows: "the pleasant and relaxing feeling this thought may produce, together with,

---

[7] The term 'proprietary' is due to D. Pitt (2004). I use it in such a way that allows for exceptions: a state or episode of one type can have the phenomenology characteristic of another.

[8] This conception is discussed by J. Prinz (2002). It is, I think, often implicitly assumed, as when the notion of phenomenology is introduced by reference only to the character of sensory experiences, such as seeing red, smelling coffee, or orgasm, and (less commonly) by reference to affective experiences as well.

perhaps, a strong sense of confidence" (ibid., p. 22). At work here seems to be an assumption that the judgement itself is apt to be phenomenally conscious only by virtue of accompanying phenomenally conscious feelings. Such accompanying feelings would not reliably identify the event they accompany as a judgement. No wonder, then, that Coliva finds this conception of consciousness inadequate to support the reasons account.

Many philosophers reject this conception of phenomenology, claiming that non-sensory and non-affective episodes of conscious thought can count as having phenomenology in their own right, and not merely by virtue of being accompanied by sensory or affective phenomenology (including Flanagan, 1992; Goldman, 1993; Siewert, 1998; McCulloch, 1999; Peacocke, 1999; Horgan and Tienson, 2002; Pitt, 2004; Strawson, 2004; Klausen, 2008). On this view, when a subject consciously judges that p, or entertains an occurrent hope that p, there is something it is thereby like for that subject to do so, and what it is like depends (in part) on the type of the episode. By contrast, there is nothing it is like for a subject to engage in unconscious cognition regarding p.

This view can be illuminated with reference to the notion of a stream of phenomenal consciousness. As William James (1890) noted, there appears to be a unified stream of consciousness that plays host, not only to sensory episodes and states, but also to episodes and states in thought. The idea that there is such a unified stream, encompassing diverse kinds of episodes and states, is supported by the fact that thoughts and sensory perceptions seem to be able to compete with each other for occupation of the stream at a particular time. This occurs, as both James (1890) and Peacocke (1999) point out, via the mechanism of attention. You can, for example, be attending to some object via sensory perception, and then find your attention captured by a propositional content that occurs to you. Here, it seems that what has happened is aptly described in terms of what occurs within your stream of consciousness: the thinking of the propositional content displaces, or shifts to the background, the sensory awareness.

On the view of phenomenology that I am discussing, the goings-on in a subject's stream of consciousness contribute to (or perhaps exhaust) phenomenology—to what it is like for the subject. This applies equally to sensory, quasi-sensory, affective, and cognitive goings-on.[9]

Thus, we seem to have a conception of phenomenology that makes room for the idea of a proprietary phenomenology of conscious thoughts of various types.

There is reason to think that conscious thoughts do indeed have a proprietary phenomenology, when we conceive of phenomenology in this way, and that this proprietary phenomenology can make a difference to what is rational from the subject's point of view. Consider a subject who engages in an activity of conscious reasoning. Suppose the subject judges that p, and, inferring q from p, judges that q. The

---

[9] For a rich discussion of the relations between phenomenology, thought, and the stream of consciousness, not all of whose conclusions are friendly to the present proposal, see M. Soteriou (2007).

subject makes the latter judgement in part because the previous episode was one of judgement, and not some other type. The subject would not (we can suppose) have judged that q if she had merely supposed that p. This sensitivity, to whether we have judged or merely (say) supposed that p, is something that we all display effortlessly.[10] Now, conscious reasoning of this kind seems to be a case where the subject is doing what is rational from her own point of view. So it seems that the first episode's being, specifically, a judgement, makes a difference to what is rational from the subject's point of view. And it seems that it does so because it is a particular sort of occupant of the stream of consciousness. It is because the subject's stream of conscious thought contains an event characteristic of judging that it is rational from the subject's point of view to judge the content inferred from the content of that event.[11]

This contribution, on the part of a judgement, to what is rational from the subject's point of view, does not seem to depend on the subject's having some distinct higher-order awareness *of* the judgement as such, or on her making some higher-order judgement *about* that judgement. She need not, in arriving at the judgement that q, proceed via awareness or self-ascription of the judgement that p. She need only infer q from p. It is the conscious occurrence of the judgement that p, as such, that makes the judgement that q rational from the subject's point of view.

Similar points apply to other types of conscious episode. Subjects can engage in conscious reasoning from something that is supposed, something that is imagined, or something that is wished for. In each case, what is rational from the subject's point of view depends on the type of conscious episode or state the reasoning begins from.

I claim, then, that states and episodes in thought have non-sensory, non-imagistic, non-affective phenomenology, that this phenomenology often reflects the type of state or episode that is occurring, and that it makes a difference to what is rational from the subject's point of view.

We may of course find it difficult to *describe* the characteristic phenomenological differences between different types of state and episode. That doesn't mean there are no such differences. We find it hard to describe the phenomenological differences between itches and tickles. It may be that there is *no* informative description one could offer of the characteristic phenomenological difference between states of type T1 and states of type T2, beyond saying that it is the difference between what it is like to enjoy T1 and what it is like to enjoy T2 (Soteriou (2007) argues for a related claim). Again, that doesn't mean there is no difference. The same may be true of itches and tickles.

---

[10] A similar point is made by C. Peacocke (1999, p. 216).

[11] My intention here is not to draw an analogy with the case of self-ascription—self-ascriptions are not arrived at by inference—but rather to show that, even in the case of inference, where a relation between contents is playing the most salient role in the rationalizing relation, the occurrence in conscious thought of an event of a certain type is doing part of the rationalizing work and contributing to what is rational from the subject's point of view. This supports my claim that, in the non-inferential case, the occurrence in conscious thought of an event of a certain type can play a similar, albeit more salient role.

With this in mind, let me now address the two specific consequences that Coliva finds objectionable.

With respect to the first consequence, the question is whether our normal phenomenology is sufficiently differentiated to ground the discriminations we make in our ordinary self-knowledge—particularly discriminations between *types* of mental state and episode. The considerations above suggest that it is. Episodes such as judging and wishing occupy or have vehicles in the stream of consciousness. Their being of the types they are makes a difference to what is rational from the subject's point of view, via their contribution to phenomenology. That contribution is as differentiated as is required to explain self-knowledge in those cases where we have it.

Coliva denies that our normal phenomenology is differentiated in the right way. But, in the light of the foregoing, this just isn't compelling. Coliva gives no argument for her denial; and, furthermore, it appears to be based on an unnecessarily narrow notion of phenomenology.

The second supposedly implausible consequence of the account concerns deviant cases rather than normal ones. The consequence is that certain mistaken self-ascriptions will be rational, when intuitively they are irrational.

I think there is no problem for the account here, because the range of cases in which it must count mistaken self-ascriptions as rational is very narrow, and furthermore the account does not suggest that there is *no* irrationality or malfunction in such cases.

Consider a 'wishful thinking' case of the sort that Coliva describes, in which an occurrent hope that p is mistaken for a judgement that p (or some other manifestation of the belief that p). The self-ascription of the belief that p will be rationalized by the episode of hoping, according to the reasons account, *only* if that episode has the phenomenology characteristic of judging that p—only if what it is like for the subject to undergo the episode is just like what it is characteristically like for the subject to judge that p. What's more, the self-ascription will be all-things-considered rational only if there are no defeaters for it. Potential defeaters are not restricted to the phenomenology of the state or episode. For example, the subject must not be aware that she wants p to be true so much that she is liable to engage in wishful thinking, or be aware that the evidence in favour of the truth of p is far weaker than she would usually take to be conclusive, or be aware that she is not committed to the truth of p. If such defeaters are present, the self-ascription of belief will not be made rational by the episode of hoping.

Thus, the relevant case is one in which what occurs is genuinely not a judgement, but it is phenomenologically just like a judgement and no defeaters are present for the subject's self-ascription of belief. This is not at all like typical cases of wishful thinking; these are cases in which the phenomenology of hoping is present, or there are lots of defeaters for the self-ascription of belief, or the subject wants so much to believe p that she actually does bring herself to judge that p. Is it obvious that the *self-ascription itself* is irrational, in the unusual kind of case we have identified—where everything is, for the subject, just as though she is manifesting a belief, and she has no reason to doubt that she believes? It seems to me that it is not.

It might be insisted that there is *something* irrational, or some cognitive malfunction, occurring in these cases. This seems right—but that doesn't mean that the irrationality or malfunction is in the self-ascription. There will, presumably, be something abnormal going in the subject's first-order thought, bringing it about that she undergoes the misleading episode of hoping that *p*.

I conclude that Coliva's objection to the reasons account can be resisted.

5. Varieties of internalism

My aim thus far has been to to show that Coliva's considerations do not rule out the reasons account as a viable internalist account of self-knowledge, when that account is combined with a phenomenological conception of consciousness. But one might wish for some further positive explanation of how conscious states and episodes can give internalist reasons for self-knowledge.[12] Any further explanation will have to avoid Coliva's dilemma: it will have to portray conscious states and episodes as genuinely rationalizing the relevant self-ascriptions from the subject's point of view, without making illegitimate appeal to knowledge on the subject's part *of* those states and episodes. One might worry that no such explanation will be available. In the rest of this chapter I want to allay this worry by outlining such an explanation.

It is important to be clear on what it would be for an account to qualify as internalist. So let me step back and consider epistemological internalism as such.

The primary motivation for internalism is the thought that when a subject is warranted in believing *p*, her belief or judgement must be justified, or rational, or appropriate, *from her own point of view* (for certain kinds of warrant, at any rate). The internalist tries to capture this feature of warrant by drawing on a notion of accessibility: the subject's warrant must be accessible to her. A warrant that is accessible to the subject is a justification.[13] On this view, then, warrants are justifications.

What is it for a subject's justification to be accessible to her? There are at least two dimensions along which answers to this question can differ:

(i) What features of the subject's situation are accessible to her?
(ii) What is it for a feature to be accessible?

In response to (i), Jim Pryor has distinguished two positions that are found in the literature (Pryor, 2001, sect. 3.1; I paraphrase and alter the labels):

(Simple internalism)   The justified status of the justified belief supervenes on what is accessible to the subject.

---

[12] The need for such further explanation is discussed by Mike Martin (1998).
[13] See n. 1 above.

(Strong internalism)   The justified status of the justified belief is itself accessible to the subject.

A weaker claim is defended by William Alston (1988):

(Internalist externalism)   The presence of the justifier is accessible to the subject.

To illustrate: suppose that you believe it has rained for the reason given by seeing that the streets are wet,[14] and your belief is thereby justified.[15] In this case, the visual experience, or its content, or the fact or state of affairs it provides access to, is the justifier (justifying reason): it provides rationally justifying support for the belief that it has rained.[16] The essence of its rationalizing role is its providing truth-conducive support for the *content* of the belief. What is supported is the belief *that it has rained*, rather than a belief with some other content. And the support is a matter of the justifier's making it likely, in some sense, that the content is *true*.

Now, *internalist externalism* requires that the justifier is accessible to you. At the opposite extreme, *strong internalism* requires that your belief's being justified is itself accessible to you. That is, not only is the justifier accessible to you, but you have some access to its rationalizing role—to the fact that it rationally justifies your belief. This, presumably, will involve your having access to the connection between your reason and the content of your belief: you will have access to the fact that the justifier supports the content that it has rained, perhaps via an inductive connection between wet streets and rain. It will also involve access to the fact that this connection makes for a justified belief. This access is part of what makes your belief that it has rained justified, according to strong internalism. In the middle, *simple internalism* requires that your belief's being justified supervenes on what is accessible to you. This will involve access to the justifier and to the other features in virtue of which your belief is rationally justified—the inductive connection between wet streets and rain, for example—but need not involve any access on your part to the fact that your belief is thereby justified.

Suppose we are agreed about *which* features must be accessible to the subject—whether it is the presence of the justifying reason, the features on which the justificatory status supervenes, or the justificatory status itself. What *is it* for such a feature to be accessible? This is question (ii).[17]

---

[14] I focus on the case where the subject is justified by a reason. Perhaps there are other kinds of justifiers. I do not claim that the taxonomy of views I offer is exhaustive. It will do for my purposes.

[15] The example is adapted from W. P. Alston (1988).

[16] I leave open exactly what should be identified as the justifying reason. Even if it is the fact that the streets are wet that constitutes the justifying reason, that fact must be somehow accessible to the subject if it is to rationally justify the belief that it has rained. A full explanation of how that belief is justified will mention the visual experience that gives the subject access to that fact. The reasons account can accommodate more than one way of identifying reasons (see Section 2 above).

[17] Again, what I outline below does not exhaust possible notions of access. They are the ones that matter for my purposes. Nor do I claim that the two questions (i) and (ii) are completely independent. I will argue later that a certain version of strong internalism requires a strong conception of access.

The discussion from Section 4 above suggests one possible answer:

(P-access) The presence of the feature contributes internally to the subject's phenomenal consciousness or conscious contents.

A feature will be P-accessible when it shows up, is registered, or is manifested in phenomenal consciousness or conscious contents (i.e. contents that are tokened in consciousness, for example by being the contents of conscious thoughts).[18] In the former case, the feature's presence contributes to what it is like for the subject. This contribution is internal in the sense that it is not merely a causal factor (such as neural activity might be), but would enter into a constitutive specification of the subject's phenomenology.

Traditionally, many internalists have worked with a much stronger notion of access. For example, the following notion is explicitly at work in the classic discussion of Bonjour (1978):

(J-access) The subject has justification to believe that the feature is present.

As Bonjour, Alston, and others (including, perhaps, Agrippa) have pointed out, this conception of access as itself involving epistemic justification threatens to give rise to a regress problem, since it suggests that any justification will depend on a prior justification. One might therefore wish to find a notion of access less demanding than J-access, but still more so than P-access. Such a notion might appeal to some form of actual or potential *awareness* of the presence of a feature, or *grasp*, or *appreciation* that the feature is present, that can fall short of justification or belief, and therefore does not threaten a regress. Thus, roughly:

(A-access) The subject is aware of the feature or appreciates that the feature is present.

Here, 'awareness' and 'appreciation' can take the form of belief, including implicit belief, but also allow for non-doxastic or sub-doxastic phenomena. For example, an animal who lacks a rich conceptual repertoire might be said to be aware or appreciate that its prey is present, without possessing a full-fledged belief about the matter. The animal lacks the concepts to have a *de dicto* attitude to the relevant proposition. What it has is something like a non-conceptualized grasp of the fact that its prey is present. In some cases this may be a matter simply of perceptual awareness of the prey, together with some sort of categorization of it as such; in others it may persist in the absence of perceptual awareness. The appreciation may play a role in guiding the animal's behaviour. Similarly, it might be said, human action may sometimes be guided by non-conceptualized grasp of facts, rather than full-fledged beliefs (I will describe this in

---

[18] See n. 6 above.

more detail below). A feature of one's situation can guide one's action via one's A-access to it, rather than via J-access.

Note that one can be a pluralist about access. That is, one could hold that there is more than one legitimate notion of access, and different features can be accessible in different ways.

Let us go back to our example. Suppose we accept that your justifier—the experience as of the streets' being wet, or its content, or the fact that the streets are wet—must be accessible to you. We may claim that this access is P-access—that the justifier contributes to your phenomenology or conscious contents. Or, we may claim that it is A-accessible—you are aware of or appreciate the presence of the justifier. Or, we may claim that it is J-accessible—you have justification to believe that the justifier is present. Now suppose we accept that your justificatory status must also be accessible to you (that is, we accept strong internalism). Again, we will have to say which notion of access we have in mind. We may adopt a different notion of access for this feature.

I mentioned in Section 2 that we should prefer an internalist account of self-knowledge over an externalist one. An internalist account is one according to which the warrants for self-ascriptions are justifications accessible to the subject. But we can now see that there may be numerous varieties of internalism, as individuated by their positions along dimensions (i) and (ii).

6. Simple internalism and the reasons account

Where does all this leave the reasons account?

On question (ii), it seems clear that the defender of the reasons account must deploy the notion of P-access. The account claims that conscious states and episodes themselves typically give or constitute reasons. It is a minimal internalist commitment that reasons themselves are accessible; and, if what I have argued above (Sect. 4) is correct, conscious states and episodes (or the fact of one's enjoying them) are indeed typically P-accessible. Conscious states and episodes may be both A-accessible and J-accessible, but their being so can hardly be part of the *explanation* of how subjects know about them. A-access to a conscious state or episode just is the subject's appreciating or being aware that she is enjoying the state or episode; and J-access is her having justification to believe that she is enjoying it. To adopt either of these notions of access, in relation to the presence of conscious states and episodes, would lead towards the 'circularity' horn of our purported dilemma.[19]

---

[19] One way to escape this circularity would be to claim that conscious states and episodes are A-accessible in the sense that we have experiential higher-order awareness of them, rather than doxastic or sub-doxastic awareness. This would be to embrace an introspectionist account, and would be no more circular than the claim that perceptual beliefs are based on prior perceptual-experiential awareness. The reasons account (as I wish to develop it, at least), is not supposed to be introspectionist in this sense.

What about question (i)? One option for the reasons account would be to adopt simple internalism. The account claims that the mere presence of a conscious state or episode rationalizes the corresponding self-ascription. Nothing more than this is required as a supervenience base for the justified status of the self-ascription. After all, the presence of the state or episode provides truth-conducive support for the content of the self-ascription in a straightforward way: it is constitutively connected to its truth. The presence of the state or episode is P-accessible to the subject. So the justified status of the self-ascription will supervene on facts that are accessible to the subject. Thus, when we combine the reasons account with simple internalism and P-access, we have a way in which the reasons account can be understood as offering a genuinely internalist account of self-knowledge. We seem to have steered between the horns of the dilemma.

It might be objected that this solution fails to do justice to the motivation behind internalism. On this solution, we support the claim that conscious states and episodes can function as reasons for self-ascriptions simply by pointing out that those states and episodes (a) contribute sufficiently to conscious content and phenomenology, and (b) are constitutively connected to the truth of the corresponding self-ascriptions. It might be said that this combination is too weak to capture the requirement of *rationality from the subject's own point of view*. In particular, the fact that an aspect of the subject's phenomenology is constitutively connected to the truth of a certain self-ascription does not seem to ensure that the subject appreciates that truth-connection; it thus seems to be compatible with the self-ascription's being 'blind' in a way that the internalist finds objectionable.

Suppose this objection is right. What it seems to require is strong internalism. Let us see, then, if the reasons account can be combined with strong internalism.

7. Strong internalism and the reasons account

Strong internalism requires that the subject have access to the justificatory status of her justified belief. This will be achieved if the subject has access to the rationalizing role of her reason: to have access to the role of one's reason in rationalizing one's belief is *ipso facto* to have access to the rationally justified status of the belief. The rationalizing role of a reason is essentially a matter of its providing truth-conducive support for a proposition (i.e. the propositional content of the rationalized belief). Thus, access to the rationalizing role of one's reason will be achieved if one has access to the truth-conducive connection between one's reason and the content of the rationally justified belief. In sum, the requirement of strong internalism will be met if the subject has access to this truth-connection. Such access will surely make the justified belief rational from the subject's own point of view, and thus do justice to the motivation behind internalism.

But how is such access to be understood?

Any relation of truth-conducive support can be captured in a deductively, inductively, or abductively valid *inference* or *argument*—valid arguments just are articulations of truth-conducive support for propositions. A natural suggestion, then, is this: a subject has access to the rationalizing role of her reason when she is in a position such that she could (perhaps under certain ideal conditions of reflection) rehearse a justifying argument whose conclusion is the content of her justified belief, and one of whose premises is her reason (or states its presence).[20] This is one way of construing the strong internalist requirement. But it would be disastrous if applied to the reasons account of self-knowledge. The reasons account claims that the subject's reason is given by her conscious state or episode. On any natural understanding of what it is to rehearse a justifying argument, being in a position to do so requires a certain kind of access to the argument's premises: it requires that one be aware of the truth (or probable truth) of those premises. Thus, for a subject to be in a position such that she could rehearse a justifying argument, one of whose premises states the obtaining of a certain conscious state or episode, she would have to already be aware that that state or episode obtained. In other words, she would have to have A-access, if not J-access, to her conscious state or episode. (Here we see that the present answer to question (i) requires a certain answer to question (ii).) As I noted at the start of this section, the defender of the reasons account cannot accept a requirement of A-access or J-access to conscious states and episodes, on pain of circularity. So, on this version of strong internalism, the reasons account is indeed circular.

Indeed, this version of strong internalism is opposed to the fundamental tenets of the reasons account. It holds that rational support for beliefs consists in support by arguments that the subject could (ideally) rehearse. This kind of support is transmitted from contents, to contents. As we saw in Section 2, the reasons account claims that self-ascriptions are justified non-inferentially, and that their justification is not wholly explained in terms of relations between contents.

Should we conclude that the reasons account cannot be combined with strong internalism? I don't think so. I want to suggest that there is a less demanding way of understanding what it is for a subject to have access to the rationalizing, truth-conducive connection between her reason, R, and the content, p, of the belief it rationalizes, and thus to the justificatory status of that belief—a way that nevertheless captures the internalist requirement of rationality from the subject's point of view.

My claim is that there is a phenomenon of *non-theoretical sensitivity* to the truth-connection between features like R and propositions like p. This non-theoretical sensitivity does not involve access to an argument that could be offered for p. Rather, it involves a kind of practical grasp of the fact that features like R support the truth of propositions like p. This grasp does not require a full-fledged *belief* about R and p; the

---

[20] Something like this way of answering the question appears clearly in B. Brewer (1999, ch. 5), and is more or less explicit in the work of a number of classical internalist epistemologists, including K. Lehrer (1974) and L. Bonjour (1978).

subject may lack the concepts to have any belief about the support of R for *p*. Rather, it is a kind of capacity-constituting disposition to react to features like R in certain ways. It is not a mere disposition to react blindly to features like R with some specific range of behaviours, but rather a flexible disposition, with an open-ended range of possible manifestations in different circumstances, involving sensitivity to defeaters, and constitutive of the subject's grasp of what it is for *p* to be true. In this way (as I will elaborate below) it amounts to a practical grasp, a sub-doxastic appreciation of the truth-connection between R and *p*, and thus of the role of R in rationally justifying the belief in *p*. And thus it amounts to A-access to the justified status of that belief. Thus, when a subject's believing *p* for reason R is a manifestation of this sensitivity, the subject meets the requirement of strong internalism.

Note that 'sub-doxastic' does not mean subpersonal. It is the subject herself who grasps the truth-connection—albeit not in the first place at the level of belief and justification, but in a practical way.

I want to suggest that our self-ascriptions of conscious states and episodes meet the strong internalist requirement in just this way, and that the reasons account can therefore be combined even with a strong internalist epistemology.

In order to develop this notion of non-theoretical sensitivity to a truth-connection, I want to look briefly at the case of colour judgements. This will also help to bring out that the notion of non-theoretical sensitivity may have broad application in epistemology, going well beyond the domain of self-knowledge.

We make colour judgements on the basis of the colour appearances presented by objects.[21] There is a truth-conducive connection between colour appearances of objects and propositions about the colours of those objects: colour appearances tend, in appropriate circumstances, to make certain such propositions likely to be true. An object's appearing red in normal conditions makes it likely that it *is* red. Its appearing red thus constitutes a reason to believe that it is red.

Normally, when a subject judges or believes that an object is red on the basis of its appearance, she manifests a certain sensitivity to that truth-connection. This sensitivity involves a disposition to make certain judgements—both colour judgements and other judgements to which colours are relevant—and to behave in an open-ended range of other colour-discriminating ways, in response to colour appearances. Colour judgements are a relatively sophisticated exercise of this sensitivity. The disposition to make such judgements is partly grounded in a more basic ability to respond differentially to differently coloured objects on the basis of their appearances.

This overall disposition, or family of dispositions, including both the judgements and the more basic behaviours, is not a *mere* disposition (or family thereof). It is an *ability* or

---

[21] Strictly, it doesn't matter whether what I offer here is a correct account of colour judgements. I want to use the account to clarify and illustrate my claims about self-knowledge. What matters is whether the notion of non-theoretical sensitivity to a truth-connection *can* play the sort of role I attribute to it. The account I offer draws on Peacocke's account of concept-possession (Peacocke 1992).

cognitive *capacity* of the subject that contributes to the repertoire of ways in which she can represent, respond to, and act on the world. It involves much more than merely being responsive to certain stimuli. Our colour judgements, and other colour-discriminating behaviours, are not mere reactions to colour appearances. We take colour appearances to indicate colour properties, but we are also sensitive to the nature of that connection. We treat an object as having the same colour even though its appearance differs in different lighting conditions. We refuse to make colour judgements, or rely in other ways on colour appearances, when we know the lighting conditions to be abnormal, or when we have reason to think we are not perceiving properly. Our dispositions to make and withhold colour judgements, and to make colour discriminations below the level of judgement, constitute sensitivity to the connections between colour appearances, lighting conditions, perceptual abilities, and the identity conditions for colours.

This capacity is, plausibly, partly constitutive of possession of the *concepts* of the various colours. If a subject did not have the capacity to sort red things from others, and were not willing to judge that objects are red when they present red appearances in appropriate conditions, but also prepared to withhold judgement in abnormal conditions or in the presence of defeaters, she could not be said to possess the concept *red*.

Thus, the capacity amounts to a more or less full-fledged grasp of *truth*-conditions. When the capacity reaches the level of possession of concepts of colours, the subject grasps what it is for propositions about the colours of objects to be true.

Having such a capacity can contribute to what is rational from a subject's point of view. For a subject who has such a capacity, colour appearances can rationalize certain judgements and behaviours. But the capacity is not a *source* of reasons for the subject. It is not a store of *propositions* that the subject grasps, and that provide inferential support for the subject's colour judgements. Having the capacity does *not* require grasping, at the level of belief, a *theory* of colour—of the relation between colour appearances, lighting conditions, perceptual abilities, and the identity conditions for colours. Very many subjects have this capacity, and make appropriate colour judgements, without having a grasp of any such theory. The capacity is practical: to have the capacity is to have certain abilities that amount to a practical grasp of the connection between colour appearances and the colours of objects. The presence of the capacity provides a *context* in which certain judgements and actions are rationalized for the subject. When you make a colour judgement on the basis of a colour appearance, your sensitivity to the connection between colour appearances and colours is not a *further* reason for your judgement, but rather a context in which the colour appearance can potentially rationalize your making that judgement. More generally, possession of a concept provides a context in which certain applications of the concept are rationalized. Your understanding of what it is to be a chair (which may not involve grasping any definition of what a chair is) provides a context in which seeing an object as having certain properties can rationalize your categorizing it as a chair.

Why can such a capacity contribute to what is rational for a subject? Presumably, because of its connection to truth. Suppose you judge p on the basis of reason R, and in doing so exercise a disposition constitutive of a capacity of the sort I have been discussing. In that case, you are exercising your grasp of what it is for p to be true. In particular, you are exercising a non-theoretical grasp that p is likely to be true in the presence of R. Thus, in judging in this way, you are doing what is rational from your own point of view.

It seems that a capacity of the sort I have been discussing constitutes a kind of sub-doxastic appreciation of a truth-connection. I claim, then, that when you exercise such a capacity by judging that p on the basis of reason R, you exercise an appreciation of the truth-connection between R and p, and thus of the rationalizing role of R. This amounts to an appreciation of the rationally justified status of your belief in p. It thereby constitutes A-access to that justified status. The relevant kind of access is not J-access, because having the capacity does not require a grasp, at the level of belief or justification, of some facts that would provide inferential support for the justified belief. Rather, it is a practical grasp of the rationalization of the belief—the kind of grasp that underwrites A-access. Having and exercising such a capacity can thereby contribute to your meeting the strong internalist requirement, without involving any grasp of an argument for your belief.

This account of how a subject can meet the strong internalist requirement, without having access to an argument, has appealed to the following putative features of colour judgements:

(a) They are made for reasons.
(b) There is a truth-connection between the reason (an object's appearing a certain colour) and the proposition judged (that the object is a certain colour).
(c) The judgement manifests one of a family of dispositions to respond to the reason-constituting features in a way that requires attribution of non-theoretical sensitivity to that truth-connection, rather than a simple tendency to respond to those features blindly.
(d) The dispositions constitute a cognitive capacity that, in the case of the subject who judges, amounts to possession of certain concepts, and thus to a grasp of what it is for the judgements to be true.

When conditions (a)–(d) are met, I claim, judgements of the relevant kind will be exercises of the subject's appreciation of the truth-connection that rationalizes them, and will thus be accompanied by A-access to their justificatory status.

I want to argue that self-ascriptions of conscious states and episodes, when made in the usual way, also possess these features:

(a) Self-ascriptions are made for the reasons given or constituted by conscious states and episodes.
(b) There is a truth-connection between these reasons and the self-ascriptions.

(c) Self-ascriptions that respond to conscious states and episodes manifest one of a family of dispositions that requires attribution of non-theoretical sensitivity to that truth-connection.

(d) The dispositions constitute a cognitive capacity of self-consciousness, that, in the case of the subject who makes self-ascriptive judgements, amounts to possession of the concepts of the first person and of the self-ascribed states, and thus to a grasp of what it is for the self-ascriptions to be true.

Thus, I claim, we have A-access to the justificatory status of our ordinary self-ascriptions, just as we do to the justificatory status of our ordinary colour judgements.

That condition (a) obtains is a central claim of the reasons account. These reasons are P-accessible, I have been claiming.

Condition (b) obtains straightforwardly. When you self-ascribe the reason-giving state or episode itself, the truth-connection is that the presence of the reason makes the self-ascription true. In other cases, the connection is slightly more complex. For example, when you self-ascribe the belief that *p* for the reason given by your judging that *p*, the reason-constituting feature manifests or initiates the state of affairs that makes the self-ascription true.

The claim in (c) is that when a subject makes a self-ascription on the basis of her phenomenologically manifested state or episode, she is manifesting a sensitivity to the connection between her current phenomenology and the truth of certain self-ascriptions. Her self-ascription is not a mere blind reaction.

Evidence for the existence of such a sensitivity will come from the subject's disposition to respond to defeaters. Recall the 'misleading phenomenology' cases that we considered in Section 4 above. These are cases in which a subject has the phenomenology characteristic of, say, judging that *p*, when in fact her episode is one of occurrently hoping. As mentioned in Section 4, there may be defeaters of various kinds for the rationalization of a self-ascription of belief. We are indeed sensitive to such defeaters. In such a case, you might well realize that you do not really believe that *p*.

This sensitivity can also be seen in behavioural dispositions that do not involve full-fledged judgement or belief. Some of these dispositions have been discussed in the neo-Kantian tradition of thought about self-consciousness.[22] Consider the phenomenon, much discussed recently (cf. Ellan et. al. 2005), of joint attention. Infants within their first year can not only recognize pointing as a cue for directing their attention to something, but will also look back to the person pointing, apparently seeking feedback on whether they have identified the right target (cf. Bruner 1975; Newson and Newson 1975; Murphy and Messner 1977). What's more, infants will themselves attempt to establish a focus of joint attention, getting the other person to attend to whatever they are attending to (Leung and Rheingold 1981). These behaviours seem

---

[22] I have in mind particularly G. Strawson (1959); G. Evans (1982); J. Campbell (1994); and J. L. Bermudez (1994).

clearly to involve some non-theoretical appreciation on the infant's part of her position as a subject, and of the significance of what she is occurrently given for facts about her *qua* subject—facts that she wishes the other person to recognize.[23]

A more primitive form of this appreciation seems to be manifested in certain navigational behaviours. Chimpanzees and dogs have been shown to be able to devise efficient, novel routes to locations that have been previously visited but that are not visible from the animal's starting location (cf. Menzel 1973; Chapuis and Varlet 1987). This form of navigation requires the animal to represent a region of space, to represent itself as an object among others located at certain points in that space, and to use its current experience as a basis for representing which particular location it occupies. This, in turn, embodies an appreciation on the animal's part that what it experiences can depend simultaneously on facts about the world—how things are at a certain spatiotemporal location—and on facts about itself—her being at that location (cf. Evans 1982; Bermudez 1998, chs. 7, 8; Campbell 1994).[24]

The self-consciousness exhibited by these kinds of behaviours seems to involve a primitive form of sensitivity to the connection between what is given to consciousness and certain facts about oneself. It thus seems to be a primitive form of the sensitivity that is exhibited in more sophisticated form by self-knowing subjects.

The sensitivity in question is practical; it does not involve grasp of a theory. Subjects capable of self-knowledge do not typically possess some theory, in the form of a store of propositions that could be offered as providing inferential support for their self-ascriptions. Far less do subjects who lack the conceptual repertoire to make full-fledged self-ascriptive judgements possess such a theory. Nevertheless, this sensitivity is not a blind disposition to behave in specific ways in response to certain stimuli. It is a flexible disposition, manifested in an open-ended range of ways, and, in its more sophisticated form, involving sensitivity to defeaters. In its more sophisticated form it thus constitutes a practical grasp of the connection between what is accessible in current consciousness and facts about oneself. Such a practical grasp, like that involved in the case of colour judgements discussed above, is apt to contribute to what is rational for a subject by providing a context in which certain actions and judgements are rationalized, not by providing further reasons for those actions and judgements.

I turn to condition (d). The idea here is that the family of dispositions just discussed are a constitutive ground of possession of the concepts involved in self-ascriptions, and thus of a grasp of what it is for those self-ascriptions to be true. That is, the more basic forms of self-consciousness ground the full-fledged conceptual self-consciousness and self-knowledge that is manifested by self-ascriptions.[25]

---

[23] J. L. Bermudez (1994, ch. 9) discusses this in some detail.
[24] See also C. Peacocke (1983) on perspectival sensitivity.
[25] The defence of this kind of thesis is one of the main concerns of J. L. Bermudez (1994).

Willingness to self-ascribe certain types of state when you are in them is, very plausibly, partly constitutive of possession of the concepts of those types of state.[26] For example, a subject will not count as possessing the concept of belief if she is not disposed to apply it to herself when she makes a judgement. These self-ascriptions will also, I suggest, constitute a canonical use of the first-person concept. A subject with conceptual self-consciousness will be willing to self-ascribe conscious states and episodes, and corresponding attitudes, when she enjoys them, in so far as she possesses the other concepts that are involved in the relevant self-ascriptions. If she is not so willing, we will question whether she genuinely possesses conceptual self-consciousness. Thus, ordinary self-ascriptions are themselves a basic exercise of the subject's grasp of what it is for those self-ascriptions to be true, and in particular of the subject's non-theoretical grasp of the connection between phenomenology and the truth of those self-ascriptions.

In making such a self-ascription for the relevant reason, a subject exercises an appreciation that the self-ascription is likely to be true, given: the presence of the reason (to which she has P-access), what it is for the self-ascription to be true, and the connection between these two things. This amounts to an appreciation of the reason's rationalizing role, and thus of the justified status of the self-ascriptive belief. It is A-access to the justified status of the self-ascription. It does not involve access, at the level of belief or justification, to a theory or an argument; there is no threat of circularity for the reasons account. Thus, we have here a way in which a self-ascription, made for the reason provided by a conscious state or episode, can meet the requirement of strong internalism.

In Section 6 above, I worried that the view proposed there would not really deserve the name of internalism, since it did not seem to meet the requirement of rationality from the subject's own point of view. Is the account I have just offered subject to the same worry? I don't think so. Although reliability plays a role in the account (the dispositions I have discussed plausibly must be reliable), it is not a reliabilist account, since far more than reliability is required. Nor is it an internalist externalist or simple internalist account. These views involve no requirement that the subject have access to the justified status of her justified belief. What I have been arguing is that there is a form of A-access to the justified status of self-ascriptions, and that this form of access arises from a non-theoretical grasp or appreciation of the truth-connection between goings-on in consciousness and facts about oneself. This practical grasp is constituted by a disposition that is not blind, but is flexible, has an open-ended range of manifestations, involves sensitivity to defeaters, and is constitutive of possession of the concepts involved in the self-ascription, and thus of the subject's grasp of what it is for the self-ascription to be true.

---

[26] Again, I am drawing here on the work of C. Peacocke (2008).

The suggestion is that self-ascriptions are rational from the subject's point of view because they are exercises of this grasp. Self-ascriptions, when based on the reasons given by conscious states and episodes, will exhibit a kind of ground-level rationality, on this account. They will not be susceptible to justification by *further* reasons. But they will nevertheless be rational from the subject's point of view. Compare colour judgements based on colour appearances. Such judgements exhibit a kind of ground-level rationality. Subjects need not be able to offer any further justification for basing colour judgements on colour appearances. But such judgements, which are (I have claimed) exercises of a practical grasp of the connection between colour appearances and the truth of propositions about the colours of objects, are nonetheless rational from the subject's point of view. In the case of colour judgements, the subject exhibits sensitivity to the connection between the visually apparent instantiation of a property in the world and the truth of a certain application of a colour concept. In the case of self-ascriptions, the subject exhibits sensitivity to the connection between a type of occurrence in consciousness and the truth of a self-ascription.

It might be said that this does not count as internalism because there is no role for a higher-order *belief* about one's justifier or one's justification. The reasons account cannot be reconciled with internalism in this narrow sense, as I noted at the start of this section. But that is no great loss. The interesting category is that of theories that attempt to capture a requirement of rationality from the subject's point of view by appeal to a notion of access to one's own justification. This is what sets apart theories that fall within the internalist camp from those that do not. Within that category, various further distinctions can be made, as I have tried to demonstrate.

I have argued that the reasons account can be defended if one is prepared to accept that access to reasons can be mere P-access, rather than A-access or J-access. This is *not* to deny that you can have A-access or J-access to your conscious mental states and episodes; nor is it to deny that you can grasp arguments that articulate the justification for your self-ascriptions, or reflect on that justification. What I deny is that such access, or grasp of such an argument, is part of what makes your self-ascription justified in the first place. That is: once you know about a conscious state or episode, you will have A-access and J-access to it, and you will be able to formulate and reflect on an argument for your self-ascription. You can thereby attain a kind of self-knowledge that meets even the most demanding internalist requirements. But you can do so only because you have a prior ability to acquire self-knowledge in the less demanding, but nevertheless strongly internalist, way I have described.

8. Conclusion

I have considered an important challenge to the reasons account as an internalist account of self-knowledge. How one responds to the challenge will depend on the exact version of epistemological internalism about self-knowledge one endorses. I have argued that the challenge can be met in the context of simple internalism, and even in the context of strong internalism. The version of strong internalism I outlined promises to have application in the epistemology of other forms of knowledge, besides self-knowledge.[27]

References

Alston, W. P. 1988 "An Internalist Externalism", *Synthese* 74, 265–83.
Bermudez, J. L. 1998 *The Paradox of Self-Consciousness*, Cambridge (Mass.), MIT Press.
Bonjour, L. 1978 "Can Empirical Knowledge Have a Foundation?", *American Philosophical Quarterly* 15, 1–13.
Brewer, B. 1999 *Perception and Reason*, Oxford, Oxford University Press.
Bruner, J. S. 1975 "The Ontogenesis of Speech Acts", *Journal of Child Language* 2, 1–19.
Burge, T. 1993 "Content Preservation", *The Philosophical Review* 102, 457–88.
Campbell, J. 1994 *Past, Space, and Self*, Cambridge (Mass.), MIT Press.
Chapuis, N. and Varlet, C. 1987 "Shortcuts by Dogs in Natural Surroundings", *Quarterly Journal of Experimental Psychology* 39, 49–64.
Coliva, A. 2008 "Peacocke's Self-Knowledge", *Ratio* (New Series) 21, 13–27.
Eilan, N., Hoerl, C., McCormack, T., and Roessler, J. (eds.) 2005 *Joint Attention: Communication and Other Minds*, Oxford, Oxford University Press.
Evans, G. 1982 *The Varieties of Reference*, Oxford, Clarendon Press.
Flanagan, O. 1992 *Consciousness Regained*, Cambridge (Mass.), MIT Press.
Goldman, A. 1993 "The Psychology of Folk Psychology", *Behavioral and Brain Sciences* 16, 15–28.
Horgan, T. and Tienson, J. 2002 "The Phenomenology of Intentionality and the Intentionality of Phenomenology", in D. Chalmers (ed.) *Philosophy of Mind: Classical and Contemporary Readings*, Oxford, Oxford University Press, 520–33.
James, W. 1890 *The Principles of Psychology*, New York, Holt.
Klausen, S. H. 2008 "The Phenomenology of Propositional Attitudes", *Phenomenology and the Cognitive Sciences* 7, 445–62.
Lehrer, K. 1974 *Knowledge*, Oxford, Clarendon Press.
Leung, E. and Rheingold, H. 1981 "Development of Pointing as a Social Gesture", *Developmental Psychology* 17, 215–20.
McCulloch, G. 1999 "Bipartism and the Phenomenology of Content", *Philosophical Quarterly* 49, 18–32.
Martin, M. G. F. 1998 "An Eye Directed Outward", in C. Wright, B. Smith, and C. Macdonald (eds.) *Knowing Our Own Minds*, Oxford, Oxford University Press, 1998, 99–121.
Menzel, E. W. 1973 "Chimpanzee Spatial Memory Organization", *Science* 182, 943–5.

---

[27] Thanks to Annalisa Coliva, Adrian Haddock, Matthew Nudds, Jesper Kallestrup, Duncan Pritchard, and two readers for OUP. The chapter has benefited from the contributions of audiences at Edinburgh, Aberdeen, and Geneva, and especially from the contributions of Gerry Hough and Julien Dutant. The preparation of this chapter was supported by the Agence nationale de la recherche, under the contract ANR-08.BLAN-0205-01.

Murphy, C. M. and Messner, D. J. 1977 "Mothers, Infants, and Pointing: A Study of a Gesture", in H. R. Schaffer (ed.) *Studies in Mother-Infant Interaction*, London, Academic Press, 325–54.

Newson, J. and Newson, E. 1975 "Intersubjectivity and the Transmission of Culture", *Bulletin of the British Psychological Society* 28, 437–45.

O'Brien, L. 2007 *Self-Knowing Agents*, Oxford, Oxford University Press.

Peacocke, C. 1983 *Sense and Content: Experience, Thought and their Relations*, Oxford, Clarendon Press.

—— 1992 *A Study of Concepts*, Cambridge (Mass.), MIT Press.

—— 1998 "Conscious Attitudes, Attention and Self-Knowledge", in C. Wright, B. Smith, and C. Macdonald (eds.) *Knowing Our Own Minds*, Oxford, Oxford University Press, 63–98.

—— 1999 *Being Known*, Oxford, Oxford University Press.

—— 2008 *Truly Understood*, Oxford, Oxford University Press.

Pitt, D. 2004 "The Phenomenology of Cognition, or What Is It Like To Think That P?", *Philosophy and Phenomenological Research* 69, 1–36.

Prinz, J. 2002 *Furnishing the Mind: Concepts and Their Perceptual Basis*, Cambridge (Mass.), MIT Press.

Pryor, J. 2001 "Highlights of Recent Epistemology", *British Journal for the Philosophy of Science* 52, 95–124.

Siewert, C. P. 1998 *The Significance of Consciousness*, Princeton (N. J.), Princeton University Press.

Soteriou, M. 2007 "Content and the Stream of Consciousness", *Philosophical Perspectives* 21/1, 543–68.

Strawson, G. J. 2004 *Mental Reality*, Cambridge (Mass.), MIT Press.

Strawson, P. F. 1959 *Individuals: An Essay in Descriptive Metaphysics*, London, Methuen.

7
Knowledge of Actions and Tryings[1]

Lucy O'Brien

1. Introduction

A background motivation to this chapter is to try to understand what philosophers who believe in them, and their ubiquity, believe that tryings are, and how they understand what explanatory role they are supposed to have. I am skeptical that there are tryings, understood as personal level mental kinds involved in all actions. My suspicion is that tryings understood in that way are philosophical creations designed to soak up the problems we do not know how to solve, picking up the explanatory burden that more familiar mental phenomenon are supposed not to be able to bear.

However, my immediate concern, and the one that this chapter will be focused on, is the question of the extent to which an appeal to trying is helpful in our attempts to explain our knowledge of our actions. To this end I will consider two models for knowing our actions that centre on tryings. I will argue that if we allow that there are mental actions, there are problems with both models. If we think there are mental actions, we are, I argue, going to have to give an account of our knowledge of them that does not appeal to trying. So, if we hope to give an account of our knowledge of our actions which is uniform across mental and physical cases, we have reason to avoid appealing to tryings in our attempt to do so.

So, what are the two models? The first aims to account for our knowledge of our actions via our knowledge of our tryings.[2] The second is Peacocke's recent account,

---

[1] Many thanks to Annalisa Coliva and Gianfranco Soldati for organizing and inspiring the ongoing Self-knowledge and Self project out of which this volume grew. I have learnt a tremendous amount from Annalisa and Gianfranco, as well as Dorit Bar-On, Akeel Bilgrami, John Campbell, Fabian Dorsch, Chris Peacocke, Jim Pryor, Carol Rovane, Paul Snowdon, Martine Nida-Ruemelin, Barry Smith, and Crispin Wright. This chapter was started a long time before it was finished; but before finishing it I ran a graduate class at UCL on 'Mental Actions'. Thanks are due to the terrific students who helped me to get clearer about these issues. Particular thanks also to Matt Soteriou for talk about these matters over a period, and also to Chris Peacocke for comments on this chapter.

[2] Who subscribes to the first model? Perhaps nobody accepts it in quite this simple form. However, theorists like J. Hornsby (1980) and B. O'Shaughnessy (1980) who appeal to tryings are committed to something like it. In particular, both need to hold that our knowledge that we acted is dependent on our

which aims to account for our knowledge of our actions in terms of a form of awareness of our actions, where tryings are taken to be the joint cause of the action and the awareness of the action. My knowledge of my actions on the two models can be set out roughly as follows:

> Model 1. I try to act. My trying causes an action. I know what I tried to do. I know that my tryings cause my actions. Therefore, I know that and how I acted.
> Model 2. I tried to act. My trying causes my action. My trying causes action awareness. I know that, and how I acted, in virtue of my action awareness.

2. Knowing our actions in virtue of knowing our tryings

I do not think that Model 1 can be right. The argument will go via a consideration of what account to give of our knowledge of our mental actions. I argue that the account embodied in Model 1 does not work for our knowledge of our mental actions and, if we want an account of our knowledge of our actions that is uniform across mental and physical actions then we must give up the claim that we know our actions by knowing our tryings.

At first blush, the hypothesis that there are tryings which are the causal antecedents of the movements of our bodies when we act, seems to serve two useful functions in our epistemology of actions. It can explain both our knowledge of our action and our failures of knowledge:

1. We can know that our bodies moved in a certain way, by knowing that we tried to move our bodies in that way, and that we are entitled to take our bodies as functioning normally.
2. When we think we have acted in a certain way, but have in fact failed to, our thought can be explained by the fact that we tried to act in that way.

More precisely, we can make the following two claims:

> Claim 1. If ϕ-ing is an action and A knows that she ϕ-ed, she knows by knowing that she tried to ϕ.
> Claim 2. If A thinks that she ϕ-ed, but due to some failure did not ϕ, her thought is usually explained by her knowing that she tried to ϕ.

---

knowledge that we tried. Given that O'Shaughnessy has a metaphysical view on which tryings extend to include what they cause, it is slightly deceptive to say only that he takes tryings to cause actions—they cause the action they become. Hornsby's view that the action *just* is the trying which causes a movement of the body means she does not hold, as Model 1 does, that the trying causes the action—rather it causes a movement of the body. Nevertheless, knowledge that I raised by arm, does on her view rest on knowledge that I tried to raise my arm in a context in which I have reason to hold that my arm thereby rose.

2.1 The regress problem

It is not difficult to show that a regress problem emerges from a consideration of Claim 1 if we allow that there are mental actions. It follows from Claim 1 that if ϕ-ing is an action and if A knows that she is ϕ-ing, then A knows that she tried to ϕ. If on a given occasion ϕ-ing is a mental action and A knows that she is ϕ-ing, then on the reasonable assumption that trying to ϕ must be something we do and as such also a mental action, we are able to get a regress.

We can set out the argument like this:

1. For all x, if x is an action, and A knows that she x's, then A knows that she tried to x. (A)
2. ϕ-ing is a mental action. (A)
3. A knows that she is ϕ-ing. (A)
4. For all x, such that x is an action, trying to x is a mental action. (A)
5. A knows that she tried to ϕ. (from 1, 2, and 3)
6. Trying to ϕ is a mental action. (from 2 and 4)
7. A knows that she tried to try to ϕ. (from 1, 5, and 6)
8. Trying to try to ϕ is a mental action. (4, 6)
9. A knows that she tried to try to try to ϕ. (from 1, 7, and 8)

and so on...

There is a tendency in action theory that appeals to tryings, not to worry much about regress problems. I suspect that this is partly because they will so obviously arise: after all if we require tryings for all actions, and tryings are themselves actions, then they must themselves require tryings, and so on. So, appealing to tryings as things we do when we act was always going to require treating them as a special case if we were not to face a regress. Similarly, if we are going to appeal to knowledge of tryings to explain knowledge of action, and hold tryings to be actions, then it looks like we are going to have to treat knowledge of tryings as a special case. However, the familiarity and clear recognition of a problem does not in itself make the problem go away. We need either to be shown that the problem can be dispensed with, or need some developed explanation of what it is about tryings that means we are entitled to take them, and in particular our knowledge of them, as a special case.

Faced with the regress, the theorist who appeals to our knowledge of our tryings to explain knowledge of our actions must choose between the following four options:

(i) Accept the regress.
(ii) Deny that there are any mental actions.
(iii) Deny that tryings are mental actions.
(iv) Revise Claim 1.

The first option, accepting the regress, seems pretty much out of the question in this case. The option involves accepting not just that there is an infinity of knowledge states which may be open to a dispositional construal, making it acceptable.[3] Rather, it involves accepting an infinity of mental actions—tryings—the postulation of each one being required to explain our knowledge of the one before. Since, I take it, we think of mental actions as temporally located and extended events, requiring the efforts of a finite agent, we would be hard put to explain how a subject could carry out an infinite number of tryings in a limited time. It seems clear that in this case the cost of accepting the regress is far greater than the cost of revising our account of our knowledge of our mental actions.

The second option, denying that there are mental actions, seems unattractive, primarily because there seem to be relatively unproblematic examples of mental action. Consider my imagining that I am now raising my arm, or my supposing that tryings are mental actions. However, if we want to give a uniform account of our knowledge of our actions, and face a problem in extending our account to mental actions, then one possibility is indeed to deny that there are, contrary to how it seems, any mental actions to worry about. But note that the account of our knowledge of our actions invokes tryings as the basis of our knowledge of our physical actions. It, therefore, owes us a construal of tryings on which they *do not* come out as mental actions, but on which they *are* nevertheless a plausible basis as causes of, and sources of our knowledge of, our actions. It is hard to see how they can serve as the active source of our physical actions without being actions themselves—and accessible actions at that. If this is right then the third option, which involves giving up the narrower claim that tryings are mental actions is equally problematic.

Although I do not accept that we know our actions by knowing our tryings, such attraction the view does have must surely lie in the fact that we tend to see tryings as the accessible aspect, or component, of the action known. If we deny that tryings are actions in themselves, the knowledge of which requires an account, then I do not see that they will plausibly be seen as the basis of our physical actions, and so as the basis of our knowledge of our physical actions. I, in fact, deny that there are tryings whenever there are actions. Thus there is a class of putatively basic mental action that I would be sympathetic to viewing as small, if not empty. So, to that extent, I am sympathetic to the move of blocking the argument by denying that there are mental actions in the problematic class. However, obviously, that is not a move that the defender of the view that we know our actions by knowing our tryings can hold.

Our fourth option is to give up Claim 1. We can do this in two ways. One, we can keep the basic schema for knowledge of some actions, but give up the ambition of providing a uniform account of our knowledge of all our actions. Or two, we can give up the idea that we know our actions by knowing our tryings.

---

[3] I have in mind the kind of construals one sees in accounts of the infinite hierarchies hypothesized in discussions of common knowledge.

If we choose the first option we can do it either by making our knowledge of tryings a special case, or by holding that Claim 1 should apply only to physical actions—and that mental actions will require a different account.

The latter might seem a desirable move. Our physical actions—it might be said—involves the movements of our bodies, which themselves depend upon the proper workings of our motor systems which are independent of our capacity to try to act. Our mental actions are, in contrast, internal events that are autonomous in relation to the movements of our bodies. Given this we should expect, indeed seek, a different account of our knowledge of our mental and physical actions.

However, this description misconstrues things slightly. As will emerge later in the paper there do indeed seem to be mental actions for which the model applied to the standard case of physical actions seems quite wrong. However, this is not because the operations of the mind are not dependent upon the proper working of our physical hardware. The causal routes may be shorter and more secure in the case of mental actions, but we do not have a reason just on the basis of them being mental to think that there might to be failures between initiation and execution. I may decide to look out for my friend at a party and fail due to some visual disturbance to spot him. I may set about working out the sum of $25 + 33 + 47$, and through some kind of misfiring come up with 62. If there are successful mental actions that required some event as their successful completion, then they also depend on the physical hardware functioning normally.

This suggests that we ought to consider the option of treating knowledge of tryings as a special case—that while knowledge of other mental actions depends upon my knowledge of what I am trying to do, that knowledge needs to be explained in quite another way. However, what is that way to be? If there is no way given, we are left with a mystery. And if there is a successful explanation of how we know our tryings that does not appeal to knowledge of prior tryings, we ought to wonder why such a model doesn't apply to our explanation of our knowledge of actions, or at least knowledge of our mental actions, quite generally.

It seems that problems faced by this way of appealing to trying in our account of our knowledge of our actions gives us good reason to look for alternatives.

3. Knowing our actions in virtue of action awareness caused by tryings

According to the second model of what role tryings play in our account of our knowledge of our actions, our knowledge is based on my action awareness that is caused by the trying that also causes the action: I try to act. My trying causes my action. My trying causes action awareness. I know how I acted in virtue of my action awareness.

Two different versions of this model can be identified depending upon how you cash out the 'in virtue of' in the statement of the account.

3.1 The judgement dependent version of Model 2

According to this version of Model 2, our knowledge of our actions is based on action awareness and a judgement that action awareness is most easily, or most likely, explained by there being a corresponding action, given the function of the trying which is their usual joint causes. Although this is not his view, Peacocke occasionally sounds as though he has something like this in mind. He says, for example, "in taking action awareness at face value one is judging that things have come about in what is in fact the easiest way for them to come about..." (Peacocke 2009, 202).

I take it that he means here that when a subject takes action awareness at face value they judge that they have acted thus and so, and acting thus and so is in fact the easiest way for the action awareness to have come about. Although the judgement dependent view is not Peacocke's view, it seems to me to be worthwhile identifying it, if only to set it aside. The view that in order to know their actions the subject must in some way infer that they have acted from the most likely causes and effects of their action awareness is pretty implausible—we do not, and do not seem to need to, make judgements about the easiest or most probable causes of our action awareness in order to know that we have acted. A subject's knowledge of their actions seems immediate and not to be dependent upon them making judgements about what is easy or probable, even if it is true that they have the knowledge that they do in virtue of what is the easiest or most probable explanation of their having the awareness that they have.

3.2 Peacocke's immediate entitlement version of Model 2

According to Peacocke 'the distinctive way in which a subject comes to know of his own mental actions is by taking an apparent actions awareness at face value' (Peacocke 2009, 193). He holds that we have an immediate entitlement to take such awareness at face value, and that we know our actions by so taking it. Further, our account of our knowledge of mental and physical actions is *uniform*. We know our actions (both mental and physical) by taking apparent action awareness at face value. Apparent action awareness for Peacocke is:

   (i) belief independent,
   (ii) not perceptual awareness,
   (iii) independent of any perception of the action of which it is action awareness of
   (iv) such that actions are independent of it,
   (v) and can occur independently of an action.

For Peacocke, taking apparent action awareness (real or merely apparent) at face value gives us knowledge of our actions because it is caused by an initial trying. The initial trying causes the action of which, when it is real, the action awareness is awareness of.

It is in virtue of the fact that the action and action awareness are joint effects of the trying that taking the action awareness at face value gives you the knowledge you have acted.[4]

The first thing to note about Peacocke's account is that it does not run into the problem faced by the appeal to knowledge of tryings in order to explain knowledge of actions. That is, it is not left with a choice of accepting a regress of known tryings, each explaining knowledge of that which they caused, or accepting that there must be an account of our knowledge of our trying that cannot be adapted to give an account of our knowledge of our other mental actions. Peacocke makes no claim that the trying needs to be known in order that it play the role it plays in the account of the knowledge of the trying. All that is needed is that action awareness be taken at face value and:

Action awareness is... to be sharply distinguished from judgements that one is performing a certain action; and is also to be distinguished from awareness merely of trying to perform the action. (Peacocke 2009, 202–3)

Further:

Even if there is an argument that tryings must, at least in central cases, involve awareness of those tryings, the trying and the awareness of trying is distinct from action awareness. The relation between some constitutive components of the action and the action awareness of the action is causal. (Peacocke 2009, 204)

Peacocke does not need to appeal to knowledge or awareness of our tryings in order to account for knowledge of our actions, and so avoids the threat of regress of known mental actions. However, he does allow that we can be aware of, and so come to know, our tryings. Further, if tryings are themselves mental actions, then on his account of our model of our mental actions, such awareness must be a joint upshot—with the trying itself—of a prior trying to try. Thinking about Peacocke's account in relation to our knowledge of our tryings does I think lead us towards a problem for the account. The essence of the problem is that there seem to be mental actions for which it is implausible to think that there is a separation of trying from action, and for which it is hard to make sense of the possibility of failure that Peacocke's account must allow for—the possibility of trying causing the action awareness while failing to cause the action itself.

To start with, consider the supposition that I can know my tryings by taking at face value action awareness caused by my trying to try. There do seem to be cases in which it is natural to talk about trying to try to do something. Suppose I know that I have not done something difficult for a long time—like thread a needle with a small eye—and

---

[4] Peacocke does sometimes talk of 'tryings or some initiating event'. I am going to assume that he is committed to an account in terms of tryings. It is the appeal to psychological kinds other than the actions that concerns me. If by initiating event Peacocke means something sub-personal then we have a very different kind of account which would, I think, need to be evaluated separately from an account in virtue of tryings.

doubt whether I still have the ability. I may wonder if I am still able to do it and may decide to test out whether the ability has remained. In so far as my goal is to try to thread the needle, rather than simply to thread the needle, I may perhaps be naturally described as trying to try to move my arm. However, it seems that in the usual case, trying is something we do not think of my needing to try to do. I can try just like that—there seems to be no gap to be found between my trying to try and my trying. Suppose I know how to move my arm and all is functioning normally. What would it be in such a case to try to try to move my arm—what could it be other than simply trying to move my arm? Now it is possible—indeed necessary—for the theorist who appeals to tryings to claim that tryings are a special case. That you can indeed try just like that: as the explanatory primitives in the account they are accorded the privilege of being actions that need not be caused by tryings. Further, it is possible for Peacocke to claim that you know your tryings only in those cases where your trying is caused by a trying to try, that itself causes the action awareness of trying that you take at face value.

3.3 Acting without trying

The real problem for Peacocke's account, however, is that there seem to be a significant number of mental actions for which there is no possibility of a gap between trying to act and acting. They are carried out just like that—leaving no gap between attempt and success. For some such mental actions it is not just that there is no possibility of failure—given the trying, the action will inevitably follow—it is rather that it seems incoherent to think of the trying as distinct from the act. To have tried in a certain way will be to have already carried out the relevant mental action. Further, they seem to be mental actions we know easily and well. So it is not plausible to claim in their case that the lack of a prior trying means a lack of a way to know them.

In a recent paper, O'Shaughnessy distinguishes between what he terms productive and non-productive actions. Productive actions have the form 'A did X' where X is a event of which the action is 'the active bringing about'. Productive actions have a product the occurrence of which constitutes the goal and success of the action. The possibility of failure, argues O'Shaughnessy, rests in the possibility that there is only an attempt but no product. O'Shaughnessy argues that there are some mental actions which are non-productive—there is no event done which is the doing—and argues that therefore such actions do not involve tryings. The lack of a trying is evidenced for O'Shaughnessy by the impossibility of a certain kind of failure. Given these non-productive mental actions, we must give up the thesis of the omnipresence of trying. O'Shaughnessy gives two main examples of non-productive actions: talking to oneself and imagining raising one's arm. He argues that when one talks to oneself there is no resulting product which the act of talking to oneself actively brings about. And in imagining raising my arm there is no rising of an arm that takes place in imagination, and which is the event which the action of imagining raising one's arm is the active bringing about. In both cases, there is no event that constitutes the product of the action in such a way that the action could be attempted but fail, because it failed to produce a product. O'Shaughnessy is surely right when he suggests that we cannot try and fail to talk to our selves or try and fail to imagine moving one's body. To the extent that these are processes extended in time we could get distracted and cease to act—cut off from talking to oneself or imagining raising one's arm. However, to the extent that we continue to try to act we continue to succeed, because in such case to will is to succeed.

It might be thought that what is distinctive about O'Shaughnessy's cases is that the candidate products of the actions—some kind of internal speech or an act of arm rising in the imagination—are hard to make sense of. They would be ghostly, insubstantial, productions if they existed at all. According to O'Shaughnessy what is going on when one is talking out loud is that there is an event x, a talking, which is brought about by the agent in an event of 'actively bringing about x'. In such a case there is, he says:

a non-identity of the movement of the will' and the x-event which the action is the active generation of. (O'Shaughnessy 2009, 165)

If we were to construe talking to oneself on the model of talking out loud we would need to be able to identify the x event which the action was the active bringing about and which was non-identical to the talking to oneself. But, what would such a silent, ethereal production be? However, although ghostly mental products to mirror our loud physical ones would be unwelcome, this is not the core reason to deny this structure in this case—the real explanation seems to lie in features of acts of mind. The mind as a manipulator of content seems to accord us a kind of spontaneous freedom, in that to intend or try to conjure up one content or other in mind will already have been so to conjure it—the world does not need to be waited on. The problem with O'Shaughnessy's actions for the believer in independent tryings is that they seem be actions that are completed in the attempt: 'the seeming act of raising ones arm [in imagination] is one and the same thing as the act of imagining the doing of such a bodily deed' (O'Shaughnessy 2009, 170).

There is another class of mental actions which also seem not to admit of failure of the kind suggested by the distinction between tryings and actions. In these cases there is no danger in thinking that the problem has anything to do with the nature of the product, it is clear that the impossibility of a kind of failure lies in the relevant action being such as to be completed once it has been tried. Consider when I actively entertain the thought that P, or suppose that P, or consider whether P. It seems that to do those things is to bring the proposition into mind in a certain way—simply to bring to mind, bring to mind with a supposition of truth, bring to mind with a question of its truth. But to try to bring to mind, will in itself be an act of bringing to mind. And to try to bring to mind with a supposition of truth, or with a question, will in itself be an act of bringing to mind with a supposition of truth or with a question (cf. Gibbon 2009, 74–82).[5] The action and the

---

[5] Gibbons makes this point in relation to intention.

trying are inseparable. The problem of imagining a gap between the trying and the action in these cases rests not on the fact that the causal link between any trying and subsequent action would be short and secure meaning that there was less room for error than in the standard case. It is rather that the supposed trying would not be independent of the action and so could not do any explanatory work that the action itself could not do.

Peacocke holds judgements and denials—acts of assertion, as Frege calls them—also to be mental actions. It is more contentious but I think a similar point seems to apply to such cases: what would it be to complete the act of mind of trying to judge that p, or trying to deny P, without having thereby judged or denied P? The explanation in these cases might seem to be a bit different. This is partly because talk of trying in the case of judgement is problematic talk in the first place—it is accepted by both those who hold judgements to be actions and those who do not, that we cannot simply will to judge. Given that it is natural to use trying as an indicator of the voluntary—of cases in which we can will—it is odd to think of a subject trying to judge. However, Peacocke can eschew this association and hold that trying is an indicator of the active only, and that the active outstrips the voluntary. The explanation of the impossibility of a certain kind of failure in these cases does not lie in any unrestrained freedom voluntarily to manipulate our minds. As in the above cases it lies in a difficultly in making sense of the act of trying being non-identical to the act of assertion produced. If a trying is to be the immediate cause of a successful *judgement* it cannot be a voluntary act of the will—for then we could simply will to judge. Rather, like the judgement itself, it must be a non-voluntary, reason-led mental action. So, for a subject to try to judge that P, she must presumably already be resolved on the rightness of judging P and so have been led by her reasons to accept the truth of P—but what more does she need to do to judge that P? Her judgement seems already completed with the trying.

Of course, if we understand tryings to judge as something other than non-voluntary reason led actions that immediately cause judgements, then we might be able to understand talk of trying to judge in a way that leaves room for a failure of judgement. And there do seem to be cases in which we might talk about someone trying to judge that P. Suppose a subject strongly desires that P, or suppose a subject has been informed that good consequences will come from judging that P. Might a subject declare: "I am trying to judge that the doctor's diagnosis is wrong: it would be so painful to accept it" or "I am trying to judge that the doctor's diagnosis is wrong: I have evidence that I am marginally more likely to recover if I do"? It seems possible, but how are we to understand what is going on in these cases? What would the subject do to realize her aim? Perhaps the subject might keep trying to think that the doctor's diagnosis is wrong, or she could keep repeating "she is wrong, she is wrong" to herself in inner speech. But that is not directly to try to *judge* that the diagnosis is wrong. It may be to try to put herself in a position that will make her more susceptible to judging in the future, but it cannot be to try to judge then and there. Perhaps, she will try to seek out evidence for the diagnosis being wrong, or the doctor being unreliable, but that is to try to find grounds for the diagnosis being wrong, not to try to judge in the light of current evidence that it is.

It is true that it can be very difficult to get a subject to judge that P, or to adopt a certain belief despite the evidence being overwhelming. And that might seem to suggest that a subject could try to judge P, but fail. However, it seems to me that in fact there are two possibilities here, neither of which amounts to a case of a subject trying directly to judge and failing. One possibility is that the subject judges P, but the judgement does not 'take': the dispositions to act that would be conditions of believing P are dispositions the subject does not have, and perhaps could not have. The second possibility is that the subject has excellent reason to accept P, decides to make up her mind whether P, but is unable to commit to P being the case. But this does not seem to be a case in which she tries to judge P—what she tries if she tries anything is to not judge P, to not make up her mind.

Perhaps it will be said that we do not need the trying to be a trying to judge that P, rather we can settle with the trying being a trying to judge *whether* P? Trying to judge *whether* P is non-identical to the judgement that P itself, and it may be that judgements are proceeded, and indeed caused, by prior tryings to judge whether P. This, however, will not help Peacocke. Peacocke needs the action awareness caused by the trying to *match* and be as content specific as the action of which it gives knowledge. Trying to judge whether P will precede both a judgement that P, and a denial that P, but will, in having the same nature and content in both cases, produce action awareness of the same character in both cases. It will therefore be unable to ground the subject's knowledge that she is judging P rather than denying P.

There is a third class of problematic cases that have a slightly different structure. They are mental activities rather than discrete mental actions, but they also seem to be non-productive in that they lack an event non-identical to the attempt which constitutes the satisfaction of the goal they are aimed at. Consider the activity of watching or listening to something one is seeing or hearing. There is not an event of hearing or seeing, say, or picking up some information rather than another, which constitutes the event of successfully watching or looking. Rather they seem to be aimed at the maintenance of perceptual contact with that being watched or listened to.[6] On the other hand despite not having an end point in this way, we can say that we can try and fail to watch a bird in the garden, or try and fail to listen to a piece of music. However, the kind of failure that is possible here does seem distinct from the kind of failure that is possible when the subject is non-distractedly focussed on her action, but where the conditions required for the completion of the action fail to be met. Rather the possibility of trying and failing in these cases seems to be the possibility of failing to keep acting, to keep focussed on maintaining perceptual contact with the object or scene. If perceptual contact with the object or scene were not available one could not

---

[6] This is argued by T. Crowther (2010).

even start to try to watch or listen. Thus, there does seem to be a kind of failure that is impossible in these cases. One cannot be trying to watch or listen while having an uninterrupted visual or auditory contact with the object in question and not succeed. But such contact is not sufficient for watching or listening. I can have had an extended and uninterrupted visual contact with my computer screen without having watched it. And given such an uninterrupted contact even if we are watching we might find it hard to keep trying, because we are distracted or tired, but if we are continuously trying there seems to be no further event that is required to constitute our succeeding.

Let me try to sum up in relatively broad terms the features that have come out of the cases we have considered:

Pre-figuring the specific nature or content of one's actions. In physical actions, for the most part, the act of mind that causes the action can determine, or pre-figure, in detail the content or nature of the action it is to bring about, but still fail. In some mental actions, to so pre-figure the action will already have brought the action about. This will be because the act of pre-figuring will constitute the act being brought about.

Non-productive actions. As O'Shaughnessy argued, not all actions can be naturally construed as the active bringing about of some event distinct from a trying. In the case of physical action cases, even if one is suspicious of the claimed ubiquity of tryings, one can make some sense of what event it is that is missing when someone has tried to raise her arm, but due to a neurological failure of some kind, has failed. There was no arm rising which would have been the satisfaction of the supposed trying. However, how are we to understand the failure in the judgement or denial case: there was no judgement made even though there was an act of mind that constituted the trying to make it? It is difficult to see what impediment there could be to the judgement made that was not *ipso facto* an impediment to the trying to judge.

Antecedent vs Consequent possibilities for failure. The possibilities of failure present in some cases of mental action seem only to be *antecedent* rather than *consequent*. For many physical actions it seems possible for the action to fail after the agent has played her part. The subject can try to move her arm but the neurological system can fail, or the arm be held down. However, for some mental actions the only possibilities for failure seem to be antecedent to the subject's part. An envisaged or desirable action may fail to occur because the initial conditions are such that it could not even be attempted. And were it possible to attempt it, it would be successful. Suppose A cannot entertain, suppose, consider, judge, deny the thought that P. Perhaps A does not have the concepts required, or is insufficiently sophisticated to be led by reasons, or her reasons make it irrational. All such causes of a failure to be able to act in the envisaged ways are antecedent causes which will equally bedevil any trying or attempting on A's part.

As O'Shaughnessy puts it, we seem to have discovered "that the concept of trying has a strangely circumscribed application in the mind" (O'Shaughnessy 2009, 166).

And if we are right to think that there is a significantly sized class of mental actions for which it makes little sense to think of there being trying or tryings independent of the action or activity, then Peacocke's account will be worryingly incomplete. One of Peacocke's avowed aims is to give a *unified* account of our knowledge of mental and physical actions. If it turns out that a significant number of mental actions, and if mental actions from significant types, prove inconsistent with his basic model, it must put pressure on his account.

Peacocke could and indeed does respond to this by accepting that in those cases for which there is no distinction between trying and action, the trying just is the action.

But we do then have a question: given that action awareness is caused by the trying, we then have input of a non-conceptual phenomenal character from the event that is the object of our knowledge. Why does this not amount to a perceptual model of our knowledge of our mental actions? And if we can get the case for judgement to stick, since for Peacocke our knowledge of our beliefs in general depends on our knowledge of our judgements, why don't we in effect have a perceptual model of introspection? Now that, in itself, is not a criticism—it is just an observation.

3.4 Apparent action awareness

Finally, I want to look at how we are to understand the nature of apparent action awareness—that which we take at face value when we know our actions—particularly if we think of apparent action awareness as caused by tryings. Peacocke wants to leave open a disjunctivist approach to action awareness, and to what grounds a knowledge self-ascription. Thus, he wants to allow that apparent action awareness could come in two types, real and apparent, and that the explanation of why we know when we know be that we had factive awareness of the action.

First let me note that there is a slight inconsistency in the way that Peacocke uses 'apparent action awareness'. In introducing his account we saw that apparent action awareness is that which one takes at face value in knowing one's actions ("the distinctive way in which a subject comes to know of his own mental actions is by taking an apparent actions awareness at face value" (Peacocke 2009, 193)) and saw that it allowed of two types: real and merely apparent. For example, he says "when an apparent action awareness that you are ϕ-ing stands in the right complex of relations to your ϕ-ing, the apparent action awareness is genuine action awareness" (Peacocke 2009, 199). However, he also talks later of a distinction between real and apparent action awareness: "the real or apparent action awareness lies on a different causal pathway from the action itself (Peacocke 2009, 204). We can take it that what is intended is the former use: apparent action is what we take at face value, it can be real or merely apparent, and whether it is real or merely apparent depends upon the relations in which it stands to one's acting, or not.

I want now to consider whether Peacocke can in fact leave open, as he wants to, the question as to whether real action awareness and apparent action awareness are distinct kinds. If they are allowed to be distinct kinds, then the account of our knowledge of our actions would be available to the epistemologist who holds that the grounds of a *knowledgeable* belief cannot be such that they are available in both good and bad cases: cases in which the belief is true and cases in which it is false. If real action awareness and apparent action awareness are subjectively indistinguishable, but epistemologically distinct kinds, then a knowledgeable self-ascription based on real action awareness will be based on distinct grounds from the mistaken self-ascription based on merely apparent action awareness. I am not suggesting that Peacocke *needs* to adopt such an epistemology. However, he declares a desire that his account be compatible with such a 'McDowellian approach' (Peacocke 2009, 199–200). Further, in being so compatible it would increase the marketability of his view of our knowledge of our actions.

The first stage in an objection to treating real action awareness as fundamentally different in kind from merely apparent action awareness comes from the thought: how can real action awareness and merely apparent action awareness be distinct if they are both caused, as they are on Peacocke's account, by a trying which is of the same type of event in both the cases in which it is successful and which it is not? There may be a contrast here to the disjunctivist about perception who holds that the kind of awareness involved in real perception is distinct from that involved in merely apparent perception. In the case of the disjunctivist about perception, at least the distal *causes* of the distinct kinds of awareness are different, but in the case of the disjunctivist about apparent action awareness when such awareness may be understood as caused by tryings, the causes of the distinct kinds of action awareness (real and merely apparent) may be the same all down the line.[7]

One could easily keep a disjunction between real and merely apparent action awareness if one thought that the action itself, or whatever happens when the action fails, caused the action awareness. However, if tryings of the same type give rise to both, the task is harder. The obvious next possibility is to allow for the matching of distinct effects with distinct causes by leaving open the possibility of being a disjunctivist, not only about apparent action awareness, but about tryings also. The story would be that the successful trying (which gives rise to real action awareness that enables us to know that we are acting) is distinct in kind from the mere trying (which gives rise to merely apparent action awareness and is what make it seem that we are acting when we are not).

However, this move, while it responds to the problem about apparent action awareness coming in distinct types, leaves the explanation of our knowledge of our actions oddly positioned. We now have distinct types of trying, distinct types of action awareness, and finally distinct types of effect of the trying (an action, and no action) in the successful and unsuccessful cases.

The natural question to ask now is: given that the trying in the successful case is distinct from the trying in the unsuccessful case, is the *trying* in the successful case also

---

[7] If we bracket distal causes and look at the proximal causes of the perceptual experience in veridical and non-veridical cases, there is a parallel problem for the disjunctivist about perception.

distinct from the *action* in the successful case? If it is distinct from and independent of the action, then it is puzzling why it is not also invoked to play an explanatory role in the unsuccessful case. When tryings are seen as operating across the successful and unsuccessful cases, explaining what is missing and what is left in the unsuccessful, it is clearer what function they might be thought to be playing. Postulating a trying which is common across the successful and failed action cases enables us to explain why it is that it can seem to one that one is acting, but failing to. But if they are not common across the cases they start to look quite redundant in the success case. Indeed they look slightly worse than redundant, they look costly—there is a standing problem for those who hold that we act by trying to act, to the effect that we thereby act twice, or that we are in some way displaced from our actions by the prior intermediate tryings. These costs may be necessary and got around—but if the trying is doing no obvious work, then it is a puzzle as to why one should try to accommodate them in the account. Of course, we do not have a problem if what we are calling the trying in the successful case *just is* the action. But if the trying just is the action, is not distinct from the action, then given that apparent action awareness is caused by the trying which *just is* the action, then we are really explaining our knowledge of our successful actions as based on action awareness caused by the action itself. And then it is not clear what useful role the appeal to tryings to explain our actions has played.

In fact, Peacocke himself seems to be committed to taking tryings to be common across the successful and unsuccessful cases. His explanation of the content of merely apparent action awareness—as apparent awareness of clenching one's first, say—is that it is caused by a trying, which causes the action—of clenching one's fist—when all is functionally normally:

What makes an apparent action awareness one of clenching one's fist, or raising one's arm, or judging or deciding some particular thing, is that when these and the subject's other mental states are properly connected to the world, they are caused by events (tryings) that cause a clenching of the fist, a raising of the arm, or a judging or deciding of some particular content. (Peacocke 2009, 201)

This explanation requires the trying to be held fixed across the cases of normal and abnormal function: the trying that causes the apparent action awareness of clenching one's fist must be, when the subject is properly connected to the world, what causes the action of clenching one's fist. So apparent action awareness has the content it has by being caused by tryings that cause actions when things are connected up properly. If the tryings were not common across the cases in which they cause merely apparent action awareness, and cause a clenching of the fist etc, then this explanation of the content of apparent action awareness would not be available.

It seems that Peacocke is either going to have to give up this account of the way in which the content of apparent action awareness gets fixed, or give up neutrality with respect to the claim that there is a fundamental disjunction between real and merely apparent action awareness.

Let me conclude by noting two things. One, that if we are attracted by the view of tryings on which the successful trying *is just the action*—then tryings cannot play the explanatory role in our account of our knowledge of our actions that Peacocke would have them play. However, some kind of action awareness might still play that role.

Two, if tryings are to play a role in explaining our knowledge of our actions, it is hard to see how they are to do so unless something like Peacocke's account is right. However, if his account is right we must either give up the assumption that we can give a uniform explanation across mental and physical actions, or accept that in the case of those mental actions for which there is no distinction between the trying and the action, we know the action in virtue of an action awareness *caused* by it. To accept that looks very much like accepting a perceptual account of our knowledge of some of our mental actions. If such awareness is not perceptual we need an explanation as to why it is not.

References

Crowther, T. 2010 "The Agential Profile of Perceptual Experience", *Proceedings of the Aristotelian Society* 101/2, 219–42.

Gibbons, J. 2009 "Reason in Action", in L. O'Brien and M. Soteriou 2009, 72–94.

Hornsby, J. 1980 *Actions*, London, Routledge & Kegan Paul.

O'Brien, L. and Soteriou, M. (eds.) 2009 *Mental Actions*, Oxford, Oxford University Press.

O'Shaughnessy, B. 1980 *The Will*, Cambridge, Cambridge University Press.

—— 2009 "Trying and Acting", in L. O'Brien and M. Soteriou 2009, 163–172.

Peacocke, C. 2003 "Action: Awareness, Ownership and Knowledge", in J. Roessler and N. Eilan, N. (eds.) *Agency and Self-Awareness: Issues in Philosophy and Psychology*, Oxford, Oxford University Press.

—— 2009 "Mental Action and Self-Awareness (II): Epistemology", in L. O'Brien and M. Soteriou 2009, 192–214.

8

Conscious Events and Self-Ascriptions: Comments on Heal and O'Brien

Christopher Peacocke

The editor of this collection, Annalisa Coliva, has kindly invited me to comment on Jane Heal's chapter 'Consciousness and Self-Awareness' and Lucy O'Brien's chapter 'Knowledge of Actions and Tryings' just before the volume goes to press. My comments focus on the points at which Heal and O'Brien most closely engage with some claims in my earlier writings. There is much more material of great interest in their chapters (and on which I have views) than I can discuss here.

I

Jane Heal discusses this principle:

> (C) Whenever someone consciously Fs and also has the concept F then she will be able to judge explicitly, with non-inferential justification, that she Fs (p. 128).

She writes that "(C), just as it stands, is false" (p. 129). Her reason for saying so is that there are cases in which a person meets three conditions: (a) the person has the concept of fear; (b) he has an unconscious fear of authority figures; but (c) he may nevertheless have a distinctive conscious phenomenology resulting from this unconscious fear, a phenomenology involving suffering "acute unpleasant episodes when in the presence of authority figures" (p. 130), finding anticipation of some situations uncongenial, and so forth. I agree that cases of this kind are possible and commonplace.

We should distinguish sharply between someone who has a fear with various manifestations in consciousness and someone who consciously fears. Only someone who consciously fears instantiates the antecedent of principle (C). In ordinary English, the expression 'consciously fears' covers both occurrent fearings and the disposition to experience such occurrent fearings. As Heal makes clear in her discussion, principle (C) is part of a wider discussion of a proposal about the way in which occurrent conscious events can make rational certain self-ascriptions of mental events. Only the occurrent fearings are relevant to this proposal.

An occurrent fear that *p* is a conscious mental event with a representational content, a content that is evaluative and negative, having to do with some kind of danger. The event is representational in the strong sense that in suffering the event, it seems to its subject that the world is a certain way, even if that seeming is overruled by rational judgement. Someone who fears heights may suffer an occurrent fear when on the fully enclosed observation floor at the top of the Willis Tower in Chicago, even though he judges, indeed knows, it is perfectly safe. Here the negatively evaluative representational content of the occurrent fear is that he is in a dangerous situation (cf. Peacocke 2004, sect. 8.3; Gendler 2008). A person who suffers such an occurent fear and rationally judges, because he has that experience, "I fear heights", instantiates principle (C).

By contrast, consider a person who sincerely denies that he fears heights, but always finds excuses for not taking visitors to see the view from the top of the Willis Tower, never takes a route in a building that involves a view from high up, and finds it acutely uncomfortable when he is at a great height, however safely. He may not experience this discomfort as fear. Only what is experienced as fear is relevant to the truth of (C) in the case in which 'fears' or something of the form 'fears such-and-such' is substituted for 'F' in the principle. It is fear, experienced as fear, that can give a thinker reason for self-ascribing fear. Fearing "in a phenomenologically distinctive way" (Heal's phrase, p. 131), if the phenomenologically distinctive way involves only unspecific discomfort, however acute, and such matters as finding the anticipation of certain situations to be unpleasant, is not sufficient for experiencing something as fear.

In describing her example, Heal does at one point include, in her list of phenomenological manifestations of her subject's unconscious fear of authority figures, his "experiencing some episodes of acute occurrent fear, when actually confronted with authority figures" (p. 130). If this acute occurrent fear is experienced as fear, then the subject has a noninferential justification for judging that he fears. If he does not in fact so judge, when the question arises, then either there is some independent factor interfering with the proper and normal functioning of his cognitive faculties (such as panic, for instance); or else he does not have the concept of fear. If the acute episode is not one in which the subject experiences anything as fear, then it will not be in the scope of principle (C) as intended in previous discussions of these issues. In neither case do we have reason for modifying (C), so understood, provided it includes the qualifications about proper functioning of cognitive faculties (a qualification on which Heal was not applying pressure). So understood, principle (C) is true.

These points would not be available if experiencing fear had to be elucidated in terms of a willingness to judge that one fears. Under such an attempted elucidation, conscious fear would already involve the notion of judging that one fears. But that proposed elucidation seems incorrect. There is no greater difficulty in conceiving of a creature that suffers occurrent fears without having the concept of fear than there is in conceiving of a creature that is in pain without having the concept of pain. This is not only conceivable, but seems to me to be the actual situation of many creatures that lack concepts and even nonconceptual notions of psychological states. Experiencing something as fear, or as pain, both states that seem to me metaphysically more primitive than anything involving conceptual mastery, can make rational a judgement that one fears, or that one is in pain.[1]

Heal and I stand on the same side on an important issue, that of whether a mental event or state can itself make a judgement rational. On the other side are those who hold that only an intentional content in a certain mode (judgement, perception, emotion,...) can make a judgement rational. Of course not any event or state can be a reason. It is conscious events and states of a thinker, in contributing to what it is like for the thinker and to his perspective on the world, that can make rational judgements about those very events and states.

Heal moves on to consider what might be involved in noninferential justification. She includes some discussion of the idea that it is justification by a state that, as Jim Pryor puts it, does not "assertively represent a proposition" (p. 133; Pryor 2005). Heal develops the idea primarily in connection with perception, and compares a failure to recognize one of one's own states as fear with a failure "to spot a tiger, amid the shifting stripey lights and shadows of the jungle, even when the tiger is, in a sense, there in full view" (p. 135). I would make three points about this comparison.

First, in the case of perceptual justification (or as I would prefer to say, entitlement) to judge, what the perception makes it rational to judge is either part of the very content of the perceptual state, if you follow McDowell, or some conceptual content about the world individuated in part by its relation to the nonconceptual representational content of the perceptual state. A perception as of the carpet as blue entitles the thinker, other things equal, to judge *that's blue*, where the demonstrative is perceptual, referring to the carpet. Now the representational content of an occurrent fear is some content such as *It's dangerous to stand at this height*. There is no rational transition from that content to *I fear standing at this height*. Any such transition would be a non-sequitur, something that is not generally truth-preserving. So any proposed parallel with the perceptual case must be loosened at least in this respect.

Second, Heal's comparison between failing to spot the tiger and failing to identify one's state as fear will work only if fear can be analyzed into components in the way being a tiger (or at least tiger-like) can be analyzed into being a creature of a certain characteristic shape and size, with stripes. It is not at all obvious that any such analysis is possible. Although conscious fear has to have a certain restricted kind of intentional content (when it has any at all), I strongly doubt that there are other phenomenologi-

---

[1] See the further elaboration of the generalization of such a position in the chapter 'Reasons and Self-Knowledge' by Conor McHugh in this volume. I am in agreement with the broad thrust and structure of his defence of the position.

cally present properties and relations, not themselves involving fear, whose combination is sufficient for something to be fear. Fear is more than a conscious thought that there is a danger something bad may occur; it is not the same as anxiety; and so forth. If there are no such properties and relations which suffice for something to be fear, then the comparison with failing to perceive the tiger will not go through. If there are no such component properties and relations that together amount to fear, then the subject with unconscious fear, but with some conscious manifestations thereof, cannot be described as failing bringing a set of components under the concept *fear*.

Third, an intended parallel with perception may nevertheless be sustainable at a different and much more general level. The idea may rather be that in a range of cases, one's being in a state of kind K with content p may noninferentially entitle one to judge one is in state K, thought of in some canonical way, with content p, also thought of in a canonical way. Thus, a subject's having a visual experience as of it's being the case that p can noninferentially entitle him to judge that he has a visual experience as of it's being the case that p. In that case I am more sympathetic: provided the range of such cases and states K is restricted to the phenomenally conscious, then principle (C), defended in the way I have suggested, is an instance of precisely such an account.

II

Lucy O'Brien initially characterizes my conception of apparent action awareness accurately and concisely when she writes that apparent action awareness is, for me, "(i) belief independent, (ii) not perceptual awareness, (iii) independent of any perception of the action of which it is action awareness of (iv) such that actions are independent of it, (v) and can occur independently of an action" (p. 169). She then attributes to me the thesis that "if tryings are themselves mental actions then on his [i.e. on my—CP] account of our model of our mental actions, such awareness must be a joint upshot—with the trying itself— of a prior trying to try" (p. 170). This last is certainly not my view. Tryings themselves are one of the best counterexamples to the thesis that for an event to be an action, it must be caused by a prior trying. In fact the immediately preceding sentence "Tryings themselves are one of the best counterexamples..." is a direct quotation from my paper 'Mental Action and Self-Awareness (I)' (McLaughlin and Cohen 2007, 362). O'Brien also offers me, as a way out of her objection, the option of saying that there is no knowledge (so presumably no action-awareness) in cases in which a trying is not caused by a preceding trying. But there is action awareness, and knowledge too, of the mental action of trying in those cases too; so I would not want, and do not need, to take that offered option. Such tryings cause apparent action awareness of themselves, and of any basic actions of which they are constitutive components.

As O'Brien's chapter proceeds, it becomes clear that she is disputing a further claim which is independent of her point in the quotation above. The further claim is one I really did make when I wrote, "Every mental action involves success in something at which one may in principle fail" (Peacocke 2007, 361). O'Brien agrees with Brian O'Shaughnessy's thesis that some types of action are ones at which it is impossible to fail.

I was not convinced by all her examples. For instance, one of her examples is that of talking to oneself (silently, internally). She writes, "O'Shaughnessy is surely right when he suggests that we cannot try and fail to talk to ourselves" (p. 172). By contrast, it seems to me that you may reasonably say to a severely depressed person "Start talking to yourself in thought, you might find that something interesting occurs to you, something worth pursuing". I think we can conceive of the severely depressed person sincerely trying to do this, but with no train of thought, or internal talking, taking place for him at all, and so failing in what he is trying to do. O'Brien's and O'Shaughnessy's best example is that of trying to bring something consciously to mind. First, if there are unconscious tryings, such a trying to bring something consciously to mind may fail. Second, the explanation of the impossibility of failure in the case of conscious tryings follows simply from the fact that such a trying already involves bringing the thing consciously to mind. The source of the impossibility is the consciousness of the trying, not the nature of trying itself.

Even if, however, there are cases which show that there are action-types at which one cannot fail, and even if we draw from them O'Shaughnessy's conclusion that in those cases there are actions without tryings, I do not think this would undermine the fundamental structure of the account of knowledge of one's own actions that I was presenting. It would require only the modification that the apparent action awareness, on which one's knowledge rests, be caused by some kind of initiating event in the subject. In ordinary cases, that initiating event would be a trying. In the case of those actions that are of an alleged type for which failure is impossible, the initiating event would not be a trying. But it would still exist, and have the role in explaining apparent action awareness that I described. Indeed the whole account could be formulated in terms of initiating events rather than tryings, for those who are uncomfortable with the more general application of the notion of trying.

On the account I have offered, some tryings cause action awareness of those very tryings. Of those cases, O'Brien writes: "we do then have a question: given that action awareness is caused by the trying, we then have input of a non-conceptual phenomenal character from the event that is the object of our knowledge. Why does this not amount to a perceptual model of our knowledge of mental actions?" (p. 176). That an apparent action awareness is caused by what it is an apparent awareness of does not suffice to make it perceptual awareness. Action awareness and perceptual awareness are both phenomenologically and metaphysically distinct. Here are some of the differences.

Action awareness in its nature always involves a content of the form *I am ϕ-ing now in this event*. In this content, the first person, the present tense and the ϕ-ing are nonconceptual notions of a subject, a time, and an action-type. The component *this event* is a demonstrative notion of the event (if any) which is the object of the apparent action awareness, a demonstrative made available by that awareness, rather than by any perceptual awareness. For subjects who do possess concepts, the action awareness may contain conceptual versions of each of these several nonconceptual notions. In enjoying the apparent action awareness, it seems to oneself that one is acting. This awareness does not rest upon any acceptance or presumption of an identity of oneself with something given in a certain way in perception. If one takes the apparent action awareness at face value, and possesses the requisite concepts, one will judge the conceptualized content that one is performing an action of such-and-such kind. This is what I called "the use of *I* as agent" (Peacocke 2007, 370).

It is true and important that there is such a thing as perceiving an event as an action—as a grasping, a reaching, a jumping. One can visually perceive an event as a reaching for an object, even when one's visual point of view is that of the subject who is reaching. One can perceive the event as one's own reaching for the telephone to one's left, say. That does not make such a visual perception into action awareness. One could visually perceive one's own hand as reaching for the telephone without any action awareness as of reaching for the telephone. Perhaps some neuropsychologist is making one's hand move that way, or perhaps it is a case of alien hand syndrome; and this could all occur even if there were no proprioceptive feedback. Even when there is no proprioceptive feedback, there is a difference between one's having a visual experience as of one's hand reaching for the telephone, and having that experience while it also seems (action awareness) that one is doing it oneself. Both kinds of case are possible. Apparent action awareness is possible even when there is no sensory feedback from the relevant limbs at all. Even when one's action awareness is not of a bodily movement, but merely of a trying, it falls within the same subjective category as other cases of action awareness, rather than perception.

The preceding points are all at the level of phenomenology. But there are also some individuative, metaphysical differences between perceptual states and states of action awareness. Genuine perception always involves some kind of computation from merely sensory states. It is this that makes error possible in perception even when the organism is functioning internally as well as it possibly can. O'Brien's argument targets the proper subcase of apparent action awarenesses that are apparent awarenesses specifically as of the agent's tryings. Those apparent action awarenesses of the subject himself trying to ϕ are type-individuated in part by their being events of a type (with a content *I am ϕ-ing now in this event*) produced, when all is functioning properly in the organism, by the subject himself trying to ϕ. Error in such states is not possible when all is functioning properly, because there is no analogue here of sensory states on which otherwise well-functioning computation may operate. Genuine perceptual awareness of the subject, even when it has a content specifically concerning action, may have a false content, consistently with the subject functioning as well as he possible can, internally. That is one consequential difference between perceptual awareness and action awareness of one's own tryings (and other mental actions too), in addition to the intrinsic difference in the form of perceptual content and the contents in action awareness.

Internal malfunction is of course possible for both apparent action awareness and for apparent perception. Malfunction in radically abnormal circumstances is the source of the possibility of a kind of illusion in which there is apparent action awareness but no trying (and no relevant initiating event by the subject either). The illusions that Wilder Penfield induced in his subjects, that they had spontaneously decided to make some movement, when in fact he had induced the movement with an electrode inserted in a carefully chosen part of the brain, may fall under this general head. Certainly, such cases of incorrect apparent action awareness, even of one's own mental actions (including decisions), seem to be in principle possible.

The remarks in the past few paragraphs about the differences between apparent action awareness and apparent perceptual awareness constitute the initial resources on which I would draw in addressing the request in O'Brien's final section, to explain why my account is not a perceptual account. All the same, consistently with everything I have said in these comments, there remain at the level of epistemology some legitmate parallels with the (different) perceptual case. In attaining perceptual knowledge we take the content of apparent perceptual states at face value; in attaining knowledge of our own actions, we take the content of apparent action awareness at face value. In both cases it is a task for epistemology to explain our entitlement to do so. In both cases, an appeal to the nature of the individuation of the respective representational states in question is an essential part of carrying out that epistemological task. At this level of generality in epistemology, the tasks are parallel. Apparent action awareness has factive subvarieties, as does apparent perceptual experience. I myself do not in fact hold any kind of epistemologically significant kind of disjunctivism. I did intend to point out that the issue of whether action awareness plays a part in an account of how we know what we are doing is orthogonal to that of whether disjunctivism is correct. It is open to both parties disputing about disjunctivism to acknowledge the significance of action awareness as a distinctive category of representational state, and as a state explanatory of our knowledge of our own actions.

References

Gendler, T. 2008 "Alief and Belief", *Journal of Philosophy* 105, 634–63.
McLaughlin, B. and Cohen, J. (eds.) 2007 *Contemporary Debates in Philosophy of Mind*, Oxford, Blackwell.
Peacocke, C. 2004 "The Emotions and Moral Rationalism", in C. Peacocke (ed.) *The Realm of Reason*, Oxford, Oxford University Press, 252–7.
——2007 "Mental Action and Self-Awareness (I)", in B. McLaughlin and J. Cohen 2007, 358–76.
Pryor, J. 2005 "Is There Immediate Justification?", in M. Steup and E. Sosa (eds.) *Contemporary Debates in Epistemology*, Oxford, Blackwell, 181–201.

PART THREE

Self-Knowledge: Robust or Fragile?

9

Externalism and Skepticism: Recognition, Expression, and Self-Knowledge

Dorit Bar-On

According to *external-world skepticism*, were I now to think: There's water in this glass, I wouldn't *know* that there is water in the glass, even if there was water in the glass, my eyes were wide-open, etc. This is because, for all I know, my way of telling what is in front of me does not allow me to rule out the possibility that I am only under some kind of illusion about what is in front of me. Surely, though, I know that I'm now thinking *that* there's water in the glass? According to *content skepticism*, I do not. This is because, for all I know, my way of telling *what* I am thinking does not allow me to rule out the possibility that I am only under some kind of illusion about what I am thinking. Yet, as commonsense would have it, my ordinary belief about what I am presently thinking is remarkably secure—at least much more secure than my ordinary beliefs about my extra-mental world. My first aim in this chapter is to examine whether the commonsense confidence about ordinary knowledge of content can be sustained in the face of a skepticism that proceeds by analogy to external-world skepticism. It might seem that we could get the right analogue, by enlisting the doctrine known as *content externalism* (externalism, for short). On the most straightforward construal of this move, the use of content externalism by the content skeptic betrays an implicit reliance on a suspect *recognitional conception* of our ordinary basic self-knowledge. Once this conception is made explicit, it should be clear that we ought to reject it. My second aim will be to sketch an alternative to it, which would allow us to sustain the commonsense idea that ordinary self-knowledge is not threatened by a skepticism that is analogous to external-world skepticism.

1. External-content skepticism meets external-world skepticism

Suppose I now say, or think:

EW: There is water in the glass.

For purposes of raising her doubt, the *external-world* skeptic will allow me, at least initially, to suppose that I do know that I now have a thought with the content of EW. Still, she invites me to question whether EW represents something I actually know.[1] Full symmetry would require the *content* skeptic to invite me to doubt that I now have a thought with content *p* while at the same time holding fixed, or at least not questioning, my belief that *p*. But it is not clear how I am to proceed. How can I confidently affirm that there is water in the glass, even as I doubt that I am now thinking that there's water in the glass? Am I to think to myself: "There's definitely water in the glass. But, for all I know, I may not now be *thinking* that there's water in the glass"? This seems like a version of Moore's paradox (namely, "*p*, but I am not thinking that *p*"). Moreover, just as I cannot doubt *p* without thinking that *p*, so I cannot affirm *p* without thinking that *p*; and this too is something I can easily recognize. Explicitly entertaining a doubt about whether some external-world proposition *p*, which I believe is true, as well as expressing confidence that *p* is true, are both inconsistent with simultaneously entertaining a doubt about whether I am thinking that *p*. But this suggests that content skepticism cannot be entertained in a fully explicit form that parallels the way (Cartesian) external-world skepticism is entertained. Each of us can internalize the external-world skeptic's challenge, and pose it in the form: as I am thinking that *p* is the case, for all I know, *p* may not be the case. But it seems we cannot rationally pose to ourselves the content skeptic's challenge in a parallel form, namely: as I am thinking that I am thinking that *p*, for all I know, it is not the case that I'm thinking that *p*.

It is also worth noting that the commonsense conception of the content of a mental state does not readily furnish us with skeptical alternatives. It takes some fairly sophisticated philosophical stage-setting to bring us to appreciate the kinds of alternatives that would support a skeptical doubt concerning what we are currently thinking. This is precisely what the view called *externalism* (or anti-individualism) about content is supposed to have provided. The thesis of content externalism says, roughly:

EXT: The contents of our thoughts (and other mental states) depend for their individuation on the nature of our physical or social environment. Whether an individual is in a mental state with one content rather than another depends in part on relationships between that individual and her extra-mental environment.[2]

Now, the commonsense view of our knowledge of the contents of our mental states can be summarized as follows:

---

[1] An extreme skeptic could of course later turn around and question my knowledge of the content of my thought, as well.

[2] The *loci classici* are H. Putnam (1975) and T. Burge (1979) (which applies the externalist thesis to mental contents). Note that the externalist thesis as presented so far concerns specifically the *content* of thoughts and other propositional attitudes, not their attitudinal aspect (namely, thinking vs wishing vs fearing, etc.). Correlatively, the content skepticism we are considering concerns our knowledge of the content of our states, not our knowledge *whether* we are in a given type of state. (Later on, however, we shall turn to the latter.)

Content Self-Knowledge (CSK): Normally, when we ascribe to ourselves occurrent contentful mental states (in speech or in thought), our self-ascriptions do not rely on observation, evidence, or inference. Nonetheless, our self-ascriptions are especially secure and privileged, and they represent genuine knowledge we have of the content of the relevant states.[3]

Though CSK does not imply absolute infallibility, incorrigibility, or self-omniscience regarding content, it does imply that our pronouncements regarding *what* we think, want, hope, etc. carry special weight and represent some kind of privileged knowledge.[4]

EXT is often claimed to be incompatible with CSK. Suppose I make the following Self-Ascription of a Contentful state

SAC: I am thinking that there's water in the glass.[5]

For SAC to constitute something I *know* requires not only that it be *true* that I am thinking there's water in the glass, but also that I be *warranted* in holding it true. If EXT is true, then it seems that, to ascertain the truth of SAC, it is necessary to verify that I stand in the right relation to my extra-mental environment. Yet according to CSK, my own self-ascription of the thought doesn't rely on *any* kind of study or observation. So how could I possibly be warranted in my self-ascription?[6]

2. Is externalism compatible with self-knowledge?

However, assuming that the alleged problem for CSK that is based on EXT is *not* supposed simply to follow from a more general skeptical problem about extra-mental

---

[3] As I explain in Bar-On (2004, ch. 1), I think we ought to separate two claims in the commonsense view: a. that our self-ascriptions of occurrent mental states is *secure and privileged*; and b. that such self-ascriptions are instances of genuine *knowledge*. This separation makes room for a substantive explanation of the security of such self-ascriptions that does not *presuppose* that we possess privileged self-knowledge. Once we have such an explanation on hand, we can (and should) address separately the question of knowledge. My own view (Bar-On 2004, ch. 9) is that spontaneous mental self-ascriptions such as SAC *do* represent privileged (even if not infallible) knowledge of *both* the content and the type of the self-ascribed mental state.

[4] We are leaving open, for now, the degree to which common sense is committed to our having privileged knowledge of the *type* of state we are in when making self-ascriptions of occurrent mental states, that is, knowledge *that* we are thinking, hoping, fearing that p (as opposed to knowledge that *that p* is the content of our state we're in).

[5] SAC is to be understood as a self-ascription of a *presently entertained thought*—the occurrent passing of a thought through one's mind, as opposed to the occurrent affirmation, or belief. See Section 5 below. For additional discussion and references, see Bar-On (2004a).

[6] Following Davies in C. Wright et al. (1998), who distinguishes between the "achievement problem" for content externalism which he says "does not pose any insuperable achievement problem for first-person authority" (p. 342), and "the consequence problem" which he thinks is more difficult. The 'consequence problem' is the subject of Bar-On (2004a), where I reference a number of authors who address alleged problems posed by externalism for self-knowledge. Although I agree with Davies that what he calls "the achievement problem" is not insuperable, I think solving it takes some doing. In any event, the achievement problem is my main focus in this chapter.

knowledge, it is not as yet clear what the problem is. Granted, if externalism is true, contents have essential features—a kind of nature, if you will—that are not transparent to us purely in virtue of our being thinking subjects; they admit of theoretical understanding. But if I can normally know I am drinking water, even in ignorance of chemistry, why is it that I cannot know that I am thinking *that I am drinking water*, even in ignorance of the correct theory of thought content?

In general, for any range of truths, there may be different ways of knowing those truths, not all of which involve a theoretical probing into the underlying nature of the known items. Still, even in the absence of such theoretical understanding, if someone is said to know some truth p, it is because she has *some* positive way of telling that p is the case. And that *seems* to imply that she must go by some features of the relevant situation that are somehow correlated—and reliably so—with the obtaining of p. Thus, if I can be said to know that the man I see is George, even though I have conducted no DNA tests, this is because visual recognition represents a reliable method for correctly identifying people. Similarly for knowing that there's water in the glass, or that a shirt in front of me is red. But if externalism is true, how can there be *any* telltale signs by which we could immediately recognize what our own thoughts are about?[7]

However, even if it's true that, to know some truth p, we must have some reliable epistemic access to the worldly conditions that render p true, it is not clear that this access must afford us *counterfactual discrimination*. If there is no twater, but only water in my environment, can I not know that there is water in the glass, even though *had* I been confronted with a glass of twater, I *might* have been fooled? If so, then why could I not know that the thought I am having is that there's water in the glass, even though, had circumstances been different, I might have been fooled into thinking that that's what I was thinking?

Note that skepticism about the external world can proceed without trading on an implicit counterfactual discrimination requirement. The Cartesian external-world skeptic invites us to consider alternatives that may *in fact* obtain for all we know, ones that (so the challenge goes) we are unable to rule out. Such an inability to rule out alternatives is supposed by the skeptic to undermine our claims to know external-world propositions, insofar as it shows a diminished capacity for discrimination in actual, and not merely counterfactual, situations. And such diminished capacity does seem to bear on epistemic warrant. If I am to have perceptual knowledge that this man is George, or that the liquid in my glass is water, for example, I must be able to tell George apart from other individuals I know, and water from other liquids, respectively, through perception. Such discriminative abilities are necessary if I am to *know which*

---

[7] The present suggestion has obvious affinities to what is known as epistemological reliabilism, which is usually presented as an externalist view of knowledge. It has often been observed that, to avoid the charge of incompatibility with self-knowledge, content externalism can (perhaps must) be coupled with epistemological reliabilism. I have avoided the label 'reliabilism' here, since I am not certain that the proposal I am working with here qualifies as a purely reliabilist proposal. See below, Section 3.

individual is George, or which liquid is water, which in turn seems to be a precondition of my being warranted in thinking that this man here is George, or that the liquid in the glass is water.[8] (Of course, how good my ability to discriminate must be in order for me to be warranted is open for debate. The safe answer for our present purposes would be: good enough so that it is not a sheer coincidence that I hold the relevant claim true, but not so good that it would allow me to rule out counterfeits in all imaginable situations.) As it happens, I am quite good at discerning George by his looks, voice, manner, etc., and am quite adept at telling water apart from other liquids by its color, smell and taste (or lack thereof). But now suppose that George in fact has an identical twin brother; or suppose twin-Earth is discovered, and we begin to import twin-Earth's twater (XYZ) to Earth. My world in such cases encompasses actual candidate counterfeits. If I still cannot perceptually tell George apart from his twin, or water apart from twater, could I nevertheless be warranted at times in thinking that I am looking at George, or that I am drinking water? Arguably not. If so, then the external-world skeptic could legitimately mount a challenge to our knowledge of the external world by trying to offer actual alternatives that we cannot rule out.[9]

To preserve the analogy with external-world skepticism, then, the external-content skeptic would have to challenge content self-knowledge as described by CSK without relying on the counterfactual discrimination requirement. The external-content skeptic needs to persuade us of the following: As I ascribe a thought with a certain content to myself, there are in fact, though perhaps unbeknownst to me, actual *counterfeits* of that thought; that is, thoughts I may now be having which differ in content, and which I could not tell apart from the thought I take myself to be having. This would be a situation in which, given how things are in the world I live in, I could be fooled into thinking, or could be merely under the impression, that I'm having a particular thought. But this is not as easy to accomplish as in the case of external-world skepticism (where one can trade on familiar phenomena such as dreaming, or hallucination, to generate the threatening possibility). Specifically, the external-content skeptic needs to describe a situation in which I do ascribe to myself a *water*-thought, but where it is possible, for all I know, that I am instead having a *twater*-thought. The trouble is that, if my present situation is one in which there is (and has always been) only water around, then I can only *have water*-thoughts, and so I cannot go wrong by ascribing to myself a *twater*-thought. And any situation in which I fail to meet the conditions for having genuine *water*-thoughts, will be a situation in which I cannot so much as *think* that I am having a *water*-thought. This is just the familiar point that, if my first-order intentional states are all about twater, since I have only ever been in contact with XYZ, then none

---

[8] Russell proposed that this "knowing which" requirement must be satisfied by anyone who is able even to *think* about an individual. For a construal of the requirement in terms of an ability to discriminate the object of judgment from other things, see G. Evans (1982, ch. 4).

[9] Whether the dream or the evil demon/brain-in-the-vat hypotheses qualify as legitimate, such alternatives can of course also be debated. For relevant discussion, see A. Goldman (1976).

of my higher-order self-ascriptions can involve erroneously assigning *water* contents to my intentional states. By contrast, a situation involving counterfeit glasses of water is *not* one in which I cannot think (or believe, or be under the impression) that there is a glass of water.

At this point things get a bit complicated. Briefly, to envisage the right situation, it is not enough to imagine, for example, that twater is brought to Earth, since such a change will not automatically render false my belief that I am thinking there's water in my glass. I do not cease to have *water*-thoughts, or begin to have *twater*-thoughts upon the introduction of twater into my environment, or even upon first encounters with twater. Similarly, if I undergo a "fast switch"—I suddenly get transported to twin-Earth I will still be thinking that there is water in my glass. Since there is no water on twin-Earth, my thought is bound to be false. But my self-ascription to the effect that that is what I am thinking will still be true. So now suppose that I undergo a "slow switch": I am unwittingly transported to twin-Earth and stay there long enough to have acquired the concept *twater*. (And maybe I even start travelling between Earth and twin-Earth with some frequency.) This description of the scenario is not sufficient by itself either; we must add that I stay long enough on twin-Earth to acquire the concept *twater*, but I do not thereby lose my concept *water*. For only if I have *both* concepts simultaneously in my cognitive repertoire, would it be possible for the contents of my first-order thought and my self-ascriptive thought to pull apart in the requisite way.[10]

This suggests that the content skeptic is less well placed than the external world skeptic to mount a challenge to our ordinary knowledge. However, recall that the commonsense expectation is that content self-knowledge should be *more* resistant to skepticism than knowledge of the external world. In particular, we might expect that our ability to know what we are thinking should *not* be threatened *even* in slow switching situations. And indeed, some externalists—Burge, for example—assures us that even in slow switching cases "there is no possibility of counterfeits," because basic self-knowledge is "self-referential in a way that ensures that the object of reference just is the thought being thought" (Burge 1988, 659).

But we may wonder: What is it about basic self-knowledge that makes it "self-referential" in Burge's sense? That is, what guarantees that the content of the ascribed thought and the ascribing thought will still interlock even in cases where a thinker has both twin-contents in her actual, active cognitive repertoire? I will offer an answer to this question later on. But before doing so, I want to bring out something that is easily obscured by focusing too narrowly on the compatibility of externalism and content self-knowledge. The most straightforward use of content externalism in mounting a skeptical challenge to content self-knowledge that is modeled after external-world skepticism would, it seems, implicitly rely on a certain conception of content self-knowledge in particular, and of self-knowledge more generally. If we adhere to this

[10] For a discussion of 'slow switching', see P. Ludlow (1995).

conception, which I will call the *recognitional conception,* it will turn out that the skeptic's challenge has nothing to do especially with content, nor is it exclusively threatening to externalists. Once the recognitional conception is made explicit and rejected, and an alternative to it is put in its place, we can see our way out of content skepticism. Or so I will be arguing.[11]

3. Content skepticism and the recognitional conception of self-knowledge

The content skeptic's challenge can be put as follows:

> How could a thinker know what content her present thought has, if it is possible, for all she knows, that the content her thought *really* has is different from the content it *appears* to her to have?

Put this way, however, it should be clear that the challenge potentially faces not only externalist views of content, but *any* objectivist view of content, whether externalist *or* internalist—any view that allowed for a possible gap between what objectively makes it the case that a thought *has* a certain content and what content the thought *appears* to anyone, including the individual herself, to have. To meet the skeptical challenge it is not enough simply to insist that contents depend for their identity only on facts internal to the individual. We have to be assured that the relevant internal facts will always somehow be immediately available to the subject who has contentful mental states. But mere acceptance of content internalism does not provide this assurance. As long as what makes it the case that someone has states with certain contents includes objective facts that are not directly available to her, then, regardless of whether they concern things "inside" or "outside" her head, we will have the makings of an appearance/reality gap with respect to content. Where there is such a gap, there is a possibility of imposters: mental states that appear to us to have contents that are different from the contents they actually have. It is this possibility that is relevant for generating content skepticism on the model of external-world skepticism.

The analogy with external world skepticism, however, may invite an additional idea. This is the idea that, in the normal case, our ability to tell correctly the relevant facts—who the person in front of us is, or what liquid is in a glass, on the one hand, and *what* we are thinking, or hoping, etc., on the other hand—depends on characteristic ways things appear to us. The contribution made by content externalism is that it

---

[11] As noted by an anonymous reader, there are no obvious contemporary authors who endorse what I describe as the recognitional conception in its baldest form. This should not be surprising if the reasons I outline below for rejecting the conception are correct. My aim here is not the interpretive one of documenting explicit appeals to the recognitional conception. Rather, as I explain in what follows, I aim to identify the sort of conception that would be needed to generate a straightforward analogue of external-world skepticism (using content externalism), and offer an alternative to it that could help vindicate CSK.

allegedly shows that there can be circumstances, however extraordinary, in which a thinker would simply be unable to discriminate among alternative thought contents available to her, given how things *appear* to her 'from the inside.' But note that this would be problematic *only if* having ordinary knowledge of content *requires* thinkers to be able to make such discriminations. Only if one's ability to tell knowledgeably what content one's thought has depended on one's *assigning* content to one's thought and on one's being able reliably to pick it out as the correct one, would the possibility of counterfeit contents pose a threat to one's knowledge of content.

According to the commonsense doctrine of content self-knowledge (CSK), recall, self-ascriptions of present contentful states are special, in that they do not rely on the use of ordinary epistemic means such as ordinary observation, evidence, or inference. Still, on what I have dubbed 'the recognitional conception', if such self-ascriptions are to constitute some kind of knowledge, we still must have at our disposal *some* epistemic means or method that we deploy in obtaining the information they convey. Moreover, *to be able to tell* that a state of mine has a certain content c, *I must be able to tell apart* states with content c from states with other contents that are available to me, using some characteristic 'signs' that allow me to recognize content c as the content my state has, as opposed to any other content that is available to me. And, in keeping with CSK, my way of telling must be especially secure and unique to me. So, even if I do not need to ascertain directly that I satisfy the conditions necessary for my entertaining content c, still, my ability to know that a present state of mine involves c, as opposed to some other content, depends on my being able somehow to recognize distinctive characteristics of my state or its content.

In the sorts of cases we looked at earlier—knowing that this is George, even without checking his DNA, or knowing that there is water in the glass, even without running chemical tests—I clearly have certain recognitional abilities with respect to the relevant items, which allow me to tell them apart from other items. I can *distinguish* George from other people (even from one who looks quite a bit like him) by certain characteristic features. Applying this idea to the case of content self-knowledge, we would suppose that there must be some recognitional ability that allows us to tell that a present mental state of ours has a specific content, as opposed to some other candidate contents. To accommodate the (alleged) privileged character of self-knowledge, we'd have to maintain that each of us possesses a *proprietary* way of distinguishing between her being in a state with content c as opposed to c' (and ascertaining the correct content assignment). Thus, perhaps—as introspectionist views would have it—in my own case, I have a special form of inner perception that delivers reliable verdicts on the contents of my present mental states.[12] Yet, according to externalism, there can be situations in

---

[12] At the very least, whatever internal mechanism is said to play the role of 'inner perception' would need to enable the *tracking* of the content of one's own mental states. If such tracking is not to be a matter of happy coincidence or pre-established harmony, it would seem to require some kind of sensitivity to characteristic features of the first-order states. (For discussion of a variety of introspectionist views and their limitations in explaining the security of ordinary mental self-ascriptions, see D. Bar-On (2004, chs. 4 and 5).)

which an individual will inevitably fail to meet this recognitional requirement; so she will fail to know what she is thinking. And this threatens the idea that ordinary knowledge of content can be *more secure* than ordinary knowledge of the external world.

By now, I think we should be in a position to appreciate that the dialectical situation will remain essentially the same if we broaden our focus and consider basic self-knowledge in general—including knowledge of the kinds of occurrent mental states we are in, and not just knowledge of their contents. *Content skepticism is but a special case of a more general skepticism that has nothing specifically to do with content.* The true analogue of external-world skepticism is then *internal world skepticism*, which poses the following generalized challenge:

How could a subject know what mental state she is in (as well as what content it has), if it is possible, for all she knows, that the state she is actually in is different from the state that it appears to her she is in?

(Let me note in passing again that this internal-world skepticism is indifferent to the specific view one holds regarding the nature of mental states, be it "externalist" or "internalist". Skepticism thrives wherever we combine an appearance/reality distinction with a conception of non-theortical knowledge as epistemically mediated by some recognitional ability.)

As regards ordinary self-knowledge, what this means is that, if we want to adhere to the idea that we possess an especially secure and privileged kind of knowledge of our present states of mind, we must *either* reject the appearance/reality distinction as it applies to one's own mind *or* reject the recognitional conception of ordinary self-knowledge. I myself do not see how we can have an objectivist view of mentality while denying that it is possible for things in the mental realm to be different from the way they appear on any given occasion to *anyone*, including oneself. But we have another option: to deny that ordinary self-knowledge is a matter of recognitional judgments that represent how things appear to one.[13] This seems to me, in any event, a plausible route to take, since I don't think the recognitional model is an appropriate model on which to understand ordinary, basic self-knowledge.[14]

---

[13] I see a prima facie difficulty in reconciling the following three claims:
  (i) There is an objective difference between, e.g., my being in M and my being in M'.
  (ii) We normally tell which state we are in by recognizing it introspectively.
  (iii) When ascribing a state to ourselves introspectively we cannot be fooled.

Holding (i) and (ii) has the effect of portraying what is in one's mind as, in a crucial sense, like what is in one's extra-mental world, in being epistemically external to one, whereas (iii) attempts to recover some kind of distinction between the mental and the extra-mental world. I am inclined to think, but cannot argue here, that the distinction cannot be preserved without rejecting the recognitional conception. In any event, it should be clear that accommodating all three claims would require more than adopting an internalist conception according to which mental states supervene on an individual's internal organization.

[14] See footnote 12 above. Although what I am calling the recognitional conception does not feature explicitly in arguments purporting to show that content externalism threatens basic self-knowledge, the upshot of the foregoing discussion is that it is required in order to sustain a strict analogy between extern-world skepticism and content skepticism.

4. The security of self-knowledge: immunity to error

Ordinary present-tense mental self-ascriptions that are not made on the basis of therapy, careful reflection, self-interpretation, or scientific findings—what are often called "avowals"—seem to enjoy a special security. As I ascribe to myself in the normal way, say, a desire for a glass of water, I seem to *know* that I want water. I do not seem vulnerable to certain skeptical doubts about the content of my state. Could it be that I really want a glass of *twater*, rather than water? Somehow, the question seems to have no grip. My self-ascription seems secure also as regards its being water *rather than gin* that I want. Furthermore, I can tell securely, not only that it is water that I want, but also that I'd *like* some water right now, rather than merely speculate that there's water in the glass, or that I have some other water-involving attitude. Indeed, I would argue that the security of content-assignment is but a special case of a more general security we enjoy when making mental self-ascriptions in the normal way.

Now, I have suggested that, if we accept a recognitional conception of ordinary self-knowledge, then skeptical alternatives abound, and the apparent security of avowals may be illusory, *quite apart from any commitment to content externalism*. However, since the recognitional conception may seem to be our best model for understanding non-theoretical knowledge, then, if we answer the skeptic by *rejecting* the recognitional conception, we may be saving self-knowledge from skepticism by embracing *deflationism* about self-knowledge:

> If avowals are not open to doubt in view of alternatives, this is not at all because they represent an especially secure form of knowledge, but because they represent *no* knowledge whatsoever.

In what follows, I want to sketch a *non*-deflationist view of what allows ordinary spontaneous mental self-ascriptions to be *both* especially secure *and* to be instances of knowledge, even though they do not rest on recognitional determination.[15]

I propose that we understand the knowledge I have of what content a present mental state of mine has on the model of the knowledge I have that it is *I myself* who is instantiating a certain property. In "Self-Reference and Self-Awareness," Sydney Shoemaker makes an observation regarding certain self-ascriptions that use a first-person device such as 'I':

> The statement "I feel pain" is not subject to error through misidentification: it cannot happen that I am mistaken in saying "I feel pain" because, although I do know of someone that he feels pain, I am mistaken in thinking that person to be myself....

---

[15] See footnote 3, where I mention my distinction between the question of avowals' security and the question of their being instances of knowledge.
 For presentation of the deflationist challenge in terms of self-knowledge involving "no cognitive achievement", see Wright, Boghossian, and Fricker in C. Wright et al. (1998). The explanation I offer below is the briefest sketch of a view I develop at length in D. Bar-On (2004, ch. 9).

If I say "I feel pain" or "I see a canary," I may be identifying for someone else the person of whom I am saying that he feels pain or sees a canary. But there is also a sense in which my reference does not involve an identification. My use of the word "I" as the subject of my statement is not due to my having identified as myself something of which I know, or believe, or wish to say, that the predicate of my statement applies to it. (Shoemaker 1968, 557–8).

Shoemaker offers the notion of *immunity to error through misidentification* by way of characterizing the special epistemic status of self-ascriptions of the kind he describes in these passages (a notion also discussed by Gareth Evans and others) (cf. Shoemaker 1968, 82–3; Evans 1982).[16] The following features of judgments that are immune to error through misidentification (IETM, for short) are important for my present purposes. First, such judgments are not in general incorrigible. "I see a canary," "I am sitting down," "My legs are crossed," can all be plausibly said to be IETM, yet no one would be tempted to take them as incorrigible. Further, the class of self-ascriptions that are IETM includes *nonmental* self-ascriptions. Second, when an ascription is IETM, then, even if it can be mistaken, it is not open to a certain kind of error: an error of mistaking *me* for another because of a mistaken identification. Third, whether or not a self-ascription is IETM depends not on its semantic content, but rather on its "epistemic pedigree".[17] One and the same (semantically individuated) self-ascription can be IETM or not, depending on the *basis* on which it is made. If I tell that I am sitting down by seeing in a mirror, or on a video screen, someone who is sitting down, and whom I take to be me (perhaps mistakenly), my self-ascription will *not* be IETM, even though it is IETM when it is made in the normal way. Finally, if I issue a true self-ascription "I am F" that is IETM, I can be legitimately said to *know that it is I myself* who has the property F. However, my knowledge is not based on some recognitional identification of myself as the "right" subject of my ascription.[18]

This last point bears elaboration. Suppose I'm asked how I know it's a canary that I see at the bird-feeder. I may cite my ability to recognize canaries. This ability provides my epistemic grounds for the judgment that it is a canary I see. By contrast, when I say or think in the usual way: "I see a canary," it is not as though I think of someone in particular that she sees a canary, and take it to be me, or recognize that there is someone who sees a canary, and take it to be me who sees it. Indeed, I have *no* grounds or basis

---

[16] For a recent discussion that distinguishes two different kinds of immunity to error through misidentification, see J. Pryor (1999). Since, as far as I can see, nothing hangs on this distinction for my purposes here, I will ignore it in what follows.

[17] Also, being IETM is not unique to first-person ascriptions. Both Shoemaker (op. cit.) and Evans (op. cit.) think that demonstrative thoughts such as "This is moving fast" are IETM (though clearly not infallible or incorrigible).

[18] There is a "thin" sense in which I do identify myself as the subject of the ascription, for I do manage to *refer* to myself as opposed to someone else. But my ascription does not rest on a recognitional judgment of the form "I = r" (where "r" stands for some identifying description or demonstrative representation of an individual), or of the form "I am the individual who is F" (where I have an independent reason to think that someone is F). It may be useful to distinguish between the referential notion of identifying (a semantic notion) and the recognitional notion of identifying (an epistemic notion). Compare G. Evans (1982, 218).

for thinking it is me who is the correct subject of my ascriptions, over and above, or separately from whatever grounds I have for thinking that *I* see a canary. And whatever knowledge I have that it is me who is F, for the relevant Fs, does not rest on any independent knowledge that *someone* is F; for in the normal case, my only grounds for thinking that someone is F is whatever grounds I have for thinking that *I* am F.

But what about counterfeits? Suppose I say or think: "I am sitting down." Couldn't it be, for all I know, that it is my identical twin who is sitting down? Well, that possibility would seem entirely irrelevant in this case, given that I do not tell that it is me who is sitting down by telling myself apart from other candidates. Since in the normal case, my self-ascription does not rest on any recognitional judgment identifying me as the individual who is sitting down, there is no room for me to doubt whether it is me, rather than someone else, who is sitting down.

Evans suggests (see quotation) that the *reason* why in certain cases it will make no sense to wonder: "Someone may be F, but is it I who am F?" is that, in these cases, there is no way to doubt that *I* am the one who is F without doubting that *someone* around is F. To put it somewhat awkwardly, in these cases, there is no stable judgment of appearances concerning who is F that I can hold onto so as to raise a doubt about how things really are. This is because the only reason it *appears* to me that someone is F is that it appears to me that I am F. I can, of course, be wrong that I am F. But Evans denies that this is sufficient to show that my knowledge that I am F must rest epistemically on my (correct) recognitional identification of myself as the individual who is F. What, then, allows a self-ascription of the form "I am F" to represent something I *know* about myself? Evans notes in this connection that we possess two general and distinctive capacities for gaining information about some of *our own* states and properties. First, we possess "a general capacity to perceive our own bodies" (which includes "our proprioceptive sense, our sense of balance, of heat and cold, and pressure"), and second we also have a capacity for determining our own "position, orientation, and relation to other objects in the world... upon the basis of our perceptions of the world" (Evans 1982, 220–2). It is the exercise of these capacities that gives rise to self-judgments that are IETM and which represent a certain kind of bodily self-knowledge.

If we accept Evans' analysis, then we have an interesting and powerful model that is useful for understanding the epistemic status of content self-ascriptions (and mental self-ascriptions more generally). On this model, there are epistemically secure self-ascriptions that have the following features:

(i) Though not absolutely infallible, they are *immune to a certain kind or error and doubt* (concerning the identity of the subject of ascription)
(ii) They represent *knowledge* that something is the case (namely, that *I* am F)
(iii) The knowledge is *non-recognitional*, in the sense that it does not depend on the subject's having direct recognition of that which is the case (i.e. the judgment that I am F does not rest on a recognitional identification of myself)

I think we can fruitfully enlist this model to understand what I call the distinctive *ascriptive security* of the mental self-ascriptions earlier referred to as avowals. Specifically, I maintain that

> When making a self-ascription of a contentful state in the ordinary way, my self-ascription enjoys a special *immunity to error through misascription* and it can constitute knowledge I have about my state, even though the intentional content of my state is not for me a *recognitional target* (and neither is my state).

It is often tacitly assumed that I could only be said to know the content of my state if I had a separate epistemic reason for taking the content to be this rather than that. The idea of recognitional identification could be invoked to supply the relevant reason: I know c rather c' to be the content of my state because I can *recognize* c as the right content; I have a good way of telling when it's c rather than c'. In analogy with ordinary perceptual judgments, this recognitional ability could be used to explain what epistemically grounds the self-attribution of the content part of self-ascriptions. However, consideration of judgments that are immune to error through misidentification opens up the following possibility. When I simply avow being in state M with content c, I have no epistemic grounds for the content component of the self-ascription that is not at the same time grounds for the self-ascription as a whole. But from the fact that I don't have separate grounds for thinking that *it is c (rather than c') that is the content of my state* it doesn't follow that I couldn't be said to *know* that I am in state with content c. (And, similarly, if I were to have no epistemic grounds for ascribing to myself, specifically, for example, being worried—*as opposed to* wishing—that p, over and above whatever grounds I have for the self-ascription "I am worried that p"—as a whole, it wouldn't follow that I couldn't be said to know that I am worried that p.)

When I make content ascriptions to others, my ascriptions *do* rest on such separate grounds. I see by your behavior that you are scared of *something*, and I look around to figure out what it is you are scared *of*. I conjecture that it is the dog you are scared of by noticing that you're looking at the dog. And I can sensibly wonder whether it is the cat, not the dog, that you are scared of, while not questioning that you are scared of *something*. This can be true even of content *self*-ascriptions. If I were to determine that *it is my neighbor* that I am annoyed at, using indirect methods such as reviewing the circumstances as well as my behavior, consulting with friends, or submitting to costly therapy, then I *would* be relying on specific grounds for taking *my neighbor* to be the intentional object of my annoyance that are not at the same time grounds for simply thinking I'm annoyed at my neighbor. But this is clearly not the normal case.

As regards the content part of spontaneous self-ascriptions of occurrent contentful mental states (what I've been calling "avowals"), my proposal is this. We should regard avowals of contentful states not only as immune to error regarding *who* it is that is in the relevant contentful state (that is, as IETM), but also as *immune to error through content misascription*. When assigning content c to a present state of mine in the ordinary way,

I have no reason for taking my state to have content c other than whatever reason I have for taking myself to be in contentful state M. If my self-ascription of the contentful state M is false, which it *can* be, this will not be due to my mistaking the state's content for another, say, because it *appears* to me a certain way. Whereas I can go wrong in my proprioceptive report "My legs are crossed" precisely because my legs may merely appear to me to be crossed when they're not (just as I can wrongly judge a colored patch in front of me to be blue, simply because it merely appears blue to me), when avowing a contentful state I cannot go wrong through mistaking one content for another due to its merely appearing to me to have that content.

To forestall a common misunderstanding, let me clarify that, to say that a self-ascription is immune to error through misidentification is *not* to say that it is infallible, or even incorrigible. It is just to say that *if* it is false, the falsity is not *due to an error of misidentification*—that is, due to the self-ascriber mistaking someone else for herself. Similarly, to say that a self-ascription is immune to error through misidentification is also not to say that it cannot be false. It is just to say that its falsity is not due to the self-ascriber mistaking content c for content c' (or state M for another, M').[19]

5. The security of avowals: a neo-expressivist account

We saw that, on Evans' analysis, although self-ascriptions that are IETM are immune to a *certain kind* of epistemic error, they can nonetheless represent knowledge that we have about ourselves, obtained through the exercise of distinctive capacities for gaining information about some of our own properties and states. If we are to insist, as against the deflationary view, that avowals can be instances of knowledge we have about our mental states and their contents, we would do well to identify what is it that allows avowals to represent knowledge that we are in a state with a particular content. My proposed answer is that, here too, we can appeal to a distinctive capacity that we deploy when issuing avowals. The proposal is as follows:

> When ascribing to myself a state with content c in the normal way, I exercise an *expressive* capacity: the capacity to *use* content c (rather than content c') to articulate, or give voice to my present state. When avowing, say, a present thought that is crossing my mind, I tell what content the thought has by telling *it*, i.e., that content. If I "identify" the content c, it is not by recognizing c to be the content I take my thought to have, but rather by using *that* content in the course of giving voice to my thought.

---

[19] If avowals are immune to both errors of misidentification and errors of misascription, one may wonder *how* they could be false. The short answer is that an avowal such as "I am hoping that my aunt will come to visit" will be false, quite simply, if either I am not hoping that my aunt will come to visit (but rather, say, am dreading it) or if, say, what I'm hoping is not that my aunt will come to visit but that my uncle will. How could I come to make such a false self-ascription, if not through confusing one content (or one state) with another? There can be any number of *psychological* explanations for avowing falsely. For my neo-expressivist account of false avowals, see D. Bar-On (2004, ch. 8). (And see the discussion of failed natural expressions, below.)

I shall first explain this expressivist proposal in connection with the case of content self-ascription with which we began, and then explain how we can actually see this case as but a special case of a more general phenomenon.

So let us return to

SAC: I am thinking that there is water in the glass.

Understood as a self-ascription of a presently entertained thought, rather than something one affirms, or judges to be true, SAC is maximally secure. For, when making it, I cannot misidentify the subject of my ascription, but I *also* cannot misascribe to myself the specific thought that there is water in the glass. Indeed, on a natural reading of self-ascriptions of this special kind, that is, self-ascriptions of presently entertained thoughts, they are *self-verifying*—they make themselves true.[20] Now contrast SAC with: "I am thinking something boring," which clearly does not seem self-verifying. What makes "I am thinking that there is water in the glass" self-verifying is the fact that the very act of self-ascribing the thought summons up the ascribed thought, as it were. Here what renders my self-ascription true is the fact that, in ascribing the entertained thought, I directly spell it out.

When the state ascribed is simply one of entertaining a certain thought, all I need to do in order to succeed in *truly* ascribing to myself the entertaining of a thought with content c is to entertain a thought with that content, which I am bound to do if I ascribe the thought explicitly. As I spell out the content, I cannot but entertain the very thought I ascribe to myself, which is why my avowal is self-verifying. This is not true of all intentional avowals. However, although intentional avowals are not in general self-verifying, they do typically articulate their content. When avowing, say, the hope that dinner will be served soon, I do not obliquely describe my hope as when I report: "I am hoping for the same thing you are hoping." Rather, I explicitly articulate the content *that dinner will be served soon*, in the course of giving voice to my hope. And, I maintain, when I *avow* a contentful mental state, as oppose to ascribing it to someone else, or even ascribing it to myself indirectly, on the basis of some specific epistemic basis—when I self-ascribe a state in the 'avowing mode,' as we might put it—the explicit articulation of the state's content does not rest on an independent assessment of a feature of my first-order state.[21] Rather, it is the upshot of putting to use the very same resources I would put to use in saying, or thinking "Let dinner be served soon" *hopefully*.[22] (And

---

[20] For an analysis of self-verifying thoughts that is designed to be consistent with content externalism, see T. Burge (1996).

[21] When I assign content to another's state by explicitly articulating it, I still rely on a recognitional judgment; the content is for me still a recognitional target, whereas in my own case, as I explain below, the articulation of the content is made in the course of giving voice to the contentful state. For more discussion, see D. Bar-On (2004, ch. 6).

[22] Burge (1979) remarks that "[w]hen one knows that one is thinking that p, one is not taking one's thought (or thinking) *that p* merely as an object. One is thinking that p in the very event of thinking knowledgeably that one is thinking it. It is thought and thought about in the same mental act"

as regard the state ascribed, if I am avowing, then I issue the self-ascription by way of expressing my present hope itself.)

Semantically speaking, a self-ascription that is IETM, such as "I am sitting down," *specifies* a particular individual who is said to be sitting down. However, what allows such a self-ascription to qualify as a piece of *knowledge* that *I* am sitting down is not the fact that I have correctly recognized myself as the one who is sitting down. Rather, it is the fact that in issuing the self-ascription I put to use certain capacities for gaining information, which I have only with respect to certain of my own states. I am making an analogous claim regarding self-ascriptions that are, as I put it, immune to content misascription. Semantically speaking, an avowal such as "I am hoping that dinner will be served soon" specifies a state I am said to be in as well as assigning it a specific content. However, what allows it to qualify as a piece of knowledge I have about my present state is the fact that in issuing the self-ascription, I put to use a distinctive capacity that I have only with respect to my own mental states: the expressive capacity to give articulate voice to my present state of mind, or to *speak from* it.

6. Neo-expressivism expounded

The account I am invoking here—my *neo-expressivism*—is in the first instance an account of the distinctive security of avowals—the *epistemic asymmetries* between the way we treat certain present-tense self-ascriptions of mental states and the way we treat all other ascriptions. Unlike traditional epistemic accounts of this security, my account does not appeal to the security of a special epistemic method, or basis, or access on which I rely when avowing. Like more familiar expressivist accounts, it appeals instead to the notion that avowals, unlike ordinary reports, serve directly to express the avower's present mental states. However, unlike "simple expressivist" views, my neo-expressivism is motivated in a non-traditional way, without appealing to similarities between, for example, saying "I have a headache" and wincing, or saying "I feel so happy!" and giving a big grin. Rather, I approached the expressivist idea by considering a sort of case that is a far cry from paradigm cases of naturally expressive behavior (yelping, wincing, gasping). I used the case of self-ascribing an articulate presently entertained thought (our SAC). The advantage of doing so is that it can help forestall a standard complaint against "simple expressivism", namely, that it compromises the *semantic continuity* between avowals with ordinary reports. My neo-expressivist account, unlike its predecessors, is designed from the start to accommodate the idea that, when issuing an avowal I make a genuine self-ascription that can be true or false, and can be interchanged in context with reports about the mental state I am in, in virtue of its semantic content. Indeed, I believe the expressivist insight is best

---

(ibid., 70). Peacocke (1996) also appeals to the idea of a self-referential or reflexive element in self-verifying self-ascriptions. The expressive take I offer on knowledge of content can help explain how this idea can be generalized.

approached by focusing on the epistemology of avowals and their use, rather than their semantics.

Although I have appealed to the expressivist insight in connection with the security of self-verifying self-ascriptions, I think it is applicable to non-self-verifying cases of avowals, and more generally, to all avowals, whether intentional or phenomenal. The general expressivist claim I endorse is that avowals derive their special security not from being based on some special epistemic method or access, but rather from being expressive acts in which subjects directly give voice to—share, air, vent—a self-ascribed mental state. A subject who issues an avowal, like one who says: "This is great!" or "How gross!" or "God, please no!" *speaks from* her state, instead of giving a nonverbal, natural expression to her state. Although the avowal proper tells us that the self-ascriber is in some state, just like a report of that state (by someone else or by the avower herself), in the circumstances, it may still play an expressive role similar to that played by a natural expression of the state.

To bring out the various aspects of similarity and dissimilarity between avowals and natural expressions, we need to make some distinctions. Specifically:

(I) Sellars' three senses of "expression":

a-expression: in the *action* sense a *person* expresses a state of hers by intentionally doing something;

For example, when I intentionally give you a hug, or say: "It's so great to see you," I express in the action sense my joy at seeing you. One may also express one's feeling of sadness in the action sense by *letting* tears roll down one's cheeks, instead of wiping them out and collecting oneself. (Note that a-expression requires doing *something* intentionally, not necessarily *expressing* intentionally.)

c-expression: in the *causal* sense an *utterance* or piece of behavior expresses an underlying state by being the culmination of a causal process beginning with that state;

For example, one's unintentional grimace or trembling hands may express in the causal sense one's pain or nervousness, respectively.[23]

s-expression: in the *semantic* sense, for example, a *sentence* expresses an abstract proposition, thought, or judgment by being a representation of it.

For example, the sentence "It's raining outside" expresses in the semantic sense the proposition that it is raining at time [*t*] outside place [*p*].

The similarity I find between avowals and natural expressions concerns a- and c-expression, *not* s-expression. Natural expressions do not express anything in the semantic sense. And avowals s-express a proposition/judgment that I am M. But it's

---

[23] As I understand it, expressing 'in the causal sense' is not a purely causal notion. For discussion, see D. Bar-On (2004, ch. 7–8).

still possible that in the causal and action senses an avowal, just like a natural expression, expresses the state it ascribes. Indeed, to give full purchase to the expressivist idea, we should focus more narrowly on the comparison between avowals and natural expressions that fall under a-expression—that is, cases where one produces a facial expression or a gesture intentionally, and where we can think of the expressed mental state, not only as the 'brute cause', but also as the rational cause of, or reason for, one's expressive behavior. And more narrowly still, the crucial comparison that really matters is between avowals and *non-self-ascriptive utterances* through which speakers are said to express their present feelings, emotions, and other occurrent mental states. (We'll come back to this shortly.)

(II) Avowals as acts and avowals as products:

As we consider cases of intentionally producing expressive behavior, we should distinguish between an *act* of expressing and its *product*. The important similarities between avowals and other intentionally produced expressions require thinking of avowals as acts, whereas the salient dissimilarities come to the fore when we think of avowals as products.

The product of an act of avowing, unlike a smile or a wince, or even a verbal cry such as "Ouch!", is a semantically articulate self-ascription, an item with semantic structure and truth-conditions. It is a product whose properties allow it to serve, and be caught up, in other kinds of distinctively linguistic (and mental) acts. Importantly, avowals, understood as products, s-express (in Sellars' semantic sense) self-ascriptive propositions, to the effect that the avower is in some state. And the mentalistic terms that constitute parts of avowals semantically represent the relevant states. Natural expressions understood as products—a facial expression, a gesture, bodily movements or demeanor, an inarticulate sound, however produced—do not s-express anything. There are no semantic conventions in virtue of which laughter represents amusement, no linguistic rules in virtue of which a hug signifies, or refers to, joy at seeing the person hugged. Moreover, it could perhaps be argued that natural expressions *show* the expressed mental states, whereas avowals only *tell* of the states. This too should be understood as a claim about the respective products. But we should keep in mind that we often take linguistc acts—saying "What a mess!" or "How gross!" or "This is great!"—to be a-expressive of speakers' mental states, even though they have semantically articulate products, and even though these products do not mention the mental states they a-express. So we can agree that there are notable differences between the products of avowals and of acts of natural expression while retaining the expressivist insight.

Let's consider another example. A linguistic utterance such as "It's so good to see you!" which typically serves to a-express the speaker's joy, does so with an expressive vehicle that s-expresses the proposition or thought that it is very good to see one's hearer, in virtue of the rules of English. If, as I maintain, one can also a-express her joy by avowing "I am so glad to see you!" this would involve using a sentence which, in virtue of the rules of English, s-expresses the *self-ascriptive* proposition or thought that I am very glad to see her hearer. The minimal expressivist claim is that these are two acts that equally serve to a-express the agent's joy, though they use different expressive vehicles (both linguistic, but only the latter self-ascriptive). I think that once we see how to understand the similarity claim, we should be more open to seeing that these two linguistic acts can be in turn similar, in point of the act performed, to an act of giving your friend a cheerful hug. The product of the latter act is not governed by any syntactic or semantic rules of English, and it does not s-express anything. Still, in all three cases we can see the agent as performing the same kind of act—that is, giving expression to (a-expressing) her joy at seeing someone.

(III) Expressing M vs expressing one's M:

The third distinction I want to call on is between expressing *a* mental state and expressing *my* mental state. An actor on stage may express anger making use of a variety of expressive vehicles, from growling to throwing her hands in the air, to uttering: "Darn it!" to saying: "I am so angry". But she will typically not be expressing *her* anger.[24] The distinction is equally applicable to both natural and linguistic expressions. Intentionally produced natural expressions exhibit a certain measure of 'expressive autonomy' (a feature regularly exploited in the arts). A disgusted face, a scared shriek, a yawn of boredom, can all be produced on occasion in the absence of the relevant feelings or emotions.

Natural expressions cannot only be simulated on purpose, but they can also be 'pressed' from someone even when the person is not in the relevant mental state, due to unusual circumstances. A person on a dentist's chair with a long history of painful dental work may emit a gasp of pain as the drill approaches her mouth, *as well as* say: "Ow!" or "My tooth hurts!" even though in reality she feels no pain. Circumstances conspired to squeeze out of her an inappropriate expression. We need not suppose her to be insincere, nor do we need to suppose that her verbal or non-verbal emissions were due to a recognitional mistake she's made regarding the state she is in. A *psychological* explanation of what led to the inappropriate expression is ready at hand. It would allow us to make sense of the possibility of false avowals without resorting even to a non-Cartesian *recognitional* story and yet without giving up the expressivist explanation of avowals' security. (Standard cases of so-called wishful thinking and self-deception can be treated along the same lines. See Bar-On (2004, ch. 8))

A strand of the neo-expressivist account that has so far remained in the background can now come to the fore. We saw that the account invokes the expressivist idea to

---

[24] Perhaps the *character portrayed* by the actor is expressing her anger (if we think Romeo can die in the play, even though the actor portraying him doesn't, there's no obvious reason why Romeo can't express 'his' anguish, even if the actor portraying him doesn't). We may, however, think that the actor only *pretends* to be a-expressing his anger. (And, while no one can c-express a state she's not in, one can presumably *pretend* to c-express such a state—an actor pretending to stub her toe, when portraying a character who is stubbing her toe, can pretend to c-express feeling a sharp pain). For discussion, see D. Bar-On (2004, ch. 8).

explain the distinctive *ascriptive* immunity to error of avowals. But the expressivist idea, properly understood, can also help explain why avowals are governed by a strong presumption of truth (even though, as indicated above, this presumption *can* be overridden; for we can make sense of cases of false avowals). If we take someone's behavior to be an act of genuine—as opposed to pretend—(a- or c-) expression of a mental state, we take it that she is *in* the mental state that we perceive in her behavior. Except under non-standard circumstances, if we think that someone is engaged in behavior expressive of, say, fear, we take it that not only does the behavior show us fear, but also that it shows us the *agent's* fear. The verb "express" shares in the facticity, or 'success' aspect, of the verb "show". In the special case of avowals, though, the product of the act actually *tells* us that the agent is in a certain mental state. Thus, to take the avowal to be expressive of the agent's mental state *just is* to take the avowal to be *true*. Avowals are unique among expressive acts in that their products semantically express a proposition that ascribes to the agent the very same mental state that we take her to be expressing in the action sense in the act of avowing. If someone says: "This is so boring!" we can take her to be a-expressing her boredom *without* presuming her utterance to be true. (We can perfectly consistently suppose her to feel bored by something that isn't boring at all.) But to take the utterance: "I feel so bored" to express the utterer's boredom *is* to take the utterance to be true. (As hinted above, though, there is a certain slack between a-expressing c-expressing, a slack characteristic of all intentional acts; and herein lies the possibility of false avowals.)

To sum up: On the neo-expressivist account, when avowing, a person issues a self-ascription of a mental state in the course of speaking directly from her present condition, rather than reporting her finding regarding her present state of mind. Unlike the person who grunts, or smiles, she is *speaking* her mind. And unlike the person who says "Darn it!" or "How awful!" or "This is great!" she speaks self-ascriptively. On the present account, to regard someone's self-ascription as an avowal is to take her to be a-expressing her self-ascribed state. This is why it would make little sense to contradict or correct her self-ascription. For, to take it that she has (successfully) a-expressed her state just is to take it that she has given voice to a state she is in. Recognizing an expressive element in all avowals thus contributes to a non-recognitional explanation of avowals' distinctive security. Insofar as we think of all avowals as enjoying a special security that goes beyond the epistemic security of well-grounded or highly reliable self-reports, it is *because, or to the extent that,* we regard them as acts in which the speaker successfully a-expresses the very conditions ascribed by the proposition the avowal as product s-expresses.

7. Self-knowledge

Back to self-knowledge. On the neo-expressivist account, the *security* of the self-ascription does not come from the epistemic security of the avower's recognition of the presence and character of her state, but it is rather a consequence of the fact that the avowal is a successful act of a-expressing the self-ascribed state. But if this is so, one may worry that the deflationist challenge has still not been met. For, even if avowals are not vulnerable to "internal-world" skepticism, they are altogether poor candidates for genuine knowledge that the avower has about herself. This worry can be perspicuously couched in terms of the familiar notion that to know *that p* one must have a *warranted belief that p*. Now, if an avowal (a- or c-) expresses the mental state it ascribes, doesn't that mean it does *not* (a- or c-) express the avower's *belief* or judgment that she is in the mental state? But then how could it possibly represent something she knows? This is a good question to ask, and I have addressed it at length elsewhere (cf. Bar-On 2004, ch. 9). Here I can only offer a few brief remarks. Notice, first, that the question presupposes that, for example, if an avowal (a- or c-) expresses my hope that *p*, it cannot at the same time *also* (a- or c-) express my belief, or judgment that *p*. This exclusivity claim can be denied. My expressivist account denies that my avowal represents a recognitional self-judgment that is based on the way my present state or its content appear to me. And it maintains that my avowal a-expresses my first-order state. But it can allow that my avowal *also* a-expresses something I *hold true* about myself, and not only in the weak dispositional sense that *if* I were to consider what the avowal says I would affirm it. For I can also be said to make the relevant occurrent judgment, at least in the sense that I intentionally produce the relevant self-ascription. Granted, since my self-ascription is not based on any recognitional judgment, and it is certainly not based on any observation, evidence, or inference, it doesn't seem that I could have *justification* for holding-true the self-ascription, at least not in any traditional sense. However, this does not mean that I cannot be warranted in my belief, in the sense of being *entitled* to hold-true the self-ascription. Perhaps, as the subject of the relevant mental state, who is speaking from the mental state—who is giving it articulate voice—I am simply warranted by default, as it were, since no defeating alternatives to the ascription I make are in the running. Or perhaps my self-ascription, though not based on any recognitional judgment, is grounded in the very same state that gives reason for the act of avowing, namely, the mental state that I self-ascribe (cf. Peacocke 1996). If any of these options works, then we could think of avowing subjects, not only as expressive beings capable of speaking their mind, but also as *knowing* selves, capable of giving articulate voice to warranted beliefs about their present states of mind.[25]

★ ★ ★

If the neo-expressivist account is right, we can agree with Descartes that our ordinary mental self-ascriptions are not open to the same skeptical threat as our ordinary claims about extra-mental reality. Should this tempt us to Cartesian dualism? Wittgenstein describes the temptation to postulate Cartesian Egos as follows:

---

[25] The general point behind the last remarks is that the neo-expressivist account of avowals' security is *compatible* with any number of non-deflationary views of self-knowledge. In Bar-On (2004, ch. 9) I argue for the compatibility, and tentatively offer an account of privileged self-knowledge that I regard as an improvement on several existing accounts. (In ch. 10 (pp. 405–10), I take up the objection that my account does not explain how subjects like us can have privileged basic self-knowledge of their present states of mind regardless of whether they *avow* those states.)

We feel then that in the cases in which "I" is used as subject, we don't use it because we recognize a particular person by his bodily characteristics; and this creates the illusion that we use this word to refer to something bodiless, which, however, has its seat in our body. In fact *this* seems to be the real ego, the one of which it was said, "Cogito, ergo sum".

(Wittgenstein 1960, 69)

Wittgenstein's "uses of 'I' as subject" are precisely what Shoemaker and Evans try to capture with the notion of immunity to error through misidentification: uses of "I" in judgments that rest on no recognition of "a particular person by his bodily characteristics." But, Wittgenstein warns us against concluding that they rest on recognition of someone by *non-bodily* characteristics. We should equally resist an analogous temptation in the case of the ascriptive part of mental self-ascriptions. We often issue such self-ascriptions spontaneously and without any reliance on recognition of physical (or even functional) features of our mental states. Though our avowals enjoy immunity to error through misascription, we should not conclude that avowable mental states have *nonphysical* qualitative features that only we can securely recognize in our own case and on which privileged self-knowledge is based. Once the recognitional conception of self-knowledge is made explicit, exorcized, and replaced, we can also see how our commonsense notion of privileged self-knowledge can withstand the skeptic's threat.[26]

References

Bar-On, D. 2004 *Speaking My Mind: Expression and Self-Knowledge*, Oxford, Oxford University Press).
——2004a "Externalism and Self-Knowledge: Content, Use, and Expression", *Noûs* 38, 430–55.
Boghossian, P. A. 1989 "Content and Self-Knowledge", *Philosophical Topics* 17, 5–26; repr. in P. Ludlow and N. Martin 1998, 149–74.
——1997 "What the Externalist Can Know A Priori", *Proceedings of the Aristotelian Society* 97, 161–75; repr. in C. Wright, B. Smith, and C. Macdonald (eds.) 1998, 271–84.
Burge, T. 1979 "Individualism and the Mental", *Midwest Studies in Philosophy* 4, 73–122; repr. in P. Ludlow and N. Martin 1998, 21–83.
——1988 "Individualism and Self-Knowledge", *Journal of Philosophy* 85/11, 649–63; repr. in Q. Cassam (ed.) 1994, 65–79.
——1996 "Our Entitlement to Self-Knowledge", *Proceedings of the Aristotelian Society* 96, 91–116; repr. in P. Ludlow and N. Martin 1998, 239–64.
Cassam, Q. (ed.) 1994 *Self-Knowledge*, Oxford, Oxford University Press.

---

[26] My thanks to Ram Neta, Dylan Sabo, and Ted Parent for comments on earlier drafts of this chapter. Thanks to audiences at MIT, Davidson College, University of Maryland, Auburn University, University of Western Ontario, and to the participants at the Self-Knowledge and the Self Workshop in Bigorio, Switzerland (2003) for helpful questions and comments.

Davies, M. 1998 "Externalism, Architecturalism, and Epistemic Warrant", in C. Wright, B. Smith, and C. Macdonald 1998, 321–61.

Evans, G. 1982 *The Varieties of Reference*, Oxford, Clarendon Press.

Fricker, E. 1998 "Self-Knowledge: Special Access Versus Artefact of Grammar—A Dichotomy Rejected", in C. Wright, B. Smith, and C. Macdonald 1998, 155–206.

Goldman, A. 1976 "Discrimination and Perceptual Knowledge", *The Journal of Philosophy* 73/20, 771–91.

Ludlow, P. 1995 "Externalism, Self-Knowledge, and the Prevalence of Slow-Switching", Analysis 55/1, 45–9.

——and Martin, N. (eds.) 1998 *Externalism and Self-Knowledge*, Stanford, CSLI Publications.

Peacocke, C. 1996 "Our Entitlement to Self-Knowledge: Entitlement, Self-Knowledge and Conceptual Redeployment", *Proceedings of the Aristotelian Society* 96, 117–58; repr. in 265–303 in P. Ludlow and N. Martin 1998, 265–303.

Pryor, J. 1999 "Immunity to Error Through Misidentification", *Philosophical Topics* 26/1–2, 271–304.

Putnam, H. 1975 "The Meaning of 'Meaning'", in H. Putnam, *Mind, Language and Reality*, Cambridge, Cambridge University Press, 215–71.

Shoemaker, S. 1968 "Self-Reference and Self-Awareness", *Journal of Philosophy* 65/19, 555–67; repr. in Q. Cassam (ed.) 1994, 80–93.

——1994 "Self-Knowledge and 'Inner Sense'", *Philosophy and Phenomenological Research* 54/2, 249–314.

Wittgenstein, L. 1960 *The Blue and Brown Books: Preliminary Studies for the "Philosophical Investigations"*, 2nd Edition, New York, Harper and Row.

Wright, C. 1989 "Wittgenstein's Rule-Following Considerations and the Central Project of Theoretical Linguistics", in A. George (ed.) *Reflections on Chomsky*, Oxford, Basil Blackwell, 233–64.

——1998 "Self-knowledge: The Wittgensteinian legacy", in C. Wright, B. Smith, and C. Macdonald 1998, 13–45.

——2001a *Rails to Infinity*, Cambridge (Mass.), Harvard University Press.

——2001b "The problem of self-knowledge (I) and (II)", in C. Wright 2001a, 319–73.

——Smith B. C., and Macdonald C. (eds.) 1998 *Knowing Our Own Minds*, Oxford, Clarendon Press.

10

One Variety of Self-Knowledge: Constitutivism as Constructivism[*]

Annalisa Coliva

It is a commonplace that we know our own minds, namely that we know our own sensations, feelings, perceptions, imaginations, and emotions, as well as propositional attitudes, such as beliefs, desires, intentions, hopes, wishes, and so on. Still, there is little consensus over what would count as a sound philosophical explanation of our knowledge of each of these kinds of mental states. For, on the one hand, a variety of competing encompassing theories of self-knowledge are available nowadays.[1] On the other, given the intrinsic differences among the various kinds of mental states we can enjoy, it may well be that the most apt attitude towards self-knowledge should in fact be *pluralistic*—that is, such as to allow for different accounts of how we know each of these various kinds of mental states.

Sydney Shoemaker[2] and Crispin Wright[3] have been among the first theorists to propose a so-called "constitutive" account of self-knowledge. Constitutive accounts

---

[*] I would like to thank people in attendance at various presentations of previous versions of this chapter such as the participants to "The Self and Self-Knowledge I" conference, held in Bigorio (CH), and kindly supported by the Fonds nationals Suisse (Project number 1115-05572): Dorit Bar-On, Akeel Bilgrami, Jane Heal, Martine Nida-Rümelin, Lucy O'Brien, Eva Picardi, Jim Pryor, Carol Rovane, Gianfranco Soldati, and Crispin Wright. My thanks also to Achille Varzi for helpful discussions, to Paulo Faria, Elisabeth Pacherie, Joelle Proust, Barry Smith, Isidora Stojanovic, and to the rest of the audience at Institut Jean Nicod, Paris, as well as to people in attendance at King's College London, in particular Charles Travis and Keith Hossack. I would also like to thank the audience at the ECAP conference in Lisbon 2005, at the Italo-Spanish workshop in Bologna in 2005, and at the SIFA conference in Genova in 2004. I also take this opportunity to express my gratitude to my colleagues and friends at COGITO Research Centre, in particular, Paolo Leonardi, Eva Picardi, Sebastiano Moruzzi, Giorgio Volpe, Delia Belleri, Michele Palmira, as well as Carla Bagnoli and Mario Alai for helpful discussion on the penultimate draft of this chapter. Most of all, however, my thanks go to the Italian Academy at Columbia University (NY) and the Alexander von Humboldt Stiftung for generous support, and to my host in Heidelberg, Professor Andreas Kemmerling, for providing ideal settings in which much of the research that eventually led to the present chapter was conducted.

[1] See, for instance, D. Bar-On (2004). Another potentially encompassing account of self-knowledge is the one presented in C. Peacocke (1999, ch. 5) See also Peacocke (2004, chs. 3, 8) for an account of self-knowledge of perceptions and an account of the emotions, which would be compatible with Peacocke's other pronouncements on self-knowledge.

[2] See also S. Shoemaker (1968, 1986, 1988, 1990, 1996a, 1996b); Heal (2002).

[3] C. Wright (1989a, 1989b, 1998, 2001a, 2001b).

are designed to apply mainly to knowledge of our own propositional attitudes. For it is a tenet of this kind of account that having knowledge of one's first order mental states is (at least) a necessary condition for having those mental states. Clearly, this would make little sense for sensations and perceptions, as well as for some kind of emotions, which we may want to grant to creatures such as infants and higher-order mammals whom, however, we think would lack knowledge of their own mental states. This, therefore, invites the idea that self-knowledge as a whole should be explained in a variety of ways.[4]

Despite Akeel Bilgrami's new vigorous and thought-provoking attempt at defending a constitutive account of our knowledge of propositional attitudes (cf. Bilgrami 2006),[5] constitutive accounts have recently come under attack,[6] for many theorists working in this area are getting increasingly uneasy with the idea, which has by now become the central tenet of constitutive accounts, that the immediate and authoritative way in which each of us knows her own propositional attitudes is *not* the result of any cognitive achievement, consisting, rather, in a pair of two conceptual truths which can be variously redeemed. In fact, many theorists are now trying to defend the idea that, although self-knowledge of propositional attitudes is neither observational, nor inferential, just as constitutivism holds, it nevertheless counts as a genuine kind of knowledge: for it would consist in having true beliefs about one's own first-order propositional attitudes, which would exist independently of one's knowledge of them, for the *reason* that one has them. So, self-knowledge, despite its being neither observational nor inferential, would not be *baseless*,[7] or *groundless*,[8] for one's second-order (true) beliefs would in fact be based on, or grounded in the corresponding first-order mental states and held because one is somehow aware of them.[9]

An initial difficulty with these latter accounts is that it is quite hard to see how *one's own available reason* or *warrant*[10] for one's psychological self-ascriptions could be anything else but the avowal itself. For, if asked "How do you know that—say—you believe that P?" I could only answer by repeating my avowal, namely, by saying "Because I do believe that P". Hence, it is not clear how subjects could provide

---

[4] As Patrizia Pedrini kindly pointed out to me, recently Matthew Boyle has argued for this very conclusion. See M. Boyle (2009).

[5] Bilgrami's account allows him to connect self-knowledge, agency, value, and intentionality, which he sees as fundamentally integrated.

[6] See C. Peacocke (1999, 2004); R. Moran (2001); D. Bar-On (2004, ch. 9) which, interestingly aims to combine this view with expressivism; L. O'Brien (2007). Much of the inspiration for these accounts comes from Burge (1996).

[7] The expression is J. McDowell's, although not used in the context of providing a positive account of self-knowledge (cf. McDowell 1998, at p. 48 and *infra*).

[8] This is Wright's way of characterizing self-knowledge in his works. (cf. fn. 3).

[9] Notice that what would be baseless or groundless is the self-ascription of the relevant mental states, according to the constitutive account, not the first-order mental states themselves, which may indeed be based on grounds and evidence, as we shall see at much greater length in the following.

[10] All these accounts are advertised as internalist.

independent reasons for their avowals. More generally, as I have argued elsewhere,[11] if, in order for first-order mental states to function as reasons of the corresponding self-ascriptions, subjects need to be aware of them, depending on what notion of awareness one favours—propositional or phenomenal—it may well turn out either that self-knowledge of the basing state be presupposed, or else that awareness of it falls short of providing one with a genuine reason for the self-ascription. Thus, I think constitutive accounts remain the most promising way of looking at our knowledge of our own propositional attitudes. In this chapter, I will present a new brand of constitutivism which, while finding its inspiration in the works of Wright and Bilgrami, seems to me to have the resources to do better than its predecessors on a number of fronts.

1. The constitutive thesis

According to constitutive theorists, self-knowledge can be based neither on observation nor on inference for either would fail to account for two features of it which seem intuitively compelling, namely, so-called "transparency" and "authority". Transparency amounts to the idea that at least in a large class of cases the occurrence of one's own mental states is of a piece with one's awareness of their kind and content. If, for instance, I were asked "What are you thinking of right now?" I would be able to answer immediately, without conducting any inquiry. Whatever kind of thought is now crossing my mind, it would seem to be immediately known to me, both with respect to its kind—its being a belief, a desire, a wish, etc.—and its content. It seems to make no sense to suppose that I should somehow find out what I am now thinking of by observing myself and my behaviour. Nor would it make sense to suppose that such knowledge would in fact depend on observing mental states somehow luminously presented in my mental arena. After all, mental states are not kinds of objects we may observe, and to think otherwise would in fact depend on holding on to a Cartesian conception of the mind, whose limits and intrinsic incoherence have been variously exposed.[12] Authority, in contrast, consists in the fact that, at least in the vast majority of cases, one's sincere and competent avowals can't rationally be challenged. It makes no sense, at least in most cases, as we shall review in the following, to challenge a subject who sincerely avows "I believe that summers in Greece are really too hot" and is competent with respect to the relevant concepts, by saying "How do know that you believe it?—Give me your grounds for your claim", and so on.[13]

---

[11] For a detailed criticism of Peacocke's position, see A. Coliva (2008). Some qualms are raised also in Bilgrami (2006, 134–9). See also the essay by J. Heal in this volume.

[12] See, for instance, C. Wright (2001b, 331–40); D. Bar-On (2004, ch. 2, 37–46); A. Bilgrami (2006, 3–8). Most criticisms rely on Wittgenstein's considerations against the very intelligibility of a private language. A different kind of criticism can be found in Shoemaker 1996a, Lecture I in particular.

[13] Obviously what wouldn't make sense is to challenge a subject's psychological self-ascription, not her grounds for holding that summers in Greece are really too hot (cf. fn. 9). Furthermore, as the qualifications suggest, it wouldn't make sense provided there were no reasons to think that such a subject may be self-deceived. There will be more on self-deception in the following.

Furthermore, transparency and authority seem to be a priori and necessary features of our knowledge of our own mental states, not just mere contingencies,[14] for there is at least a general presumption that people will know their own mental states and that their avowals will be correct. We may think of exceptions both to transparency and authority, such as unconscious mental states, which will be there but won't be self-known, or cases of self-deception, where a subject might think she has a given mental state she doesn't really seem to have. But either exception seems peculiar. Not knowing that one has a serious hatred towards all other male subjects as the result of one's Oedipus complex is not quite like ignoring what one is thinking of right now. The first kind of ignorance would not impair the idea that we are dealing with a human being capable of a real mental life. The latter, in contrast,[15] would: it seems to be part and parcel of our own conception of adult human beings' mentality that they have knowledge of their own occurrent mental states. Furthermore, supposing that subjects could routinely self-ascribe beliefs and desires they don't really have would hinder the idea that they possess the relevant psychological concepts, and, arguably, that we are dealing with rational subjects at all.

So bar these peculiar (and perhaps only seeming) exceptions, there seems to be a general presumption that mental states are transparent to the subjects who have them and that when they avow their own mental states they are correct. To stress, transparency and authority don't seem to be just empirical generalizations. Rather they seem to be of a piece with our conception of ourselves and others as endowed with a real and normal mental life, as rational agents, and, finally, of a piece with our linguistic practice of making avowals, in which our conceptual mastery is deployed.

Yet, no bit of knowledge based on observation is either "transparent" or "authoritative". For, by definition, it will always be based on a however minimal empirical

---

[14] The fact that transparency and authority are held to be a priori and necessary features of self-knowledge as opposed to mere contingencies sets constitutivists apart from other theorists, such as functionalists, who may think that it is part of the functional role of propositional attitudes that they give rise to a correct second-order belief about them. Indeed, David Armstrong (1968), though no functionalist at all, is prominent for holding such a view. Notice, however, that on his picture, failures at self-knowledge, either for lack of transparency or of authority, would be due to the malfunctioning of a subpersonal cognitive mechanism, which either does not produce second-order beliefs, or gives rise to erroneous ones. It should be noted, however, that such failures would not impair a subject's rationality—not any more than being colour-blind should impair one's rationality in using colour concepts. Constitutivists, in contrast, maintain that failing to know one's own mental states or being massively mistaken with respect to them would rightly make us suspicious of dealing with a subject who is rational and in possession of the relevant conceptual repertoire. On this issue, see, for instance, D. Bar-On (2004, 95–104); A. Bilgrami (2006, ch. 1); C. Wright (1998, 17). I discuss and criticize Armstrong's position in more detail in A. Coliva (2006, esp. at pp. 104–6). True, as an anonymous referee has pointed out, there may be other accounts of self-knowledge, beside constitutive ones, which exclude massive failures of self-knowledge, if subjects are to be granted with the relevant conceptual repertoire. These proposals would have to be discussed on merit and, in particular, it should be seen whether they would be compatible with the claim—which seems to me distinctive of constitutivism—that radical failures of self-knowledge would impair a subject's rationality. In any event, the considerations proposed in the main text are merely meant to make an at least prima facie case for the plausibility and interest of constitutive positions.

[15] Under certain constraints I will indicate in the following.

inquiry, and will remain open to rational challenges, at least in principle. Similarly, our inferential knowledge will always be based on connecting our observations with some kind of theory, thus failing to be transparent, and, obviously, it will always be amenable to rational scrutiny. Since we don't have any other way of knowing empirical truths, other than by observation or by inference, we should conclude that self-knowledge is in fact based on *nothing* (cf. Boghossian 1989, 5; Wright 1989b, 312). To repeat, what this means is that so-called "self-knowledge" is not a kind of cognitive achievement after all, consisting in holding a true belief on the basis of having reasons for it—no matter how you might construe these reasons. Therefore, if knowledge is understood in such a usual way, it is somehow a misnomer to call it "knowledge". Rather, what we call "self-knowledge"—that is the distinctive kind of authority we recognize to our fellow humans (and to ourselves) over their own mental states, as well as the distinctively immediate, or transparent way in which they are aware of them—are guaranteed to hold a priori.

In more detail, all constitutive theorists agree that a suitably qualified version of the following thesis holds a priori and that, in fact, it is true as a matter of *conceptual necessity*.

> Constitutive Thesis: given certain conditions C, S believes/desires/intends/wishes/hopes that P if and only if S believes (or judges) that she believes/desires/intends/wishes/hopes that P.[16]

However, constitutive theorists debate the following:

(i) what the *grounds* of the constitutive thesis are—for example, is it grounded in the linguistic practice of making psychological avowals (Wright); or in the notion of rationality (Shoemaker); or, else, in the notion of deliberative agency (Bilgrami)? Depending on their answers to such questions, they will return different characterizations of the C-conditions which are supposed to constrain the constitutive thesis. Furthermore, what they debate is

(ii) how to interpret the thesis and, in particular, what kind of *metaphysical implications* it has. On some constitutive accounts, to judge that, say, one believes that P does (at least partially and in some cases) bring about the corresponding first-order propositional attitude (Shoemaker, Wright, and myself, as we shall see). Hence, enjoying the latter is actually *constituted* by one's believing to be in such a state. On some other, weaker constitutive views, such as Bilgrami's, the relevant self-ascriptions are not intended as bringing about the corresponding first-order propositional attitudes. Hence, the constitutive thesis is read as merely entailing that self-knowledge is both a necessary and a sufficient condition for the corresponding first-order mental states.[17]

---

[16] I think that the formulation of the second half of the constitutive thesis is irrelevant, as long as one holds that judgement brings about belief. This view can be found, for instance, in C. Peacocke (1999, 238), as well as in T. Scanlon (1998, ch. 1); but also in R. Moran (2001, 116).

[17] Sometimes people worry about the fact that such a position could really qualify as constitutive (O'Brien in conversation). Insofar as constitutivism is taken to be individuated by its adherence to the

Here, however, I won't look at the details of other constitutive accounts and will simply let my (dis)agreement emerge in the course of the presentation of my own positive proposal.

2. Transparency

Let us focus on the left-to-right side of the constitutive thesis, which elevates transparency to the rank of a conceptual truth. Clearly, we should specify the C-conditions so as to impose the obvious constraint that the biconditional should hold only for a lucid and sincere subject. Even so, however, it remains that maintaining it is a conceptual truth that if such a subject has a given first-order belief/desire/intention/wish/hope and so on she will believe she does, seems to be bound to generate some critical reactions. Two are most likely.

As we have already anticipated, there are unconscious mental states. If one allows for them,[18] then they would be there even if one is in no position to self-ascribe them. Furthermore, we are now conversant with the practice of ascribing at least beliefs and desires to higher-order mammals and infants to explain their purposive behaviour that can't be explained simply in a causal-nomological manner.[19] Still, we don't want to say that these creatures have knowledge of their own mental states. So, this would be another case where there would be first-order propositional attitudes but no second-order beliefs about them.

2.1 Mental states as commitments

In order to answer these objections I think it is useful to point out that, on reflection, and contrary to what mainstream philosophy of mind seems to hold, our notion of an intentional mental state isn't univocal. On the one hand, there are intentional mental states that we might call "mental states *as dispositions*" or "*non-judgement-sensitive* mental

view that self-knowledge is not the result of any cognitive achievement and that it consists in maintaining that the constitutive thesis holds as a matter of conceptual necessity, I think we can embrace Bilgrami's position within the scope of constitutivism. So, we could distinguish between "weak" and "strong" forms of constitutivism: they would all hold that self-knowledge isn't the result of any cognitive achievement, but only strong ones would add that first-order mental states are (at least partially and in some cases) constituted by having the corresponding second-order ones. Notice, moreover, that weak forms of constitutivism would be applicable also to phenomenal self-knowledge (as long as we were dealing with creatures endowed with the relevant conceptual repertoire and we characterized the C-conditions accordingly, with obviously no reference to propositional attitudes as commitments). By contrast, I don't think strong forms of constitutivism could sensibly carry over to our knowledge of our own sensations and other non-propositional mental states. For the fact that we share them with infants and at least higher-order mammals seems to me incompatible with the view that these mental states could be at least partly constituted by the judgement that one has them.

[18] Personally I am not skeptical with respect to them. But, in case one were so skeptical, one possible counterexample to transparency would disappear.

[19] Again, someone might deny the legitimacy of such a practice. Although I think we shouldn't be too cavalier in ascribing beliefs and desires to these creatures, I think that qualified ascriptions of beliefs and desires to them are fine. In the following I will be more precise about the form these qualifications should take.

states".[20] Admittedly, this would be a very heterogeneous class, whose width may be hard to determine exactly. However, what will characterize the mental states that belong to it is at least the following:

(a) these mental states aren't the result of a conscious deliberation, that is, a judgement, on a subject's part, based on considering and, in particular, on *assessing* evidence in favour of P (or of P is worth pursuing, it would be good if P happened, etc.);
(b) these mental states aren't within one's direct control, being rather something one finds oneself saddled with;
(c) hence, these mental states aren't something one will be held rationally responsible for.

Some examples of mental states that will satisfy these conditions are: (i) mental states that aren't formed by being able to *assess* evidence in favour of P (in the case of beliefs) or of P would be good to have (in the case of desires, intentions, and hopes), though one may form them in response to available evidence in favour of P, or of P would be good to have, if presented with it;[21] (ii) mental states that are attributed to subjects to make sense of their behaviour, of which they themselves may be entirely *ignorant*; (iii) the latter class of mental states may comprise, but isn't exhausted by, *unconscious* mental states of a Freudian kind, which, however, can be operative in shaping a subject's behaviour; (iv) also mental states that are self-attributed on the basis of an act of *self-interpretation*, by finding them out through the observation of one's own behaviour and other immediately self-known mental states, will fall into this category. For self-interpretation, when successful, makes one aware of a mental state that is already there, yet isn't "one's making", but, rather, something one finds oneself saddled with.[22] Finally, and as the converse of self-interpretation, (v) there may be mental

---

[20] Bilgrami (2006, ch. 5) in particular, distinguishes between mental states as "dispositions" and as "commitments"; Scanlon (1998) and Moran (2001, 2003) between "brute" or "non-judgement sensitive" and "judgement-sensitive" mental states.

[21] Brute urges and needs would fall into this category; but also, I think, those dispositional mental states we may ascribe to a-conceptual creatures to make sense of their intelligent behavior, which, while responsive to some evidence, aren't dependent on its appraisal.

[22] A nice example, although not a case of propositional attitude, is provided by Jane Austen in her novel *Emma*, when the protagonist finds out about her love for Mr. Knightley, her long-lasting friend, by reflection and inference on her own immediately available feelings of jealousy at the prospect that Mr. Knightley could return another woman's feelings. The example is presented and discussed in C. Wright (1998, 15–16), borrowed from J. Tanney (1996). (Notice, however, that Tanney is concerned with the kind of construction of one's own mind which could occur in self-interpretation. Here, in contrast, I will be concerned with constructivism regarding one's own immediate avowals of propositional attitudes.) Analogous examples could easily be construed for the case of propositional attitudes. Giorgio Volpe has kindly pointed out to me that also Schopenhauer in *On Freedom of the Human Will* holds the view that a person's character traits are known to him through reflection and inference on his past behaviour.

states, which one can inferentially *predict* will assail one, in given circumstances, which, however, *won't be within one's direct control*.²³

Yet, manifestly, adult human beings also have different kinds of mental states, namely, mental states that depend on a judgement based on the *assessment* of the evidence at subjects' disposal, and that, for this reason, are within their control and for which they are held rationally responsible. Call them "intentional mental states as *commitments*", or "*judgement-sensitive* mental states" (cf. Bilgrami 2006, 213; Scanlon 1998, ch. 1; Moran 2001, 116). Although the word "commitment" may have become common currency in philosophical literature nowadays,²⁴ I think there is still little agreement among its users about its meaning. In my view, what is essential to commitments such as to make them, in effect, very close to "judgement-sensitive" beliefs, desires, intentions, wishes, hopes, and so on, is the following:

(a) that they are the result of an action—the mental action of *judging* that P is the case (or worth pursuing/having)—on the subject's part, on the basis of considering and hence of *assessing* evidence for P (is worth pursuing/having);²⁵
(b) that these mental states are *normatively constrained*, that is, they must respond to the principles governing theoretical and practical reasoning;
(c) and, in particular, they are so constrained (also) *from the subject's own point of view*;
(d) that they are mental states for which the subject is held *rationally responsible*.²⁶

---

²³ Perhaps, due to one's long-lasting self-observations, one will know that if one were to work in an unsupportive environment for a while, one would start losing one's self-confidence and believing that one's work is meaningless, or of poor quality. The characteristic feature of these mental states is that one would seem to find oneself *saddled with them*, even if one were rationally able to find reasons which should make one think differently.

²⁴ Bilgrami makes extensive use of the term; Robert Brandom too, although he is more interested in stressing the social dimension of commitments, than the former (or indeed myself). Furthermore, it is not my contention, somehow built in in the very notion of a commitment, that one should have knowledge of all the logical consequences of one's own beliefs and further propositional attitudes. As Bilgrami points out (2006, 371–2, fn. 7, but see also 376–7, fn. 20), the origin of the use of this term to refer to intentional states (or at least to a class of them) goes back to Isaac Levi.

²⁵ This is the main difference between my account of commitments and Bilgrami's. For, on his view, commitments aren't dependent on a subject's judgement.

²⁶ This is the constraint Bilgrami identifies as essential to commitments, from which, on his view, (b) and (c) follow. However, he gives a moral or evaluative twist to it I would resist. For, on his view, not only would one be held *rationally* responsible for one's commitments, but also *accountable* at large. For instance, one might be *reproached* or *resented* for having certain commitments (cf. Bilgrami 2006, 226). To my mind, however, specified in the way Bilgrami characterizes it, (d) is not sufficient to mark out the contrast between commitments and dispositions, because one can criticize or be criticized, and accept to be criticized, also (for) one's own dispositions, such as the disposition to smoke, or, to take a more loaded example, for wanting to get rid of other male opponents as a result of an unresolved Oedipus complex. But, surely, neither mental state is the result of a subject's action, for which one can be held rationally responsible, although one may be considered "badly"—in Bilgrami's extended sense of the term—for having it. It is then not by chance that, as a matter of fact, Bilgrami ends up endorsing the view that "we do have transparent self-knowledge of mental dispositions" (Bilgrami 2006, 287). I find this conclusion unpalatable, for, surely, when we do get knowledge of our unconscious mental states we obtain it through a process of self-interpretation or of analysis (that may or may not be guided by a therapist) relevantly similar to the ways in which we may come to attribute mental states to others. So, it seems to me that whatever knowledge we may eventually gain of our unconscious

So, in my view, mental states as commitments depend on a subject's *deliberation* with respect to P, in the case of belief, of "P ought to be pursued" and of "It would be good (for me) if P were the case" in the case of desires and intentions, hopes and wishes, and so on, based on considering and evaluating evidence for P or for "P ought to be pursued", etc.[27] Furthermore, should countervailing evidence come in, then a subject *ought* to withdraw from holding P, "P ought to be pursued" and "It would be good (for me) if P were the case" etc., thus, withdraw from one's belief that P is the case or from one's desire/intention/hope/wish that P should obtain. Finally, precisely because such "oughts" would have to be appreciated by the subject herself, were she not to withdraw from her beliefs and further propositional attitudes as commitments in light of counter-evidence, she would not only incur *rational criticism*, but she should also *accept* to incur it, since she wouldn't have—the phrase comes in handy—"lived up to her commitments".

Now, some clarifications are in order. First, to say that beliefs (as well as other propositional attitudes) as commitments are the result of a deliberation and fall within one's responsibility doesn't "involve us in any sort of voluntarism about [their] formation [...], any more than we need to see ordinary argument with others as aiming at getting one's interlocutor somehow to adopt a new belief by sheer act of arbitrary will" (Moran 2001, 120, cf. Moran 2003 and Shoemaker 2003, postscript). That is to say, forming certain mental states by considering relevant pieces of evidence is a rational action, yet not an act of arbitrary will. Indeed, being aware of evidence in favour of P, and being unaware of countervailing evidence, ought to give rise to one's judgement that P is the case, and thus to the corresponding belief (similar considerations would hold for other propositional attitudes and the kind of evidence with respect to which they are the rational response). Hence, it would be a sign of irrationality not to form that belief, given favourable evidence for P.[28] If one did not

---

mental states it is not transparent, and is actually grounded in observation and inference. Moreover, in the case of dispositions such as the disposition to smoke, we certainly don't want to account for their transparency by mobilizing something like the constitutive thesis, read in a strong sense (see fn. 17, above). For that would have the unattractive consequence of making one's own dispositions the result (at least partly) of one's beliefs about them. So, in the case of dispositions such as the disposition to smoke a cigarette, when they are known immediately—that is, when the corresponding *urge* manifests itself—I would rather account for that knowledge along purely expressivist lines. The kind of more general knowledge of one's own generic disposition to smoke, in contrast, would be self-known through a process of self-observation and interpretation; hence, in a third-personal way.

[27] This is a sketchy account that, however, doesn't prevent obvious forms of local holism between mental states from arising. Indeed, viewing also desires, intentions, and other propositional attitudes, beside beliefs, as commitments, tightly connects them with *believing* that their contents are worth-pursuing or would be good for one if actualized. This, in my view, is a plus and not a deficiency of the present proposal.

[28] I said that it would be a sign of irrationality not to form certain mental states as commitments, given certain pieces of evidence, and this might invite the objection that, at least in the case of intentions, one could fail to form them, upon having suitable evidence in their favour, as a result of mere weakness of will. My view is that weakness of will could only prevent one from *acting* on the basis of a given intention, but would not impinge on its formation. One might then suggest that despite having evidence in favour of "It would be good (for me) if P were the case" a (lucid and attentive) subject could fail to form the corresponding intention

form such a belief, one should incur and ought to accept to incur criticism. Conversely, forming the belief that P when no evidence in favour of P is at one's disposal, let alone contrary, undefeated evidence is available to one, would not be the rational thing for one to do. If one did, one should accept and ought to agree to accept criticism.

Second, it is important to emphasize that a subject may not always arrive at her beliefs and further propositional attitudes as a result of *conscious* consideration of the evidence for P (or else, for P ought to be pursued, or for "it would be good (for me) if P were the case"). All the present account of commitments requires is that she must be able to offer her evidence in support of her beliefs and judgement-sensitive desires and other propositional attitudes if asked to give her grounds for them—that is, the reasons why she holds them, not the reasons why she *believes* she does (cf. Moran 2001, 116). This is part of what distinguishes commitments from dispositions, which while perhaps based on evidence, aren't based on the assessment—not even the potential assessment—of such evidence.

Third, it may sound surprising that also desires could be seen as brought about by rational deliberation. But I think it is important to keep in mind that here I am not concerned with what we might call "brute" desires such as lust or hunger, but only with rationally held ones.[29] For instance, one may rationally desire to provide one's child with the best possible education. If one does so, it will be for reasons, which, as such, may be further assessed. Were it to turn out—quite implausibly—that countervailing considerations should outweigh that desire, one should withhold from it, if rational.

Finally, it has to be registered that although the distinction between mental states as commitments and as dispositions may be misleading, insofar as it might suggest the idea that commitments *exclude* having behavioural dispositions (at large),[30] on my

---

because of other considerations. Hence, rationality doesn't require forming the relevant intentions upon having at one's disposal certain pieces of evidence. I think that is all right, but that it merely shows that the subject didn't have *sufficient* reasons to form a given intention. Hence, it is obvious, though I haven't so far added nor will in the following add such a qualification, that when I claim that there are intentions as commitments that are based on evidence, I am in fact talking of those intentions we form on the basis of *sufficient* reasons for them. Again (cf. fn. 27), this shows that, inevitably, there will be forms of local holism in the formation of one's mental states, which is all to be expected.

[29] See also T. Scanlon (1998); R. Moran (2001, 116); and A. Bilgrami (2006, 214). These "oughts" are what distinguishes beliefs and desires as commitments from mere drives and brute dispositions: if I believe/desire that P as a commitment, then I *ought* to do so on the basis of *evidence* and ought to *withhold* from it in case contrary evidence came up. Obviously no such "oughts" hold for drives, e.g. the urge to smoke a cigarette after dinner, which will persist no matter what amount of counterevidence will be considered against the advisability of such a practice; or brute dispositions, such as the disposition to form a certain thought upon hearing a given word, tune, etc. As already remarked (see fn. 26, above), it may well be that the best account of our knowledge of our "brute" desires, which are not known through self-interpretation, should be given along expressivist lines.

[30] I am not sure Bilgrami really avoids this risk (see for instance, 2006, 210, 226), although, on his view, commitments consist in having the (second-order) disposition to be self-critical or to accept criticism from another person, if one fails to live up to one's commitments (see Bilgrami 2006, 226). Bilgrami seems to see commitments and (first-order) dispositions as mutually exclusive types of mental states mostly because of his preoccupation to avoid naturalism. A discussion of this topic will have to be postponed to another occasion.

understanding of them, mental states as commitments will in fact *have to* be accompanied by the relevant set of dispositions:[31] for instance, if I believe that P as a commitment then I ought to be disposed (*ceteris paribus*) to use P as a premise in a piece of practical or theoretical reasoning, to assert "P", to give grounds for my claim if challenged, as well as to withdraw from it in case contrary evidence came up. Similarly, in the case of a desire as a commitment that P, I ought to be disposed (*ceteris paribus*) to seek means to make P happen, or withdraw from it if it were shown that it is not worth-pursuing, and so on.[32] If I didn't actualize such dispositions, I should then be prepared to accept criticism for having failed to live up to my commitments.

Now, let us go back to the apparent counterexamples. First of all, it seems safe to hold that while infants and higher-order mammals may of course have "brute" desires and be able to react and interact in intelligent ways with their environment, thus (perhaps) justifying the fact that we may want to attribute beliefs and desires to them, they certainly don't have mental states as a result of judgement and of actively bringing evidence and practical considerations to bear on what they believe and desire, by considering and assessing such evidence and practical considerations, not even potentially. Hence, whatever kind of mental states they can actually enjoy, they can't have mental states as commitments.[33] Similarly, unconscious mental states aren't, obviously, brought about by judgements sensitive to epistemic evidence and practical considerations. They are produced, rather, by experiences we have had, mostly in early years, but aren't formed by consciously assenting to certain contents in light of assessed evidence for them. Hence, they aren't commitments. Thus, infants' and animals' mental states as well as unconscious ones won't be counterexamples to the

---

[31] Here is another difference between Bilgrami's understanding of commitments and mine. For, on his view, although commitments *may* be accompanied by dispositions they *need not* be. See A. Bilgrami (2006, 214–15, 225). So, on his account, one could have a commitment to help the poor, say, even if one lacked any disposition to do so. I beg to disagree. I think one ought to have that (first-order) disposition, in order really to have that commitment, although, of course, one may fail to live up to it—that is, one may *on occasion* and *in clearly specifiable conditions*, fail to actualize it. There will be more on this in Section 3.1.

[32] I don't think, contrary to what theorists often suppose, that acknowledging this will impair the characteristic authority of propositional attitudes' avowals. See fn. 68, below.

[33] Of course this might invite the idea—put to me by an anonymous reader—that at a later stage in their development they might have these very same mental states together with the ability to assess the evidence on which they are based and be able to offer it, if requested. Thus, commitments would just be a different mode of presentation of the very same kind of mental state originally held as a disposition. While I am comfortable with this idea in the case of some mental states as dispositions—those presently under scrutiny—I don't find this view very plausible when the dispositions at stake are unconscious mental states of a Freudian kind. Whether this should be taken as a recommendation to split the category of mental dispositions at least in two, or else to resist the idea that commitments are ontologically identical to mental states as dispositions, even in the apparently harmless case, is not something I am able to expound on at present. Be that as it may, it seems to me that either way it is important to recognize the role of mental states as commitments, if only as different ways in which an ontologically unique kind of entity may be given to a subject, contrary to the dominant tendency in the philosophy of mind, whereby all (propositional) mental states are usually treated in a functionalist, hence purely dispositional way.

left-to-right side of the constitutive thesis, once that thesis is appropriately qualified. That is to say, if it is taken to hold *only* for mental states as *commitments*. Yet, we must still explain why having beliefs and desires as commitments, that is to say, as brought about by judgement in the way described, should entail that they are known to a subject who has them.

Here's a first, partially unsuccessful shot:[34] in order to have beliefs and desires as commitments one should be able to withhold from them in case contrary evidence or countervailing considerations came up. So, for instance, to have the belief as a commitment that it is raining now one ought to withdraw from it if it were shown, say, that the street is wet because it has just been cleaned. Now, that information wouldn't require one to change one's mind if one were just imagining that it is raining or were so hoping. So, that information can make one change one's mind just in case it is taken by a subject to bear on her *belief* that it is raining now. Hence, having mental states as commitments—that is to say, as mental states that are within one's control and for which one is rationally responsible—entails that one knows them because it is only if one does that one can actually have them. So, having mental states as commitments would entail that the subject who has them would know them.

This move, however, taken as such, is unsuccessful for (at least) two reasons. First, because I think we can at least conceive of a self-blind subject, namely a subject who is capable of mental states as commitments, that is able to withdraw from her assertion of "It's raining now" in light of new counter-evidence, or that is able not to use that piece of information in her deliberations to action, if she got that new information—and yet, if asked "Do you believe that P?" would be unable to answer. Thus, while having beliefs as commitments, she would lack knowledge of them.[35] Second, because even if we had managed to establish the desired connection between commitments

---

[34] This is Bilgrami's move (2006, 160–6, 175–205). Notice, however, that I disagree with Bilgrami only insofar as he holds that the ability to engage in belief- (and other mental states-) revision *and nothing else* is sufficient for self-knowledge. As we shall see in Section 2.2, in my view, this is one necessary condition which, when combined with another one, adds up to a sufficient condition for self-knowledge.

[35] Self-blindness has been extensively discussed and criticized by S. Shoemaker (1996, 226–45). Notice, however, that Shoemaker is taking for granted that a subject who *already has the relevant psychological concepts* can't be self-blind. As he writes very clearly in an earlier essay "...second-order belief, and the knowledge it typically embodies, is supervenient on first-order beliefs and desires—or, rather, it is supervenient on these plus a certain degree of rationality, intelligence *and conceptual mastery*" (Shoemaker 1988, 34; emphasis added). Bilgrami thinks that self-blindness is inconceivable, when we are considering commitments, because of his specific understanding of that notion, as a second-order disposition to criticize oneself, or to accept to be criticized for not having lived up to them. Here, however, I have proposed a different account of commitments. But, at least on the face of it, it seems to me that one could criticize oneself or accept criticism from others for not having lived up to one's commitments without thereby having knowledge of them *as the mental states they are*. Consider a subject who has the desire as a commitment to help the poor, and is therefore able to judge "One should help the poor", give evidence for this, etc., but didn't have the concept of desire. Now, it seems to me perfectly conceivable that if someone told him "You are doing badly. You said the poor ought to be helped, but you aren't doing anything to that end", he would (have to) accept criticism, without thereby having knowledge of his desire *as such*. So I think self-blindness is metaphysically possible also for subjects capable of propositional attitudes as commitments. It is a further issue whether it is, or may actually be, instantiated.

and self-knowledge, we would have merely shown that the latter is a *necessary condition* for the former, but we wouldn't have provided any *substantive* account of it.[36]

2.2 Conceptual mastery as the result of blind drilling

In order to meet these objections, I think we have to introduce a further ingredient into the picture so that we will have two substantive[37] constraints on the C-conditions that, once *jointly fulfilled*, will make the left-to-right side of the biconditional hold as a matter of conceptual necessity. The missing ingredient—I submit—beside the capacity of having propositional attitudes as commitments, is *conceptual mastery*. This may come as no surprise, since one would have imagined from the start that in order to judge and therefore believe that one *believes* (or desires/intends/wishes/hopes) that P, one would have had to possess the relevant psychological concepts. Hence, in my view, self-blindness is inconceivable only once we are dealing with a subject who is rational, that is, capable of propositional attitudes as commitments, is sincere, cognitively lucid and, finally, equipped with the relevant psychological concepts.

However, I think it is only by giving a substantive account of what such a conceptual mastery may consist in that we can actually both avoid surreptitiously falling back into unwanted models of self-knowledge, and say something more meaningful about self-knowledge itself, in such a way that we won't be left with the impression that there is still some explanatory work to be done. So the question is: how does one conceptualize one's first-order mental states? Obviously, the answer can't be: either by having such states in view, as it were, and by recognizing and labelling them as the mental states they are; or else, by *self-consciously* applying the rule that if I *judge* that P is the case (or is worth pursuing) on the basis of evidence, then I believe (or desire) that P. For, in the former case, we would be back with the observational model of self-knowledge, and, in the latter, we would presuppose knowledge of our own judgement, which is nothing but a mental state (or, in fact, an action). Furthermore, we would presuppose the possession of other intentional psychological concepts, such as the concept of judgement, which, arguably, will have to be explained along the same lines as the possession of the concept of belief (and desire). Finally, the self-conscious application of the introduction rule for the concept of belief (in this case) would presuppose the possession of the latter concept. Hence, the explanation would be hopelessly circular. It is

---

[36] This criticism can in fact be leveled against Bilgrami's account of self-knowledge, although I suppose he would dig in his heels and insist that he has done all the explanatory work there is to be done, as long as he can redeem the left-to-right side of the constitutive thesis by placing it within the scope of an "agency" condition, complexly characterized as involving reference to justifiable reactive attitudes (see Bilgrami 2006, 119), that reveal the connection between transparency and agency so characterized. Bar-On (2004, 346–50) makes a similar critical point in connection with Wright's constitutive account.

[37] Recall that there are also two non-substantive constraints; namely: cognitive lucidity and sincerity (as we will see in Section 3.3, sincerity is not entirely trivial).

therefore crucial to come up with a different account of what mastery of the concepts of belief and desire (in the first person present) consists in.[38]

Here's a tentative view. Take a subject who is able to judge that P, give evidence in favour of it, use it as a premise in her reasoning and withdraw from it if required, and has, therefore, the first-order belief as a commitment that P. Suppose you ask her "Do you *believe* that P?" and she is unable to answer. So you would conclude that she doesn't have the concept of belief. In which case, you could simply train her to the use of that verb by *drilling* her into using the *expression* "I believe that P".[39] Similarly, take a subject who says "My children's proper education is worth pursuing" and is disposed to offer considerations in its favour, does what she can to help bring that about, and withdraws from it if those considerations did (incredibly) no longer seem compelling; but if asked "Do you *desire* that your children should have proper education?" didn't know how to answer. Then again you could drill her to use "I desire that P" as an alternative expression of her mind—of her judging "My children's proper education is worth pursuing".

Let me stress that it is absolutely essential in order for the present proposal to steer away from any observational model of self-knowledge or from surreptitiously assuming such knowledge of our own mental states, that one should be adamant that "I believe/desire (intend/whish/hope) that P" are taught *blindly*: they are *ingrained* as an alternative way of expressing one's first-order beliefs and desires (and further propositional attitudes as commitments), other than by asserting "P", or "P is worth pursuing", or "It would be good (for me) that P be the case".[40] So, on the present account there would really be no inner epistemology—just a substitution of one form of behaviour with another. But—and this is crucial—the kind of behaviour which would get replaced would already be quite rich. For, in order to have beliefs (and other propositional attitudes) as commitments, a subject will already have to have the *ability* to differentiate between, for instance, believing P and P's being the case, by being sensitive to the fact that her point of view may be challenged—thus responding with reasons in favour of it—or proved wrong—thus abandoning it. It is only on the background of this already

---

[38] As to the possibility of having *tacit* knowledge of the conceptual role of the concept of belief, it must be noticed that it would still presuppose tacit knowledge of one's first-order judgement. How, then, would we account for this form of self-knowledge in its turn? I develop this objection in my 2008.

[39] This account seems to me to be in keeping with Evans' point according to which all is needed to make self-ascriptions of belief is to judge that P is the case and preface that with "I believe that". Evans, however, isn't explicit about how the concept of belief in the first person present would be acquired. See G. Evans (1982, 225–6).

[40] Indeed, this seems to me to be the right development of Wittgenstein's idea that avowals substitute behaviour. It is just that when we move from avowals of sensations to avowals of propositional attitudes the behaviour we must take into account is not merely physical but also linguistic. I was pleased to find a similar suggestion in D. Bar-On (2004, ch. 7). However, Bar-On makes this point in the context of articulating a purely neo-expressivist account of psychological avowals that explicitly rejects the constitutive model. As we shall see in the following, I think this is just the beginning of an account of the role of "I believe/desire that P". (An expressivist account of Wittgenstein's views on avowals is given in R. Jacobsen (1996). As we shall see in the following, to my mind, it actually provides equal scope for a *constructivist* reading of Wittgenstein).

complex pattern of behaviour, which, however, doesn't seem to require the concept of belief (or of any other propositional attitude), but merely the capacity for first-order beliefs (and other propositional attitudes) *as commitments*, that I think we can maintain that "I believe that P" may be taught blindly. "I believe that P" would then be taught as an alternative way of making the commitment to P other than judging that P. But what "I believe that P" would make *explicit*—to the subject herself and others—is the fact, which remains only implicit in judging P, and in forming the corresponding commitment, that that is just her own point of view among other possible ones, which need not be correct. This would happen by telling the subject, for instance, "See, you have said that P, but it is not the case that P. So you merely *believe* it".

An important feature of the present account is that it tights first-person and third-person uses of "to believe" together from the start. For it is only by being taught *by someone else* to replace the direct expression of one's mind—of one's beliefs as commitments—by means of asserting "P", while being disposed to retract it, if shown wrong, with appropriate psychological self-ascriptions, that one acquires the concept of belief, though not the ability of having beliefs as commitments. Once endowed with the capacity for making explicit her belief that P as a commitment, the subject can *then* articulate the conceptual role which individuates the concept of belief: for she can now express the difference between believing that P and its obtaining, both in her own case and in the third-person case. But the newly acquired ability to articulate that difference—which displays her conceptual mastery—shouldn't obscure the fact that she may well have been already practically sensitive to it, and that her grasp of the concept of belief may not have depended on any substantial cognitive work.

2.2.1 Objections from empirical psychology Coming from the psychology camp, various objections may be raised against this proposal; first and foremost that empirical evidence shows that children take time to acquire the concept of belief and that that goes hand in hand with the development of a theory of their own as well as of other minds.[41] This evidence wouldn't sit well with my proposal and would rather favour an account of concepts' possession, according to which to possess a concept—and, in particular, the concept of belief—consists in knowing its conceptual role.

In response it may be said that, quite apart from the conceptual problems that would pose, such as presupposing self-knowledge and the possession of a lot of intentional concepts, here I haven't tried to present a *psychological* theory of concepts' possession. After all, what I have suggested is simply how someone who is already able to have first-order mental states as *commitments* may come to acquire such a concept. It may be that young infants simply don't qualify. Nonetheless, I think it is an entirely empirical issue if the psychological data currently at our disposal, like the age at which children

---

[41] The *locus classicus* is A. Gopnik (1993). Gopnik's paper gave rise to an enormous literature. However, it doesn't look as if the case of desires and other propositional attitudes has been studied as extensively as that of beliefs.

pass the false-belief test in their own case as well as in the case of other subjects,[42] should be taken to show that it takes time for them to learn how to use "*I believe*" (and acquire the corresponding concept), or else should be taken to show that it takes time for them to become capable of *beliefs as commitments*. For, as I understand it, they come to pass the false-belief test in their own case when they actually understand that their own point of view about the world (or that of other subjects) may be wrong. This, I take it, is at least a necessary condition for having beliefs as commitments. Furthermore, the ability to pass the false-belief test in the case of others may be explained differently than by appeal to the fact that children would possess a theory of other minds. For it would be enough to explain their correct answers to suppose that they issue them as if they themselves were in the other person's shoes. So, the ability to pass the false-belief test need not show that children possess a theory of their own minds as well as of others'. In fact it may actually just be taken to prove that they are capable of first-order beliefs as commitments and to project themselves onto others and therefore issue the correct answer to the false-belief test, without thereby having any explicit knowledge of their own and other minds, which, in my view, crucially depends on the possession of the relevant psychological concepts.[43]

The reason why I think the data at our disposal doesn't tell us clearly what is the case is that—quite understandably—the experiments haven't been designed to test the possibility I am advocating here, for, usually, children will be exposed to talk in terms of belief when they are actually in the process of acquiring the ability to have beliefs as commitments. This may well have confused the issues: we may have mistaken the fact that it takes time for children to learn to have beliefs as commitments as a sign of the fact that they need time to acquire the concept of belief. Furthermore, we may have imputed that difficulty to the fact that mastery of that concept would depend on the acquisition of a theory of one's own as well as of others' minds. A more telling test, then, would be to look at children who haven't been exposed to psychological talk up to the age of 3 or 4 (which is the age at which they allegedly come to have a theory of the mind and the concept of belief); see if, around that age, they pass the false-belief test in their own case as well as in others'—where, crucially, the test

---

[42] The test, first designed by H. Wimmer and J. Perner (1983), usually consists in showing children a Smarties' box. Asked what there is inside it, they answer "Smarties". They are then shown that there is a pencil instead and asked what another person, who hasn't seen the content of the box, would answer. They pass the test if they say "Smarties".

[43] I don't think this makes me automatically side with simulation theorists. For one thing, I am suggesting that children need not have the relevant psychological concepts, not even in the first person, in order to pass the false-belief test. Among simulation theorists, Robert Gordon's proposal avoids the attribution of psychological concepts to children. Simulative abilities, in his view, would be hard-wired and connected to the operations of so-called "mirror neurons". I myself am sceptical of the fact that mere appeal to hard-wired mechanisms can fully account for such cognitive abilities, though it can certainly manifest some of their material preconditions. I am also sceptical of his recent proposal (Gordon 2007) of explaining the acquisition of propositional attitudinal concepts through ascent routines that are based on the expressive, though dumb use of the very words that would later on come to signal the possession of those very concepts. I can't, however, pursue these points here.

shouldn't be phrased in terms of beliefs—; and *then* introduce them to talk in terms of belief (and other propositional attitudes). If, at that stage, it actually takes them a short amount of time to learn how to use "I believe", then I think we would have shown that the account of concepts' possession I have been proposing would in fact be compatible with human psychological development.[44,45]

Furthermore, it has to be noted that the conceptual role of the concept of belief is what theorists of concepts offer as an *abstract* individuation of that concept that supervenes on a *practice* of its use which, however, may come about in different ways. In particular, since on my proposal the commitments undertaken by asserting "P", as an expression of one's belief as commitment, and by asserting "I believe that P" would actually be the same (save for the fact that the latter would make explicit what the former leaves implicit, namely that the assertion of "P" expresses one's own point of view that need not be correct), it may well be that the conceptual role of the concept of belief in the first person present specifies the rules for the use of that concept which, in practice, may have been acquired by becoming able to have first-order beliefs as commitments first, and by then being blindly drilled to express them by prefacing one's assertion of "P" with "I believe that".

Assuming that what I have been proposing is along the right lines, it is perhaps worth-noticing that it is a consequence of the suggested account of conceptual mastery that, while it may be an open issue if and to what an extent language is necessary in order to have first-order propositional attitudes as commitments, on my view language is indeed necessary for one's knowledge of them. So, while pre-linguistic (or non-linguistic) creatures might still have the former, I am committed to the view that only linguistic creatures can have self-knowledge.[46]

---

[44] Should this test prove impossible, one might see if there are languages which don't have talk in terms of belief and other propositional attitudes. If speakers of those languages were in fact capable of beliefs as commitments, as I think there is no reason to be sceptical of, we could then test how long it would take them to acquire the ability to express their minds by self-ascribing beliefs and other propositional attitudes in a different language which contained these devices.

[45] The apparently difficult case, for my own proposal, would in fact be constituted by autistic patients affected by Asperger syndrome. While they don't fail the false-belief test, they seem not to have a theory of their own minds, and to lack a theory of other people's minds (Frith and Happé 1999). But several things must be noted: 1) when we look at their reports, what they show is that subjects affected by this syndrome have different kinds of *experiences* particularly of speech, and different *sensations*, if not an altogether lack of painful sensations (pp. 15–18). None of this would show anything relevant with respect to their propositional attitudes and their knowledge of them. 2) The only report which has a bearing on this issue (from Donna Williams 1994) in fact seems to imply that she didn't have, as an autistic child, desires as commitments (she writes (p. 15): "Autism had been there before I'd ever known a want of my own, so that my first 'wants' were copies of those seen in others (a lot of which came from TV)"). In such a case, it would not be surprising that they would have to gain knowledge of their own minds in a third-personal way, and that this would require some kind of theory of other minds. Finally, all the data is based on personal reports and, obviously, this wouldn't have any bearing on the possibility of having, and of having knowledge of, one's occurrent commitments. For much of what they say could actually be due to forms of self-interpretation.

[46] In fact, I would be inclined to maintain that only linguistic creatures can have mental states as commitments, since that would require the ability to articulate and defend their basing reasons, at least in

In this connection, it is worth stressing that the psychological literature on self-knowledge in non-linguistic creatures I am aware of is both difficult to interpret and actually potentially irrelevant. For what has been tested, particularly in chimpanzees, is merely the ability to know others' *perceptions*, such as seeing, and not their propositional attitudes—let alone the highly specialized class of propositional attitudes as commitments I have been trying to make plausible so far. Moreover, these studies also show crucial discrepancies. For instance, researches conducted by Povinelli and his associates deny that chimpanzees have knowledge of other subjects' perceptions, while those conducted by Tomasello and his lab support the opposite interpretation.[47] So I think we can actually conclude that, at the present stage of the inquiry, the empirical data currently at our disposal has in fact no bearing on the issue of whether only linguistic creatures can have knowledge of their own propositional attitudes as *commitments*.

To recap and conclude: in order to account for transparency (and hence to exclude self-blindness), the C-conditions figuring in the constitutive thesis must include reference to a lucid and sincere subject, who is capable of having propositional attitudes as commitments, and who is endowed with the relevant psychological concepts, acquired through blind drill.

3. Authority

Now our problem is: how can we account for free, as it were, for the claim that when a sincere and conceptually competent subject self-ascribes a mental state, she has it? And even before engaging in this task, what grounds would there be to accept that any sincere psychological self-ascription made by a conceptually endowed subject capable of the corresponding first-order mental states as commitments is correct? Aren't cases of self-deception, however rare they might be, just a clear counterexample to that half of the constitutive thesis? So, no matter how good our qualification of the C-conditions was in guarding against possible counterexamples to the left-to-right side of the constitutive thesis, its other direction doesn't seem to hold—let alone to hold as a matter of conceptual necessity. Thus, the constitutive thesis in its entirety would have to be rejected.

3.1 Self-deception

One might, with Wright (cf. Wright 1989a, 200–1), add to the C-conditions that the subject shouldn't be self-deceived (or anyway, that it is reasonable to assume that she is not). But, quite apart from sounding an ad hoc move, it seems that the very possibility of self-deception would show that constitutive accounts don't have much of

---

principle, while allowing that pre- or non-linguistic ones may have propositional attitudes as dispositions. I can't, however, pursue the point here.

[47] See D. Povinelli and J. Vonk (2004); followed by an *Appendix* with replies to objections coming from the other camp, at pp. 24–8. M. Tomasello et al. (2003a, 2003b).

a point: after all, how could one be mistaken about one's own immediately available mental states if not by somehow going wrong in identifying them? Wouldn't such room for error be compatible only with non-constitutive accounts of self-knowledge?[48] So, it would come as really good news if we could account for self-deception differently, thereby showing that its existence wouldn't constitute a threat to constitutive accounts.

Bilgrami[49] has come up with an idea that I find illuminating: on his view, self-deception is a case where a subject self-ascribes a mental state and has it as a *commitment*, yet she also has *another*, opposite unconscious mental state. The irrationality is brought about by the clash between her commitments and her dispositions (in Bilgrami's sense of this term).[50] So, for instance (the example is mine), take a jealous wife who openly and sincerely asserts with her friends that she believes that her husband is totally faithful to her—and has all the reasons in the world to do so—but, then, once at home, is often inquisitive, searches his belongings, etc. According to Bilgrami, what we should say is that she believes, *as a commitment*, that her husband is faithful—after all she is prepared to assert it with friends and has all the reasons to think so.[51] Still, she also has the unconscious belief, *as a disposition*, that he is unfaithful to her, which is operative in her inquisitive behaviour. So, she is "self-deceived" all right, in the sense that she sincerely avows a belief and partly behaves in ways that run contrary to it. Yet, it isn't the case that she has a false belief about her own beliefs. Rather she has two, different—both in nature and content—beliefs that give rise to her distinctively irrational behaviour.[52]

---

[48] Wright (2001b, 324) seems to me to underestimate the implications of allowing for cases of self-deception, and so I think does Heal (2002, 276.)

[49] See A. Bilgrami (2006, 140–57, 278–80). (Cf. also Stoneham 1998.) It must be stressed, in order to avoid confusions, that I am endorsing Bilgrami's account of self-deception with respect to those mental states one would *not* attribute to oneself on the basis of inference and observation of one's own behaviour and further available mental states. I think in the latter cases one could make genuine mistakes and self-attribute mental states one doesn't really have. If, then, one were to restrict self-deception, properly so-conceived, only to these cases, as Wright suggested to me in conversation, then the fact that one might go astray in self-*interpreting* oneself would not represent a counterexample to the view that *non-observational* or *immediate* self-ascriptions of propositional attitudes aren't open to failures of authority. The authority of immediate attitudinal avowals would then remain unchallenged.

[50] Notice that, in contrast, the opposition between two incompatible commitments wouldn't count as a case of self-deception, but of overt, fully conscious conflict.

[51] Notice, however, that for Bilgrami this wouldn't be necessary. See fns. 31–2.

[52] One may object that there are also cases of "negative" self-deception. Cases, that is, in which a subject says "I don't believe that P" yet behaves in ways that are explainable only by attributing to her the belief that P. Stretching the example slightly, but just because that would help make the point more vividly, think of Pascal who would say "I don't believe that God exists (nor that he doesn't)" and yet would behave as an irreprehensible Christian. In this case one wouldn't be self-ascribing any belief. Hence, the only option seems to say that one falsely believes that one doesn't believe that God exists (nor that he doesn't). But I think we can recast the example in such a way that it ceases to be a counterexample to authority. Here's how. We could say that the avowal is still the expression of the subject's mental state, namely, of her commitment to not using "God exists" (nor its negation) as a premise of her practical and theoretical reasoning, which runs against the disposition to behave as a kosher—if I may say so—Christian and thus use that belief as a premise of her practical reasoning. Bilgrami (2006, 147–54) elaborates on this kind of difficulty in somewhat

Here are some considerations I can put forward in favour of Bilgrami's account of self-deception. First, I agree with Bilgrami that his account is better suited than its rival to explain cases of *motivated* self-deception, namely cases in which self-deception is the outcome of a conflict in the subject between, say, believing that P and believing that not-P. In these cases, one of the two mental states gets suppressed, while the other is endorsed. Yet the former can remain operative in shaping (at least part of) the subject's behaviour and lead her to various forms of inconsistency. Second, and more generally, what makes us say that a subject is self-deceived is a *conflict* between her psychological self-ascriptions and (some other part of) her behaviour. Now, conflict is usually brought about by the fact that there are *two opposite parties* (or more) *at fight*, neither of which need be wrong, but be simply responding to different motivations and concerns. In the case at hand, it then makes sense to think that while one part of the subject's personality is entirely confident and mature, the other is full of insecurities, which lead her to be suspicious of the behaviour of those around her. Of course there may be reasons for both attitudes: on the one hand, the fully open and trust-worthy behaviour of the husband; and, on the other, a perhaps (well-)motivated sense of insecurity about one's own power to attract a person and to involve him in a stable relationship. Finally, suppose the subject realizes, either through self-analysis, or through the aid of a therapist, that she has such an unconscious belief about her husband's infidelity. Now, if it were just a matter of realizing her own mistake, she should simply correct her psychological self-ascriptions. After all, when I get to know that the wall I am looking at isn't red, but white and lit by a red light, I would immediately correct my belief—that is, I would *substitute* it with the new one. But clearly this is not what would happen in the case we are considering. For the subject would presumably still believe as a commitment that her husband is faithful to her. What she would (or, at any rate, should) do, rather, is to try and realign her behaviour with her commitments. Obviously, this can take a lot of time and personal effort and may indeed never fully succeed. For all these reasons, it seems to me that Bilgrami's account of self-deception is by far preferable to the traditional explanation of this phenomenon in terms of false psychological self-ascriptions. As a result, self-deception is entirely compatible with the fact that a subject is authoritative with respect to her own mental states, as long as it is clear that the mental states she is authoritative about are merely those as *commitments*.

3.2 Constructivism

Having dispensed with the counterexample to authority—indeed, with what is usually regarded as the only counterexample to it—let me turn to the problem of explaining why it holds. Recall that we want an account of authority that does not make it the

---

different terms, essentially because he is considering the matter from the point of view of a third party that attributes self-deception to a given subject. It seems to me that looking at a subject's own avowal *simpliciter* allows us to clarify what is going on in these apparently difficult cases in a simpler way.

result of any cognitive achievement. For any cognitive achievement may, in principle, go wrong and, therefore, there could be counterexamples to authority. But we have just seen that there aren't any.[53] Indeed, there can't be any if we want to be serious about the fact that the biconditional holds as a matter of *conceptual necessity*. So, the account *must* dispense with the result-of-a-cognitive-achievement picture, *tout court*. For, so long as psychological self-ascriptions are seen as reports on one's own mental states, the question arises of whether they are true or false. Unless one is prepared to suppose that our cognitive faculties may be infallible,[54] one couldn't account for the claim that authority holds as a matter of conceptual necessity.

One—I think unsuccessful—attempt at explaining authority may consist in holding a purely expressivist position, whereby "I believe/desire/intend/wish/hope that P", being just expressions of one's propositional attitudes, would always be "correct". Better, by default they wouldn't be open to error, because they wouldn't be in the business of semantic evaluation.[55] However, this proposal still doesn't explain why *necessarily* if one asserts "I believe/desire that P" one is right about it. For, after all, one could be merely sounding off. Or else, if some kind of "seriousness" constraint were imposed, what would exclude, on this picture, that one may sometimes say "I believe/desire/intend/wish/hope that P" "spontaneously and in good faith" (Heal 2002, 180) and yet not have the corresponding propositional attitudes at all?[56]

Another strategy may consist in maintaining that since there aren't counterexamples to authority, any competent and sincere assertion of "I believe that P" (or of "I desire/intend/wish/hope that P") would entail that one has the corresponding first-order belief (or other propositional attitude, as a commitment). Still this would hardly be an explanation of *why* authority holds, but, rather, a simple acknowledgement, or a consequence, of the fact that it does.[57]

---

[53] This is not to say that one's own avowals of one's mental states as commitments are always correct, but only that they are open to a very limited form of error: either they are incorrect because of conceptual incompetence, or because of slips of the tongue. (It remains an open issue, which I can't take up in this chapter, whether these failures could have analogues in thought.)

[54] An assumption that Descartes was happy to make but that wouldn't find many supporters nowadays.

[55] Notice that contemporary expressivists in this domain, like D. Bar-On (2004, ch. 8) and R. Jacobsen (1996), do not deny that "I believe that P" has the meaning and the truth conditions it is usually taken to have, while not having the role of asserting that one has that belief but of expressing it. There will be more about this in the following section, although in the context of defending a performative account of avowals. That move, however, makes it even more difficult to explain why there should be a presumption that one's avowals be correct.

[56] It is not by chance that expressivists are usually happy to account for self-deception along traditional lines. But, then, how can they account for authority? In particular, how can they hold that it is an a priori feature of our linguistic practice involving psychological avowals? Or, at any rate, that there is an "asymmetric presumption of truth governing them" (Bar-On 2004, 403)? What would make such a presumption asymmetric with respect to the presumption of truth which we may grant to judgements that, for instance, are based on reliable observation or inference? If, in contrast, they maintain that authority is "only apparent—an illusion fostered by the descriptivist assumption that self-ascriptions express second-order beliefs about mental states" (Jacobsen 1996, 16), how can their position be reconciled with the fact that authority seems to be a constitutive feature of avowals?

[57] I think this would be Bilgrami's strategy. In this connection, see fn. 36.

In fact, I think the most promising way of explaining authority, in keeping, to some extent, with Wright's original proposal of conceiving of self-ascriptions of propositional attitudes as *judgement dependent* (cf. Wright 1989a), would consist in inverting the direction of fit and in holding the following—*constructivist*—picture: psychological self-ascriptions such as "I believe/desire/intend/wish/hope that P" do *bring into existence* the corresponding first-order mental states, for example, the belief/desire/intention/wish/hope that P. On this model, there would be a sense in which it is literally true that we *make up* or *create* our minds. Moreover, since one's judgements would bring into existence the relevant first-order mental states, those judgements would necessarily be *true*. In fact, self-verifyingly so.[58] Furthermore, there would be no temptation to think that one should have the first-order mental state in view first, in order to make one's judgement or avowal, which would thus result in knowledge. For, if there is no mental state *before* making the relevant assertions or judgements, then of course there is nothing to know, or be aware of, in the first place, which should be tracked in judgement.

No doubt this proposal is going to meet objections. In what sense do we create mental states? How could asserting or judging "I believe/desire/intend/wish/hope that P" suffice to bring about the corresponding first-order mental state? These are all legitimate worries, but I think this proposal has some considerable attractions too, once phrased a little differently. What should be claimed is *not* that we create *all* of our own mental states. For mental states as dispositions would be there independently of our ability to self-ascribe them. Still, there is a clear sense in which we do create our minds as we have been reviewing in the previous section, namely, by *judging* that something is the case (or is worth pursuing or having) we do create our beliefs (and other propositional attitudes) *as commitments*. The crucial point is that when "I *believe/desire/intend/wish/hope* that P"—that is, the corresponding psychological self-ascriptions are acquired along the lines I developed in the previous section, as ways of making the same commitments as the ones undertaken by judging and asserting "P" or "P is worth pursuing/having", while having in view reasons in favour of P (is worth pursuing/having), it then becomes possible to use "I believe/desire/intend/wish/hope that P" *en lieu* of asserting (or judging) that P (is worth pursuing or having), in order to form one's first-order belief or desire that P *directly*. The difference between forming the first-order mental state by means of the second-order judgement, instead of forming it by means of the first-order one, is just the fact that "I believe/desire/intend/wish/hope that P" makes explicit what the first-order judgement leaves implicit, namely that that is just one's own particular standpoint on P (or its being worth-pursuing or having). Hence, we can bring about the relevant first-order belief and other propositional attitudes (as commitments) *either* by judging that P is the case (or is worth-pursuing or having), *or* by judging "I believe/desire/intend/wish/hope that P" (while having in

---

[58] Also the corresponding assertions would have the same effect, as long as sincerity is granted. For an account of what this means, in the present context, see Section 3.3.

view reasons in favour of P (is worth pursuing/having). For, to repeat, given the role of the latter locutions (either in speech or in thought) and of "P (is worth pursuing or having)", I can commit myself to P (is worth pursuing or having), thus bringing about the corresponding first-order beliefs or other propositional attitudes, either by simply judging the latter; or else, by judging the former, thus simultaneously making explicit my commitment to P's being the case (or to its being worth pursuing/having).[59]

Before turning to a defence of the view that "I believe/desire/intend/wish/hope that P" are performatives (at least on occasion), let me address one possible objection to constructivism. Some theorists have argued against it on the grounds that it would entail the *unreality* of first-order mental states:[60] if such mental states do not pre-exist their self-ascription, then they don't have *real* and *independent* existence. Since this is implausible, constructivism is doomed from the start. In response, I think it should be stressed that my brand of constructivism entails only that mental states *as commitments* don't *necessarily* have independent existence of the corresponding second-order judgements. So, the kind of constructivism I am advocating allows for (first-order) mental states *as dispositions* to exist independently of the corresponding self-ascriptions. Moreover, it also allows for the conceivability of the independent existence of (first-order) beliefs and desires as *commitments*, when they are merely brought about by judging that P (is worth pursuing or having), by subjects who don't have the conceptual resources necessary to make the corresponding second-order judgement. Notice in fact that, as already remarked,[61] strong forms of constitutivism merely hold that self-ascriptions of propositional attitudes as commitments can (and often do) bring about the corresponding first-order mental states. They need not claim, however, that the latter can't possibly exist without the former, for instance in subjects who did not possess the relevant psychological concepts. Yet, strong (as well as weak) forms of constitutivism are united in claiming that, to suitably conceptually endowed subjects (who are also lucid and sincere), first-order propositional attitudes as commitments are transparently

---

[59] Obviously it would always be available to one to justify one's judgement—"I believe/desire/intend/wish/hope that P", say—*ex post* by appealing to the fact that one's evidence allow(ed) one to judge that P (is worth pursuing or having), thus giving rise to one's belief/desire/intention/wish/hope that P (as a commitment). The possibility of giving such a justification for one's judgement "I believe/desire/intend/wish/hope that P", however, shouldn't obscure the fact that the commitment to P (is worth pursuing or having) was actually made by judging "I believe/desire/intend/wish/hope that P". My account of attitudinal avowals then explains why philosophers, most notably Wittgenstein in *The Philosophical Investigations* II, x, have been tempted to reduce "I believe that P" to "P". Their mistake was due to failing to see that the *contents* of those judgements are different, while their insight was to recognize that the *commitments* undertaken by making those judgements (or the corresponding assertions) are virtually the same. I take up the issue of Moore's paradox in Coliva (2005).

[60] See, for instance, D. Bar-On (2004, 412–13). Notice how Bar-On finds support for the untenability of this view in general, from its untenability in the case of those mental states "we share with non-human animals and pre-cognitive children". But judgement-dependency shouldn't, I think, be meant to apply to the latter cases. See also J. Heal (2002, 286).

[61] See fn. 17 and Section 2.2.1.

known. Hence, their occurrence is of a piece with subjects' awareness of them as the mental states they are with the content they have.

Be that as it may, it has to be stressed that the fact that the existence of certain beliefs and other propositional attitudes—those as commitments—is taken to depend on judging I believe/desire/intend/wish/hope that P does not make those mental states less *real*. The crucial point is that judgement-dependence is a claim about the *provenance* of first-order mental states, not about their *(un)-reality*. What I have been urging is that there are two kinds of judgements that can bring about the *same* result (i.e. a belief/desire/intention/wish/hope as a commitment), namely either judgements that are outright about the world (or what is worth doing or having) or else, judgements that make explicit the particular standpoint from which the world is conceived to be thus-and-so.

It may sound surprising, if not altogether alarming, that in my view first-order judgements and second-order ones play such an interlocking role. But to dissipate the resistance to such a view, consider that any judgement/assertion that P (is worth pursuing or having) is always made by *someone,* and hence is necessarily the expression of a subject's point of view, even when its subject matter is, as it were, the world. By being drilled to the use of first-person present-tense psychological *vocabulary*, subjects are simply endowed with the means to make that "grammatical" fact *explicit*. Once they are conversant with that practice, they can use second-order judgements or assertions directly, as ways of forming the same commitments they would form by making the corresponding first-order ones. It then seems to me that the point of our psychological self-ascriptions is first and foremost to make explicit to ourselves and others the fact that the world, broadly conceived, is always described or assessed from a particular standpoint—one among potentially many. Their further performative role is simply a result of having being trained to take part in a linguistic practice where the same commitments can be undertaken in two different ways. This, I take it, is also the deep truth in Wittgenstein's and Wright's positions: psychological avowals—and their equivalents in thought—are the result of being trained to take part in a *linguistic practice*, and have their main point in making any participant aware of the fact that her specific point of view is just one among other possible ones.

3.3 *Performatives and commitments*

When understood in the way proposed, a judgement (or a sincere assertion[62]) such as "I believe/desire/intend/wish/hope that P" is like a *performative*, namely like "I promise to buy you an ice-cream", "I hereby thee wed", "I hereby name you so-and-so", etc.: it

---

[62] Notice the sincerity condition placed upon second-order assertions, which cannot, however, be carried over to judgements, since judgements are—when made—*necessarily* sincere. This seems to me enough to dispel the worry, raised by an anonymous reader, that one may judge or assert "I believe that P" and yet not form the corresponding first-order mental state as a commitment. Of course what remains entirely possible is that I don't act on the basis of such a commitment and thus fail to actualize the connected disposition. But this is no objection to the view which is being proposed here.

makes a certain thing *happen*, for it does create the first-order propositional attitude as a commitment. Where this, to repeat, is possible precisely because judging "I believe/ desire/intend/wish/hope that P" becomes just an alternative way of undertaking the same commitments one would make by judging that P (is worth pursuing or having), save for the fact that the former kind of judgement would also make explicit what the latter leaves implicit, that is, that the judgement just reflects a subject's own point of view.

Many have argued against such a view of psychological self-ascriptions by maintaining that it would commit one to the implausible claim that they would lack content and couldn't, therefore, be sensibly prefaced by negations, or be embedded in suppositions, and otherwise wider contexts.[63] But this objection, if sound at all,[64] could be raised only in the case of *implicit* performatives—that is, those which don't make explicit the kind of commitment one is undertaking, for *explicit* performatives, like "I *promise* to buy you an ice-cream" and "I *believe* that P", are speech-acts, which can have *more than one function at the time*: they can make things happen but they can also say what is being done by means of them.[65] In this latter sense, they would retain truth-evaluable content. For instance, "I promise to buy you an ice-cream" is both a way of *making the promise* of buying you an ice-cream and of *saying what I am doing*, that is, promising to buy you an ice-cream. Of course, what I am saying could be *false*, since I could be insincere. Similarly, "I believe/desire/intend/wish/hope that P" would be both a way of forming the commitment that P (is worth pursuing/having) and of saying what I am doing. Moreover, what I am saying, that is, that I believe/desire/ intend/wish/hope that P (as a commitment), could be false, since I could in fact not be making that commitment and simply trying to fool you.

---

[63] The *locus classicus* is P. Geach (1965).

[64] The counter is usually that they could retain *minimal assertoric content* as well as *minimal truth*. Accordingly, it would suffice for minimal assertoric content that performatives can be embedded in negations and suppositions, and that they can undergo the usual tense transformations. Obviously they can. For "I am not going to buy you an ice-cream", or "Suppose I bought you an ice-cream", and "I did buy you an ice-cream" are perfectly sensible things to say. Minimal assertoric content then pairs with *minimal truth*—with the idea that it is enough to qualify as a truth-predicate that some platitudes and, in particular negation and the T-schema, are respected. It would then be a further issue whether these statements should be taken as *descriptions*, or else, as *expressions of commitments one is (or isn't) undertaking thereby*. This strategy can be found in Hacker (1986, 90); as well as in Wright (1992, 28); and in R. Jacobsen (1996). P. Hacker (1986, 298), however, denies that minimal assertoric content would be compatible with truth-evaluations. Be that as it may, when we consider judgements (and assertions) of "P" (is worth pursuing/having) we could distinguish between the *content* of the judgement (or of the assertion), which obviously is truth-assessable, and what is being done by means of the *act of judging it*. It is the act of judging that P that brings about the corresponding belief (or further propositional attitude) as a commitment, which can get *expressed* in one's assertion of "P (is worth pursuing/having)", although the *content* of one's assertion would remain P (is worth pursuing/having). A similar distinction can be found in R. Jacobsen (1996, 26) and in D. Bar-On (2004, 251–64).

[65] A similar point can be found in J. Heal (2002, 282–8). But also in R. Jacobsen (1996, 23–8). Strangely enough, Jacobsen who, officially, sets out to characterize an expressivist account of avowals, in fact ends up defending the claim they are performatives. See R. Jacobsen (1996, 26–8). So I find myself in agreement with much he says, although I would insist on the difference between expressivism and constructivism: on the former, first-order mental states are already there and get simply expressed by the relevant utterances; on the latter, in contrast, utterances (if sincere) bring about first-order mental states, at least in some cases.

However, whenever sincerity conditions are introduced, one might suspect that, perhaps surreptitiously, reference is being made to the fact that one's assertions or judgements should track one's pre-existing mental states. Hence, the whole point of the performative account I am proposing would be pre-empted, for its main contention is precisely that first-order mental states can be brought into existence by one's making the relevant psychological judgements or assertions, leaving no room for the idea of tracking a pre-existing mental reality. But, in effect, this account of what sincerity would consist in is not compelling. For the sincerity condition, in the case of performatives, just amounts to *one's lack of the intention to fool one's interlocutor*—and does not consist in a correspondence between one's pre-existing (first-order) mental states and utterances (or judgements about such mental states). By contrast, when I do wish to deceive my interlocutor, it is not the case that I first check within myself whether I have the belief or the desire that P, find out I don't, say, and then say the opposite. Rather, I utter the performative sentence without respecting one of its felicity conditions—since I have *another* mental state, namely, the intention to fool you. Thus, although I utter a performative sentence, I don't thereby bring about the corresponding first-order mental state.[66] That is why "I believe/desire/intend/wish/hope that P" can be performatives and yet, on certain occasions be false, since what would make them true hasn't in fact been brought about. (Conversely, once the sincerity condition is satisfied, "I believe/desire/intend/wish/hope that P" is true because what would make it true has been brought about by that very judgement or assertion).

One frequent objection raised against performative accounts of avowals is that they would introduce a difference in *meaning* between the first-person, present-tense use of the relevant psychological verbs and their third-personal use (as well as their first-personal non-present-tensed use) (cf. Geach 1965, 260). Since this seems absurd, one should reject such an account of psychological avowals. However, I don't think this objection is compelling. For, if the meaning of a word is what is offered as an *explanation of its meaning*,[67] then we will offer just one kind of explanation for "believe", "desire" and so on, for instance, that to believe that P means to be disposed, *ceteris paribus*, to use P as a premise in one's practical and theoretical reasoning; that in order to believe that P one needs evidence in favour of P, that if one believes that P, then, *ceteris paribus*, one will assert that P, etc. But nowhere did the performative account suggest that in the first person case things should be any different. After all, on the present proposal, all is being suggested is that the commitment to P can be *formed* by judging (or asserting) "I believe that P", where it is part and parcel of making such a commitment

---

[66] Notice that here an asymmetry between assertions and judgements may arise. For the performative judgement can't be overridden. So, one way of putting the point is that when I am insincere I utter a performative sentence without making the corresponding judgement.

[67] See also R. Jacobsen (1996, 18) for a similar point, which can be traced back to Wittgenstein (cf. *Philosophical Investigations*, sect. 560).

that one should have the kind of *dispositions* just mentioned.⁶⁸ So, allowing for the performative nature of first-personal, present-tense avowals merely entails that there are two ways in which a subject can come to have certain dispositions (or in fact ought to come to have them): either because she is somehow finds herself saddled with them; or else, as in the case at hand, because she actively brings them about—or tries to bring them about—as an implementation of her own deliberations. Obviously, on occasion, a subject could fail to behave accordingly, but one shouldn't confuse the fact that sometimes a disposition may not be actualized with the fact that there is no real or genuine disposition at all. To offer what I think is an instructive analogy: the fact that occasionally a crystal vase can be struck and not break doesn't show that it doesn't have the disposition to break if struck. So, the fact that sometimes one could fail to implement one's own deliberations doesn't show that one lacks the relevant disposition.

However, what this suggests, in its turn, is that there is another, perhaps more important distinction to be drawn—that is, a distinction between self-, as well as other-directed ascriptions of beliefs and other propositional attitudes as *commitments* and as *dispositions*. True, we can *bring about* commitments only for ourselves, by judging or asserting "I believe/desire/intend/wish/hope that P". Yet, we may nevertheless ascribe this kind of mental state to other people. Suppose you are listening to a subject who asserts that P, gives a lot of evidence in its favour, bets her own head on P, as it were, etc. When you then report on her by saying "S believes that P", obviously what you would be correctly attributing to her is a belief as a commitment. If, in contrast, you were interpreting S's behaviour by attributing to her a mental state she has never avowed (and might never be in a position to avow), which, however, would be helpful to *you* to make sense of what S is doing; or else you were engaging in deep analysis of a Freudian kind of her behaviour, then you would be attributing to her a belief as a *disposition*.

Furthermore, not all uses of "believe" (or other propositional attitudinal verbs) in the first person present are performatives. For, sometimes, the same judgement or assertion, can be used as a simple *description*, like when one finds out about one's own beliefs or desires through a process of self-interpretation. Conversely, both past and otherwise embedded uses of "believe" (or or other propositional attitudinal verbs) in the first person, although not themselves performatives—for they can't bring about a commitment—may nevertheless be an *ascription* of a *commitment* one had in the past, based on the memory of having made it, or, for instance, of a commitment one is supposing to be making.

⁶⁸ Hence I wouldn't be too keen to endorse the kind of dilemma Wright thinks there is in the fact that, on the one hand, avowals are authoritative and, on the other, they self-ascribe a disposition whose obtaining is assessable from a third-personal point of view. See Wright (1987, esp. at pp. 122–3). R. Jacobsen (1996) and J. Heal (2002) too seem to be highly struck by it. The dilemma, however, seems to me very much a function of a simplistic description of the situation. So, it calls more for a dissolution—for an account of why it doesn't really stand—than for a positive solution.

So, what we witness here is a variety of uses of self- as well as other-directed psychological ascriptions: although it remains that we can bring about commitments only in our own case by means of first person present avowals, we can ascribe commitments both to ourselves and others and, moreover, we can ascribe both to ourselves and to others mental states as dispositions. The reason why it is so is simple: each of us can deliberate only for herself, but we can, and obviously do see also other people as deliberative agents—that is, we do know when they are making commitments as opposed to when they are simply acting on the basis of mental states they may be saddled with, but which are not the result of any deliberation of theirs. The same, however, applies to ourselves too, so we can report on previously made (and perhaps already abandoned) commitments, or engage in the supposition of undertaking them; but we can also self-ascribe mental states as *dispositions*. What self-interpretation and psychoanalysis help us do is to acquire that kind of (third-personal) knowledge of the latter kind of mental states. What they can't do, however, is to turn us into deliberative agents with respect to them, for no amount of theoretical knowledge about ourselves will, by itself, ever transform the mental states we thereby become aware of into commitments.[69]

So what should be claimed—in keeping with one of the main theses of this paper—is that we have two different notions of belief and other propositional attitudes—those as commitments and those as dispositions—that cut across the first-person/third-person divide. Indeed we do explain their meanings differently, as we have seen in one of the previous sections of this chapter (Section 2.1). Nevertheless, the propensity to see them as two different species of the same genus, instead of altogether different kinds of mental states—beliefs and "shbeliefs", say—and thus to talk, in both cases, of beliefs—specified "as commitments" or "as dispositions" respectively—would then be explainable by reference to the fact that both beliefs (and desires) as commitments and as dispositions could be responses to evidence (although only beliefs and desires as commitments would depend on actively assessing it) and could have similar effects at least on our *non-linguistic* behaviour: in the case of either kind of belief, a disposition to behave on the basis of P and, in either kind of desire or intention, a disposition to bring about P. What is relevantly different is the way in which the respective self-ascriptions are made. For when "I believe/desire/intend/wish/hope that P" is judged or sincerely asserted to make a commitment, it is a performative and brings about the corresponding first-order mental state. But the same words or mental content can also be a report on one's dispositions, known to oneself through observation and inference on one's own behaviour, hence in a third-personal way.[70]

---

[69] In fact they may make action and deliberation even more difficult to attain.

[70] Notice, moreover, that they can also be used to report a commitment previously undertaken. In such a case they are based on remembering having made such a commitment and certainly not on inspecting one's own mind, as it were. Also, it may be possible to find out about one's own dispositions in a third-personal way and self-ascribe them, and subsequently form a corresponding commitment. All this would require two different mental actions, though the final self-ascriptions may be identical in form.

A related point has to do with an oft-made observation that "the mark of the mental" would be the first-personal, present-tensed use of psychological verbs.[71] Well, on the face of it, this remark is simply wrong. For some psychological *self*-ascriptions are made in a *third*-personal way, as we have seen, and are such that one is self-ascribing a mental state as a disposition. By contrast, we have already noticed that there can be third-personal, present-tensed ascriptions of mental states which, while not performatives, are nevertheless ascriptions of commitments. What I think is distinctive about (most) adult human beings' mentality, then, is both that we can *make commitments* and that we can actually *see others as mental deliberative agents*—that is, as subjects who are capable of making commitments.

Finally, another objection often raised against performative accounts of avowals is that "P" and "I believe that P" would turn out to have the same *content*.[72] This objection, however, is wrong because, obviously, the truth-conditions of the two sentences are different: "It's raining (at *l* at *t*)" is true iff it's raining (at *l* at *t*); whereas "I believe it is raining (at *l* at *t*)" is true iff I believe it is raining (at *l* at *t*). Clearly these are quite independent states of affairs—it may be raining (at *l* at *t*) and I may be ignorant of it; or else, I may believe it is raining (at *l* at *t*) and be wrong. What, however, would be identical in the two cases, according to the performative account of (as we can now say) *some* uses of "I believe that P" (and of other avowals) are simply the *commitments* one would undertake by *judging* or *asserting* either.[73] This is why, at least certain occurrences of "I believe that P, but it isn't the case that P" would be *Moorean-paradoxical*. For when "I believe that P" is an expression of a commitment to P's truth, it would be (at least) irrational to commit oneself to P's falsity, *as well*.[74]

4. Conclusions

The constitutive account of our knowledge of our own propositional attitudes I have proposed, if correct at all, shows how constitutivism worth its name will have to take a rather radical constructivist twist. This makes constitutivism a viable explanation of self-knowledge only for very specific and limited kinds of mental states we can enjoy—those as commitments—and, connectedly, only for specific kinds of self-ascriptions of propositional attitudes—those which amount, in fact, to performatives. These, in their turn, seem to me to be the only attitudinal self-ascriptions, which deserve to be called "avowals" and to be granted a distinctive authority, for they themselves do bring about

---

[71] With the usual caveats having to do with difficulties in exegesis, Wittgenstein seems to have had this view, as R. Jacobsen (1996, 14–17) reminds us.

[72] This idea may be suggested by some of Geach's observations (1965, 259). Wittgenstein is obviously considered the chief-holder of this view, for his well-known remark that "I believe that P" is just a tentative assertion of "P" (cf. Wittgenstein 1953, II, x, esp. 190–1).

[73] In order to undertake these commitments one obviously need not have the concept of a commitment. Nor should this claim be understood as implying that the content of "I believe that P", say, is "I commit myself to P".

[74] This is the account of Moore's paradox I gave in my 2005 chapter.

those first-order mental states they are about. To my mind this is no sign of irrelevance, though. For what this long and winding road has led us to see is that we do have a variety, not just of mental states, but also of propositional attitudes, as well as of ways of knowing them. Thus, for once, it is perhaps not mere rhetoric to conclude by saying that a full account of self-knowledge—that is, an account of the different ways in which we have knowledge of the varieties of mental states we can enjoy, as well as of the varieties of psychological self-ascriptions which will express that knowledge—will have to be deferred to another occasion.

References

Armstrong, D. 1968 *A Materialist Theory of the Mind*, London, Routledge.
Bar-On, D. 2004 *Speaking My Mind. Expression and Self-Knowledge*, Oxford, Oxford University Press.
Bilgrami, A. 2006 *Self-Knowledge and Resentment*, Cambridge (Mass.), Harvard University Press.
Boghossian, P. 1989 "Content and self-knowledge", *Philosophical Topics* 17, 5–26.
Boyle, M. 2009 "Two Kinds of Self-Knowledge", *Philosophy and Phenomenological Research* 77/1, 133–64.
Burge, T. 1996 "Our Entitlement to Self-Knowledge", *Proceedings of the Aristotelian Society* 96, 1–26.
Coliva, A. 2005 "Moore's Paradox and Commitments. On this Very Complicated Concept of Belief", in P. Leonardi and J-J. Açero (eds.) *Facets of Concepts*, Padova, Il Poligrafo, 233–52.
——2006 "Self-Knowledge: Another Constitutive View", *Preprint Dipartimento di Filosofia Università di Bologna* 28, 101–21.
——2008 "Peacocke's Self-Knowledge", *Ratio* 21/1, 13–27.
Evans, G. 1982 *The Varieties of Reference*, Oxford, Oxford University Press.
Frith, U. and Happé, F. 1999 "Theory of Mind and Self-Consciousness: What is it Like to Be Autistic?", *Mind and Language* 14/1, 1–22.
Geach, P. 1965 "Assertion", *The Philosophical Review* 74, 449–65; repr. in J. F. Rosemberg and C. Travis (eds.) *Reading in the Philosophy of Language*, Englewood (N.J.), Prentice-Hall, 1971, 250–61.
Gopnik, A. 1993 "How We Know Our Minds: The Illusion of First-Person Knowledge of Intentionality", *Behavioural and Brain Sciences* 16, 1–15.
Gordon, R. 2007 "Ascent Routines for Propositional Attitudes", *Synthese* 159, 151–65.
Hacker, P. 1986 *Insight and Illusion: Themes from the Philosophy of Wittgenstein*, Oxford, Clarendon Press.
Heal, J. 2002 "First Person Authority", *Proceedings of the Aristotelian Society* 102; repr. in J. Heal, *Mind, Reason and Imagination*, Cambridge, Cambridge University Press, 2003, 273–88.
Jacobsen, R. 1996 "Wittgenstein on Self-Knowledge and Self-Expression", *Philosophical Quarterly* 46, 12–30.
McDowell, J. 1998 "Response to Crispin Wright", in C. Wright, B. Smith, and C. Macdonald 1998, 47–62.
Moran, R. 2001 *Authority and Estrangement*, Princeton, Princeton University Press.

Moran, R. 2003 "Responses to O'Brien and Shoemaker", *European Journal of Philosophy* 11/3, 402–19.

O'Brien, L. 2007 *Self-Knowing Agents*, Oxford, Oxford University Press.

Peacocke, C. 1999 *Being Known*, Oxford, Clarendon Press.

——2004 *The Realm of Reason*, Oxford, Oxford University Press.

Povinelli, D. J. and Vonk, J. 2004 "We Don't Need a Microscope to Explore the Chimpanzee's Mind", *Mind and Language* 19/1, 1–22.

Scanlon, T. 1998 *What We Owe to Each Other*, Harvard (Mass.), Harvard University Press.

Shoemaker, S. 1968 "Self-Reference and Self-Awareness", *Journal of Philosophy* 65, 555–78.

——1986 "Introspection and the Self", *Midwest Studies in Philosophy* 10, 101–20; repr. in S. Shoemaker 1996a, 3–24;

——1988 "On Knowing One's Mind", *Philosophical Perspectives* 2, 183–209; repr. in S. Shoemaker 1996a, 25–49.

——1990 "First Person Access", *Philosophical Perspectives* 4, 187–214; repr. in S. Shoemaker, 1996a, 50–73.

——1996a *The First Person Perspective and Other Essays*, Cambridge, Cambridge University Press.

——1996b "Self-Knowledge and Inner Sense. Lectures I–III", in S. Shoemaker 1996a, 201–68.

——2003 "Moran on Self-Knowledge", *European Journal of Philosophy* 11/3, 391–40.

Stoneham, T. 1998 "On Believing that I am Thinking", *Proceedings of the Aristotelian Society* 98, 125–44.

Tanney, J. 1996 "A Constructivist Picture of Self-Knowledge", *Philosophy* 71, 405–22.

Tomasello, M., Call, J., and Hare, B. 2003a "Chimpanzees Understand Psychological States—The Question is Which Ones and to What an Extent", *Trends in Cognitive Science* 7, 153–6.

—— —— ——2003b "Chimpanzees versus Humans: It's Not that Simple", *Trends in Cognitive Science* 7, 239–40.

Williams, D. 1994 *Somebody Somewhere*. London, Corgi Books.

Wimmer, H. and Perner, J. 1983 "Beliefs About Beliefs: Representation and Constraining Function of Wrong Beliefs in Young Children's Understanding of Deception", *Cognition* 13, 103–28.

Wittgenstein L. 1953 *Philosophical Investigations*, Oxford, Basil Blackwell.

Wright, C. 1989a "Wittgenstein's Rule-Following Considerations and the Central Project of Theoretical Linguistics", repr. in C. Wright 2001a, 170–213.

——1989b "Wittgenstein's Later Philosophy of Mind: Sensation, Privacy and Intentions", repr. in C. Wright 2001a, 291–318.

——1998 "Self-Knowledge: The Wittgensteinian Legacy", in C. Wright, B. Smith, and C. Macdonald 1998, 13–45.

——Smith, B., and Macdonald, C. 1998 *Knowing our own Minds*, Oxford, Oxford University Press.

——2001a *Rails to Infinity*, Cambridge (Mass.), Harvard University Press.

——2001b "The Problem of Self-Knowledge (I) and (II)", in C. Wright 2001a, 319–73.

11

How to Think about Phenomenal Self-Knowledge

Paul Snowdon

I want to discuss some suggested properties of self-knowledge, and to propose myself some properties for certain cases. I take as my initial stalking horse in this discussion suggestions that Professor Wright has made in his Whitehead Lectures (of 1996), entitled 'The Problem of Self-Knowledge', which form chapters 10 and 11 of his book *Rails to Infinity* (2001; cf. Wright 1998)[1] My engagement with Professor Wright's rich and substantial discussion has, alas, to be highly selective. I have chosen Professor Wright's writing because of its interest and clarity, but also because his overall approach attempts to build a defensible account of self-knowledge on lines which are supposedly faithful to Wittgenstein's insights, and it seems to me that an as yet undecided but very important question is how acceptable recognizably Wittgensteinian theories of self-knowledge are.[2] Out of the consideration of his views will emerge, I hope, the threefold conclusion that the properties he suggests do not in fact apply, that he specifies his candidate properties at the wrong level, and that when they are re-formulated in what I suggest are the right terms their attribution remains a mistake. However, even if these negative conclusions are correct, one difficult problem related to what Wright has said remains and I shall try to make some progress with that. Discussing self-knowledge of the kind I shall focus on is an odd activity at the moment, in that it is not clear whether there is anything approaching a consensus about these matters amongst philosophers, and so it is not clear whether what one is saying will

---

[1] Wright's (1998) paper is wholly contained in the lectures and itself contains everything in Wright's view that I shall be considering.

[2] I try to say some things about Wittgenstein's own approach in "Wittgenstein on Sense Data and Privacy" (forthcoming). It will not have escaped notice that within the camp of those trying to propound accounts of self-knowledge which are faithful to the spirit of Wittgenstein there are what one might call, with pardonable understatement, trenchant and internecine disagreements. John McDowell's (1998) paper represents one such disagreement with Wright's attempt. It is not my intention to take, in this chapter, a side over their disagreements.

strike people as obviously right, obviously wrong or, maybe, disputable but at least interesting.[3] Let me begin, however, with a few, fairly uncontentious remarks about the general topic.

1. General remarks

(1) Self-knowledge stands for knowledge which has that sort of content that if it were to be expressed by the subject possessing the knowledge it would involve the employment of the first person pronoun, characteristically in English the word 'I'. It is not sufficient for knowledge to count as self-knowledge on the part of S that S knows that Fa, where, in fact, it happens that a is identical to S. Further, there is, I think, a fairly widely accepted and plausible non-equivalence thesis to the effect that there is no type of designator D, other than the first person pronoun, such that someone's accepting what he or she would express as 'D is F', is equivalent to knowing or believing that he or she is F.[4] This non-equivalence thesis is, of course, stronger than the previous non-sufficiency claim. We can summarize this by saying that thought and knowledge with first person content is a basic mode of thought (cf. Davidson 2001, 85).[5]

(2) We need, however, to liberalize our conception of the problem in one direction, and to narrow it in another. First, let me introduce the liberalization. I want to talk about some suggested properties of *beliefs* about oneself, as well as of *knowledge* about oneself. According to some philosophers some beliefs about oneself have certain special properties (they are, for example, claimed to be incorrigible), and these claims need discussing. So I propose not to restrict myself solely to generalizations or claims about self-*knowledge,* but also to let the discussion range over beliefs about the self. It should be clear at any point whether it is knowledge or belief that is the topic.

(3) Given the understanding here of what self-knowledge is, knowledge of a subject with that distinctive content, the striking thing is how diverse such knowledge is, at least in the case of a normal, relatively mature human. Thus I know how I am in many respects both physical and psychological, and how I have been in those ways, and how, to some extent, I shall be. I know, too, what I have done, who I am, and what my social history and role is and has been, etc. This variety means, I suggest, that the only generalizations that will apply across so called *self-knowledge as a whole* are, first, those, if

---

[3] This has arisen in part because recent discussion of self-knowledge has tended to focus on knowledge of one's beliefs or of one's so called propositional attitudes generally. That is not the case I am interested in here.

[4] I owe to Josh Parsons the observation that as a speaker, when I attribute self-knowledge to someone else, I can do so without myself employing the first person pronoun. I can say 'He believes he is F'. It may not be that this attribution has to be understood as attributing a belief with first person content but it certainly can be.

[5] Davidson (2001) endorses this claim. We need to distinguish between the claim that we cannot equate first personal content with another type of content, and the claim that we cannot provide an analysis of what it is to have first personal content. The non-equivalence thesis supports the first but not the second irreducibility.

any, involved in the content's being first personal, and, second, in its amounting to knowledge, that is, in its fulfilling the conditions required for being knowledge.

(4) The chances of some significant generalizations about properties of self-knowledge/ belief are obviously significantly increased if we narrow down the *content* of the knowledge/belief in further ways. The two narrowings that are normally made are: (i) to consider self-knowledge which is present tensed, which relates to the time it is possessed; and (ii) which relates, roughly, to psychological or mental features.[6] Frequently when philosophers discuss what they are calling self-knowledge (when they work, that is, under that title), they restrict themselves to such cases. However, having made the second restriction it is obvious that the category (or categories) of the psychological/mental ranges over states or features which are themselves significantly *different*. So the chances of locating significant generalizations will be improved by working with sub-categories of the psychological. What subcategories should we choose?

2. Wright's subcategories: the phenomenal and the attitudinal

In his Whitehead Lectures, Professor Wright makes one distinction, and conducts the discussion in terms of it. On the one hand there are what he calls *phenomenal avowals*, examples of which are 'I have a headache', 'My feet are sore', 'I'm tired', 'I feel elated', 'My vision is blurred', 'My ears are ringing', 'I feel sick', and so on' (Wright 2001b, 321). The contrast is with what Wright calls 'content bearing states' or '*attitudinal avowals*', about which he says 'that the psychological characteristics, processes and states which they concern are partially individuated by the propositional content or intentional direction, which they contain' (ibid., 322). His examples are; 'I believe that term ends on the 27th', 'I hope that noise stops soon', 'I am frightened of that dog', and 'I am thinking of my mother' (ibid.).

Now, one very important thing to note about Wright's list is that he is talking about the content of *avowals*, whereas I have been talking about the content of knowledge (or belief). An avowal is a speech act; it is an explicit affirmation of some sort. In fact, or so it seems to me, (and despite its employment in philosophy) the term 'avowal' is one the *ordinary meaning* of which is hard to pin down. Is just any statement or assertion an avowal? Or does 'avowal' stand for a special, distinctive, sub-class of assertions? If so, what class? Again, does the use of the term 'avowal' by philosophers correspond to its normal use, or does it incorporate or rest on some special theory? The answer to this last part of that question is relatively clear. When Wright talks of avowals, he does seem to build in that an avowal must be an 'authoritative non-inferential self ascription'

---

[6] This second narrowing is, of course, in effect expressed in the title *Knowing Our Own Minds*.

(ibid., 320). On this use, if no first person ascriptions actually fulfill these conditions there are no avowals, even if in the ordinary sense people do constantly avow things about themselves. It is surely also clear that I can avow to such things as having seen a certain act or having been at a certain place. There is nothing authoritative or non-inferential about such claims. If so the use by Wright *is* a technical one. Still, the vital and surely agreed point is that avowals (in both the normal and technical sense) are *speech acts*. Knowledge and belief are not speech acts, or indeed acts of any kind at all. This contrast is one I shall come back to, because it raises the absolutely fundamental question as to why we should regard the problem of self-knowledge, as Wright does, as a problem about avowals (rather than, say about knowledge or belief of certain kind). I want, though, initially to consider Wright's distinction simply as a distinction of *content*.

It is somewhat unclear what Wright's attitude to the distinction is. He writes; 'It seems safe to suppose that we must begin by distinguishing two broad classes of avowals' (ibid., 321). This presumably means the categories are meant to be exclusive, but are they meant to be exhaustive? One would have assumed that was the intention. What stands out, though, is that the examples cited to illustrate the categories are far from exhaustive. Strikingly, ordinary reports of perceptual experience (such as 'It looks to me as if there is a city ahead') are not mentioned at all. Now, Wright could respond at this point by saying, completely correctly, of course, that his conception is that he is drawing a distinction within the class of *avowals*. He would be entitled to exclude cases which fall outside *that* category.

There is though no obvious reason, as far as I can see, to place first person perceptual experience reports (appearance reports) outside that category, if the others on the list are included. So I take it, on reflection, that they must belong to the sub-category of attitudinals, since such claims do exhibit intentionality, and that is definitive of attitudinals. Understood this way, the phenomenal list must be defined as all the rest, whatever they are, the content of which, whatever it is, does *not* exhibit intentionality. We then have guaranteed the categories are exclusive and exhaustive. We are, though, far from having guaranteed that the categories are felicitous. Let me mention some infelicities. It is odd to call the attitudinals 'attitudinals'. In particular, 'I am thinking about my mother' does not express or pick out an attitude to anything. If a psychoanalyst promoted you to give your attitude to your mother, it would be an evasion and not an answer to avow that one was at least thinking about her. Such a report does not register an attitude such as belief or fear. Again 'It looks to me as if there is a city ahead' does not, in any normal sense, express an attitude either. Appearances are not attitudes, though one might form attitudes in response to them. Further, the attitudinal category is extremely heterogeneous. In particular it contains some states or occurrences which are or involve experiences, such as thinking about one's mother, and being frightened of the dog, and others which are not, and do not involve experiences at all, such as believing that term ends on the 27th, and hoping that the noise will stop. It seems to me that it is very likely, from the point of view of self-knowledge, that these will have to be treated differently. The fact that these contents are all in some sense intentional is very likely not as important as their differences. In fact, the heterogeneity of the category is just what one would expect, in part for the reason that the term 'intentional' is itself standardly defined disjunctively, as involving a (propositional) content *or* bearing on an object.

The heterogeneity of an initial category is not inevitably a problem since one can subdivide it into further and perhaps more closely unified categories, for the purposes of theorizing. That is not Wright's approach though. His idea is that attitudinals are, as a class, different from (what is I shall, for the moment, call) the phenomenals. The difference is, or seems to be, twofold. First, attitudinals can be advanced (or delivered) as part of what Wright calls a self-interpretation. This activity arises when one is trying to make sense of oneself. The example used is that of Jane Austen's Emma coming to realize in the light of her own reactions that she wants Mr. Knightley to marry her. In such a case her remark that she wants this is based on grounds; it is not such that the subject has to be regarded as right, and it is something about which the subject might at some stage aver ignorance. According to Wright, as we shall see, with the phenomenals none of these represents a possibility. Now, one might wonder at this point why Wright does not say that Emma's remark is not an actual avowal at all in his sense. (Perhaps he does somewhere.) The thing he stresses, however, is that the claim itself can in other contexts qualify as an avowal. In the activity of self-interpretation, claims about oneself are made with epistemological features that in other contexts the very same claim would not have. However, in these other contexts there still remains a distinction between phenomenals and attitudinals, which is that with attitudinals there is the space for mistakes in self-ascription opened up by, or represented by, the concept of *self-deception*, but with phenomenals there is no such possibility of mistake (Wright 2001b, 321–5).

At this point, though, it is reasonable to worry that something has gone wrong. First, are all attitudinals, simply in virtue of exhibiting intentionality, claims that can be used in what Wright is calling self-interpretation? It is hard to think that 'It looks to me as if there is a city' can be the result of self-interpretation. It is also hard to think that 'I am thinking about my mother' could do so either. Second, Wright gives no reason for thinking, nor does it seem plausible, that non-intentional psychological reports cannot be grounded by the data of self-interpretation. Think of 'I am elated' or 'I am full of shame'.

Third, it is not obvious that the possibility of self-deception exists for all attitudinals. It is not standard to treat perceptual reports in such discussions. Nor do reports of whom you are thinking about figure in the literature of self-deception.[7] Fourth, there is no reason for thinking that some phenomenals cannot come under the category of topics of self-deception. Think again of 'I am elated'. The suspicion has to be that the

---

[7] To someone who made the following confession, 'I have just suffered a bad bout of self deception—I thought that I was thinking about my own mother when in fact, as I now realize, I was thinking about yours', we would not, I suggest, rush to confirm his self-diagnosis.

way that Wright cuts up avowals does not correlate neatly with the characterizations he gives.

Having developed these problems for Wright somewhat, I want to return to the task of how to impose a limitation on the content of self-knowledge so that it looks more likely that we shall have an interestingly unified category. I am attracted by the idea of limiting the content of the self-knowledge to be investigated here roughly to what Wright calls the 'phenomenal', or, rather, to what his central examples represent. But what is that? Since Wright leaves out descriptions of perceptual experience, and includes in the attitudinals such experience as fear and the experience of occurrent thinking, something does not qualify as phenomenal simply by being or involving experience. The phenomenal is a type of experience, but which type? The best suggestion that I can make is that phenomenal judgements concern the way experiences are, irrespective of what they indicate or seem to mean. Thus if you characterize how you feel as being 'as if my leg is bent' you characterize your experience in terms of what it indicates is the case (though without committing yourself to its being that way), whereas if you characterize what you feel as simply a pain or an itch that is not in terms of what the experience indicates or means. I take it therefore that descriptions of your after images as, for example, blurry or red should count as phenomenal. (Wright's list does not mention such cases.) Now, I do not think that this is a completely satisfactory characterization, but it is the best I can currently do.

So, insofar as I am in this chapter going to focus on one particular sort of self-knowledge, it will be on that branch of knowledge of one's current experiences which Wright terms phenomenal. There is, it seems to me, something strange about giving that kind of knowledge particular philosophical attention. That is that for a large part, and usually, it is not knowledge which we would employ in our practical or theoretical reasoning or thinking. Or, at least, so it seems. Of course, such knowledge can assume enormous importance for us if certain phenomenal conditions, for example, extreme toothache, obtain, or threaten to obtain. But in the absence of such extreme cases our phenomenal condition is not a matter of especial interest. It is of less interest than our perceptions, environmental beliefs, and goals. However, in fairly recent philosophical discussion of self-knowledge, it has in fact attracted considerable attention. I am thinking of the employment of the example of pain by Wittgenstein in his discussion of the privacy of experience, which has meant that people responding to, or engaging with that discussion and his ideas, have inevitably employed the same cases. One justification, therefore, for concentrating on this sort of experience knowledge is that it has attracted philosophical scrutiny. It may further seem that this scrutiny can itself be justified. What has often seemed to be the case to philosophers is that such self-knowledge (of the phenomenal) is, in some way, what one might call especially good knowledge. We are particularly well placed to get such knowledge. Now, it is hard not to think that if, on reflection, there is nothing, as one might put it, special at all about so called phenomenal self-knowledge (and belief), then there is going to be nothing special about psychological self-knowledge in general. If that conditional claim is plausible, to see this sort of phenomenal self-knowledge is a crucial test case. But, although such a conditional claim seems plausible, it is by no means obvious that it is true. Why should not other cases of self-knowledge or belief be special even if these phenomenal cases are not? I cannot currently think of any good answer to that question, so base my choice not on the idea that it is crucial test case but rather on its popularity and intrinsic interest.

A crucial question remains if the criticisms of Wright's approach are correct. If we are dividing the content of psychological self-knowledge up so that the division might be theoretically valuable, how best should that be done? I want, in contrast to Wright's proposal, to suggest that the first basic distinction we should draw (under the general category of the mental or psychological), even though it is in some ways rough, is between self-knowledge of experiences, and self-knowledge which is not of experiences. The most interesting case of the latter sort would be knowledge of one's own attitudes, for example, that one believes that P. In the former category, that is self-knowledge about experiences, we should include the cases Wright calls phenomenal, for example that I am in pain, but also appearance knowledge and knowledge of occurrent cognitive activity, such as that one is thinking about X, or running through a tune in one's head. The reason that this twofold distinction seems significant is that self-knowledge of non-experience-states is not in any plausible way to be treated as grounded in or derived from what might be called inner observation or inner scrutiny. How we know or form beliefs about what we believe or want or hope is surely not by observing or scrutinizing such states in ourselves. In fact, we would not know how to recognize a belief or a desire if, as it were, we encountered one.

3. Wright and avowals

If we are to make progress in the philosophical description of self-knowledge and self-belief, how should we proceed? Wright makes the proposal, which will initially strike many as plausible, that we first of all describe some general properties of self-knowledge and then seek for a good explanation why it possess these properties. This will reveal, or may reveal, some more basic, less obvious, theoretically interesting, properties. Now, if I understand him, Wright is, in the final analysis, sceptical of this strategy because he has doubts, which he would dub as in a Wittgensteinian spirit, about the explanatory project. However, part of his case for such skepticism is the claim, grounded in trying to carry out the strategy and discovering no adequate explanation, that there is no explanation. Wright, thereafter, tries to see what strategy is available once one drops the explanatory demand. Still, it seems that he thinks the general strategy is the best first strategy.

I want to argue, or suggest, that if it is the best first strategy, then Wright's way of carrying it out is mistaken. Wright's approach is to lay down three initial properties for which an explanation is going to be sought. They are these (in a somewhat abbreviated form). (i) Phenomenal avowals are *groundless*. This is the claim that the demand, in response to an avowal, that the subject produce reasons or corroborating evidence for their claim is always *inappropriate*. Wright also seems to express this as the claim that the question 'How can you tell?' (or 'How do you know?') in response to an avowal is also inappropriate. As he puts it: 'The demand that somebody produces reasons or corroborating evidence for such a claim about themselves—"How can you tell?"—is always inappropriate' (Wright 2001b, 321). (ii) Such avowals are *strongly authoritative*. This is explained as the claim that if someone doubts what the avower says then that doubt has to resolve into either a doubt about the subject's sincerity or about his or her understanding. Wright's words are these: 'A doubt about such a claim has to be a doubt about the sincerity or the understanding of its author' (ibid.). Some care, though, needs to be taken about quite what this means if it is not to be incorrect. If it is to be true it must be consistent with the possibility that the skeptical observer cannot decide which of the two alternatives obtains, but does think that one or the other does. There need be no resolution deeper than the disjunctive doubt.[8] Wright also says: 'Since we standardly credit any interlocutor, absent evidence to the contrary, with sincerity and understanding, it follows that a subject's actually making such a claim about themselves is a criterion for the correctness of the corresponding third-personal claim made by someone else: my avowal that I'm in pain must be accepted by others, on pain of incompetence, as a ground for the belief that I am' (Wright 2001b, 321). This remark which seems intended to note a consequence of the claim about doubt, itself raises many questions. It employs the terminology of 'criterion' to state the consequence, but there is no received understanding of that term. Is it being suggested that doubts about phenomenal avowals must rest on evidence? This ignores the existence of the distrustful, of the mildly paranoid, and those, perhaps including Descartes, who follow the motto 'Once bitten, twice (or always?) shy'. It is better to ignore this claimed consequence. (iii) Such avowals exhibit *transparency*. This is the claim that it is *absurd* to profess ignorance of the form 'I do not know whether P or not', where 'P' would be a phenomenal avowal.[9]

I wish to make four initial comments.

(1) What stands out is that Wright's characterization has two distinctive aspects. First, it about avowals and the reaction to *avowals*. It formulates its claims as theses about things of that sort. Second, the theses are, in a sense, *normative*. The claims are about what it is

---

[8] A further doubt about Wright's claim is this. Is it somehow ruled out that an observer cannot simply have grounds for suspecting that an (apparent) avowal is incorrect without him or herself articulating the doubt further, that is without realizing what the two alternatives are? I do not really see that this is ruled out, but whether Wright's claim is intended to rule it out I am not sure. I shall ignore this problem.

[9] Wright, at this point, advances a qualification. He says; 'there are contexts in which I might be uncertain of a precondition—(for instance, whether I have feet)' (op. cit., 321). What is unclear is why Wright treats this as a case of an avowal to which transparency does not apply, rather than a reason for not treating claims which require for their truth that one has feet as not having the status of avowals at all. Another example on Wright's list of avowals which seems clearly not to exhibit transparency is 'My ears are ringing'. The problem is that it may possibly be that one is hearing a ringing sound. Thus one can say, 'I don't know whether my ears are ringing or there is actually a ringing sound'.

appropriate or absurd to do at, or in reaction to things at, that level. Now, if this characterization is correct, it simply forces us yet again to ask: why should we study self-knowledge (our awareness of ourselves) via theses with *that character*? I want, though, for the moment, to face up to them as theses of the kind they are. Should we agree with them?

(2) Whether *after a thorough review* we agree with Wright or not, it seems to me remarkably incautious to simply state straight off that phenomenal reports have all these properties. It is hardly obvious that such strong universal and unrestricted claims are correct. In fact, this worry, if sound, should probably lead one to rethink how sensible the general strategy is that Wright proposes (albeit ultimately to reject). It is highly unlikely that we are in a position to reasonably assert, as it were, straight off, that self-knowledge (of the phenomenal kind) has such general properties as this. It is simply not enough that a scrutiny of a few central cases (e.g., 'I am in pain' or 'I am in severe pain') seems to fit them.

(3) It is hard to know quite what Wright is claiming in that, although he has listed some central cases of so called phenomenal avowals, that listing gives us no real guidance as to how extensive the category of phenomenal avowal is. For example, does it include 'I have an afterimage which is yellowy brown on the left and bluish green on the right'? I am assuming that it does, but Wright makes no effort to persuade us that his properties apply to such judgements. (In fact, he makes no serious efforts to persuade us that they apply to any judgements at all, but for some, though not for all, he can reasonably expect agreement.)

(4) It seems to me that there are quite plausible counterexamples to, or problems with, Wright's three properties. In order to develop these problems I need to confront an interpretative issue. I have said that Wright's theses qualify as normative. They concern what are appropriate acts, or acts that we must perform, or acts that it would be absurd to perform. But how does Wright view these normative claims? There are, it seems to me, two alternatives. The first is that they represent normative claims that he himself for some reason accepts. His claims would then be like those of someone who said; 'Although lots of people have bought ISAs I myself consider it an absurd or inappropriate thing to do'. The second interpretation is that Wright holds that the norms are ones that we all accept (or have internalized) in relation to how to respond to avowals or in respect of making avowals. Now, I take it that Wright views his norms in the second way. It therefore becomes relevant to assessing his claims to ask whether they correspond to how *we* (in general) do view things. Do we share the sense of absurdity or inappropriateness that Wright is alleging we do?

Consider first a case relevant to authoritativeness. A teenager on amphetamines crashes a car and is hurled through that window and ends up under the car. The doctor tries to locate the injured areas in a systematic way, by first pressing the areas which do not seem damaged. However, the boy screams and claims that he is in pain. It seems to me that it would not be at all irrational for the doctor to hold that the boy was so confused and frightened and disordered that he thought that the pressure gave him pain when it did not. The doctor could think this without hypothesizing that the injured boy was either lying or did not understand English. In circumstances such as these there is no norm about avowals corresponding to Wright's concept of authoritativeness.[10] Next, consider transparency. It seems to me that there is no norm against professing ignorance. For example, when having my eyes tested I am asked which of two lenses results in the greater blurring. It can be very hard to say, and I can aver that I do not know which is blurrier. Now, this is a comparative judgement which relies on memory, but it would not be true to the experience to suppose that the worry is generated by not remembering. The problem is, rather, that it is hard to judge which is blurrier. This seems to be a phenomenal judgement about which one can aver ignorance.

Finally, consider groundlessness. When explaining this, Wright makes two remarks. The first is that it is inappropriate to demand evidence or reasons that the avower has for his or her avowal. Now, it seems to me that if we understand evidence in the normal sense, then this claim by Wright is correct. Evidence or reasons are things that indicate to someone that a claim is correct. If, however, someone feels a pain and in virtue of that, or in response to it, judges that he or she is in pain, it is not the case that the judger has any evidence to think they are in pain. It is rather that they can simply tell that they are in pain: they simply recognize what is pain as pain. The case seems like the one described by Austin who remarked that someone can have evidence that there are pigs ahead, for example the smell or the sounds, but when he sees the pigs he no longer needs evidence that there are pigs. There are the pigs! However, Wright seems to equate the inappropriateness of asking for evidence with the inappropriateness of asking how the subject can tell. In fact, unless we always tell what is the case by considering evidence, this would not follow, and the point of the remark by Austin is to bring out that we do not always tell by having evidence. Further, it seems plausible to think that wherever there is knowledge there is a method whereby the knowledge is acquired. This method is, presumably, what the question—how can you tell, or how do you know?—is, or seems to be, asking for. It seems, then, that the question—how can you tell?—is appropriate, simply in virtue of thinking of the subject as having knowledge. Of course, actually asking the question would be inappropriate in most cases of phenomenal avowals because, as one might say, the question does not really arise. But it seems to me that asking the 'how' question is not per se inappropriate; rather it is appropriate in light of the thought that knowledge is based on methods.[11]

---

[10] I owe the description of this medical case to Dr Victoria Snowdon, who was in fact a doctor in the story. I have embellished it somewhat for dialectical effect!

[11] My criticism of Wright at this point corresponds to McDowell's observation that, although Wright at times speaks of such avowals being non-inferential, he really seems to hold the stronger claim that McDowell formulates as the claim that they are baseless. In McDowell's terminology (or something close to his terminology), my point is that non-inferentiality does not entail baselessness. See J. McDowell (1998, 48). Having drawn this distinction McDowell himself uses it to demonstrate that the so-called Cartesian

My general conclusion is that each of Wright's properties is dubious. Authoritativeness and transparency seem wrong, and groundlessness is confused.

However, I want next to develop a different question about the approach. We can start by noting a feature of the way Wright specifies the initial properties. Two of the properties are specified in terms of what might be called admissible or legitimate *responses* by someone to avowals of someone else. Now, avowals are speech acts. Thus, groundlessness and authoritativeness are properties fixed in terms of legitimate responses to speech acts by another. Transparency is different; it is not a matter of the inadmissibility of an interpersonal response. It is, however, specified in terms of the *illegitimacy* of a certain speech *act*. All three properties, therefore, singled out by Wright are a matter of what we might call the acceptability of certain acts. Two of the acts amount to responses to the (speech) acts of others, and one amounts to the performance of a certain speech act characterized in terms of its content. I want to call the thought that this level is the correct level at which to formulate theses about self-knowledge (in the broadest sense) *the speech act thesis*. Having formulated this, three further points can be made.

(1) It can be asked, first, why the supposed philosophically fundamental properties of self-knowledge (which we must explain or simply accept) should be specified in terms of the admissibility of certain speech acts. It seems to me that given that knowledge, awareness, belief, recognition, etc., are *not* speech acts, some strong justification is needed for setting up the debate about these cognitive phenomena at the level of theses about speech acts. Now, I cannot myself see what the argument for this approach would be. Certainly, Wright provides no reason to debate matters at this level.

At this point, though, I can envisage two alternative lines of reply on behalf of Wright. The first response is that an interpretative mistake is being made in supposing that Wright is committed to the speech act thesis. It has to be agreed, I think, that within his complex discussion Wright does not always formulate matters in terms of speech acts.[12] In particular there is the following interesting passage.

A different way of seeing the unplayability of the expressivist position is to reflect that the content of an avowal is always available to figure in a subject's thoughts, without public expression. You may sit reading and think to yourself 'My headache has gone' without any outward sign at all. And anyone versed in ordinary psychology will accept that *if* you have that thought, not by way merely of entertaining it but as something you endorse, then you will be right (Authority); that there is no way that your headache could have passed unless you were willing to endorse such a thought (Transparency); and that your willingness to endorse it will not be the product of

---

model, which postulates a special form of inner observation, is not even a candidate explanation for the property of baselessness.

[12] Wright's example of Emma's self interpretation also does not concern an avowal strictly speaking. In the story, as quoted, Emma does not avow her conclusion to anyone (at least not initially). What the story reveals therefore is hardly something about the status of avowals.

inference or independently formulable grounds (Groundlessness). Thus analogues of each of the marks of avowals that pose our problem engage the corresponding unarticulated thoughts.

(Wright 2001b, 364)

I am not interested here in the truth of Wright's claims in this passage, an issue to which I shall return, but in what it shows about Wright's attitude to the speech act thesis. The answer is that it leaves it hard to understand what his attitude is. At the end of the passage Wright has clearly returned to the idea that 'our problem' concerns avowals, but in the light of the acknowledged possession of analogous properties by non-avowals, one can only wonder why the shape or content of the basic problem does not deserve to be modified. One also wonders why the thought seems not to figure in the conception of the problem that perhaps the analogous features on the part of non-avowals might be considered as candidate explanations for the features of the avowals.

The second possible reply concedes that, maybe, there is no need or special reason to formulate the initial properties in terms of speech acts, but that it is, for all that has been really shown, an acceptable way to capture some properties for which one can look for an explanation. It is true that I have not shown that it is illegitimate or wrong to suppose that there are speech act properties and appropriate to ask for an explanation of their presence.[13] It is also true, I suggest, that something more than this needs to be said by way of justifying a concentration when stating the problem of self-knowledge on speech acts. One surely needs more than the mere thought that it has not been refuted to be *justified* in setting up the problem that way.

(2) I want, though, to generate rather stronger grounds for skepticism about starting with Wright's speech act properties. What solution does ultimately Wright favour? Where is he trying to persuade us to end up? He claims that there is no explanation as yet available for the presence of the properties he has cited but he appears to think, more strongly, that it is reasonable to conclude that there is no explanation. He says: 'We must not underestimate our colleague's resourcefulness, of course, but the smart money will bet we are not going to get one' (Wright 2001b, 371). Wright's proposal seems to be that one ought to remain satisfied simply by saying something along this line: 'But these marks are part of 'grammar' and grammar is not sustained by anything. We should just say 'This language game is played' (ibid., 372). The main lacuna that Wright feels exists is that no reason has been advanced to think that this *should* be enough. That is, as it were, a task for the future. Now, my conjecture or suspicion is that anyone inclined to end up here, has a strong motive to formulate basic features in terms of principles governing acts. For then it might at least look as if the basic features correspond to rules (of grammar) that have simply been adopted or chosen (and as such do not depend on anything else). ('This is how we play'.)

---

[13] For the purposes of the discussion in this section I am bracketing off the objections already presented in the last section against Wright's actual speech act theses.

However, although there may be a sort of fit between the final theory that Wright is tempted by and characterizing things in terms of acts which are admissible, there is also, I believe, a significant tension. What strikes me is that Wright expresses the properties of the speech acts by using words like 'it is *absurd* to profess ignorance', or, 'asking "how do you know?" is *inappropriate*'. Now, it seems to me that such ways of putting it do not fit with the idea that the inadmissibility is grounded in something like the existence of a rule or procedure that we have adopted. Thus, compare what is said here with how we would speak about a case where a prohibition is, or is close to being, grounded in a rule. It is contrary to the rules of chess for a bishop to change the colour of square it occupies however it moves. This is not the case for any other piece (or indeed pawns). It would however be very weird to report this by saying 'It is *absurd* for a bishop so as to change the colour of square it is on', or, 'It is *inappropriate* for a bishop to change the colour of its square'. We would say, rather, 'A bishop cannot change the colour of square it is on' or 'You must keep your bishops on squares of the same colour'. Not only is Wright's way of talking totally unnatural if the act is regarded as excluded by a rule, but the way he speaks fits much better with cases where it is felt that there is some real reason or basis *against* the act in question. Thus, to be absurd, there must be something that makes it absurd, and to be inappropriate there must be something that makes it inappropriate. So the way that Wright captures the properties suggests that, even if he is right about those properties, they cannot, in some sense, *just correspond to ways we would not proceed*.

(3) Instead, I want to suggest that there are certain true conditionals that describe the basis of Wright's properties, if that is, they have a real basis. Thus, if it is true that it is inappropriate to ask for the evidence upon which an avowal is based that can only be because the belief (or knowledge) to which an avowal gives expression is not itself based on evidence. Again, the idea that an expressed doubt about an avowal must become either a doubt about the avower's sincerity or the avowers understanding of their language, can be right only if the belief that the avower is giving expression to must be right. If it were really possible for someone to be mistaken, then a doubt might amount to thinking that the avower is simply wrong, and neither insincere nor verbally confused. Of course, this property of the belief is what is called incorrigibility. Finally, if it is correct to think that one cannot appropriately say 'I do not know whether P or not' (where P would correspond to an avowal), then that can only be because it is not possible for P to be the case and the subject not realize it. If it is in the nature of the case possible for P to apply to someone and the subject in question not be aware of it, then an admission of ignorance would not be ruled out. This property is sometimes called the self-intimatingess of psychological features. My suggestion, then, is that Wright's properties specified in terms of speech acts could hold only if there are, and in virtue of, more basic properties applying to the cognitive states (of knowledge and belief) themselves. If that is correct then I think that the focus on avowals turns out to be mistaken, and we should rather ask if those cognitive theses are true.

There is one complication that needs to be mentioned. Moore showed that there are certain claims which it is absurd to make even though what is claimed corresponds to a possibility. It is not therefore completely obvious that if it were possible for P (or not P) to obtain without the subject knowing which then it must be appropriate for the subject to affirm that they do not know which obtains. The affirmation may exhibit an absurdity of a special kind. However, having alerted ourselves to this possibility, I do not see what the source of such a special absurdity would be. So I am inclined to affirm that Wright's speech act property of transparency cannot obtain unless self-intimatingness obtains.

4. Some properties of self-knowledge

I have argued that we should not formulate the properties of phenomenal self-knowledge/belief in the terms that Wright favours. What candidates should we consider? I want to consider those which I argued would have to obtain if Wright's suggestions hold. There are three properties that we need to focus on. We can distinguish them in accordance with the direction that the conditionals defining them take.

The first suggested property is this: necessarily, if any phenomenal condition C applies to S, then S knows that he/she is in C. This conditional goes from the obtaining of the phenomenal condition to the presence of knowledge. It is what used to be called 'The self-intimating nature of experience'. I have argued that this is the property that must obtain if Wright's Transparency property holds.

The second property rules out error. With it, the conditional goes in the other direction. It says: necessarily, if S believes that he/she is in C, then S is in C. This is standardly called incorrigibility. No correction is possible because no error is possible. Now, incorrigibility is the more directly specified property that is such that only if it holds can strong authoritativeness, in Wright's sense, hold, and vice versa.

Now, I want to argue that the two properties of self-intimation and incorrigibility do not apply to ordinary knowledge of our phenomenal experiences.

Before I start to argue for those claims I want to draw a contrast between self-intimation and incorrigibility. Self-intimation goes from the presence of the phenomenal state to the presence of awareness of it, involving a belief that it is occurring. Incorrigibility goes from belief in a phenomenal condition to its presence, thereby making the belief true. Now, the contrast is that a problem arises for the former idea which does not arise for the latter idea. That is that if there are creatures who have phenomenal states without a matching belief, and we could be like them if certain things happened, then self-intimation fails. However, because incorrigibility is a property defined for subjects who have beliefs, the existence of belief-less creatures does not threaten that. Such cases are not relevant.

Let us start with self-intimation. I list some objections and counterexamples. These are not strikingly novel but are variations on fairly well-known themes.

(1) As it stands the self-intimatingess thesis is problematic because it seems there can be creatures who have experiences of a phenomenal kind but who are not aware that they do. I have in mind sub-human animals, infants, and adults suffering from severe dementia. It is plausible to say that they do not know what is happening to them even though it includes phenomenal experiences. They have and react to such experiences without knowing that they themselves have them. I think that we have to modify the thesis so that such cases are not counterexamples. The best way to do this is to reformulate the claim as: if phenomenal condition C applies to S and S possesses the relevant concepts, then S will know that C applies to him/her. (Of course, if non-possession of the concept was the only problem for the basic self-intimatingness thesis, then one could deny self-intimatingness even though one accepts Wright's transparency property.)

(2) We can, I suggest, draw a important distinction between features we can detect only via the operation of a systematic procedure and ones we can detect (relatively) immediately. Thus, if I see a group of three objects then I can detect immediately that there are three, but if I look at a group of twelve objects then I cannot immediately detect that it is a group of twelve, but must resort to a procedure of counting. (I am not assuming that this division between features that can be detected immediately and those that cannot is fixed across people, or within the lives of single people.) Now, surely there are phenomenal features which cannot be detected immediately, for example, whether this after-image has twelve spots on it or not. If you do not engage in the procedure you can fail to know this. Further, there could be creatures whose ability to take things without a procedure is much more limited then ours. So the range of features that this can affect is very hard to determine. I take it that this shows that phenomenal conditions are not per se self-intimating. Clearly, too, someone could say; 'Well, I do not know whether my after-image has twelve spots on it or not'.

(3) These two arguments are intended to show that someone can fail to know truths about their own experiences. Its character is not, as such, self-intimating. I want, however, to offer a more general argument. The first claim in the general argument is that knowing how your experience is, recognizing its character, requires some uptake on the subject's part beyond the occurrence of the experience itself. To this claim we add the general naturalistic assumptions that the occurrence of the experience requires a physical realization, and that the occurrence of the extra uptake or recognition does so as well. Now, this second physical occurrence must presumably be causally related to the physical occurrences which constitute the experience itself. Finally, understood this way, the physical causal processes involved in the uptake is such that it need not occur of necessity. In principle, something could happen to stop it occurring. It seems to follow that the knowledge of the experience need not occur. Experiences are not self-intimating.

(4) As well as these general arguments there is what night be called a fairly common-sensical and received understanding of the possibility of ignorance, possible grounds for

failures to know or realize something, which can be applied to our knowledge of our own experiences. These grounds include simple lack of attention, where one's attention is firmly on something else; an inability to attend grounded in one's general psychological states—the source might be, for example, panic, fear, drug-induced jitteriness; an inability to take things in accurately due to being primed to expect something else, which might indeed be somewhat similar to what is the case; and also a mistrust of one's cognitive faculties. It seems to me that all these conditions can be present and ground ignorance in the sorts of case we are interested in.

(5) It might be replied or responded to these examples that surely at least if I have a severe pain then I must know about that. Now, before objecting to the truth of this claim, I want to point out that the argument has taken an odd turn. Proponents of self-intimatingness surely wish to advance a *general* theoretical claim. It cannot be that their thesis is one about pain or severe pain. So, someone tempted by such a remark should pause and wonder quite what the significance of their claim about pain is. However, I want to bring against it, when it is understood a certain way, a further kind of example which has fairly general application. Suppose that S is feeling a severe pain in his or her right foot. Must S know that that is so? In the normal event it certainly would be odd if S did not realize this. But holding the severe pain in the foot constant, imagine that S had all sorts of other severe pains added to his condition. As things get worse and worse must S still know about the pain in the right foot? I cannot see why anyone should think that S must remain aware that he has such a pain in a condition of pain overload. I call these important examples 'overload cases'.

(6) I want to sketch a further sort of case which seems possible to me. I cannot cite actual cases, but I do not see how to rule it out as impossible. The case seems possible to me in the light of what we should say about other types of case. Consider these examples. Some people have what are called religious experiences. They feel they can sense a divine presence. The environment or happening is, as they might say, infused with God. A second case is that of people who fail to recognize their own extent. When shaving, for example, looking at themselves in the mirror, they shave half their face and fail to realize they have only half shaved. They do not see the unshaven part as theirs. How should we think about such cases? At a very general level, I am tempted to suggest, we can characterize them in causal terms. In the example of religious experience, perceptual occurrence triggers the application of the god-concept, so the subject has a sense of god. Whereas in the second case, a causal link between experience and concept which would be present normally has been lost. A perception which would trigger an application of the self-concept fails to do so. This is, of course, a very general and pretty uninformative description. It provides no explanation as to why the causal links are as they are; nor does it say in any informative way what it is to trigger the application of a concept. However, if it is, despite its generality and general uninformativeness, a reasonable description, then we can envisage the following sort of case. A subject has a phenomenal experience which, however, fails to trigger the application

of the self-concept. The subject fails to recognize it as his or hers. Although the subject might recognize a pain, say, he or she fails to recognize whose it is. If this is possible, then a subject might not realize that an experience belonged to them. Now, I do not see how to rule this out.

I want next to make a case for thinking that incorrigibility is not a property of phenomenal self-knowledge. The case here resembles the case against self-intimatingness in two respects: first, the same or more or less the similar cases to those that were relevant are still relevant; second, the argument is primarily case or example based. Here, then, are some points.

(1) My first example is intended to weaken the hold on you of the idea that we do assume that first person present tense phenomenal judgements are incorrigible. The case is a variant of one I learned from C. B. Martin. Imagine you are having troubling pains in your stomach. The doctor after an examination says: 'It is one of two complaints. There is a test to determine which. I shall apply pressure to a region and it will cause pain in two areas—one left and one right—and which ever hurts most tells us what the problem is.' He then applies the pressure and you judge that the left area hurts most. The doctor then says: 'Oh dear, that means that you have a very serious condition, requiring drastic treatment. If it had been the right side then it would have been minor.' Confronted with this, do you say: 'Since my judgement is incorrigible go ahead with the drastic treatment'? Or might you say: 'Do you mind if we repeat the test? Maybe I was a little bit hasty—I would like to make sure and check things'? The final claim is that we would indeed opt for the second response, and not the first. We would not view anyone doing so as overlooking some basic principle that we cannot make mistakes in these sorts of judgements.

(2) If the distinction drawn earlier between knowledge or conviction based on a procedure and non-procedure-based knowledge is sound, then there seems no reason why beliefs about the phenomenal which result from procedures cannot be wrong. The outcome of such procedures depends on keeping track of the different stages of the procedures, and there is no reason to assume that we cannot lose track, leading to an erroneous final judgement.

(3) In discussing self-intimation we saw that circumstances can explain failures to recognize things. It seems fairly clear though that such circumstances can equally explain the occurrence of error. What is the problem about the following rather hackneyed case? Suppose that someone is extremely frightened and nervous at the prospect of torture by having acid dropped on their skin, and to the accompaniment of misleading noises, etc., is very suddenly doused in water. It is highly likely that they will be under the impression initially that the acid torture has started, and along with it the horrible pain. I have not filled in all the details, but I cannot see why a mistake in such a case can be ruled out. Indeed, it would seem a highly likely outcome.

(4) One problem in discussing incorrigibility is how broad its application is supposed to be. But if having visual images counts as phenomenal experience, then another ground for error flows from our ability to mistake other occurrences for such occurrences. In the famous Perky projection experiments a roomful of Harvard students thought that they were having visual images when in fact they were seeing a pattern projected onto the wall. Here, they affirmed a phenomenal claim which was erroneous.

6. Grounds and ways

I have argued now that phenomenal beliefs are not incorrigible, nor are phenomenal states self-intimating. These conclusions undermine strong authoritativeness and transparency. Now, it does not follow from this that there are no modified versions of these two properties which do apply to phenomenal states and beliefs. That would be worth investigating, but what I want to finish by considering is Wright's Groundlessness property. Consideration of this, I believe, generates some difficult problems.

In relation to groundlessness I have so far argued that Wright appears to compress two different features. It is true that in the normal sense one does not have evidence or a reason to suppose that, for example, one is in pain, or one's after-image is red. However, it does not follow from this that the question—how do you know?—is not appropriately askable, and in principle, has a correct answer.

It is possible to hold that, although the distinction between having evidence or reasons and there being a way that you know is a distinction, in the case of phenomenal self-knowledge there is in fact *no such thing* as the way that one knows. There is no answer to the question, 'How do you know?'.

It is hard to show that this option is incorrect, but on balance it seems dubious to me.[14] The best I can say is that, thinking naturalistically, knowledge *comes to you somehow*; so there will be an answer to the 'How?' question. Second, it seems intuitively plausible that 'How do you know?' is always answerable if there is knowledge. That seems to be one defining feature of knowledge. Third, there is no commitment in thinking that just because there is an answer to the question 'How do you know?' that the subject possessing the knowledge must be in a position to provide the answer. This last remark is intended to block an argument the other way. Fourth, one might ask someone who wishes to endorse this option of knowledge where there is no answer to 'How do you know?' why they think there are such cases. As far as I can see, the only reply they have is that they cannot say what the answer is in the kind of case we are investigating. But this reason provides no real ground to say that an answer is not possible rather than that it is difficult.

---

[14] Discussion with Dr Lesley Brown made me realize this.

Let us assume, then, that the question is askable. What is its answer? Now, one suggested answer is: you know you are in pain by feeling the pain. This suggestion has the appearance of being right because it is grammatically parallel to many plainly correct answers to 'How do you know?' questions. Thus I know there is a cat by seeing the cat. However, there is a disanalogy too. This is that there seems to be an equivalence between being in pain and feeling a pain. If there is such an equivalence, then the suggested answer reduces to: I know I am in pain by being in pain. Now, so formulated that does not seem a correct answer, because what we want to know is how the fact that you are in pain, that is, feeling a pain, is known. It seems no more plausible than saying: I know that I am standing up by standing up.

A second suggested answer that philosophers would give is: by introspecting. The initial problem is—what does this mean? What is introspecting (or introspection) supposed to be? Either it means something like an inner perceptual mechanism, or it means nothing more than some distinctive method (whatever it is) whereby we know such things about ourselves. The main difficulty, it seems to me, for the idea of an inner perceptual mechanism can be brought out by considering this. Suppose that you are asked to make something that has and feels pain. Let us suppose that you have done that. Now, you are asked to add to it so that the creature knows that it has pain. It does not seem that you would need to add another inner perceptual mechanism in some sense perceiving the pain. *Ex hypothesi*, the creature already feels the pain, already has as much pain experience as it needs. As one might say: you do not need to increase or add to the experiences of the creature, but rather to give it the means of somehow knowing how those experiences are.

If that argument is correct, then we end up saying rather uninformatively that there is some internal mechanism generating knowledge or awareness of how it is (which we can if we wish but without thereby characterizing it in any way called 'introspection'). Can we say what nature this mechanism has? We can add, I believe, some manifest *functional* properties that the mechanism must have. It must be such that the subject can do what we describe as attending to, concentrating on, scrutinizing the experience, as part of a process of improving its knowledge of the experience. But the real nature of this mechanism, it seems we must say, is not known to us. This is, in some way, not a surprise. Our knowledge of how we know about the external world arises because we get to know about the mechanisms operating there, systems involving such things as our eyes and ears and bodies, and how to some extent the information we have depends on them and their states, and on many occasions at least we can tell which mechanism is operating. We are not, as normally equipped observers, in a similar way, acquainted with our *internal* mechanisms. Their nature will therefore be revealed by science.[15] If there is a 'how' in such cases, that is the best we philosophers can say.

---

[15] The tense in this sentence might be careless. Maybe science knows!

7. Conclusion

I have tried to make a case for saying that it is an incorrect research programme to treat the problem of self-knowledge as a problem about avowals and norms. Instead, we should look at the properties of beliefs about and knowledge of our own phenomenal states. After considering some examples, I have concluded that we can make mistakes and be ignorant about such matters. Our privilege in part consists in having a distinctive method of learning about such features in ourselves, but the nature of this method requires elucidation by empirical science. That may not be our only privilege, but it is the only one emerging here.

I introduced in the very first paragraph one motive for the direction taken in the present paper, which is to contribute to an evaluation of accounts of self-knowledge within the Wittgensteinian tradition. How far has that goal been achieved in this discussion? Two things, of different relative importance, have, perhaps, been achieved. The first is that a case has been made against formulating matters in terms of appropriate responses to avowals or norms about making avowals. However, even if this skepticism is reasonable, its significance is not clear, since it is not obvious that a Wittgensteinian response has to be formulated in those terms or at that level. More significant, I believe, is that by accepting the ideas that the phenomenal judgements we make about ourselves can be incorrect and that we can be, and even profess ourselves to be, ignorant, some assumptions that seem to have shaped Wittgenstein's own approach have been rejected. Quite how significant this is remains as a question for another occasion.[16]

References

Davidson, D. 2001 *Subjective, Intersubjective, Objective*, Oxford, Oxford University Press.

McDowell, J. 1998 "Response to Crispin Wright", in C. Wright, B. Smith, and C. Macdonald (eds.) *Knowing Our Own Minds*, Oxford, Clarendon Press, 47–62.

Snowdon, P. (forthcoming) "Wittgenstein on Sense Data and Privacy", in M. McGinn (ed.) *Wittgenstein Handbook*, Oxford, Oxford University Press.

Wright, C. 1998 "Self-Knowledge: the Wittgensteinian Legacy", in C. Wright, B. Smith, and C. Macdonald (eds.), *Knowing Our Own Minds*, Oxford, Clarendon Press, 1998, 13–45.

——2001a *Rails to Infinity: Essays on Themes from Wittgenstein's Philosophical Investigations*, Cambridge (Mass.), Harvard University Press.

——2001b "The Problem of Self- Knowledge", in C. Wright 2001a, 319–73.

---

[16] The main influence on my thinking has been conversations over a long period with the late Professor C. B. Martin. More recently, I have benefited greatly from reading the chapter at UCL, Howard Robinson's discussion group in Oxford, ANU, the University of Otago, and the University of Waikato, and the stimulating discussions in all those places. I would also like to thank Professor Wright for his comments on the chapter at the London conference, which were illuminating and helpful.

12

The Unique Status of Self-Knowledge

Akeel Bilgrami

The term 'privileged access', on the lips and keyboards of philosophers, expresses an *intuition* that self-knowledge is unique among the knowledges human beings possess, unique in being somehow more direct and less prone to error than other kinds of knowledge such as, say, our knowledge of the physical world or of the mental states of others. These notions of 'directness' and 'immunity to error' do, of course, need to be made more precise and may need more qualification (and even revision) than is provided at the level of intuition. Those are the familiar tasks of the philosophical *refinement* of an intuition. But these tasks must nest in a more basic philosophical question, which is to consider, as with all intuitions, whether the intuition can be *justified* in the first place by philosophical argument or whether, on scrutiny, it should be discarded as insupportable.

It is my view, one for which I have argued at greater length in my book *Self-Knowledge and Resentment* (Harvard University Press, 2006), that the intuition of privileged access in the limited domain of self-knowledge of intentional states, such as beliefs and desires, could be redeemed philosophically if we acknowledged in general, the close and integral relations between four different notions—value, agency, intentionality, and self-knowledge, and in particular the irreducibly normative nature both of human agency and of the intentional states of human agents. Without such an acknowledgement, it is more plausible and more honest to concede (to those who are skeptical of the soundness of the intuition) that self-knowledge is not distinct, except in matters of degree, from these other forms of knowledge.

The integration begins with a characterization of two properties of intentional states which amount to the special character of self-knowledge. 1) *Transparency*, a property possessed by first order intentional states (restricting myself, as I said, to beliefs and desires); and 2) *Authority*, a property possessed by second order beliefs about the existence of these first order intentional states. Beliefs and desires are transparent if—not as a matter of contingency, but by their very nature—they can be said to be known by their possessors. And a second order belief about the presence of a first order belief or desire is authoritative if, by its very nature, it can be said to be a true belief.

Authority, if true, would certainly capture something of what is intuited in the idea of 'immunity to error'; and the intuition of 'directness', which presumably has to do with the fact that paradigmatic cases of self-knowledge of intentional states do not require of their possessors that they undertake analogues to 'looking' or 'seeing' or 'checking' as ordinary *perceptual* knowledge of the world does, is captured by the idea that it is because of their very nature rather than via these cognitive activities, that intentional states are known (to their possessors)—something we would not say about physical objects and facts, nor even about intentional states as they are known by those who do not possess them.

If these properties do make explicit the special character of self-knowledge, a bold initial move would be to begin by putting down two conditionals in a stark form, one for each property:

(T): If one desires or believes that p, one believes that one desires or believes that p.
(A): If one believes that one desires or believes that p, then one desires or believes that p.

These primitive conditionals need to be accounted for and qualified in various ways that I will explain below.

The main argument by which it is established that these properties hold of intentional states such as beliefs and desires turns on a preliminary point of central importance.

There is a deep ambiguity in the very idea of intentionality. It is widely (though not universally) thought that beliefs and desires are states that are in some sense deeply caught up with *normativity*. But they are also widely thought to be *dispositions* to behaviour. As some, for instance Saul Kripke (1982), have pointed out these are not entirely compatible ways of thinking of them. Much needs to be sorted out about this, which I won't try and do here, but the general thrust is that we need to disambiguate the terms 'belief' and 'desire', making clear whether we mean to be talking of normative or dispositional states, when we use these terms. So, for instance, the term 'desire', when it describes an urge or a tendency I have, might be understood to have the dispositional sense. But it need not always be used to describe my urges and tendencies. It may be used to describe something more normative, something I think that I should do or ought to do. This latter is 'desire' qua *commitment*, not disposition. Thus an intentional state of mind that we might describe as the 'desire that I smoke a cigarette' could be an urge or a commitment on someone's part, and there is a distinction of principle between intentional states, conceived as one or other of these. (The desire that I smoke can, of course, be both an urge—or tendency—*and* a commitment, but in being so it is two things, not one, and that is why the term 'desire' is genuinely ambiguous.) As with desire, so with beliefs. Beliefs can be viewed as dispositions, which when they nest with desires (also conceived as dispositions) *tend*, under suitable circumstances, to cause behavior describable as appropriate to the propositional contents by which those beliefs and desires are specified. But they can also be viewed as commitments. Thus, a belief that there is a table in front of me is a commitment I have. If I believe it, I *ought* to believe various other things that are implied by it, such as, for instance, that there is something in front of me, or (more materially) that if I run hard into it, I will be injured. It is a commitment in the sense that it commits me to believing these other things, even if I don't actually believe them, just as my desires commit me to do various things, even if I don't do them.[1]

How does a commitment contrast with dispositions (our urges and tendencies)? To put it in very brief summary: A commitment, being a normative state, is the sort of thing we can fail to live up to, even frequently fail to live up to, without it ceasing to be a commitment. After all it is in the nature of norms that we might fail to live up to them. By contrast, the very existence of a disposition would be put into doubt, if one did not act on it, if what it was disposed or tended to bring about did not occur (given, of course, the suitable conditions for its occurrence). When we fail to live up to a commitment, even under suitable conditions for the performance by which we live up to it, it does not put into doubt that one has the commitment—rather, all that is required is that we try and do better by way of living up to it (quite possibly by cultivating the dispositions necessary to live up to it.)

---

[1] To many, it seems much less intuitive to think of desires as commitments than it does beliefs. An objection might go as follows: "As far as beliefs are concerned, it is quite easy to see how beliefs are normative commitments, but when it comes to desires, someone might desire something without at the same thinking of the object of his desire as something that is normatively desirable. Take, for example, having the desire to smoke. That desire does not seem to commit me normatively towards smoking. If I am clear-headed, I understand that I should not try to act on this desire." The response to this, as I said above, is that the term 'desire' is indeed ambiguous between commitments and urges or dispositions. I may have the desire, qua urge or disposition, in this way, to smoke, but no desire, qua commitment, to smoke. Just because someone (many more today than before) may not have the desire, qua commitment, to smoke, it does not mean others *can't* have the desire, qua commitment, to smoke. Perhaps the skepticism about desires as commitments is of a more general kind and shouldn't be linked to the specific example of smoking. The objection could go like this: "The objects of one's desires are not desirable because that would imply that the world would contains desirabilities, i.e. values or value properties, and that goes against naturalism. (No similar objection arises in the case of beliefs, it might be said.)" There are several things to say about this: first of all, one can presumably hold onto the notion of desires as commitments without insisting that the objects of one's desire are desirable (i.e. desirabilities in the world). Someone like Robert Brandom, who believes that desires can be commitments, nowhere, for instance, claims that there are desirabilities in the world. My own view, however, is that the world does contain desirabilities and values, and our desires are often responses to those properties in the world. And I am quite unfazed by the charge of not being in tune with naturalism. I am avowedly not a naturalist in that sense. Why do I think that there are desirabilities or value properties in the world? I can't possibly argue for the view at length in a footnote, but let me just say this. Gareth Evans once insightfully said: If someone is asked, "Do you believe that it is raining?", he does not typically scan the interiority of his mind to see if it contains the belief that it is raining. He looks outside and answers. I think it can be exactly so with desires. If someone is asked, "Do you desire X?" he does not typically scan the interiority of his mind to see if it contains that desire, he considers the *desirability* of X. If this were not so, if all the objects of our desires were given to us as desired rather than as desirable, we would not be agents at all. We would always be spectators of our own minds rather than agents, to put it in terms of a Spinozist distinction that I make much use of in my (2006) book. For a longer elaboration of this deep link between agency and value properties in the world, see also Bilgrami (2010).

This disambiguation of the very notion of intentional states is important, not only in itself,[2] but because the properties of transparency and authority distribute quite differently depending on whether intentional states are conceived as dispositions or as commitments. How so?

Authority holds of second order beliefs *only* if the first order intentional states they are about are conceived as commitments. Transparency holds of first order intentional states, whether they are conceived as commitments or dispositions, but it only holds of the latter under a crucial further condition—it holds of those dispositions that are tied to one's agency, where by 'agency' I mean a notion of accountable human action, itself conceived in thoroughly normative terms. Thus, under this condition, transparency has wider scope of application since it takes in a wider class of mental states.

Let's consider transparency first. That intentional states, conceived as commitments, should be transparent is due to the very nature of commitments. I had characterized commitments above, as requiring that we try and do better to live up to them, when we fail to do so. That, in part, is what makes a commitment, a commitment. If that is so, then I cannot fail to know my own commitments since I cannot try and live up to something I do not know I possess. But transparency, as I said, holds not just of intentional states conceived as commitments—it also holds of dispositions. And it is here that the relevance of notions of human agency and responsibility enters. I will briefly elaborate the by a modification and application of the innovative ideas in P. F. Strawson's essay (1962).

Strawson had argued that human freedom and agency are not non-normative metaphysical ideas having merely to do with issues of causality. Rather they are constituted by the *normative* practices surrounding notions of responsibility, such as blame and punishment, and these practices are, in turn, grounded in our normative reactions ('reactive attitudes' such as resentment and indignation) to each other's behaviour.

---

[2] It is important in itself, but like anything significant, it brings questions with it that need to be addressed. First, is the question of the somewhat different relations that hold between commitments (as opposed to dispositions) and actions. When one has a commitment, one acts so as to live up to it, if one also has the correlative disposition towards that action. If one lacked the latter one would not act on the commitment. That is why, often when one fails to act so as to live up to the commitment, one often tries to cultivate the disposition to act on it, or fights the disposition that makes one act in ways that fail to live up to it. All this should suggest, not only that commitments and dispositions are two different kinds of states, but that the relations between commitments and actions are different from the relations between dispositions and actions. I discuss these differentials at much length in chapter 5 of my (2006) book. A second question has to do with whether commitments, even if they are distinct from dispositions, do not themselves, as states, involve dispositions in some form or another in their characterization. In my book, mentioned above, I discuss how (and why) a commitment, because it is a normative state, does indeed get characterized as possessing a built-in second-order disposition to try and do better to live up to the commitment, whenever one fails to live up to it. And I try and show why, because this is a second-order disposition of a kind that is necessarily specified by specifying a commitment with which it nests, it is not to be thought of naturalistically as first-order dispositions standardly are.

I extended this line of thought on freedom along the following lines to the notion of self-knowledge. For Strawson, the freedom of human action is a *presupposition* of our practices surrounding responsibility and the reactive attitudes that underlie them. To blame or resent another is intelligible only to the extent that he or she is capable of free action, and the blame and resentment only targets those free actions. To blame or resent a particular action is to presuppose that it has been freely enacted. My extension of this insight is this: Free and accountable human action, in this Strawsonian sense, *in turn, presupposes* that each such action is *also self-known*. And if that is so, the intentional states (whether conceived as commitments or dispositions) that potentially go into the production of such action, are also self-known. In short, any intentional state of mind of a human agent that is tied (or potentially tied) to her actions which are the (potential) targets of justified reactive attitudes, is necessarily known to that human agent. To put it differently, we cannot justify having reactive attitudes (say, resentment) to actions/ intentional states that are not self-known. This last may seem controversial since it seems to rule out any moral-psychological counterpart to the legal idea of strict liability, but a range of considerations can be advanced to justify taking such a view, though I will not try and do so here since I have done so at length in the book I mentioned earlier.

Transparency, argued for along these lines, holds of intentional states qua dispositions. I am justified in resenting intentional actions (for instance those that cause harm) that flow from someone's dispositions, only if she has self-knowledge of those dispositions. Thus intentional action flowing from dispositions (that is, flowing not just from one's commitments but also from one's urges and tendencies) is free and accountable in Strawson's sense, so long as the dispositions are self-known. If we are justified, say, in blaming and resenting certain actions, then those actions (if Strawson is right) are free, and (if I am right) are self-known, as are the intentional states (even if conceived as dispositions) from which they flow.

Transparency can now be fully characterized in the following refinement of conditional (T): To the extent that an intentional state is part of a rationalization (or potential rationalization)[3] of an action or conclusion, which is or can be the object of justifiable

---

[3] In this context, I use the term 'potential' here and elsewhere in the text, to talk about intentional states rationalizing actions, and it is a very general term that can cover a lot of things. But it should be obvious that by 'potential' in this context I mean something very specific and tightly controlled. By an intentional state 'potentially' rationalizing an action, I mean an 'intentional state, if *in its present status* in the moral psychology of an agent, were to rationalize an action, which it has not actually so far done.' What I do not mean by it is, 'if it were to rationalize an action which it has not actually done so far, *after having altered its status*.' I mention this for the following reason. Mental states which are not self-known have a status *different* from the states whose potential to rationalize I am claiming is caught up with agency. Yet these unself-known mental behavior states may *come to be* self-known by cognitive (e.g. psychoanalytical) inquiry, and then they too might rationalize, which they have not actually so far done. When they do become self-known and when they then actually rationalize an action, those actions would be the object of justifiable reactive attitudes. So while they are still unself-known, in one sense of the term they still have the 'potential' to rationalize actions that are the objects of justifiable reactive attitudes. However, they would have this potential only in the sense that in order for the potential to be actualized, they would have to first change their status from unself-known

reactive attitudes, or to the extent that an intentional state itself is or can be the object of justifiable reactive attitudes, then that intentional state is known to its possessor. Since the antecedent 'to the extent that...' relies on considerations of agency (as deriving from the Strawsonian ideas I mentioned), we can abbreviate the conditional for the sake of convenience and apply it to beliefs and desires in particular, as follows: *Given agency*, if someone desires (believes) that p, then she believes that she desires (believes) that p. This conditional (T) captures our intuitive idea that *by their very nature*, intentional states are self-known to their possessors.

I repeat: in this conditional, intentional states such as beliefs and desires may be conceived as commitments, but, *with the crucial antecedent in place*, they can be conceived as dispositions as well. Thus the proviso about agency, understood along Strawsonian lines, in the antecedent, is essential to this more capacious scope of transparency.

Authority next. Authority, the idea that our second order beliefs about our first order intentional states are always true, has seemed to many philosophers to be a very tall claim, given the widespread fact of self-deception and other Freudian phenomena.

Here is a necessarily brief and rough version of the argument for why we may concede the ubiquitous fact of self-deception and other such phenomena (a concession that distinguishes 'authority' and 'privileged access', as I and others who have written recently about self-knowledge present it, from traditional Cartesian claims), while denying that that fact undermines authority. When one believes that one believes (or desires) that p, and one is self-deceived, it is not that one *lacks* the first order belief (or desire) that p, and therefore it is *not* that the second-order belief is false, it is rather that one *has another* first order belief (or desire) which is *not consistent* with the belief or (desire) that p (let's say, taking the clearest case, not-p). And, if the second order belief is not false, then this strategy has provided a way of viewing self-deception such that it leaves authority intact.[4]

---

to self-known, otherwise the actions they rationalize would not be the objects of justifiable reactive attitudes. That is a sense of potential quite different from the one I intend. What I intend is a distinction between actual and potential within the same status of intentional states. Perhaps one should drop the word 'potential' and find another, if this distinction is easily lost sight of.

[4] My claim here cannot be faulted on the grounds that it attributes *blatantly* inconsistent intentional states to an agent (just in order to save an agent's authority), and that it therefore is a violation of the principle of charity which forbids one to attribute blatantly inconsistent attributes to an agent. Blatant inconsistencies fall afoul of charity because there are no explanations given of why the inconsistencies exist. But when there are explanations for why there is an inconsistency, there is nothing uncharitable about attributing it. Sometimes the explanation is that the subject is unaware of one of the inconsistent beliefs. At other times, a subject may be (severally) aware of two inconsistent beliefs but has not brought them together, having compartmentalized them and their surrounding implications. And so on. In the case of self-deception, there will always be some such explanations of the inconsistency invoked by my strategy for saving authority. In cases of self-deception, it is perhaps most often (though not necessarily always) the former explanation that is in play. Assuming it is in play, we can admit that, though it would be uncharitable to say of someone that she has inconsistent beliefs if she has self-knowledge of both the beliefs involved, in the inconsistency, in our example both of the inconsistent pair of beliefs are *not* self-known. In particular, the belief that not-p, mentioned above, is not self-known to the agent. It is not a belief, transparent to its possessor. And if that is so, there is *no* lack of charity involved in attributing inconsistent beliefs in this way to save authority, since lack of charity only holds

To put it less abstractly, let's take a standard sort of case of self-deception. Suppose someone has the following second order belief: she believes that she believes that her health is fine. But let's suppose that her behaviour suggests to others around her that she is full of anxiety about her health. Let's suppose that she does not recognize her behaviour as being anxious in these ways, but any analyst or even friend can tell that it is so.[5] One view to take of this sort of familiar case is that her second-order belief is simply false. It is the simpler view, and it is wrong. I think the right view is more complicated: her second order belief is true, which means she has the first order belief that her health is fine, but she also has another belief that she is not aware of, the belief that she is sick (or might be sick). So authority is not unsettled by the phenomenon of self-deception, rather *transparency* is missing regarding one of the two inconsistent beliefs (i.e. it is missing of the belief that not-p; in our example it is missing of the belief that she is sick). Perhaps she has suppressed her belief that she is sick because it is discomfiting to her to think of herself as sick, or because she does not want to be bothered with it in her busy life, and so on. If this is right, then allowing for self-deception clearly does not undermine *authority*. And, at the same time, for reasons mentioned in footnote 4 below, we have saved it from being undermined without any lack of charity in the attribution of inconsistent beliefs to the agent, since lack of charity in inconsistent attribution only holds if (among other things) the person is aware of both inconsistent beliefs. If she is unaware of one of them, it cannot be uncharitable to be attributed an inconsistency. In the example above, we have even offered specific possible explanations for the lack of awareness of one of the pair of beliefs in the inconsistency, so there is nothing uncharitable about finding her inconsistent.

Of course, there is an immediate and obvious point regarding this strategy. First a bit of terminology: call the first order belief (the belief that one is healthy) in our example an 'embedded' belief since it is what the second-order belief takes as its object. In my strategy, in order to save the *authority* conditional I have allowed that the *transparency* conditional does *not* hold for the first order intentional states which are inconsistent with the 'embedded' first order intentional states of the second-order beliefs, whose authority is saved. This strategy saves authority of second-order beliefs about first order intentional states by insisting that in cases of self-deception these 'embedded' first order beliefs are indeed always present and therefore the second-order belief is always true—it's just that in each such case there is always another first order intentional state which is inconsistent with the 'embedded' first-order state and which is *not transparent* to its possessor. But to admit such a lack of transparency is all right since I have said that transparency (as captured in (T)) holds only when the proviso for agency, in the

---

of cases of blatant inconsistencies, where there are no extenuating explanations of them in terms of lack of transparency of one of the inconsistent beliefs, or in some other terms.

[5] Often such a person may have a *half*-awareness of her anxiety regarding her health. Though that complicates things, it doesn't change the basic issues. In my book, mentioned earlier, I do discuss *grades* of self-knowledge while discussing self-deception, but for the sake of brevity and simplicity, I won't here discuss cases of half knowledge that someone might have in such cases of her belief that she might not be healthy.

Strawsonian sense, holds—and we can grant that the relevant intentional states fail to meet that proviso.

But a question now arises, why should one deal with self-deception along the lines I am suggesting rather than as a less complicated phenomenon which is incompatible with the claim that we have first person authority over our intentional states? The answer lies in the intrinsically normative nature of intentional states conceived as commitments, as I have characterized them earlier.

As I said at the outset, authority holds only of first-order intentional states conceived as commitments and not dispositions. If we keep faith with the distinction between commitments and dispositions, we can say this: the behavioral evidence that is evidence of self-deception does not provide any evidence that the person lacks the *commitment* which is the 'embedded' intentional state of his second-order belief. It only shows that he has not lived up to the commitment in his behavior. His behavior reflects some of his dispositions, which of course he may not be aware of. And these will conflict with his commitments. All we need to find in order to attribute the *commitment* to him, is that when and if he does become aware of his dispositions and notices his failures to live up to his commitments, he accepts criticism for not living up to his commitments, and tries to do better by way of living up to them, by perhaps cultivating the dispositions to do what it takes to live up to them, etc. And so, even when he is not aware of his dispositions and his failures, so long as he is *prepared* to accept criticism etc. were he to become aware, that is sufficient to attribute the commitment to him. If he meets these conditions for having the commitment, (i.e. if he has this preparedness), his behavior can no longer be seen as evidence for his second order belief being false, only of him not having lived up to his commitment.

Why exactly does the behavior not *also* refute the claim that he has the first-order belief, *qua commitment*, that he is healthy, thereby falsifying his second-order belief that he has such a commitment? Here is another way of putting my argument that makes it more explicit why not. Let's stay with our example and add that the protagonist not merely has the second order belief that he believes that he is healthy, but that he *says* he believes that he is healthy, that is, he *avows* the first-order belief. (There is an elementary distinction between second-order beliefs and avowals that should not be lost sight of—the latter are not second-order beliefs, they are expressions of second order beliefs in words.) Now, two things must be established to conclude that there is authority: his avowal must be sincere (otherwise there is nothing—there is no second-order belief—to be authoritative, since avowals express second order beliefs only if they are sincere avowals), and he must have the first order belief being sincerely avowed, which, of course in turn, requires that the defining conditions for his having the first-order commitment, must be met. Let us assume that the avowal is sincere, despite the behavioral evidence, because if it were not, there would be no question, as I said, of something being either authoritatively true or being false, and hence there would be nothing to dispute, since authority is a property of second-order beliefs. Assuming the avowal to be sincere, we must ask, what are the conditions that would establish this sincerity of his avowal, given the behavioural evidence which suggest anxiety on his part about his health? The answer here is crucial and highly revealing: there can be no conditions which would establish the sincerity of his avowal *which would not also be the conditions which establish that he has the commitment he is avowing*. The conditions for having the commitment, I had said earlier, would be his preparedness (were he to become aware that he is not living up to his commitment) to accept criticism for not having lived up to it, and his preparedness to try and do better by way of living up to it. These preparednesses, I am now saying, are the *very conditions* which would establish that his avowal of the commitment is sincere. What else could establish its sincerity?

So, if a sincere avowal is an indication that one has a second order belief that one possesses an intentional state, then it follows that our second order beliefs are always true because the conditions which allow us to say that she has the second order belief (that her avowal is sincere) are the very conditions under which we say that she has the intentional state she avows. To the extent that it has been established that an avowal of an intentional state is sincere and, therefore, that a second-order belief really exists, then (even in the cases of self-deception), so must the intentional state it is about really exist, thus making the second-order belief true. No doubt, an agent may make insincere avowals. But what that shows is that we don't really have a second order belief, since sincere avowals and second order beliefs stand or fall together. And if there are no second-order beliefs, then the subject of authority is not yet on the table, since authority is a claim about the truth of second-order beliefs, not the truth of insincere avowals. But, if and when authority *is* on the table, self-deception need not be seen as overturning it. Second-order beliefs need not be seen as having any role in a psychological economy without the presence of the first-order beliefs they are about.

On this basis, we can claim that (A), the conditional for authority, is established, but its reach is more limited than (T) since, on the argument I have offered, it holds only of first-order intentional states, conceived as commitments, not dispositions.

That summarizes some of the more basic refinements to be made on the intuitions regarding privileged access—showing the intuitions to be captured in two properties of intentional states such as beliefs and desires that are, in turn, captured in two conditionals, and giving the arguments for the truth of those conditionals.

As I said, the argument only goes through for the property of authority, *if we assume that intentional states are themselves normative states such as commitments*, and though the argument for transparency goes through for both commitments and dispositions, it only goes through for the latter, *if we assume a normative notion of agency that owes to Strawson's notion of freedom and modifies it in one fundamental aspect*. Those are both large assumptions on large topics, and since they each drive the two arguments for the special character of self-knowledge via these two properties of authority and transparency, I will close this essay, with a very brief indication of why I think we should make both those assumptions.

1) For the first assumption, it is important to understand the idea that normativity is central to intentionality in a particular way, in a way that has it that intentional states such as beliefs and desires are *themselves normative states* (since that is what the idea of commitments are). Davidson, who was something of a pioneer in arguing for centrality of normativity to intentional states (and thereby repudiating various forms of naturalism about intentional states, such as physicalism and functionalism) fails to see just this point and, despite his claims for the relevance of normativity to intentionality, he views beliefs and desires as *dispositions*, not commitments. For him the normativity allows these states to be dispositions but views these dispositions as being 'governed' by normative principles (principles of deductive, inductive, and decision-theoretic rationality). That, by my lights, is insufficient, and we need to give reasons for why we should require something stronger by way of normativity, viewing beliefs and desires, not as first order dispositions governed by normative principles, but rather commitments that are themselves normative states. To establish this, an argument is needed against the naturalistic equation of intentional states with dispositions. Here, in outline, is what I would call a "pincer" argument for this stronger (than Davidson's) claim.

One arm of the pincer invokes and adapts G. E. Moore's open question argument that targets the reduction of value or norms to natural properties in general, to a more specific target: the reduction of intentional states to dispositions in particular, which are, as Kripke rightly points out, states that cannot be thought of normatively and can only be given a naturalistically descriptive characterization since they are causal *tendencies*. The relevance of the open question to a view which takes beliefs and desires to be dispositions would be roughly that someone can always *non-trivially* ask: "I have all these dispositions to Φ, but *ought* I to O?" If this is a genuinely non-trivial question, if it is not like asking, say, "Here is a bachelor, but is he unmarried?", then that would suggest that intentional states such as beliefs and desires are internal oughts (commitments) not to be reduced to first order dispositions.[6]

The other arm of the pincer is motivated by a limitation of the first arm. The Moorean argument works only if one assumes that there is a *definitional* equation of intentional states with dispositions. But much of contemporary philosophy of mind has aspired to something much less strong. It has been quite satisfied with something like an assertion of an a posteriori identity of intentional states with dispositions, on the model of other a posteriori identities such as water = H_2O or Hesperus = Phosphorus. Here the Moorean argument will not be effective since it targets only definitional reductions. These identities, being a posteriori, turn not on the meaning or definition or 'sense' of the terms involved ('water', 'Hesperus', etc.), but on their reference,

---

[6] I say first order dispositions deliberately. Second-order dispositions may well be involved in the characterization of commitments. In characterizing commitment, I say that failures to live up to commitments require of an agent that she tries to do better by way of living up to them; and it might well be asked if this requirement is satisfied by the exercise of a disposition to try and do better. I can allow such second-order dispositions, pointing out that it does not amount in any way to reducing.

usually elaborated in the last forty years or more in causal-theoretic terms. So, the second arm of the pincer drops the Moorean considerations and invokes at this stage a Fregean argument to supplement it. The argument has a familiar pattern. Someone can deny that intentional states are dispositions (or, better, deny that some particular intentional state is some particular set of dispositions—even when it is identical with it) without being inconsistent or irrational. But if that is so, then to account for the fact that such a person's mind represents a completely consistent state of affairs, the terms on each side of the equation being denied will need to have a sense over and above a reference. If one restricts oneself to the reference or extensions of the terms, the person would seem to be inconsistent. But we know that he is not. He merely lacks some information, he fails to know a worldly identity. So just as the terms 'water' and 'Hesperus' would need to have a sense if we were to make it come out that someone who denied that water = H_2O or denied that Hesperus = Phosphorous was not being irrational and inconsistent, we will need to posit that the intentional term in the identity or equation being denied by him has a sense. But this raises the question: what is the sense of the intentional term expressing?

Here we have a choice in answering this question, a choice that amounts to a dilemma for the naturalist who wants to equate the intentional state with a naturalistic property like a disposition. Either it is expressing a naturalistic property or it is expressing a non-naturalistic property. If it is expressing the latter, then of course, it straightforwardly undermines naturalism. So one assumes that the naturalist will insist on the other option and claim that it is expressing a (further) naturalistic property. At this stage, the first arm of the pincer re-asserts its relevance and closes in on the naturalist once again. For now, if it is the *sense (or meaning or definition)* that is given in terms of the naturalistic property, then that is precisely what the Moorean open question consideration is once again effective against. Moore's argument, as we said, is geared to target definitional reductions.

Thus a Moorean argument, supplemented by a Fregean argument, together construct a pincer effect against the naturalistic equation of intentional states with dispositions. We start with Moore, then introduce Frege to deal with a posteriori identities, which in turn *returns* us to the Moorean argument, if the naturalist appeals to senses that express *naturalistic* properties. And the effect of such a pincer argument is to make room for the assumption that my argument for authority requires, namely, that intentional states are internal 'oughts' or commitments, not dispositions. Someone might persist: but what *motivates* in the first place your insisting on the difference between a conception of beliefs as states that are governed by normative principle and as states that are inherently normative? Why is the first (Davidsonian) option insufficient? Surely, a belief is a state that is governed by consistency principles. In addition, it can be criticized in light of such principles. Why do we need more to grasp the normativity of a belief? Here is one way of presenting a motivation, over and above the argument I gave via Moore and Frege. Suppose someone believes that p. Then, in a fit of distraction, he assents to something inconsistent with p, say (to keep things simple), 'not-p'. Now on Davidson's view the advice he should get is: Get your logical act together, get consistent, and either give up your belief that p or withdraw your assent to 'not-p'. But given, how I've set up the scenario, he needs more specific advice, he needs the advice: Withdraw your assent to 'not-p'. But he can only get this advice if belief itself is a commitment, that is, if normativity resides in the belief-state itself and not just in the consistency principles that govern it.

2) The assumption of a normative notion of agency, which presupposes that one's intentional states (whether conceived as commitments or dispositions) are transparent so long as they fall within the purview of such agency, owes to Strawson's re-orientation of the notion of agency towards a norm-based metaphysics. Without it, the presupposition of transparency would not go through.

Strawson was speaking to a traditional debate about human freedom in which two opposing doctrines shared a common background commitment—that freedom was incompatible with the universal sway of causality. Determinism (or 'hard determinism' as it was sometimes called), one of the two opposed doctrines, took the view that universal causality put into doubt that freedom was so much as possible, while Libertarianism, the other doctrine, took the view that the fact of freedom depended on a 'contra-causal' capacity of the human subject or will which put into doubt that causality did have universal sway.

Strawson rejected the shared background commitment of these two opposing doctrines and thereby formulated a version of what is often described as 'compatibilism'. But his compatibilism was quite different from traditional forms of compatibilism in introducing an explicitly normative element that they lacked. Traditional ways of resisting the shared background commitment took the form of saying that though causality may be universal, not all causes were coercive or 'compulsive' or 'constraining' causes (to use Hume's terms). Those which were coercive causes thwarted human freedom, but many causes were not coercive and that left open the possibility of free human action, even within universal causality. One can understand Strawson's version of the doctrine of compatibilism as emerging out of a criticism of this more simple version of it. Suppose we ask the question: What about a coercive cause makes it coercive and what about a non-coercive cause makes it non-coercive? His view would be that just staring at the causes in question won't help to answer this question. We have to look at our practices of such things as blame and punishment, and their underlying moral-psychological basis, which consists in our reactive attitudes of resentment, indignation, etc., to even so much as identify which causes of actions are coercive and which non-coercive. It is not as if causality (i.e. the distinction between coercive and non-coercive causes) is irrelevant to freedom, it is rather that there is no identifying these causes as distinct types of causes without appeal to some *normative or evaluative* considerations, such as our practices of blame and punishment and the reactive attitudes that underlie them. Thus for instance a harmful act that issues from a non-coercive cause would go hand in hand with our attitudes of, say, resentment towards the act, whereas an act that issues from a coercive cause goes in tandem with our attitudes of excusing that act. It is not as if one identifies the coerciveness and non-coerciveness of the causes of the act independently of these attitudes towards the act, and then comes to have these attitudes on the basis of that identification. Rather these occur together. There is no norm-independent identification of these causes as distinct types of causes.

This innovative move on Strawson's part was a real advance in the philosophical account of human agency, but I think that it stops a little short of the full extent of the normative dimension of agency that is needed. The uncompromisingly committed determinist might still argue that what Strawson presents as the deepest grounds of human agency—our reactive attitudes—are themselves unjustified. For such a determinist, given the fact of the universal sway of causality, our moral psychology in which the reactive attitudes figure so centrally is indulgently judgmental, and determinism requires that we should really be suspending our reactive attitudes. This would, of course, in turn affect how we conceive of the practice of punishment (since for Strawson that is grounded in the reactive attitudes), which would now be thought of on a more medical model, something purely instrumental, a model of 'repairing someone' rather than blaming them, and reacting to them with attitudes of resentment and indignation.

Strawson's predominant response to such a view in his celebrated essay is to frankly and simply say that this is to fail to understand who we are. We cannot imagine a human life that is a life entirely rid of a moral psychology in which the reactive attitudes are central. In my discussion, I quote passages where Strawson makes this response and I argue that it is complacent on his part to simply plunk down the unimaginability of such a pervasively judgment-free mentality. People under conditions of alienation (whether from social or psychological sources) often don't care to be judgmentally reactive and we *can* imagine a comprehensive extension of such a condition that will exemplify the determinist's scenario of kicking the ladder of agency (of the reactive attitudes) away from under one. And even if we cannot perhaps easily *achieve* such a comprehensive surrender of agency, we *can* decide to commit such agential suicide *by* committing *biological* suicide. So long as the underlying motive is to commit the former, that still leaves it as a moral psychological possibility that we can actualize.

If suspending the reactive attitudes is not unimaginable, how, then, might we justify the possession and the retention of the reactive attitudes (and therefore, of our agency) against the extreme determinist who asks us to suspend them as far as we can? I argue that we can justify the reactive attitudes (and, therefore, agency) not by going to something *more* fundamental and general than agency, but from *within* agency itself. In other words, we need not try and justify the reactive attitudes and the agency they ground foundationally. We can justify our being agents with reactive attitudes, that is agents who are normative subjects, by citing *particular* norms or values that they further. Thus specific norms and values we have can justify the much more general idea of the very possession of norms and their exercise in judgments and reactive attitudes. This is an internalism in justification, a form of normativist coherentism of practical reason to match coherentism of beliefs in theoretical reason, where propositions of a high generality may be confirmed by propositions whose content is specified in much more specific terms.

How is this insistence on my part that we must go further in the normativist direction than Strawson's stopping point relevant to my account of self-knowledge, in particular my account of the property of transparency that intentional states (whether thought of as commitments of dispositions) possess? In other words, what role does my further demand for the *justification* of the reactive attitudes themselves play in accounting for transparency?

Strawson does not need nor want further justifications of the reactive attitudes because he merely claims that *freedom* is presupposed whenever the reactive attitudes are in play. But I want to say, not merely that freedom is presupposed when the reactive attitudes are in play, *but self-knowledge (transparency)* of intentional states is also presupposed. Now, there is a common view that we may have reactive attitudes of resentment (and even blame and punishment) towards someone who does another harm unself-knowingly. Krista Lawlor, in a critical comment on my view, has claimed: "When the self-deceived person harms another out of spite, we find fault with more than her *ignorance-of-the-harm* she causes, but also fault her *spitefulness*" (Lawlor 2008). If this is right, then resentment and blame do not presuppose self-knowledge on the part of the subject who is resented and blamed. My view is that though we do often *have* such reactive attitudes, there is no *justification* for such reactive attitudes, when we have them. But to even so much as raise this issue, we have to raise the prior issue as to whether and when the reactive attitudes themselves are justified. And to raise that issue is to be set on a path, a quite general path, that takes one further down the normativist path I described earlier, than anything found in Strawson, who shuns that path by saying we cannot imagine not doing without the reactive attitudes, so there is no question of seeking some justification of them.

These two assumptions—that of the more than usually radically normative nature of intentional states as well as of our agency—may seem, on the face of it, to be far-flung from the theme of self-knowledge. But I hope this essay has gone some distance towards showing that one cannot establish what makes self-knowledge unique among the knowledges we possess unless we see it as having these distant connections to wider themes in the philosophy of mind and the moral psychology of agency. It is my presiding claim that it is the network of relations that self-knowledge bears to these detailed and radically normative elements of agency and intentionality that allows one to account for self-knowledge without turning to any perceptual or other routine forms of epistemological explanations. Indeed, it goes further than other 'constitutive' accounts of self-knowledge by denying that even some of the recent talk of the 'entitlement' to self-knowledge on the basis of our first order intentional states giving us reasons for the relevant second order beliefs, has any particular aptness within the sort of account on offer here (cf. Burge 1996; Peacocke 1996). Such talk has real bite and point when one is pursuing a more substantial epistemological project, such as is found paradigmatically in a perceptual account. Philosophers who have discarded the perceptualist model should be discarding this kind of residual talk of 'entitlement' as well. In perceptual knowledge there is a crucial element of a *dynamic transition* involved in the warrant that is provided by facts and objects in the world for our veridical perceptual beliefs about them. I make a much more radical claim than other 'constitutive' views of self-knowledge precisely because I don't think it is apt to say that self-knowledge involves a dynamic transition in which our first order intentional states give us *reason* to form our beliefs about them. Though it is true that neither the concept of a reason, nor even the concept of an entitlement, *as such*, imply such a dynamic transition, the very specific 'reasons' claim (sometimes made by philosophers) mentioned in the last sentence, which underlies the idea of an entitlement to self-knowledge on the basis of our possessing intentional states, *does* imply it. Claims of that specific sort and the rhetoric of 'entitlement' they have generated—reflecting, as they do, this dynamic element rather than stressing, as I do, not the dynamic but the *integral* connections that self-knowledge bears to a range of normative notions that characterize our agency and our intentionality—has no suitable place in my account.

But, then, this puts a *great* burden on what I have called the 'integration' of self-knowledge with these other notions, so much so, that it is only a slight exaggeration to say that four problems, sometimes even called 'mysteries' by a certain kind of naturalist, that have vexed philosophers for so long—the possibility of agency and freedom in a deterministic universe, the place of value or norm in a world of nature, the relation between intentional states and the central nervous system, and the special character of self-knowledge—are really, in one sense, at bottom, the *same* mystery. At any rate they are so highly integrated that there is no understanding any one of them without coming to grips with all.

If one thought instead that self-knowledge, being *knowledge* after all, was just another narrow epistemological theme, I don't think we could account for our intuitions about privileged access. Viewed in purely epistemological terms, without integration with questions of agency, norm, or value, and the irreducible nature of intentionality, the widespread cases where we manifestly lack self-knowledge of our intentional states (such as self-deception, for instance), would make these intuitions seem like outdated Cartesian dogma. There is something honest, then, about those who refuse to grant anything special to self-knowledge and view it as getting a causal account based on a measurably more than usual *reliable* mechanism that will account for our intuitions misleadingly expressed as 'privileged access'. They see it as a narrow question in epistemology, they find the exceptions to be ubiquitous, and they draw their conclusion that there is nothing radically set apart about self-knowledge. Their conclusion is honestly drawn from their framework. It is their framework that is wrong. Self-knowledge *is* unique *only if* it is embedded in a much wider framework integrating very large themes in philosophy such as the normative nature of intentionality and agency that I have been expounding. Why should we pursue it in this broader rather than in a narrower framework? I will put the answer to this question flamboyantly: because it allows us to reduce four mysteries to one. In philosophy, surely that should count as some kind of progress.

References

Bilgrami, A. 2006 *Self-Knowledge and Resentment*, Cambridge, Harvard University Press.

───2010 "The Wider Significance of Naturalism", in M. De Caro and D. Macarthur (eds.) *Naturalism and Normativity*, New York, Columbia University Press.

Burge, T. 1996 "Our Entitlement to Self-Knowledge", *Proceedings of the Aristotelian Society* 96, 91–116.

Kripke, S. 1982 *Wittgenstein on Rules and Private Language*, Cambridge (Mass.), Harvard University Press.

Lawlor, K. 2008 "Review of Akeel Bilgrami *Self-Knowledge and Resentment*", *Mind* 117, 749–65.

Peacocke, C. 1996 "Our Entitlement to Self-Knowledge: Entitlement, Self-Knowledge, and Conceptual Redeployment", *Proceedings of the Aristotelian Society* 96, 117–58.

Strawson, P. F. 1962 "Freedom and Resentment", *Proceedings of the British Academy* 48, 1–25; repr. in P. F. Strawson, *Freedom and Resentment and Other Essays*, London, Methuen, Routledge, 1974, 1–28.

Author Index

Adams, R. M. 42, 72
Alston, W. P. 150–1, 162
Anscombe, E. 77
Armstrong, D. 7–8, 11, 215, 241

Bar-On, D. vii, 1, 10, 13, 137, 164, 189, 191
Bayne, T. 75–6, 100
Benovsky, J. 39, 46, 51
Bermúdez, J. L. 6, 118, 137, 158–9, 162
Bilgrami, A. vii, 1, 9, 14, 164, 212–19, 221–4, 230–2, 241, 263, 265, 278
Boghossian, P. A. 7, 198, 210, 216, 241
Bonjour, L. 151, 154, 162
Boyle, M. 213, 241
Brandom, R. 85, 100, 219, 265
Brewer, B. 154, 162
Brown, L. 260
Bruner, J. S. 158, 162
Burge, T. 2, 9–11, 17, 19, 25, 37–8, 140, 162, 190, 194, 203, 210, 213, 241, 276, 278
Byrne, A. 9

Campbell, J. vii, 6, 11, 12, 102–3, 112, 118, 158–9, 162, 164
Carruthers, P. 3
Cassam, Q. 210
Castañeda, H. N. 54, 74
Chalmers, D. 39, 42, 72
Chapuis, N. 159, 162
Chipman, S. 83, 101
Cohen, J. 183, 186
Coliva, A. vii, 1, 6, 9, 10, 13–14, 118, 123–4, 137, 139, 142–6, 148–9, 162, 164, 180, 212, 214–15, 234, 241
Crowther, T. 174, 179

Danks, D. 115, 119
Davidson, D. 37, 90, 100, 210, 244, 262, 272–4
Davies, M. 3, 191, 211
Descartes R. 22, 99, 102, 117, 119, 209, 233, 250
Dretske, F. I. 124, 137

Eilan, N. 118, 162, 179
Evans, G. 6, 8–9, 25, 59, 73, 76–7, 81–2, 85, 100, 137, 158–9, 162, 193, 199–200, 202, 210–11, 225, 241, 265

Fernández, J. 9
Fine, K. 90, 99–100

Flanagan, O. 146, 162
Frege, G. 89, 95, 100, 173, 273
Fricker, M. 198, 211
Frith, U. 228, 241

Geach, P. 100, 236–7, 240–1
Gendler, T. 181, 186
Gallese, V. 3
Gertler, B. 7, 11
Gibbons, J. 172, 179
Glymour, C. 115, 119
Goldman, A. 3, 146, 162, 193, 211
Gopnik, A. 2, 7–8, 119, 226, 241
Gordon, R. 3, 227, 241
Grice, H. P. 80, 100

Hacker, P. 236, 241
Happé, F. 228, 241
Hatzimoysis, A. 7
Heal, J. v, vii, 9, 13, 123, 180–2, 212, 214, 230, 232, 234, 236, 238, 241
Higginbotham, J. 78, 99
Hitchcock, C. 108, 119
Horgan, T. 58, 73, 146, 162
Hornsby, J. 164–5, 179
Hume, D. 11–12, 22, 89, 91–4, 96, 100, 274

Jack, A. I. 126, 138
Jackson, F. 42
Jacobsen, R. 225, 232, 236–8, 240–1
James, W. 99, 146, 162
Jeshion, R. 80, 100

Kant, I. 11–12, 84, 98–100
Kaplan, D. 62, 73
Klausen, S. H. 146, 162
Kriegel, U. 58, 73
Kripke, S. 40, 73, 76, 97, 100, 264, 272, 278

Lawlor, K. 276, 278
Lehrer, K. 154, 162
Leuenberger, S. 39, 55
Leung, E. 158, 162
Lewis, D. 21, 23, 31, 33–5, 38, 42, 73
Locke, J. 17–24, 35, 38
Lockwood, M. 80, 100
Ludlow, P. 194, 210–11
Lycan, W. 7

Macdonald, C. 7, 162–3, 210–11, 241, 262

Mach, E. 76, 100
MacPherson, F. 39, 41
Martin, C. B. 259, 262
Martin, M. G. F. 78, 99, 149, 162
Martin, N. 210–11
McCulloch, G. 146, 162
McDowell, J. 6, 17, 25, 37–8, 76, 100, 115–16, 119, 182, 213, 241, 243, 252, 262
McHugh, C. v, vii, 13, 139, 182
McLaughlin, B. 73, 186
Menzel, E. W. 159, 162
Menzies, P. 105, 119
Messner, D. J. 158, 163
Moran, R. 8–10, 213, 216, 218–21, 241–2
Murphy, C. M. 158, 163

Nagel, T. 52–4, 67, 73, 89, 101
Newson, E. 158, 163
Newson, J. 158, 163
Nida-Rümelin, J. 39, 49
Nida-Rümelin, M. v, 5, 11–12, 39, 43, 59, 67, 70, 73, 212

O'Brien, L. v, vii, 6, 8–10, 13, 99, 124, 137, 141, 163–4, 179–80, 183–6, 212–13, 216, 242
O'Shaughnessy, B. 164–5, 171–2, 175, 179, 184

Parfit, D. 17–19, 21–4, 31–5, 37–8, 51, 95–6, 101
Parson, J. 244
Peacocke, C. v, vii, 6–8, 10–14, 39, 74, 76, 85–6, 98–9, 101, 124, 127, 129, 137, 139–143, 146–7, 155, 159–60, 162–4, 169–71, 173–4, 176–1, 184–6, 204, 209, 211–15, 241–2, 276, 278
Pedrini, P. 213
Pearl, J. 108–9, 119
Perner, J. 227, 242
Perry, J. 19, 23, 38, 73
Pitt, D. 145–6, 163
Povinelli, D. J. 229, 242
Price, H. 105, 119
Prinz, J. 99, 145, 163
Prosser, S. 6
Pryor, J. 10, 14, 39, 59, 73, 79, 101, 124, 133, 137, 149, 163, 165, 182, 186, 199, 211–12
Putnam, H. 2, 190, 211
Pylyshyn, Z. 80–3, 101

Quine, W. V. O. vii, 100, 116, 119

Ramachandran, V. 88, 101
Recanati, F. 6, 99
Rheingold, H. 158, 162
Rizzolatti, G. 3
Robbins, P. 126, 138
Rovane, C. v, viii, 5, 11, 17, 20, 24, 29, 38, 164, 212

Sartre, J. P. 88, 90, 101
Scanlon, T. 216, 218–19, 221, 242
Shah, N. 113, 119
Shepard, R. 83, 101
Shoemaker, S. 8, 17, 19, 24, 33, 38, 59, 73, 198–9, 210–12, 214, 216, 220, 223, 242
Sidelle, A. 24
Siewert, C. P. 146, 163
Smith, B. 8, 14, 162–4, 210–12, 241, 261–2
Smith, P. K. 3
Snowdon, P. vi, viii, 14, 99, 164, 243, 253, 262
Sosa, E. 10, 119, 138, 186
Soteriou, M. viii, 146–7, 163–4, 179
Steup, M. 10, 137, 186
Stone, T. 3
Stoneham, T. 230, 242
Strawson, G. J. 158, 163
Strawson, P. 80, 101–2, 119, 146, 163, 266–7, 271, 274–6, 278

Tanney, J. 218, 242
Tienson, J. 146, 162
Tomasello, M. 229, 242
Travis, C. 124, 134, 138, 212, 241
Tye, M. 135, 138

Varlet, C. 159, 162
Velleman, J. D. 113, 119
Vonk, J. 229, 242

Wiggins, D. 37
Williams, B. 102, 113, 118, 119
Williams, D. 228, 242
Wimmer, H. 227, 242
Wittgenstein, L. vii, 8, 11–12, 95, 101, 134, 209, 210, 211, 214, 225, 234–5, 237, 241–4, 248, 262, 278
Woodward, J. 109, 119

Yablo, S. 39, 46

Zimmerman, A. 8

Subject Index

action v, vii, 11–13, 74–5, 79–80, 82–3, 85, 97, 105, 121, 125, 128, 156, 164–79, 183–6, 219, 239, 266
   awareness v, 11–13, 74–5,79–80, 82, 85, 97, 121, 125, 165, 168–71, 174, 176–9, 183–6
   based-approach 105
   mental vii, 13, 83, 164–76, 179, 183–6, 219, 239
     see also mental, action(s)
   non-productive 175
   physical 175
agency vii–viii, 5, 9, 14, 20, 30–1, 35–8, 86, 105–6, 108, 110, 112–14, 119, 179, 213, 216, 224, 263, 265–9, 271, 274–7
   deliberative 9, 215
agent vii, 5–6, 20, 27, 30–2, 35–7, 75, 83, 85, 96, 110, 112–13, 115–16, 137, 163, 167, 172, 175, 185, 207–8, 239–40, 242, 265, 267–9, 271–2, 275
   deliberative 5, 239–40
agentive 105, 108, 111, 112–14, 116
   approach 105, 108, 111–13
animalism 12
authority 4, 8–9, 13–14, 114, 129–31, 180–1, 191, 214–16, 222, 229–33, 240–1, 253, 263–4, 266, 268–71, 273
avowal(s) 10, 14, 130, 136–7, 198, 201–10, 214–16, 218, 222, 225, 230, 232, 234–40, 245–6, 248–9, 250–4, 255, 262, 270–1
awareness v, 5, 7, 9, 12–13, 73–5, 79–80, 82–3, 85, 91–2, 94, 97, 117, 121–5, 127–9, 135–7, 139–40, 146–7, 151–2, 165, 168–71, 174, 176–80, 183–6, 198, 211, 214, 235, 242, 251, 253, 256, 261, 269
   of actions v, 11–13, 74–5,79–80, 82, 85, 97, 121, 125, 165, 168–71, 174, 176–9, 183–6
     see also action, awareness
   introspective 7
   perceptual 13, 127, 151–2, 169, 183–6
   phenomenal 5
   self v, 13, 73, 123–4, 127–8, 135, 179–80, 183, 186, 198, 211, 242
     see also self, awareness
   solipsistic 117

belief(s) 7–10, 12, 18, 23, 26, 28, 54, 81, 98, 102–4, 111–17, 123, 125, 127, 129, 133–5, 141, 144, 151–2, 154, 176, 189, 209, 212–13, 215, 217–23, 225–8, 230, 232–5, 238–9, 242, 244, 248–9, 256, 259–60, 262–6, 268–9, 270–3, 276–7
   as commitments 220–1, 223, 225–8, 233, 238–9, 265–6, 268
   as dispositions 238–9, 264, 272
   about experience(s) 110, 115, 141, 150, 222, 248–9
   perceptual 141, 152, 277
   phenomenal 260
causal 1–2, 12, 23, 75, 97–8, 102–19, 127–8, 136, 151, 165, 168, 170, 173, 176, 205, 217, 257–8, 272–4, 277
   judgement(s) 107, 108
   process(es) 23, 205, 257
   structure(s) 103
causation 73, 105–8, 110–13, 116–17, 119, 125
cause(s) 90, 103–4, 106–8, 110–13, 117, 119, 165, 167, 169, 175, 177, 274–5
circularity 38, 142, 152, 154, 160
concept(s) 3, 24, 70, 72, 74–5, 78, 80, 85–7, 99, 101, 129, 131, 135, 151, 155–60, 163, 175, 182, 185, 194, 214–15, 223–9, 234, 241, 257
   psychological 3, 24, 129, 215, 223–4, 227, 229, 234
conscious v, vii, 6, 9–10, 12–13, 39, 41–9, 51–2, 57, 68–9, 71–2, 74–5, 77–9, 82–5, 88–92, 95–9, 118, 123–32, 134–5, 137, 139–47, 149, 151–2, 153–5, 157–8, 160–1, 163, 180–4, 215, 217–18, 221–2, 230–1
   action(s) 83
   attitudes 1, 63, 130
   being(s) 41, 43–4, 49, 69, 71–2
   belief(s) 230–1
   deliberation 218
   episode(s) 13, 140–1, 143–5, 147, 149, 152–5, 157–8, 160–1
   event(s) v, 12–13, 74–5, 83–5, 89–92, 95–9, 124, 180–2
   fear(s) 130–1
   individual(s) vii, 39, 41–8, 57, 69, 71
     see also individuals
   intention(s) 184
   judgement(s) 84, 124
   mind 128–9

conscious (cont.)
    phenomenology 123, 125–8, 180
    reasoning 146–7
    self- 9, 51–2, 118, 224
    states 6, 10, 12–13, 78–9, 83–5, 89–92, 96–8, 124–7, 129, 131–2, 134–7, 139, 142–4, 149, 152–5, 157–8, 160–1, 215, 217–18, 222, 230
    subject(s) 77, 88, 90, 98, 100
    thought(s) 9, 51, 118, 124, 146–7, 151, 183
    see also unconscious
consciousness v, vii, 6–7, 10, 12–13, 17, 20–2, 32, 35–6, 38, 40, 44–6, 55, 64, 66, 73–6, 83–4, 88–93, 99–100, 116, 118, 121, 123–36, 138, 143, 146–9, 151, 158–63, 180, 241
    manifestation(s) of 13
    phenomenal 123–7, 129–32, 146, 151
    self- 6, 22, 38, 75, 91–2, 99–100, 116, 118, 158–60, 162, 241
    see also self, -consciousness
constitutivism vi, 8, 14, 212–17, 234, 240
constructivism vi, 14, 212, 218, 231, 234, 236
content vii, 1–2, 7, 11–14, 44–7, 52–3, 62–3, 68, 72, 74–88, 92, 94, 98–9, 104, 114–15, 124, 128, 135–6, 139–44, 146–7, 150–4, 162–3, 172, 174–5, 178, 181–6, 189–204, 209–10, 214, 220, 222, 227, 230, 234–6, 239–41, 244–9, 253–4, 265, 276
    cognitive 47, 63
    conceptual 77–9, 86–7, 182
    conscious 151–3
    de re 76–7
    descriptive 62–3, 75, 77
    de se 12, 78
    of experience 85, 135
    experiential 14
    externalism 189–95, 197–8, 203
    first person(al) 74, 77, 80, 87, 244–5
    intentional 74–6, 92, 182, 201, 247
    see also intentional content
    internalism 195
    mental 190, 239
    minimal assertoric 236
    nonconceptual 76–8, 81–2, 87–8
    perceptual 87, 186
    physical 52–3
    predicative 84–5
    propositional 1–2, 143, 146, 153, 245, 247, 265
    representational 76, 86, 143, 181
    self-ascription(s) 201, 203
    self-knowledge 191, 193–4, 196
    semantic 199, 204
    -skeptic(ism) 189–90, 193–5, 197, 265
    spatial 82, 87
    truth-evaluable 236

deliberation(s) 20, 27–30, 32–3, 35, 37, 113, 119, 218, 220–1, 223, 238–9
de se 1, 12, 54, 63, 78, 89
    belief(s) 54, 63
    content(s) 12, 78
    representation(s) 89
    see also I-thoughts
desire(s) 9–11, 28, 102–4, 116–17, 129, 136, 144, 177, 198, 212, 214–15, 217–20, 222–3, 225–6, 228, 232–7, 239, 249, 263–4, 268, 272
    as commitments 219, 221, 223–4, 228, 234, 236, 239, 264–5, 268
    as dispositions 218, 221, 239, 264, 268, 272
disjunctivism 186
disposition(s) 48–9, 81–2, 130, 155–60, 167, 174, 180, 209, 217–23, 229–30, 233–5, 238–40, 264–5, 266–8, 270–4, 276
dualism v, 5, 12, 22, 39, 40, 42–6, 71–3, 209
    subject/body v, 5, 12, 39–40, 42–6, 71–3
dualist, *see* dualism

entitlement 9, 10, 11, 169, 182, 186, 210–11, 241, 276–8
epistemology vii, 8, 10, 73, 119, 137, 143, 155, 162–3, 165, 177, 179, 186, 205, 225, 242, 277
experience viii, 7, 28, 39, 50–3, 56, 58, 62, 67–76, 79–80, 84–6, 91, 94–7, 110, 112, 115–17, 123–4, 127–31, 133–7, 141, 145, 152, 159, 163, 177, 179, 181, 183, 185–6, 222, 228, 246, 248–9, 252, 256–61
    content of 85, 135
    perceptual viii, 74–5, 79–80, 86, 110, 112, 115–17, 128, 134, 141, 177, 179, 186, 246, 248
    phenomenal 256–8, 260
    subject of 52–3, 56, 67–72, 75–6, 91, 95, 123, 133
    see also subject of experience
    visual 62, 76, 97, 135, 150, 183, 185
expression v, vii, 1, 13, 44, 46, 52, 55, 57–8, 69, 71, 77, 80, 96, 134, 136–7, 180, 189, 202, 205–8, 210, 225–6, 228, 230, 232, 235–6, 240–1, 253, 255, 270
    natural 202, 205–6
externalism v, 2, 11, 13, 73, 150, 162, 189, 190–2, 194–7, 203, 210–11
    see also internalism

first person(al) v, viii, 1–9, 12, 14, 18–19, 22–5, 27–8, 34–5, 37–8, 48–55, 57–70, 74–83, 85–7, 91–4, 99, 102–4, 117–19, 141, 158, 160, 184, 191, 199, 225–8, 235, 237–42, 244–6, 259, 270
    concept 3–4, 6, 12, 75, 78–80, 85, 87–8, 160

SUBJECT INDEX 283

judgement(s) 58–9, 61–2
  mode(s) 19, 24, 49, 52, 57, 61, 63
  perspective/point of view 8, 12, 19, 34, 49, 50–1, 54–5, 60, 64, 68, 82, 242
  reference 65–8
  relation(s) 19, 22, 24–5, 35, 37–8
  thought(s) 1, 4, 6–7, 49–50, 52–5, 57–70, 91
freedom 25, 172–3, 218, 266–7, 271, 274, 276–8

groundless 7, 13–14, 213, 249, 252–4, 260
groundlessness, *see* groundless

human being(s) 5–6, 17, 20–1, 23, 29–32, 35–7, 51, 56, 215, 219, 240, 263

identity v–viii, 5–6, 11–12, 17–40, 42, 45, 51, 54–9, 61–3, 65–6, 72–3, 81–2, 90, 93, 97–100, 156, 172, 185, 195, 200, 272–3
  agent 35
  animal 17–20, 23, 36–7
  human 37–9
  judgement(s) 59, 61
  non- 55, 57–8, 63, 66, 172
  personal viii, 6, 12, 17–24, 26, 33–8, 73
  transtemporal 5, 39, 51, 73
  transworld 40, 42
ignorance 23, 57, 129, 192, 215, 247, 250, 252, 255, 257–8, 276
immunity to error 6, 58, 73, 198–9, 201, 208, 210–11, 263–4
  through misascription 201, 210
  through misidentification 6, 58, 73, 199, 210–11
incorrigibility 58, 191, 255–6, 259–60
individual(s) vii, 2, 20–2, 24, 26–7, 29–31, 36, 39, 41–8, 52, 56–63, 65–9, 71–2, 94, 100, 110–11, 116, 163, 190, 192–3, 195, 197, 199–200, 204, 210
  agent(s) 30–1, 36
  conscious vii, 39, 41–8, 57, 69, 71
  human being 20–1, 36
  perfect 71–2
  person 20, 22, 24, 26, 29
  rationality 20–1, 29–30
intention(s) 8, 24,—5, 31–2, 34–5, 43, 52–3, 85, 88, 95, 172, 184, 212, 217–21, 233–5, 237, 239, 242, 246
  as commitments 219–21, 234–5
  as dispositions 218
  quasi- 24–25, 31–2
    see also quasi-
intentional 2–5, 7–9, 74–6, 92, 182, 201, 224, 245, 247, 263–4, 266–74, 276–7
  action 267
  concept(s) 224, 226
  content 74–6, 92, 182, 201, 247
  state(s) 2–5, 7–9, 263–4, 266–74, 276–7
intentionality 2, 162, 213, 241, 246–7, 263–4, 272, 276–7
internalism 13, 139, 149–50, 152–5, 160–2, 195, 276
  see also externalism
intervention(s) 102, 108–17
  external 102
  silencing 109–12, 117
  surgical 108–10, 112, 115
interventionism 108, 111–13, 119
interventionist, *see* interventionism
irrational 30, 148–9, 175, 230, 240, 252, 273
  behaviour 230
irrationality 8, 148–9, 220, 230

judgement(s) 51–2, 58–62, 74, 80–1, 84–6, 124–5, 127–8, 131–2, 134–6, 169–70, 173–6, 181–2, 217, 219, 221, 233–7, 259, 262, 275
  conscious 84, 124
  dependent 233
  first-order 124, 233, 235
  non-sensitive 217
  second-order 234–5
  sensitive 219, 221
justification 10, 13, 124–5, 128–9, 131–7, 140, 149, 151–2, 154–5, 157, 160–1, 180–2, 186, 209, 234, 248, 253, 276
  entitlement, *see* justification, non-inferential
  non-inferential 13, 124–5, 131, 133–7, 180–2

knowledge v–vii, 1–4, 6–14, 22–3, 63, 65, 72–3, 99, 102–3, 105, 108, 110, 116–18, 121, 123, 125–6, 136–7, 139–45, 148–9, 152–5, 159, 161–70, 174, 176–80, 182–4, 186–7, 189–204, 208–17, 219–21, 223–30, 233, 239–49, 251–64, 267–9, 271, 276–8
  of actions 13, 164–70, 176–80, 184, 186
  of causal relation(s) 108, 110, 116–17
  of content 2, 189–1, 196–7
  non-inferential 7
  of our experience(s) 249, 257–8, 261
  perceptual 116–17, 186, 192, 277
  self- v–vii, 1–4, 6–14, 23, 72–3, 99, 117–18, 121, 125, 136–7, 139–45, 148–9, 152–5, 159, 161–4, 182, 187, 189, 191–8, 200–1, 208, 210–216, 219, 223–6, 228–30, 240–4, 246–9, 251, 253–6, 259–60, 262–4, 267–9, 271, 276–8
    see also self-knowledge
  of trying(s) 164–8, 170, 180

mental 1–4, 7–14, 58, 73, 76, 78, 80–1, 83–97, 100, 102–6, 110–15, 117, 119, 124–5, 130, 142, 144, 148, 161, 163–76, 179, 181–6, 189–91, 195–210, 212–22, 224–6, 228–41, 245, 249, 263, 266–7
  action(s) vii, 13, 83, 164–76, 179, 183–6, 219, 239
  causation 73, 110–12, 116–17, 119
  event (s) 14, 76–8, 84–5, 89–90, 92, 94–96, 100, 124, 181–2
  life 11, 100, 102–3, 111, 115, 215
  representation(s) 80–1, 85, 87
  state(s) 1–4, 7–10, 12–14, 77–8, 85–6, 88, 91–7, 100, 103, 105–6, 110, 114–16, 125, 130, 142, 144, 148, 161, 178, 182, 190–1, 195–8, 201–22, 224–6, 228–41, 266–7
    as commitments 217, 219–23, 226, 228–9, 231–2, 234–5
    conscious 12–13, 83–4, 89, 96, 124, 142, 161, 181
    as dispositions 217, 221–4, 239–40
    judgement-sensitive 219
    non-judgement-sensitive 217
    unconscious 13, 125, 215, 217–18, 220, 222, 230

neo-expressivism 14, 204
no-ownership view 88, 91
normativity 264, 272–4, 278

perception v, vii-viii, 12, 14, 52–3, 75–6, 79, 82–3, 85–7, 89, 91, 93–4, 97, 99, 102, 112, 114–15, 117–18, 124–9, 134, 137, 140, 146, 162, 169, 177, 182–3, 185–6, 192, 196, 200, 212–13, 229, 248, 258
  self-specifying 135
  world-specifying 135
performatives 234–8, 240
phenomenology 10, 29, 75, 84, 128, 130–1, 142–8, 151–3, 158, 160, 162–3, 180, 185
point(s) of view 11–12, 19–21, 34, 36, 78–9, 82, 119, 130, 136, 140, 142–9, 153–4, 156–7, 160–1, 185, 219, 225–8, 231, 236, 238, 246
  bodily (animal) 12, 21
  first person 12, 19, 34, 82
  phenomenological 12, 20, 144
  rational 11–12, 21, 36
  subject 140, 142–3, 145–9, 153–4, 156, 160–1, 219, 225–7, 235–6
  third-person 78
propositional attitudes 7–10, 13–14, 111, 139, 145, 162, 190, 212–26, 228–30, 232–5, 238–41, 244
psychological 3–11, 13, 14, 18, 23–25, 34, 36, 40, 48–50, 56–7, 59, 67, 69, 99, 101–3, 108, 110–12, 116–18, 123, 126–9, 131, 137, 163, 170, 182, 202, 207, 213–16, 223–9, 231–3, 235–7, 239–42, 244–9, 255, 258, 267, 271, 274–5
  abilities 3
  avowal(s) 216, 225, 232–3, 235, 237
  causation 111
  concept(s) 3, 24, 129, 215, 223–4, 227, 229, 234
  continuity 18, 24, 34
  disposition(s) 48–9
  event(s) 23, 123
  explanation(s) 202, 207
  fact(s) 40
  judgement(s) 237
  life(s) 110, 112, 123, 126
  properties 4–6, 50, 56–7, 59, 67, 69
  relations 23–4
  self-ascription(s) 3–4, 7–11, 13–14, 213–14, 226, 229, 231–3, 235–6, 240–1
  self-knowledge 248–9
  states 102–3, 108, 116–18, 127–9, 131, 182, 242, 258
  theory(ies) 3, 7, 226
  vocabulary 235

qualia 132–3, 136
quasi- 11, 19, 22, 24–8, 31–2, 145–6
  anticipate 27, 32
  attitude(s) 19, 24, 26
  first person pronoun 24
  first personal relations 22, 25, 28
  intention(s) 24–5, 31–2
  memory 19, 24, 27–8
  reasoning 11, 19, 26, 28
  remember(ed) 25, 27, 31–2
  sensory 145–6

rational 4–5, 8, 11–12, 20–2, 27, 29–31, 35–8, 51–2, 54–5, 57, 64, 83, 85, 99, 140, 142–9, 153–4, 156–7, 159, 161, 181–2, 206, 215–16, 220–1, 224
  agency 20, 30–1, 35, 37–8
  agent(s) 4, 5, 20, 30–1, 35–7, 215
  capacity(ies) 30
  cause(s) 206
  control 83
  criticism 220
  judgement(s) 181–2
  person 64
  point(s) of view 11–12, 21, 36, 143, 145–9, 153, 157, 161
  psychology 99
  self-ascription(s) 140, 144, 148, 181
  subject(s) 215, 224
  thinker 54–5, 57
  unity 5, 22

SUBJECT INDEX 285

rationality v, 11, 17–22, 26–27, 30–1, 33–5, 86, 104, 111, 153–4, 156, 160–1, 215–16, 221, 223, 272
reasons v, vii–viii, 3–4, 7–8, 10–11, 13, 17, 21–2, 26–8, 30, 34–6, 38–9, 41, 45, 48, 50, 53, 56, 59, 72, 74–5, 86, 92, 98, 100, 108, 110–11, 113, 115–17, 119, 124–5, 127, 138–46, 148–50, 152–62, 164–5, 168, 172–5, 179–82, 186, 195, 199–202, 206–207, 209, 213–14, 216, 219, 221–3, 225, 227–8, 230–1, 233–4, 241–2, 246–7, 249–55, 259–60, 269, 272, 276–7
    account 4, 139–42, 144, 146, 149–55, 158, 160–1
    epistemic 72, 201
    internalist 139, 142–3
    justifying 150
    non-inferential 141
recognition v, 13, 136, 166, 189, 192, 200, 208, 210, 253, 257
recognitional 195–201, 203, 207, 209
    abilitiy(ies) 196–7, 201
    conception 195–8, 210
    identification 199–201
    judgement(s) 199–200, 203, 209
    target 201, 203
research 1–2, 4, 51–2, 163, 211–12, 229, 241, 262
responsibility 220, 266–7
    empirical 4, 52
    phenomenological 163, 211, 241
    philosophical 1, 51

self v, vii, viii, 1,2, 3, 4,5, 6, 7, 8, 9, 10, 11, 12, 13, 14, 15, 17, 19, 21, 22, 24, 25, 27, 51, 60, 62, 67, 74, 119, 134, 139, 140, 141, 142, 143, 144, 147, 148, 149, 152, 153, 154, 155, 157, 158, 159, 160, 161, 162, 176, 177, 179, 180, 181, 183, 186, 191, 194, 196, 198, 199, 200, 201, 202, 203, 204, 205, 206, 208, 209, 210, 211, 213, 214, 215, 216, 218, 219, 220, 221, 225, 226, 229, 230, 231, 232, 233, 234, 235, 236, 238, 239, 240, 241, 245, 247, 253, 255, 256, 257, 258, 259, 260, 268, 269, 270, 271
    selves, *see* self
    -ascriptions v, 1, 3–4, 7–10, 13–14, 152–5, 157–61, 165, 176–7, 180–1, 191, 194, 196, 198–206, 208–11, 213–14, 216, 225–6, 230–6, 239–40, 245, 247
        explicit 136
        psychological 3–4, 7, 10–11, 13, 214, 226, 229, 231–3, 235–6, 240–1

-awareness v, 13, 73, 123–4, 127–8, 135, 179–80, 183, 186, 198, 211, 242
-blind(ness) 223–4, 229
-concept(s) 258–9
-consciousness vii, 6, 22, 38, 75, 91–2, 99–100, 116, 118, 158–60, 162, 241
-deception 8, 103, 129, 214–15, 229–32, 247, 268–71, 277
-identification 58–61
-interpretation 198, 218–21, 228, 238–9, 247, 253
-intimatingness 255–9
-intimation(s) 256, 259–60
-judgement(s) 200, 208
-knowledge v–vii, 1–4, 7–14, 23, 72–3, 118, 152–5, 159, 161–4, 182, 187, 191–8, 200, 208–17, 219, 223–6, 228–30, 240–1, 243–6, 248–9, 251, 253–4, 256, 259–60, 262–4, 267–9, 271, 276–8
    constitutive account of 9–10, 212–14, 216–17, 224, 229–30, 240, 276
    fragile v, 13, 187
    phenomenal vi, 14, 217, 243, 248–9, 259–60
    reasons account of 13, 139–44, 146, 148–50, 152–5, 158, 16–1
    robust v, 13–14, 187
    unique status of vi, 14, 263
-observation 219–20
-omniscience 191
-reference 25, 68, 103, 198, 211, 241
-referential 194, 204
-representation viii, 75, 85, 89, 98–9
-specifying 135
-verifying 9, 203–5, 233
skeptic(ism) vi, 13, 22, 189–90, 192–5, 197–8, 209–10, 249, 254, 262, 265
    content 189–90, 193, 194–5, 197, 265
    doubt(s) 190, 198
    external world 189, 190, 192–5, 197, 265
    internal world 197, 209
subject(s) v, 2–3, 5–13, 22, 24, 27, 29, 31, 33–4, 37, 39–46, 52–3, 55, 56, 62, 64, 66–101, 104, 110–12, 117–18, 123–61, 167, 169, 173–6, 178, 181, 183–6, 191–2, 195, 197–8, 200, 203, 205, 209–10, 213–15, 217–31, 234–6, 238, 240, 244, 247, 250, 252–3, 255–61, 268, 271, 274–6
    of authority 271
    body dualism v, 5, 12, 39–46, 71–3
    of consciousness 76, 99, 127–8, 133
    constitutive hypothesis 77
    of experience 53, 56–72, 75–6, 91, 95, 123, 133
    experiencing 70–1
    file 81–5, 87–8, 98

286   SUBJECT INDEX

subject(s) (cont.)
   human 274
   normative 275
   ontology of 12, 91–2, 97–8
   point of view 140, 142–3, 145–9, 153–4, 156, 160–1, 219, 225–7, 235–6
   reflexivity 78–9, 83–6, 89
   representation 86–8

thought(s) 17, 19, 21, 23–5, 27, 29, 31, 33–4, 39–40, 43–55, 57–70, 76, 82, 85, 91–2, 97–6, 108, 117–18, 123–7, 130–1, 134–7, 145–7, 149, 151, 158, 163, 165, 172, 175, 177–8, 183–4, 190
   counterfactual 39, 44–50, 52, 55, 57, 59–61, 65–70
   experiment 17, 23, 43, 50
   first person 54–5, 58–70, 91
   I-thoughts 63, 68, 70
   see also de se
transparency 4, 7, 9, 13–14, 214–15, 217, 220, 224, 229–50, 252–3, 256–7, 260, 263, 266–9, 271, 274, 276

tryings v, 13, 164–8, 170–80, 183, 185

unconscious 9, 13, 125, 129, 130–1, 135, 137, 146, 180–1, 183, 215, 217, 219–20, 222, 230–1
   belief 230–1
   fear(s) 129, 130, 137, 180–1, 183
   Freudian 125, 135, 137, 218
   mental states 13, 83, 125, 215, 217–20, 222, 230
   mind 129
   see also conscious

warrant 13, 139, 140, 144, 149, 152, 192, 211, 213, 277
will 12, 36, 218, 220
willingness 160, 181, 253
world 1, 6, 8, 12, 40–9, 52–7, 62, 64, 6–1, 73, 75, 77–8, 86–8, 94–5, 97, 101–2, 108, 112–18, 128, 133–4, 136, 156, 159, 161, 172, 178, 181–2, 189, 190, 192–5, 197, 200, 209, 227, 230, 235, 261, 263–5, 273, 277